INSIGHT GUIDES

Venezuela

INSIGHT GUIDE
Venezuela

Editorial
Project Editor
Angela Baynham
Managing Editor
Huw Hennessy
Editorial Director
Brian Bell

Distribution

UK & Ireland
GeoCenter International Ltd
The Viables Centre, Harrow Way
Basingstoke, Hants RG22 4BJ
Fax: (44) 1256 817988

United States
Langenscheidt Publishers, Inc.
46–35 54th Road, Maspeth, NY 11378
Fax: (718) 784 0640

Canada
Thomas Allen & Son Ltd
390 Steelcase Road East
Markham, Ontario L3R 1G2
Fax: (1) 905 475 6747

Australia
Universal Press
1 Waterloo Road
Macquarie Park, NSW 2113
Fax: (61) 2 9888 9074

New Zealand
Hema Maps New Zealand Ltd (HNZ)
Unit D, 24 Ra ORA Drive
East Tamaki, Auckland
Fax: (64) 9 273 6479

Worldwide
**Apa Publications GmbH & Co.
Verlag KG (Singapore branch)**
38 Joo Koon Road, Singapore 628990
Tel: (65) 6865 1600. Fax: (65) 6861 6438

Printing

Insight Print Services (Pte) Ltd
38 Joo Koon Road, Singapore 628990
Tel: (65) 6865 1600. Fax: (65) 6861 6438

CONTACTING THE EDITORS
We would appreciate it if readers
would alert us to errors or out-
dated information by writing to:
**Insight Guides, P.O. Box 7910,
London SE1 1WE, England.**
Fax: (44) 20 7403 0290.
insight@apaguide.demon.co.uk

ABOUT THIS BOOK

This guidebook combines the interests and enthusiasms of two of the world's best-known information providers: Insight Guides, whose titles have set the standard for visual travel guides since 1970, and Discovery Channel, the world's premier source of non fiction television programming.

Insight Guides' editors provide practical advice and a general understanding about a place's history, its culture and institutions and its people.

Discovery Channel and its extensive website, www. discovery.com, help millions of viewers explore the world from the comfort of their home and also encourage them to explore it first hand.

The Insight approach works well for Venezuela, which first gained the attention of travelers seeking far-flung adventure for its 2,500 km (1,750 miles) of Caribbean coastline; it is now a South American favorite. The country's many attractions often come as a surprise to visitors, but the dense Amazon jungles, the high Andean mountains, the Central plains, and the Caribbean beaches cannot fail to delight.

EXPLORE YOUR WORLD

ence for information on travel, hotels, restaurants, and much more. Information may be located quickly by using the index printed on the back-cover flap – and the flaps are designed to serve as bookmarks.
◆ **Photographs** are carefully chosen not only to illustrate the country and its attractions, but also to convey an understanding of the everyday activities of the Venezuelan people.

The contributors

This edition of *Insight Guide: Venezuela* has been thoroughly updated by **Claire Antell** of the Latin American Travel Association. Latin American analyst **Nick Caistor** wrote A Society Divided. The book was edited in-house by **Sylvia Suddes**.

It was originally edited by **Angela Baynham**, and builds on earlier editions produced by **Tony Perrottet**, with much of the writing shared between two US journalists, **Mary Dempsey** and **Anne Kalosh**. Perrottet himself wrote some of the chapters, including those on history and the *llanos*, while **Ed Holland** wrote about the intricacies of Venezuelan society and politics. **Eric Jennings** described spectator sports and diving.

Elizabeth Kline, one of the most experienced writers on the country, wrote the chapters on Participant Sports, Lara State, and El Litoral as well as overhauling the Guayana Region section. Kline is also a photographer, and many of her pictures are included in this guide.

Many of the photographs were taken by **Eduardo Gil**, with others from **Keith Mays**, **Tony Perrottet**, **André Bärtschi**, and **Ray Escobar**. Thanks also go to **Penny Phenix**, who proofread the book.

How to use this book

The book is carefully structured both to convey an understanding of Venezuela and its culture and to guide readers through the country's sights and activities:
◆ To understand Venezuela today, you need to know something of its past. The **Features** section covers the country's history and culture in lively, authoritative essays written by specialists.
◆ The **Places** section provides full details of all the areas worth seeing. The chief places of interest are coordinated by number with full-color maps.
◆ The **Travel Tips** listings section offers a convenient point of refer-

Map Legend

▬ ▬ ▪ ▪	International Boundary
▬ ▬ ▬ ▬	State Boundary
▬ ▪ ▬ ▪	National Park/Reserve
▬ ▬ ▬ ▬	Ferry Route
Ⓜ	Metro
✈ ✈	Airport: International/ Regional
🚌	Bus Station
🅿	Parking
❶	Tourist Information
✉	Post Office
† ✝	Church/Ruins
†	Monastery
☾	Mosque
✡	Synagogue
🏰 🏚	Castle/Ruins
∴	Archeological Site
∩	Cave
𝟙	Statue/Monument
★	Place of Interest

The main places of interest in the Places section are coordinated by number with a full-color map (e.g. ❶), and a symbol at the top of every right-hand page tells you where to find the map.

CONTENTS

Maps

Introduction

History

Features

Colorfully painted colonial residences of Ciudad Bolívar, the historical city on the banks of the Orinoco

Insight on ...

Information panels

Places

A LUST FOR LIVING

Venezuela offers beaches, mountains, rainforest and savannah,

but the real attraction is the character of its people

Venezuela: the best-kept secret in the Caribbean. This was the cunningly self-effacing theme of a promotional campaign of the national tourism corporation – and it remains true. Most potential visitors are aware that Venezuela has oil and, perhaps, have heard of Angel Falls or Isla Margarita (virtually the only parts of the country actively promoted), but beyond that... nothing. Thus, the usual reaction is one of amazement at the diversity of attractions.

After the unfortunate first image of hills covered with shanties between Maiquetía airport (where most visitors arrive) and surrounding central Caracas, the constant flow of contrasting landscapes as you explore Venezuela's interior is a marvelous surprise. You will become privy to many of its secrets: it is not just a "Caribbean country" with beaches, but a South American country with mountains, plains, and jungles; it has incredibly varied wildlife, and fascinating architecture (even among humble handmade earth-walled houses); and you can observe the ancient customs of its indigenous peoples and the colorful displays of its rich folklore.

Along with these, other great parts of Venezuela's enchantment include its people: open, friendly, in love with life; and its climate: sunny and warm, with average daytime temperatures of about 25°C (77°F) year-round.

By air, no part of the country is more than 2 hours' away. If you are driving from Caracas, within a few hours, or at most a full day, you can be on dazzling beaches, horseback riding, or birding on a cattle ranch in the *llanos* (plains); or you may be in the heart of the Andes dressed in a T-shirt but with snow-capped mountains in the background, visiting indigenous settlements in the Amazon jungle, or preparing to climb *tepuyes* (mesas of rock among the oldest on earth).

Although natives and foreigners alike despair of the prevailing "*mañana*" (or "what's your hurry") attitude, there are compensations. This laid-back approach contributes to Venezuela's allure: rather than being ruled by diaries or watches, most Venezuelans are clearly guided by the principle that life is to live – now. If you have a chance to dance until dawn on a Tuesday – go for it.

There is something infectious about the flirty smiles, warm back-slapping, or kissy-face welcomes, the boisterous laughter and people singing along with the radio on a bus. It makes such a refreshing change from the dominant "what's proper" norm (even in Latin America) that it makes you glad you came – and leaves you with a definite desire to return. ❏

PRECEDING PAGES: view from a light plane over the Gran Sabana; Spanish moss drapes the trees among tropical vegetation in the Andes; scarlet and white ibis over the *llanos*; Castillo de San Antonio de la Eminencia, Cumaná.
LEFT: facade of an old house in Maracaibo.

A COUNTRY OF SURPRISES

The contrasting lifestyles, cultures, and architecture throughout
Venezuela are as distinct as the geographical features of each region

The witchcraft of Venezuela is undeniable. Venezuelans may flock to Miami for vacations, but leave the country for ever? *No, señor*! And, if you ask foreign residents why they settled here, the answer will invariably be that they came for a short vacation or temporary job assignment and decided to stay for good.

Just what is it that charms so many people? On the surface, the answer is easy: the wonderful climate, an immense variety of geographical features, and people with a natural warmth and joy of living. But there are countless other subtle ingredients that go into the magic potion: the music and dance, marvelous wildlife, the lack of development, an absence of racial barriers, folkloric customs lovingly preserved for centuries – the list is long.

Coastal smorgasbord

As a country with some 3,000 km (1,800 miles) of Caribbean coastline, beaches are a natural focal point for diversion. Together with myriad options along the continental shore or on its hundreds of islands and cays, these beaches may be wide swathes of snowy white sand lapped by calm crystalline water, or bays framed by dramatic rock formations and cactus, perhaps ringed with palm trees, with a backdrop of mountains covered with dense tropical forest. There are solitary spots ideal for reflection and places with lively resorts. Local residents may be reserved, light-skinned fishermen or dark-skinned descendants of slaves who celebrate at the drop of a hat with their African-style *tambores* (drums) and sensual dancing. If you tire of swimming or working on a tan, there is always outstanding deep-sea fishing, windsurfing, sailing, and diving.

The majority of Venezuela's principal cities and some 80 percent of the population are also found on or near the coast: the dynamic national capital, Caracas, where you can dine in exotic restaurants and dance the night away to

LEFT: sun-worshipers at work.
RIGHT: water cacao on the Orinoco River.

the rhythms of salsa; the beach resort towns of Puerto La Cruz/Barcelona (not to mention the mega-resort haven of Isla Margarita with its duty-free shopping); Cumaná, guarded by a colonial fort; the manufacturing centers of Valencia and Maracay; Coro, with nearby sand dunes, and designated a World Patrimony City

by UNESCO for its exceptional colonial architecture; and Maracaibo, Venezuela's petroleum capital (with one of the world's largest oil reserves beneath South America's largest lake abutting the metropolis) and second-largest city, where oil tycoons rub elbows with indigenous Guajiro women in their traditional native dress and where *gaita* music fills the air.

Deserts and mountains

Westbound from Caracas, the next stop is Falcón and Lara, states with predominately desert landscapes. Often, however, these plains are broken up by verdant mountains. And Lara, despite its arid appearance, is the county's

principal source of tomatoes, onions, peppers, and other produce. Meanwhile, Yaracuy's mountains harbor everything from ancient gold and copper mines (which belonged to Simón Bolívar's family) to followers of the María Lionza cult. Continuing southwest, one passes through the western plains: rich farmlands planted with sugar cane, rice, and grains.

Mountains steeped in tradition

Traversing Venezuela's Andean states, another totally different set of sights and experiences awaits. The journey takes you from the coffee plantations of the foothills, through the barren but fascinating *páramo* (high moorland), and up to the country's tallest mountains (topped by Pico Bolívar, 5,000 meters/16,400 ft). Winding roads pass glacier-fed lakes that teem with trout and fields where farmers guide wooden plows pulled by teams of oxen. Due to the region's isolation, farmhouses with pounded-earth walls, ancient villages with cobblestone streets, and traditional rural festivals have all been preserved virtually unchanged for centuries. The way of life here remains slower and simpler.

The great plains

Moving on to the *llanos*, or central plains, you can go the easy way by road or plane – or join a group getting there by hiking across the mountains – a unique experience that is offered by various operators *(see page 314)*.

The *llanos*, in a belt roughly 100–150 km (60–90 miles) wide and 1,000 km (600 miles) long, extend north and west of the Orinoco River from its delta to the Andes. During the dry season the land is parched and cracked, but when the rainy season hits, because of the extreme flatness, it is almost totally flooded.

Apure and Barinas form the heart of the *llanos*, where the three most notable occupants are thousands of mainly beef cattle on sprawling *hatos* (ranches), an incredible quantity and variety of wildlife, and the *llanero*. The last of these, the Venezuelan-style cowboy, typically with bare feet instead of boots, has been famous since colonial times for his bravery and independence. When the *llanero* isn't tending the herds, more likely than not he will be strumming a *cuatro*, *bandola*, or *arpa criollo* to produce the local equivalent of country & western tunes.

LEFT: diamond miners await an air taxi, La Gran Sabana.

El Oriente

Northeastern Venezuela, popularly referred to as *"El Oriente,"* is best known for its beaches, but has many other attractions, including the spot on the Paria Peninsula of Sucre where Christopher Columbus first came in contact with Venezuela, declaring it to be "the land of grace" for its extraordinary beauty.

Heading inland, a favorite stop in northern Monagas is the *Cueva del Guácharo,* named after the colonies of night-flying, fruit-eating *guácharos* (oil birds), which occupy one of the chambers of this cave (the largest and best-preserved in the country).

Pushing southward, into the central Anzoátegui state, you will pass over the Orinoco Belt, one of the world's largest petroleum reserves.

Last frontiers

The Guayana region – including the Delta Amacuro, Bolívar, and Amazonas states – covers some 45 percent of the national territory. The name comes from the Guayana Shield (made up of the oldest rock on earth: 1.2–2.75 billion years old) that forms most of its base. Attractions include the *tepuyes* (or mesas) of this ancient rock, the tops of which host plants and animals found nowhere else on earth.

Delta Amacuro state, almost completely comprising the delta (among the largest in the world) of the Orinoco River, is home of the Warao. Their name, meaning "the canoe people," is most apt, as they are excellent boat builders, a vital skill given that boats offer the only practical way through the maze of *caños* (channels and branches of the river). Tourist camps in the interior of the state allow visitors to witness up-close the lifestyles of the Warao, and observe rare flora and fauna.

Bolívar state, Venezuela's largest, is also one of its richest, with vast deposits of iron, gold, diamonds, and bauxite. Moreover, harnessing the hydroelectric potential of its Caroní River, this state produces 70 percent of the nation's domestic power, plus that needed for the huge steel and aluminum plants of Ciudad Guayana.

Ultramodern Ciudad Guayana and the state's capital, Ciudad Bolívar, are both on Bolívar's northern border, the Orinoco River. Visitors can fly from these cities to Canaima (in the northwest corner of the Canaima National Park), the departure point for Angel Falls, the longest (895 meters/2,936 ft) free fall of water in the world, plunging over the side of Auyántepui.

By road, visit the mostly overlapping Gran Sabana (Great Savanna) and 3 million-hectare (7.4 million-acre) Canaima National Park in the southeastern portion of the state, following an excellent paved road. Along the full length of the park, all the way to Santa Elena de Uairén near the frontier of Brazil, travelers can delight in the majesty of the gently rolling high savannah. There are numerous beautiful waterfalls (such as Quebrada de Jaspe, with a riverbed of semi-precious jasper), and fascinating flora, ranging from ground orchids to carnivorous plants. At the southeastern extreme is Roraima *tepuy*, made famous by Sir Arthur Conan Doyle's work, *The Lost World*.

The capital of Amazonas state, Puerto Ayacucho, can be reached by road, as well as commercial flights. But from there on, exploring the depths of its virgin forests, *tepuyes* sacred to the native Piaroa, and remote villages that have changed little since the Stone Age is the stuff of adventure tours by boat or small plane.

Need you ask why Venezuela casts such a spell on people? ❏

LEFT: one of Guayana's colorful inhabitants.
RIGHT: a farmer from Mérida state.

Decisive Dates

PRE-HISPANIC DEVELOPMENT

14,800 BC First humans arrive in Venezuela.
14,800–5000 BC Paleoindian period of hunter-gatherers.
5000–1000 BC Bone and shell implements.
1000 BC–AD 300 Agriculture and ceramics develop.
AD 300–1500 Interchange of influence between groups; cultivation of grain.

PERIOD OF COLONIZATION

1498 Christopher Columbus "discovers" the mouth of the Orinoco River and lands on Paria Peninsula.

1499 Alfonso de Ojeda and Amerigo Vespucci sail from Orinoco Delta to Guajira Peninsula and name the area Venezuela; pearl beds of Cubagua discovered.
1500 First settlement in South America, Santiago de Cubaga (later renamed Nueva Cádiz) founded.
1521 Cumaná founded, the first settlement by white men on South American mainland.
1527 Coro founded; Emperor Charles V gives indefinite lease to the Welsers – German bankers.
1546 Agreement with Welsers ended.
1567 Diego de Losada founds Santiago de León de Caracas, future capital of Venezuela.
1681 By order of Felipe II of Spain, the Law of the Indies is created, which governs the colonies until Independence.

1728 The Guipuzcoana Company is formed between King Felipe V and Basque merchants: until 1785 it has total monopoly over the Province of Venezuela's imports, exports, and economic development.
1739 First political and military unification of Venezuela with creation of Viceroyalty of Nueva Granada.
1777 Captaincy-general of Venezuela is created, uniting provinces of Margarita, Caracas, Mérida de Maracaibo, Nueva Andalucía, Guayana, and Trinidad.

THE QUEST FOR INDEPENDENCE

1806 Francisco de Miranda mounts first uprising against the Spanish; Venezuelan flag flies for first time.
1810 Authority of captain-general is repudiated on April 19; the Junta Suprema de Caracas is formed to govern; the first Congress is convoked June 11.
1811 On July 5, Venezuela is the first colony to proclaim independence from Spain; the Confederación Americana de Venezuela is formed of the provinces of Caracas, Cumaná, Barcelona, Barinas, Margarita, Mérida, and Trujillo.
1812 Earthquake leaves 10,000 dead in Caracas; May 19, Miranda given dictatorial powers; July 31, Miranda taken prisoner, deported to prison in Spain.
1813 Simón Bolívar invades Venezuela from Colombia, beginning the "Admirable Campaign" on March 1; establishes the Second Republic August 7; is proclaimed Liberator and given dictatorial powers.
1819 On February 15, Congress of Angostura convenes, elects Bolívar President of the Republic; the Constitution is approved.
1821 Second Battle of Carabobo – the last great battle in War of Independence – is fought on 24 July.
1823 Battle of Lake Maracaibo fought on 24 July with Spanish captain-general surrendering in Maracaibo on August 3; Gen. José Antonio Páez liberates Puerto Cabello on November 8 and last Spanish troops leave.

NEW POLITICAL STRUCTURE

May 6, 1830 Constitutional Congress convenes in Valencia, ratifies separation of Venezuela from La Gran Colombia union, names José Antonio Páez first president of Venezuela, and creates Constitution.
December 17, 1830 Simón Bolívar dies in Colombia.
1831–35 First presidency of Páez.
1839–43 Second presidency of Páez; road between Caracas/La Guaira built – first of its kind in Venezuela.
1845 Spain recognizes independence of Venezuela with the Treaty of Madrid.
1854 Slavery abolished.
1858–63 The Federal Wars.
1864 New democratic constitution; the Republic becomes the Estados Unidos de Venezuela.

1870–87 General Antonio Guzmán Blanco is president (or behind-the-scenes ruler); in feud with Catholic Church, he establishes compulsory secular education (1870), civil birth and marriage registry (1872). He closes convents and seminaries (1874), and inaugurates Masonic Lodge in Caracas (1875).
1878 First petroleum exploitation, in Táchira state.
1899–1908 Dictatorship of Gen. Cipriano Castro, with Gen. Juan Vicente Gómez as vice president.
1908 Gómez assumes power while Castro is abroad.
1909–35 Dictatorship of Juan Vicente Gómez.
1922 Blow-out of "Los Barrosos" well in Zulia state; discovery of largest oil deposit in the world.
1936–45 Dictatorial presidencies of Gen. Eleazar López Contreras and Gen. Isías Medina.

YEARS OF TURMOIL

1945 Military dictatorship is overthrown; Rómulo Betancourt becomes provisional president of civilian Revolutionary Junta; women given the right to vote.
1948 Bloodless military coup overthrows government.
1952–58 Dictatorship of Marcos Pérez Jiménez.

DEMOCRACY

1958 On January 23, present-day democracy begins with bloodless overthrow of Pérez Jiménez; junta of combined military and civil members rules until elections; return of political exiles.
1960 OPEC (Organization of Petroleum Exporting Countries) is created through initiative of Venezuela.
1974–79 Presidency of Carlos Andrés Pérez; nationalization of iron and steel industry (1975), and then the petroleum industry (1976).

DEATH OF "SAUDI VENEZUELA"

February 18, 1983 "Black Friday" – falling oil prices force devaluation of currency. The "fat years" are over.
1984–89 Presidential term of Jaime Lusinchi is marked by corruption.
1989 Carlos Andrés Pérez elected to second term, initiates severe economic reforms; popular uprising on February 27 sparked by Pérez's reform measures brings nationwide looting and hundreds of deaths.
1992 Two coup attempts, February 4 and November 27, with rebels turned back by loyal government forces.
1993 Pérez indicted by Supreme Court for corruption; Senate suspends him from office, and elects Ramón José Velásquez interim president.

PRECEDING PAGES: a monument to the encounter between Europeans and Amerindians, Cumaná.
LEFT: indigenous Panare, Amazonas state.
RIGHT: a grenadier.

1994 Failure of Banco Latino initiates two-year banking crisis; Rafael Caldera is elected to second term as president, ordering 66 percent devaluation of the bolívar, exchange controls, return of price controls.
1996 Inflation tops 100 percent, exchange controls lifted, stock market sets record highs, oil prices hit five-year high, and the steel industry is privatized.
1997–98 Economic crisis worsens as government fails to control fiscal expenditures; oil prices and stock market plunge; wage strikes in nearly every sector.
1999 A new president, Hugo Chávez, failed coup leader, is inaugurated, although his Movimiento de la 5a República party does not have a majority. Floods devastate the country, killing thousands.

2000 A new constitution brings about major restructuring of the government and the country is renamed the Bolivarian Republic of Venezuela. Amid political chaos, Chávez is re-elected president.
2001 Despite high oil revenues, falling inflation and the implementation of increased public spending of Chávez's Plan Bolívar 2000, the president is unable to bridge the huge gap between rich and poor. Civil protests culminate in a nationwide strike and mass demonstrations in December.
2002 The bolívar is devalued by 17 percent in February. Mounting military discontent and a general strike lead to Chávez's forced resignation on April 12. Two days later he is reinstated but the country remains in political and economic crisis. ❑

BEGINNINGS

After the "discovery" of Venezuela by Christopher Columbus, the people
who had lived here for thousands of years put up a staunch defense of their lands

Many histories of Venezuela commence in 1498, when the navigator Christopher Columbus first laid eyes on the Paria Peninsula. Overwhelmed by its beauty, he called it "the land of grace." Of course, Columbus was the first European to visit South America, but it was hardly a discovery – native Americans had been living here for some 16,000 years, ever since the great migrations following the last Ice Age.

Dozens of unique cultures inhabited the vast region of mountains, desert, plains, and jungle that the invading Spaniards would eventually bring together under the name of "Venezuela." Convinced that he had found the Orient, Columbus called these inhabitants "Indians," and the misnomer has stuck (although, in Spanish, native Venezuelans prefer to be referred to as *indígenas*, or "indigenous people").

These indigenous groups did not build magnificent empires or glittering cities like those later found in Mexico or Peru. Instead, they lived in semi-nomadic, hunting and gathering societies, or small agricultural villages. Although Europeans tended to dismiss their societies as primitive, the pre-Columbian world was in fact highly complex: each society had its own language, mythology, and cultural traditions, as well as a long history of warfare and survival. Some (the Caribe for example) were fierce and warlike, descending on their enemies in canoes and turning their bones into flutes; others, such as the Arawaks, were sedentary, spending more time on farming than fighting.

No records

With no knowledge of writing, these pre-Columbian societies kept no records, and little is known about dozens of ancient cultures. Remote groups, such as the Guajiros around modern-day Maracaibo and the Piaroas in the Amazon, managed to survive the murderous onslaught of Europeans, but the majority were simply wiped out.

LEFT AND RIGHT: European visions of indigenous life.

Yet when Columbus's tiny caravels weighed anchor in the Gulf of Paria on his third voyage, there was little indication of the wholesale devastation that European contact would bring. The navigator decided that this new fruit-laden land was "the loveliest in all the world" and its people surprisingly open and friendly. Canoes

full of Paria Indians came out to greet the newcomers, and Columbus eagerly noted that they wore jewelry made of gold and pearls.

The virtual flood of explorers that followed soon abandoned Columbus's idea that the New World was Asia. After sailing up and down Venezuela's beach-lined coast, they were also decidedly unimpressed with what it had to offer in the way of riches. Apart from a few small baubles, the Caribbean yielded no quantities of precious metal, silk, or spices. One of these first explorers, the Italian Amerigo Vespucci, gave Venezuela its name – literally, "Little Venice" – when his sailors commented, no doubt ironically, that the native villages on stilts in Lake

Maracaibo reminded them of the canals of Venice. But this growing suspicion that the Americas were hardly worth bothering about changed when Cortés conquered Mexico in 1519. News of the great city of Tenochtitlán accompanied boatloads of gold to the royal court in Spain. It seemed that kingdoms of unimagined wealth might lie deep in the heart of any new territory – and Venezuela, as the most accessible part of the new continent of South America, topped the list for conquest.

WILD RESISTANCE

Paradoxically, although the huge, "advanced" civilizations of Mexico and later Peru collapsed quickly under the Spanish onslaught, the wilder shores of Venezuela proved most difficult to conquer and settle.

As a result, when Spaniards began to mount expeditions into the interior of Venezuela, the native reaction was often immediately hostile.

The invasion begins

The tone for colonizing Venezuela was set by the disastrous 1530 expedition led by one of Cortés's most trusted captains, Diego de Ordaz. Convinced that there was a link between the glow of the sun and the color of gold, the aging conquistador set off from Spain with more than 600 men toward the

The Spaniards had set up a pearl fishery on the desolate island of Cubagua, but now they decided to found a town on Tierra Firme – "the mainland," or to foreign tongues "the Spanish Main." In 1521, a few mud huts were established around a square plaza by the Caribbean and called Cumaná, the first Spanish town in continental South America. But even this outpost had to be fought for: relations with the local population had soured long before, thanks to regular Spanish slave raids. Slave traders would simply surprise indigenous families fishing on beaches and transport them to the miserable sugar plantations that were being set up in Trinidad.

hottest place then known in South America, the Equator, lying between the Orinoco and Amazon rivers.

After a difficult crossing of the Atlantic, Ordaz and his men spent several months wandering the Orinoco Delta. Tropical diseases and hunger quickly took a bitter toll among the unacclimatized Spaniards. "There were men who, from one day to the next, had their entire feet consumed by cancer from the ankle to the toes," one chronicler recorded. Finally, the desperate Spaniards found a large Arawak fishing village: the *conquistadores* went straight for the native women, who were naked except for "a rag in front of their private parts, which is loose and just long enough to cover them…Thus when they sway, or in a wind, everything is revealed."

Before long, the Spaniards became convinced that the Arawaks plotted to steal their pigs and began a fight in which the whole village burned. At another village, Ordaz put hundreds of unarmed Indians to the sword because they refused to give food (then burned the village to make sure none escaped by feigning death).

Only about 200 Spaniards were still alive when the expedition stumbled into the endless flat plains of the Venezuelan *llanos*. They wandered this near-deserted landscape, still follow-

more expeditions into Venezuela's inhospitable interior. Before long, Meta would blend with the enduring fantasy of "El Dorado," a fabulously wealthy land where a native king was covered daily with gold dust.

Dozens of expeditions set off into the Venezuelan interior, often to disappear without trace in the steaming jungles of the Amazon or succumb to starvation in the *llanos*. Strangely, many of these ill-fated groups were led by Germans. Forming a new chapter in the history of the Spanish conquest, the whole of Venezuela was temporarily granted in the 1500s to the German banking house of Welser, a

ing the Orinoco, until Ordaz finally agreed to turn back. The only good news was from an obviously terrified Indian prisoner, who announced under questioning that vast amounts of gold could be found in the nearby empire of Meta, which was ruled by a one-eyed prince.

The German conquistadors

Although Ordaz himself died on the way back to Spain, the myth of Meta inspired dozens

LEFT: the quest for El Dorado inspired the exploration of Venezuela.
ABOVE: fanciful vision of a Spanish conquistador, mounted on a llama.

group of merchant adventurers who had interests from India to Africa, patronized the artist Albrecht Dürer, and to whom the Spanish king Carlos I owed thousands of ducats.

Historians have been fascinated by the German expeditions mainly because of their cruelty, stunning even by the callous standards of the day, and their almost total futility. A wealthy young cloth merchant from Ulm, Ambrosius Dalfinger, led hundreds of finely equipped soldiers to the sandy wastelands near Lake Maracaibo, losing a third of his force without finding even a single gold earring. When he did find gold on another trip, the soldiers sent to transport it got lost, turned to

Aguirre the Mad

The 16th-century Venezuelan frontier was a remote and often desperate place, where Spaniards were as willing to turn on one another as to fight for any common goal. Spending months at sea, away from any instructions from Spain, conquistadors made their own self-serving law, and dozens of intrigues and civil wars were played out in the power vacuum.

Entering this chaotic scene in 1562 was perhaps the most notorious conquistador of them all, Lope de Aguirre, whose exploits were immortalized

for modern audiences in the 1972 Werner Herzog movie *Aguirre, Wrath of God*. The historian John Hemming has described Aguirre as "a man of unmitigated evil, cruel, psychopathic, and gripped by an obsessive grievance against the whole of Spanish society." These terms would have seemed charitable to the poor Spaniards and Indians who had to face him in a voyage of destruction that ended up in Venezuela.

Expelled from Peru after joining the wrong side of a civil war, Aguirre signed up for a large expedition leaving Cuzco for the Amazon basin. The object, as ever, was to search for the chimerical El Dorado. But as the inexperienced group of 370 soldiers stumbled through the steaming jungle,

Aguirre soon found a wellspring of discontent. He incited a mutiny and had the expedition's leader, Pedro de Ursua, murdered in his hammock. Another Spanish noble was elevated to the leadership, but his rule was short-lived: Aguirre had him put to the sword as well, and his beautiful *mestizo* mistress hacked to death.

Described as a thin, scrawny man with one lame leg, Aguirre was nevertheless one of the most experienced and ruthless fighters in the New World. Now, floating down the Amazon River on a barge, he declared his intention of leading the rebels back to conquer Peru by traveling via Venezuela around the north of South America then marching back to where they had started.

En route, Aguirre began to indulge his long-standing grudges against Spanish society and some more recently acquired psychoses, turning the expedition into a floating death camp. According to chroniclers, Aguirre "determined not to carry with him any gentleman or person of quality, and therefore slew all such persons; and then departing only with the common soldiers, he left behind all the Spanish women and sick men." The surviving Andean porters were also left to die. Aguirre then began suspecting soldiers of plotting against him, and ordered so many of them to be garrotted that before long the expedition's numbers were reduced from 370 to 230.

Aguirre's rantings and paranoia were at fever pitch when the rebel barges arrived in Venezuela, weighing anchor on the palm-fringed Isla Margarita. The Spanish governor welcomed them, but he was quickly seized and executed. Aguirre instituted a reign of terror over the island, putting to death any local citizens or his own soldiers who seemed to be "lukewarm in his service."

Aguirre moved on to Barquisimeto, his forces by now reduced by half. Between strong resistance organized by Diego García de Paredes and desertions by his troops, he realized the end was near. But, before surrender, he entered the room of his 18-year-old daughter, Elvira, killing her with his dagger, so she would not have to live being called "daughter of a traitor". When García de Paredes' soldiers entered and discovered his deed, they riddled him with bullets, then beheaded and quartered him, dividing severed members among the villages which had sent help to combat him, and placed his head in a cage displayed in the plaza of El Tocuyo for many years. ❑

LEFT: Spanish *conquistadores*.

cannibalism, then all died of starvation. Another German captain, a calculating 24-year-old named Nicolaus Federmann, became convinced that the Pacific Ocean lay not far south of Coro. He tricked tribe after native tribe into offering his men help before turning on them and either slaughtering or enslaving them as porters.

Typical was his treatment of the Guaiquerí Indians, who came to meet Federmann's men in an apparently peaceful fashion. "While I distracted them with words," the Teutonic conquistador proudly recorded, "I arranged that they should be surrounded by the horses, which would attack them."

"We took them by surprise and killed five hundred. The horsemen charged into the thick of them, knocking down as many as they could. Our footsoldiers then slaughtered these like pigs… In the end they tried to hide in the grass, or the living hid beneath the dead, but these were found and many of them beheaded after we finished with those who were fleeing."

In the end, Federmann found a race of dwarfs – only 76 cm (30 inches) tall, he reported, but perfectly proportioned – and even some golden trinkets, but little else. After about 20 years of such atrocious depredations, the Spanish Crown ordered an inquiry and revoked the German lease. With poetic justice, many of the Germans came to sticky ends: Federmann wasted the rest of his life searching for El Dorado and Dalfinger fell riddled with Indian arrows in Colombia.

The frontier secured

Although no cities paved with jewels were ever found, these misdirected quests did attract the manpower needed to secure much of Venezuela for the Spanish Crown. Giving up on El Dorado in the 1540s, colonists turned to securing more towns and routes through the Andes to the rest of the empire. It was an uphill struggle: the scattered groups of native Venezuelans were now aware of the Spaniards' cruelty and put up tenacious resistance to their advance.

In fact, Spanish colonists expected the struggle to go on for decades and ruefully looked at other American provinces, such as Peru and Bolivia, where silver mines were making penniless adventurers into grandees overnight. Then an unexpected weapon broke the native resis-

RIGHT: English pirates became the scourge of Venezuela's coast.

tance: smallpox. The disease was unknown in the Americas and wiped out entire indigenous communities. In the embattled Caracas Valley, for example, a wave of the plague in 1580 killed two-thirds of the native population.

The forgotten provinces

With this ignoble victory, Venezuela entered its long period of colonial control. These centuries as a dismal and forgotten backwater within the vast Spanish Empire are often skipped over as an unmemorable and somewhat irrelevant period, not least by modern Venezuelans. However, the structures that were set up during the

colonial era have shaped – and distorted – the fate of Venezuela to this day.

The small outposts at Cumaná, Caracas, Mérida, and Maracaibo grew to be muddy villages and then established towns as colonists began arriving in numbers from Spain. Still marking Venezuela's towns and cities is the original monotonous grid-iron street plan, spreading out from the *cabildo* (town council) and cathedral as a symbol of rational empire-building. Houses were built mainly of adobe mud, although a few of the richest settlers used brick; most were set around a patio and garden, and were kept one-story high to avoid damage by earthquakes. Attempts were made to create genteel enclaves of Hispanic style in this tropical setting: children were still married off at 14, heavy imported wine was quaffed with meals, and a long siesta after lunch was *de rigueur*.

Pirates soon replaced Indians as the main threat to Venezuela's new towns. Prowling the Caribbean coastline were packs of English, Dutch, and French corsairs waiting for gold-laden galleons but who were not above pillaging a whole town for its wealth.

Cattle and cacao

After building towns as bases, the Spaniards claimed the countryside. In the grand colonial

plan, Venezuela became half-plantation, half-ranch. Missionaries often became the shock troops of settlement: fiery-eyed Franciscans, Capuchins, and Jesuits filtered through the hinterland to make contact with the remaining indigenous groups. Many ended up martyrs, but they succeeded in setting up the missions that converted the *indígenas* and prepared for their submission to the Spanish Crown.

Across the warm valleys of the coast spread *haciendas*, semi-feudal plantations growing mostly the native South American plant cacao. Meanwhile, the grasslands of the *llanos* were opened up to cattle. *Hatos*, or ranches, began to dot this remote area and, as in the pampas of Argentina, half-wild herds were soon wandering the empty plains, unrestricted by fencing. Since beef was near-impossible to transport, *llaneros* – the breed of skilled horsemen, usually drawn from the fringes of society, who worked the *llanos* – would slaughter steers just to eat the tongue and take the hide, leaving the carcasses to rot in the wilderness.

Though there were chronic shortages of virtually every other domestic item in colonial times, leather was abundant and used for almost anything: it made the backing for chairs, replaced glass for windows, and occasionally could even be substituted for rare iron nails.

The shape of colonial society

The majority of initial settlers were young unmarried men, and coaxing Spanish women to brave the uncertainties of an Atlantic crossing and rough life in the New World would long remain a problem. Those women that did come were horrified to find they might have to share their new husbands with one or more native or black slave mistresses, and even accept a collection of bastard children. Indeed, the mixture of races was soon to be the main feature of Venezuelan society. By 1700, "free-coloreds" or *pardos* – including everyone from freed slaves to those of mixed race – would make up some 45 percent of Venezuela's whole population, with black slaves and native Americans comprising 15 percent each. *Blancos,* or whites, made up only about 25 percent of the total (and even then, as one foreign writer observed with studied prejudice, they were "rarely free of any connection to the blood of the colored class").

This white elite – often called "Gran Cacaos" in deference to the source of its power – was

SLAVE LABORS

With the native population dying out, the Spaniards brought in boatloads of black African slaves as laborers to work on the expanding cacao plantations, adding a new and lasting racial element to Venezuelan society. Slavery lasted here long after it was abolished in Europe: as late as 1840 travelers were appalled to find every Venezuelan town still had its covered slave market.

Blacks for sale had coconut oil rubbed into their skin to make it shiny and, as if they were horses, had their teeth checked by prospective buyers to confirm their age and health. Conditions on the plantations were pitiless, and slave revolts were repressed quickly and ferociously.

acutely conscious of its vulnerability, and in a primitive form of apartheid made sure that *pardos* could not wear the same Hispanic clothes as whites, could not enter the Church or study at university. There were even attempts to have *pardos* carry a certificate denoting their racial status "to avoid doubts and confusion," while the motto *Todo blanco es caballero* ("every white man is a gentleman") became the rule.

As the colonial era progressed, the *blancos* became divided between a small group of Spanish-born newcomers and the vast bulk of creoles (whites born in the New World). Both of these social groups emulated the styles and manners of far-away Madrid. The visiting German scientist Alexander von Humboldt *(see page 173)* would record of Venezuela that "in no other part of Spanish America has civilization assumed a more European character," with *blancos* holding elegant soirées, dancing, and earnestly discussing the latest French farce or Italian opera.

Still, the Venezuelans could hardly avoid some creole eccentricities: von Humboldt was astonished to see aristocratic families on hot evenings pick up their chairs and carry them into nearby rivers, chatting with friends and smoking cigars as the water flowed up to their knees, quite unfazed by the many small crocodiles splashing about their feet or the playful dolphins spraying them with water.

The chocolate empire

Despite the Venezuelans' European airs, their six scattered provinces were for almost all the colonial period among the least important, successful, or wealthy parts of the Spanish Empire. In short, Venezuela was an unknown tropical backwater. What changed all that was chocolate. When Europe and the United States developed a passion for this by-product of cacao in the mid 1700s, Venezuelan plantations geared up to meet the demand, and Venezuela was elevated from obscurity into the most valuable non-mining colony in the Spanish Empire. The Gran Cacao *blancos* could hardly believe their luck.

But this Golden Age was merely the calm before the storm. The wars of independence would soon hit Venezuela with unexpected ferocity, turning its *haciendas* into cemeteries and pushing the country's progress back more than 100 years.   ❑

LEFT: chocolate in the making: cacao pods *(mazorcas)* grow directly out of the trunk and branches.
ABOVE: African slaves at work on an 18th-century cacao plantation.

INDEPENDENCE

Venezuelans paid a high price for independence, with the lengthy period of fighting leaving their liberated country in ruins

The soporific calm of colonial Venezuela was shattered at the beginning of the 19th century by the war of independence against Spain. Although Venezuela would play a key role in liberating much of South America, most Venezuelans entered the struggle hesitantly and failed to anticipate its enormous cost. Nowhere else on the continent was the fighting more cruel and destructive: after two decades of bloodshed, Venezuela would be lying in ruins and its tenuous colonial prosperity lost.

Inseparable from this dramatic conflict is the figure of Simón Bolívar, "El Libertador" (The Liberator). Every Venezuelan village, no matter how small, now has a bronze Bolívar statue along with a plaza, main street, or municipal building named in honor of the romantic national hero who, despite his many victories, died a bitter and broken man. A heavy shroud of mythology lies over his memory. Bolívar is Latin America's Washington, Napoleon, and Hamlet all rolled into one.

El Libertador

Bolívar was notoriously short in stature, thin and wiry, a fine horseman and swimmer. He inspired the devotion of his soldiers and the praises of everyone from South American patriots to the English poet Lord Byron. Exiled twice and escaping numerous assassination attempts, Bolívar squandered one of the greatest family fortunes in the New World pursuing his dream of a united Latin America. The dream took him on campaigns across the Andes to Colombia, Ecuador, Peru, and the nation named after him, Bolivia. Looking back from the present day, few historians deny that Bolívar was a genius.

Yet as the 19th century turned, there was no indication that Venezuela would soon push for independence or that Bolívar would be involved. The rich, white creole elite rarely questioned the basis of Spanish control that had served

them so well. More worrisome was that the black and mixed-race population might rise up against them. Meanwhile, Simón Bolívar was simply another young man about to inherit a fortune from his Gran Cacao family, although on his travels to Europe, he had met Alexander von Humboldt (*see page 173*), and been

astonished by the suggestion that the Spanish American colonies were ripe for freedom.

The first push toward independence came in 1808 when sensational news arrived from the Napoleonic wars in Europe: Spain had been occupied by the French army, the Spanish king had abdicated, and Napoleon's brother had been placed on the throne. But rather than declare Venezuela independent, leading *caraqueños* formed a junta in support of the Spanish king. Only by 1810 did the wealthy elite decide that Spain was in such confusion they should try self-government. On April 19 they ousted Captain-general Vicente Emparan and constituted the Junta Suprema de Caracas.

LEFT: paying homage to Simón Bolívar at the Plaza Bolívar in Caracas.
RIGHT: the young "Liberator."

Having formed the Junta Patriótica to actively promote the cause of independence among a skeptical public, when the moment was deemed right, the date of July 5, 1811 was set to convene a National Congress. During this meeting, the Declaration of Independence was approved with only one contrary vote – not against independence, but the timing. The First Republic was formed, governed by a triumvirate. This lasted until May 19, 1812, when Francisco de Miranda was given dictatorial powers to try to save the

A MULTI-FACETED MAN

"El Libertador" Simón Bolívar could discourse as easily about the works of Rousseau as he could about military strategy.

had risen to the rank of colonel in the patriot forces, but his true leadership potential had remained untapped. Now, during his first exile, Bolívar slowly began to exert his charisma and assume command of the patriots.

First of all came what the Venezuelans call *La Campaña Admirable* (or the "Admirable Campaign"), when Bolívar and other patriot generals regrouped their forces and began a "War to the Death" against the Spaniards.

Adding to the carnage was the arrival of the *llaneros*, the wild horsemen of Venezuela's

Republic, already shaken by royalists' uprisings. Although Miranda's forces outnumbered those of the crown, disorganization, lack of funds, discontent, and desertion among patriots led him to capitulate on July 26, 1812 – which would result in him being declared a traitor. Many patriots fled into exile in the Caribbean.

The slaughter begins

One of the exiles was Bolívar, who had thrown himself into the lower echelons of the independence movement as if to help forget the tragic death of his young wife. He had gone to London as the new republic's ambassador (only to be disappointed in his pleas for support) and

interior plains who turned out to be a devastating cavalry force – initially on the side of the royalists, and later for the patriots. The *llaneros* lived off the land and took as pay what they could pillage.

By 1814, Bolívar had recaptured Caracas and declared the Second Republic. The *llaneros* mobilized against him, sweeping into Caracas and forcing the patriots, yet again, into exile, their property confiscated to add to the misery.

The *llanero* commander, José Tomás Boves, became notorious as the Spanish "butcher," personally supervising the massacre of entire villages. Boves finally met a violent end, skewered on a lance in battle.

Hiding out in Jamaica, Bolívar prepared to fight yet again. He realized the importance of the *llaneros*, and offered them land as a reward for joining his cause: the confiscated estates of royalists would be distributed among them. The *llanero* leader – a Herculean, illiterate cavalryman named José Antonio Páez agreed. And since the *llaneros* followed strong figures rather than any particular cause, Bolívar gained the backbone of a new army. The two retired to Apure and soon after Bolívar continued to Angostura for the Congress of February 15, 1819. There he was elected President of the Republic and submitted the project for the Constitution of Venezuela. Congress approved it six months later.

Meanwhile, Bolívar had returned to Apure with the idea of invading Barinas but, receiving favorable news from the west, he shifted plans to invade Nueva Granada, and led his army over the Andes into Colombia in the middle of winter. This march is considered one of the most daring strokes of Latin America's liberation. More than a quarter of the army died on the march. But, bolstered by the experienced troops of the British Legion *(see page 38)*, the campaign was a success with the triumph of Boyacá and liberation of Nueva Granada.

With this victory, Bolívar's project to form a single Republic to be called Colombia, joining Venezuela and Nueva Granada, was approved by Congress on December 17, 1819, with Bolívar named provisional president of La Gran Colombia.

The war would continue for several years more, extending across the entire territory and adjacent lands, decimating the population and destroying the countryside.

The last great and deciding battle of the War of Independence was won at Carabobo on June 24 , 1821. However, it was the patriot's triumph in the naval battle of Lake Maracaibo on July 24, 1823 that formally brought this chapter of history to an end with the capitulation on August 3 of Gen. Francisco Tomás Morales, Spain's captain general of the Costa Firme.

Twelve days later, Morales, the last representative of Spanish power in Venezuela, was ejected to Cuba, with 5,000 pesos given by the patriots to cover the cost of his trip.

The Liberator's dream

But Bolívar's career as *El Libertador* was only beginning. Forming and presiding over La Gran Colombia was hardly enough: Bolívar not only planned to extirpate the Spanish presence from Latin America, but wanted to unite all the former Spanish colonies as the world's largest nation. This vision, which drove him on to liberate the Andean nations, held together for a remarkably long time given that Bolívar may have been the only Latin American to believe in it.

Thousands of Venezuelan troops followed the general into battle among the volcanoes near Quito, the Inca ruins of Cuzco, and the bleak *altiplano* beyond Lake Titicaca. After the last Spaniards had surrendered at the Andean battle of Ayacucho, Bolívar was fêted in Lima and seemed close to achieving his dream. Yet even as he danced all night through the glittering ballrooms of South America's wealthiest city and gained a reputation as a Casanova (one cavalry officer reputedly moved out of the presidential palace because the shrieks of love-making ruined his sleep), things were going awry.

News soon arrived that the confederation of La Gran Colombia – which was then made up

LEFT: *llanero* lancers feign a retreat, only to return and attack again.

RIGHT: Simón Bolívar ponders Latin America's fate on the heights of Ecuador's Mount Chimborazo.

The British Legion

L a Legión Británica, or British Legion, is the shorthand term for the more than 5,000 English, Scottish, Irish, and Hanoverian soldiers who journeyed across the Atlantic to join Simón Bolívar's revolutionary army in Venezuela. In one of the least-known aspects of the South American wars of independence, battalions drawn from far-away London, Glasgow, and Dublin fought alongside *criollos* throughout Venezuela, with many following the Liberator even into the harsh Andes of Peru.

Recruiting in Britain began soon after 1815, when the Battle of Waterloo finally brought the Napoleonic wars to a close. Multitudes of demobilized veterans were returning to their homes, only to find few jobs and dismal prospects.

In 1817, Bolívar ordered his agent in London to recruit any officers who wanted to serve as mercenaries in South America. The response was overwhelming. An officer named Gustavus Mathius Hippisley – who, like most officers, was chafing under a half-pay army pension – immediately came forward with an officer corps ready to form a regiment of hussars in Venezuela. They were followed by three more regiments of cavalry officers, one of rifles, and an artillery unit – 1,000 soldiers in all.

Alarmed by the potential exodus, the British government decreed that any departure was prohibited. On learning the news, Hippisley ordered that the boats would leave immediately – weighing anchor so quickly, in fact, that many recruits were left behind. Although it departed unmolested, the flotilla hit a storm in the Channel and one of the troop ships was wrecked on the French coast, drowning 200 recruits.

The 800 who made it to the New World found themselves stranded in the British Antilles for months waiting for their arms. Tropical diseases hit, followed by massive desertions, and only 240 made it to Angostura (now Ciudad Bolívar) in Venezuela. They were immediately despatched to join Bolívar's army in the steaming *llanos,* where they took part in the battle of Samán. Hippisley arrived some time later, but fell out with Bolívar and soon returned to England.

Despite this inauspicious start, officers and soldiers arrived from Britain in a steady stream until the British government finally stopped the flow in August 1819. Historians estimate that some 6,500 set out for South America and 5,300 arrived. The bulk were English, although there was a battalion of Scottish highlanders and a separate "Irish Legion."

In spite of being on the winning side, very few of the British Legion would survive the gruelling years of war. The major killer was not weaponry but disease: soldiers succumbed to everything from malaria to typhoid.

The so-called "Albion Battalion," composed mostly of English soldiers, fought with distinction in Venezuela, at the battle of Boyacá in Colombia, and beneath the volcano of Pichincha in Ecuador before being disbanded in 1822 for lack of numbers. The First Venezuelan Rifles continued to march with Bolívar through the royalist stronghold of Lima and up into the *altiplano* of Peru, where it took part in the climactic Battle of Ayacucho in 1824.

The Irish contingents performed less gloriously; one group surrendered to the royalists and was executed *en masse,* others mutinied on Isla Margarita, and seized boats and fled to Jamaica. Yet one Irishman, Gen. Daniel O'Leary, stayed in South America and became one of Bolívar's most trusted confidantes, staying by the Liberator's side until his dying moments. He then wrote a 34-volume memoir, which remains the most important source of information on Bolívar's life. ❑

LEFT: contemporary drawing of a patriot in Bolívar's liberation army.

of modern Colombia, Venezuela, and Ecuador, and a cornerstone of Bolívar's plan – was cracking up. The *llanero* Páez planned to lead Venezuela to secede. Bolívar rushed back to Caracas and patched up the confederation, but it was doomed. Local interests were too strong.

Even so, Bolívar spent the last years of his life vainly staving off the inevitable. Wracked by tuberculosis, his disillusion took on a tragic dimension (brilliantly captured by the Colombian writer Gabriel García Márquez in his novel *The General in his Labyrinth*). One by one, his supporters turned against him, and his only possible successor, Marshal Sucre, was assassi-

decades of Latin American history. "America is ungovernable," he declared. "Those who serve the revolution plow the sea. The only thing to do in America is emigrate."

Repairing the ruin

For most Venezuelans, nominal independence was secured in 1821. But Venezuela had fragmented into regions controlled by *caudillos* (strongmen) and there would be another 10 years of fighting before the country was more or less under stable rule.

Although the country remained a part of La Gran Colombia for several years out of defer-

nated on a mountain highway. In Colombia, Bolívar escaped another assassination attempt only by leaping out of his bedroom window. In his home country, Venezuela, he was finally outlawed as a traitor. Jeered at in the streets by the same people who had cheered him a few short years before, the general left Bogotá for exile in Europe, but never made it. He died in 1830, almost penniless, in the small town of Santa Marta on the Colombian coast.

Shortly before his death, Bolívar penned a bitter prophecy that has echoed through the

ABOVE: the remains of Bolívar in the Panteón Nacional in Caracas.

ence to Bolívar, Páez finally declared the sovereignty of Venezuela in 1829. A Congress was convened in Valencia on May 6, 1830, which conferred Páez with leadership of the Republic, ordered the expulsion of Bolívar from the territory of La Gran Colombia and, on September 22, approved the Constitution of Venezuela, which left it definitely separated from Colombia. The new country of Venezuela began the process of reconstruction.

By any reckoning, the independence wars had been devastating: at least 150,000 Venezuelans died in the fighting; working *haciendas* were destroyed; roads and bridges were in disrepair; and livestock numbers had fallen from

4.5 million head to about 250,000. The treasury was bankrupt, and the new administration survived only on a high-interest British loan. Others besides Bolívar were beginning to wonder what it had all been for. The basic colonial social structure was still intact.

Bolívar had honored his promise to divide the lands of royalists among the *llaneros* and other veterans, on a sliding scale of size from generals down to foot-soldiers. But in a process that foreshadowed a history of failed land reform in Latin America, the impoverished soldiers sold out their smaller shares to the officers at a fraction of the real cost. The old white land-

ultimately lead to the extermination of the privileged classes." Male *blancos* tied the vote to owning property, kept important military posts and controlled everything from the presidency to the most obscure local municipal offices.

Years of chaos

The rest of the 19th century was a complicated morass of coups, civil wars and separatist movements. To some extent all these involved arguments among the white elite over who would control and profit from foreign trade. The chief participants were the educated *caraqueño* bureaucrats and a series of rougher

owning elite gained some new members, mostly white officers, whose descendants own much of Venezuelan agriculture to this day. Otherwise, their power was unbroken. Meanwhile, slavery continued to exist. Bolívar had freed his own slaves, but only a handful of other landowners followed suit.

It was only in the 1850s that they decided that slavery was actually unprofitable, and that slaves could be kept tied to plantations by making them nominally free but charging exorbitant rents. The mixed blooded *pardos* were also kept out of positions of power. Even Bolívar had dreaded the prospect of *pardocracia*, or rule by the colored masses, which he said "will

CAUDILLO WITH A CAUSE

The most famous *caudillo* (strongman) was Simón Bolívar's old ally, the *llanero* José Antonio Páez. From 1830 to 1848 he established a modicum of order in Venezuela, hunting down bandits, crushing rebellions, and, when he was not president himself, choosing exactly who should rule. The illiterate plainsman of old remained a figure in local politics until the 1860s, when he was finally exiled to die in New York City, far from his native world. Even so, Páez gave Venezuela a chance to rebuild some of its former prosperity – largely thanks to the coffee boom – and he gave it enough stability to survive the upheavals that would occur in the next generations.

caudillos who commanded armed bands left over from the wars of independence.

The legacy of two decades of brutality was that might was right in the politics of Venezuela. As in several other South American countries, the ruling elite split into two factions that called themselves the Liberals and the Conservatives – although, rather like the Republican and Democratic parties in the modern United States, their differences were more about the fine tuning of government than any serious social change. Transfers of power between the two groups occurred in violent fashion, but any hint of an uprising by *pardos* or blacks was met with ruthless, united action.

The Liberals and the Conservatives plunged Venezuela into five years of civil war after a period of economic decline in the 1850s. In theory, the argument was about whether Venezuela should have a federal system or be controlled directly from Caracas, but although the Liberal-Federalists had won by 1863, regional revolts and battles continued for decades.

Despite the turmoil, some changes were occurring. Most noticeably, the city of Caracas was growing farther apart from the rest of the country. With its direct links to the outside world, the capital became increasingly affluent and cosmopolitan: its streets, buildings, and the dress of its educated bureaucrats mimicked the styles of Europe.

A change had even taken place in the popular view toward Simón Bolívar, who was rehabilitated in the eyes of history, and his personality cult began as a symbol of national unity. In 1842, the Liberator's remains were brought back to Caracas from Colombia and installed in a national pantheon. Statues of Bolívar were erected all around the country, and Venezuela's first national currency was set up in 1879 – the bolívar.

Birth of a nation

As the 19th century stumbled to a close, the old regional *caudillo* style of politics looked increasingly outdated. Presidents could no longer be earthy and charismatic men with enough guns to fight their way to the top, but were expected to have professional credentials.

More importantly, the president was increasingly able to impose his will on the rest of the country. The central government in Caracas began to build up its armed forces and equip them with modern weapons, against which the smaller *caudillos* could no longer compete. Newly introduced communications, such as the telegraph and railroad, ensured that they could no longer plot in secrecy.

Naturally, few *caudillos* accepted these changes lying down, and the 1890s were a particularly chaotic period of regional uprisings. Eccentric presidents such as Joaquín Crespo – who built the elegant Palacio de Miraflores in

Caracas, complete with an iron-plated, earthquake-resistant bedroom – still made it to the presidency. The haphazard style of a successor, Cipriano Castro, led to such serious economic problems that the government defaulted on its European loans. Then, as today, debt default was considered the most heinous of economic crimes. Between 1902–3, England, Germany, and Italy began a naval blockade of Venezuela to make it pay up.

The era of the regional *caudillos* was finally coming to an end. With the discovery of oil in the early 20th century, a new technocratic president, Juan Vicente Gómez, would fling the country headlong into the modern age. ❏

LEFT: European-style buildings sprang up in Caracas during the late 19th century.
RIGHT: loyal troops during the civil wars.

THE OIL RUSH

The discovery of oil in Venezuela resulted in a boom that was to change
the political and economic face of the country – not always for the better

The first Spanish explorers to land on the sun-scorched shores of Lake Maracaibo noted a thick black oil oozing from the sandy earth. The local indigenous population used the sticky liquid to caulk their canoes; it could be made into candles, spread to trap animals, and even used as a medicine. But for the Spaniards it held no interest, and for the next 400 years nobody but the Indians gave the oil a second thought.

By the turn of the 20th century, the invention of the automobile had given this black fluid new value. Even so, at first Venezuelans were not enthusiastic about the costly task of crude oil extraction. Explorations around Lake Maracaibo were desultory: a few small wells were dug, a pipeline and tiny refinery built, but nobody expected much from the discoveries.

Then, in December 1922, a Venezuelan subsidiary of Shell restarted drilling at a well named Los Barrosos No. 2, near the sleepy village of La Rosa on the east coast of Lake Maracaibo. Four years earlier, drilling had been suspended in disappointment at a depth of 164 meters (538 ft). But this time the well "blew out." On the first day of drilling 100,000 barrels of oil spurted from the earth, eclipsing the entire previous Venezuelan production of 8,000 barrels a day.

A country transformed

The find was dubbed the Bolívar Coastal Field, and made immediate world news. For Venezuela, oil was like manna from heaven. Petrodollars would change the country's face forever, bringing to an end generations of stagnation and giving Venezuela the highest per capita income in Latin America. In what one writer desribed as "a compression of historical time," Venezuela was transformed by the 1960s from an agricultural society characterized by political chaos into a consumerist and relatively stable democracy.

PRECEDING PAGES: oil towers on Lake Maracaibo.
LEFT: the discovery of oil in the 1920s transformed Venezuela.
RIGHT: dictator Juan Vicente Gómez.

In the two years after that well's discovery, some 73 different foreign companies flocked to Lake Maracaibo to begin exploration, encouraged by the promise of enormous profits with minimal taxes. The skilled workers were mostly from the United States, the hired muscle Venezuelan. In a remarkably short time hard-

bitten engineers from Texas and Oklahoma had carved oil empires from the wilderness.

In the initial years of exploration, conditions were appalling: the lakeside was either virgin rainforest or bleak desert. Imported heavy equipment was unloaded on the docks of Maracaibo – with 75,000 inhabitants, by far the largest town in the area – and taken in small sailboats to the eastern shore. From there, machinery could only be dragged by oxen and mules to the oil sites, with workers following on foot.

Soon, more sophisticated oil camps were set up. The fields were fenced off and even had their own police. Makeshift towns sprouted from nowhere along the lake's shore, with all the hallmarks of a "black gold" rush: bars and brothels outnumbered food stores ten to one, and fortunes were gambled or drunk away overnight.

Techniques were quickly invented for off-shore drilling on Lake Maracaibo. Hundreds of towers soon appeared, forming a floating steel forest. These towers no longer function, but with their ghostly flames they are still one of the most vivid images the world has of Venezuela.

The iron fist

The oil boom coincided with the dictatorship of Juan Vicente Gómez, whose brutal 27-year rule marked Venezuela irrevocably and set the

Cipriano Castro to travel to Europe for a medical operation before declaring him an outlaw and seizing the presidency. Gómez quickly turned the army into his personal Praetorian Guard, with loyal officers from Andean states given positions of favor. For the more subtle tasks of social control a secret police was formed to track down anyone who plotted against or even bad-mouthed the dictator.

Having built this vast, corrupt apparatus of control, Gómez moved from Caracas – whose European pretensions he never felt comfortable with – to a cattle ranch in nearby Maracay. From there he could pronounce the major

scene for the country as it is today. In many ways, Gómez fits the classic caricature of a Latin American dictator. An ex-cattle rancher and accountant from the Andean state of Táchira, he was a colorless and taciturn figure who ran Venezuela like a latter-day Roman emperor. The country was treated like a private *hacienda*; its inhabitants like peons who needed to be looked after like children. The Gómez political philosophy was not complex: trusted friends and relatives would be given positions of power and wealth; enemies, real or suspected, were hunted down, tortured, exiled, or murdered.

In 1908, having risen through the army to the rank of general, Gómez advised President

decisions of Venezuela's fate, while allowing the bureaucrats of Caracas to look after the day-to-day details of government. Civilian ministers, foreign diplomats, and heads of local businesses all made the journey out to this rural outpost, begging cap in hand for the favors of the surly patriarch.

The carnival king

With Venezuela firmly under his control, Gómez greeted the news of the 1922 oil boom in typical imperial style. As the Uruguayan writer Eduardo Galeano has described it: "While black geysers spouted on all sides, Gómez took petroleum shares from his bursting pockets to reward his friends, relations, and courtiers, the doctor who looked after his prostate, the generals who served as his bodyguard, the poets who sang his praises and the archbishop who gave him a special dispensation to eat meat on Good Friday."

Lavish tax concessions to US oil companies meant that the Venezuelan government received only some 7 percent of the total oil profits from 1919 to Gómez's death in 1935. Even so, the money had fallen from the skies as far as Venezuelans were concerned and – to a government accustomed to surviving on minimal local taxation – it seemed like a fortune. Roads, housing, and port facilities were built, while the city of Caracas began the modernization that would wipe out its colonial past forever.

Local entrepreneurs jumped on the development bandwagon and made themselves rich, creating a Venezuelan middle class. The bolívar remained strong throughout the Great Depression, and Venezuelans began to appear in the salons of Paris and jewelry stores of New York.

Not surprisingly, everyone wanted a piece of the action. Rural peasants flocked to the burgeoning oil camps and suburbs of Caracas to pick up work. Landowners gave up their farms so they could indulge in the lucrative trade of brokering the sale of drilling rights from the State to US companies. Agriculture declined rapidly, and there was no hope of starting up a manufacturing industry: Venezuela was importing everything from beans to refrigerators.

Autumn of the patriarch

Sealed up in his remote cattle ranch, overcome by illness and senility, Gómez began to suspect his closest allies of betrayal and a new rank of secret police thugs was brought to power in the struggle. The military watched the wretched spectacle of the president's last years, biding its time until it could gain more control.

When word finally leaked from Maracay in 1935 that the patriarch was dead, riots erupted around Venezuela. Thousands flocked into the streets to celebrate the autocrat's demise, sacking the houses of the most hated *gomecistas*, and, where possible, lynching them from telegraph poles. The military was too busy getting a new government ready to protect the old fig-

LEFT: young bohemians in Caracas.
RIGHT: a chic matron promenading.

ures – having regarded them with some contempt anyway – and tacit permission was given to purge the country.

The Gómez decades had transformed Venezuela, but they also left a curious void: the dictator's brutal repression had wiped out all previous political traditions and there was hardly anyone left who was capable of running the country.

Thousands of exiles who had been living in the cities of Europe and the United States began returning to Caracas, to be greeted by avalanches of flowers and emotional reunions in the docks and airports.

The most famous and capable group were known as "the Generation of '28." As students, they had led a great anti-Gómez riot in 1928 which resulted in their wholesale exile. Now they came back with a vision for Venezuela.

It was now that many Venezuelans accepted the idea that their country could and should take its place in the First World. Modernity became a national obsession, and the national model would be the United States.

Gómez's Minister of War, Eleazar López Contreras, assumed the presidency, proclaimed a new constitution and declared that he would lead the way to the democratic future. New institutions, including a central bank, were created along with laws giving Venezuela slightly more control of its oil wealth. Some indirect elections were allowed, and the Generation of '28 figures formed a political party called Acción Democrática (AD). López's successor, Isaías Medina Angarita, used the need for oil in World War II to guarantee Venezuela a 30 percent share of the oil company's profits.

Period of upheaval

This slow process of reform came to an abrupt end in 1945, when the Generation of '28 leaders in AD convinced a group of young military officers to stage a coup. Having seen the fall

ident. Unfortunately, the author of *La Rebellión* and *Doña Bárbara* proved a better writer than politician. Too many changes were pushed through, without popular support. Reformers misjudged the traditional sectors of Venezuelan society, and failed to notice that the military officers who had led the coup of 1945 had no intention of being left out of power.

In 1948, a military junta seized power in a bloodless coup, sent the novelist-president into exile and set about undoing most of the reforms of the previous 13 years. Chief among the young bloods now in power was Gen. Marcos Pérez Jiménez. This ruthless manipulator took

of fascism in Europe, intellectuals in Venezuela felt that the time had come for drastic action against the autocrats of the south. Some 2,500 people died in bitter fighting during the coup, mostly in the streets of Caracas, but Medina Angarita stepped down. To this day, the AD decision stirs heated debate in Venezuela: the coup eventually ushered in a moment of democratic rule, but was followed by a right-wing backlash that brought on the harshest dictatorships the country has ever known.

A junta now forced through the reforms needed to change Venezuelan society to an ideal image. Free elections were held, and the famous novelist Rómulo Gallegos became pres-

over as president in 1952 after holding an election and declaring it void when it looked as if he might lose. In a throwback to the Gómez days, secret police once again patrolled the streets of Caracas in search of the regime's opponents – only this time they could use modern phone taps, radio surveillance, and electric cattle prods in the pursuit of their goals. Any union action or student demonstration was immediately crushed. AD leaders went into exile, and the party survived in hiding despite torture, assassinations, and jailings.

Strikes by oil workers were now a thing of the past, and US companies such as Standard Oil were pleased in 1954 to receive tax cuts of

US$300 million. Despite his brutality, Pérez Jiménez became a staunch ally of the United States: in the same year as the tax cuts, he was the first to recognize a CIA overthrow of the elected government of Guatemala. The regime had become the most feared and hated in Venezuelan history when US President Eisenhower awarded Pérez Jiménez the Legion of Honor.

Still, the oil money was flowing more freely than ever and Pérez Jiménez began a program with the 1984-style title "New National Ideal" for the "conquest of the physical environment." Huge public works, including six-lane highways in Caracas, the giant Humboldt Hotel, high-rise office buildings, and sumptuous clubs for military officers began to spread across the Venezuelan landscape. Corruption went hand in hand with the construction.

The regime seemed increasingly clumsy and capricious. When Pérez Jiménez finally held a plebiscite in 1958 – and again rigged the result – Venezuelans had had enough. Riots and a general strike led to the general packing his bags full of US dollars and boarding his private jet to Miami.

The new era

Venezuelans now had a second chance of forming a democracy, and this time the older, more moderate political leaders opted for slow reform. One of the Generation of '28, Rómulo Betancourt, became president in 1959 at the head of an AD government, starting a democratic era that has survived to the present.

During the 1960s, a succession of governments guided the country through threats by right-wing military officers and a left-wing guerrilla operation, but at the end of the decade stability was assured. As a major oil producer, Venezuela began taking its role on the world stage: in 1960, it took the lead in forming the international oil cartel, OPEC. Venezuela joined the Andean pact and formed a regional common market with its neighbors – although a long-standing border conflict with Guyana took the country to the brink of war.

Oil money poured in throughout the 1970s in ever greater sums. Taxes were raised so that Venezuela received nearly 70 percent of foreign oil revenues, and the Arab oil embargo of 1973 brought Venezuela a US$50 billion windfall.

Much of the money was used by President Carlos Andrés Pérez to nationalize industries, until finally oil production was taken over. Compensation was provided and the transition went smoothly. A "Venezuelization" of oil company jobs ensured that some nine-tenths of the employees were locally born. Yet even at this time of surplus, things were going awry. The middle class was drunk on oil money, while everyone else was intoxicated by the thought of getting some. Few pondered what would happen when the hangover hit.   ❑

LEFT: a petrol refinery built in the 1970s, at the height of the boom.

RIGHT: drumming up business: oil products at Paraguaná Peninsula.

A NATION ON THE BRINK

Uruguayan writer Eduardo Galeano observed in the mid-1970s: "Caracas chews gum and loves synthetic products and canned foods; it never walks and poisons the clean air… with the fumes of its motorization; its fever to buy, consume, obtain, spend, use, get hold of everything leaves no time for sleep. From surrounding hillside hovels made of garbage, half a million forgotten people observe the sybaritic scene. The gilded city's avenues glitter with hundreds of thousands of late-model cars, but in the consuming society, not everyone consumes. According to the census, half of Venezuela's children and youngsters do not go to school."

AFTER THE BOOM

The dramatic fluctuations in the country's economic fortunes over the past 30 years have left it still seeking to fulfil its potential

Since the 1970s, Venezuela has gone from being South America's richest nation to a nouveau-poor society in search of a new identity. Once known as the Saudis of the West, Venezuelans have seen their economic fortunes decline in exact proportion to the general fall in world oil prices. Even so, Venezuela's many problems were hidden from view until relatively recently, when austerity measures heralded the sort of economic crisis so painfully familiar to other Latin American countries. Runaway inflation, currency devaluations, and violent riots have marked this new phase in Venezuelan history to which the country is still trying hard to adjust.

"Saudi Venezuela"

Venezuelans still live with the memories of the oil boom years, which began in earnest with the nationalization of the petroleum industry in 1976 and ended with a crash in 1983. Government coffers overflowed with revenues. Although a good deal was spirited away by corrupt politicians, some trickled down as scholarships to study abroad, loans for small businesses, or jobs created by an expanding government bureaucracy, which would itself become a major factor in the impending fiscal crisis.

These were the days when middle-class Venezuelans grew accustomed to regular shopping trips to Miami, leaving Caracas with empty suitcases that came back packed with designer clothes, home appliances, gourmet foods, and even titles to property in south Florida. Venezuelans became known as big spenders, their slogan, *Es barato, dáme dos* ("It's cheap, I'll take two.")

Where consumer goods were concerned, "imported" became synonymous with "quality" and "national" (domestic) with "inferior." One of the richest agricultural producers during colonial times, Venezuela was importing more

than 70 percent of its food by 1983. National productivity at all levels was practically nil.

World oil prices began to slide in 1982, but Venezuelans did not feel the effect until February 18, 1983, a date now recalled as "Black Friday." Alarmed by a capital flight which had reached almost $200 million a week, the gov-

ernment of President Luis Herrera Campins imposed exchange controls and devalued the mighty bolívar, which had remained stable for more than a decade and was widely regarded as the blue-chip Latin currency.

The devaluation more than doubled the price of the US dollar. For most Venezuelans, this meant no more shopping trips to Miami and a general restriction of the opulent lifestyle. Not surprisingly, Venezuelans decided to "kill the messenger" and determinedly threw the government out in the next elections.

The more populist Acción Democrática (AD) party won the election that followed despite the lacklustre presidential campaign of Jaime

---

LEFT: unionists march to protest against austerity measures in Caracas.

RIGHT: skyscrapers and sculpture in modern Caracas.

Lusinchi, a physician by training. He maneuvered his way through the deepening crisis with measures designed to maintain social peace and bolster his ratings in the polls. Inflation was kept in check by controlled consumer prices.

Industry enjoyed a preferential exchange rate (which boosted corruption with everyone seeking cheap dollars) for raw materials and spare parts, keeping factories going and the unemployment rate down – but at the cost of burning up the country's foreign reserves.

Lusinchi's administration was sullied by the scandal arising from his much-publicized affair with his personal secretary, Blanca Ibáñez; the

A VENEZUELAN EVITA

The affair of president Jamie Lusinchi with his secretary is considered by many to be the most shameful scandal in the country's history. Blanca Ibáñez came from an impoverished family in the Andes, and sought to create an influential place for herself in Venezuela, comparable to that of Eva Perón in Argentina. With none of Evita's charisma or media appeal, Ibáñez could only emulate her role as official distributor of government largesse to the poor. "Blanquita" often played the role of first lady at presidential functions, ruffling the feathers of diplomats. In spite of her efforts, her popularity was practically nil, except among those who admired her audacity.

affair also caused a rift within Acción Democrática when the president attempted to place Ibáñez on the party's 1988 election slates, an action which subjected him to ridicule.

With soap opera flair, Lusinchi and Ibáñez got married when his term in office ended and, when charges of massive misuse of government power and funds were filed against them, skipped to Florida.

The rise and fall of "El Gocho"

Lusinchi's successor proved to be somewhat in the same mold: Carlos Andrés Pérez swept into office on a wave of popularity, with a long-time lover on the side (although with a tad more discretion), and exited under a cloud of accusations of corruption.

Pérez has been an undeniable headline-maker in Venezuela's modern democratic history. He was born on a coffee *hacienda* in Táchira state, which has produced a regular crop of Venezuela's leaders. Known as "El Gocho," a nickname for Andean natives, he was the mastermind behind Venezuela's oil and iron nationalization during 1974–79. In 1988, he won the mandate again – and immediately set about undoing reforms achieved during his first term in office.

Pérez drew up a privatization plan for state companies, followed by a harsh adjustment program to win approval and much-needed credits from the International Monetary Fund. Price controls were removed from most consumer goods causing the inflation rate to soar, and subsidies were cut from state-produced goods and services. A floating exchange rate was introduced for the bolívar, which drove the dollar price and cost of imports to new highs.

The economic shock treatment provoked a popular uprising unlike anything in Venezuela's modern history. On February 27, 1989, triggered by an increase in public transportation prices (more a last straw than the sole cause) wholesale looting and burning in key cities swept across the country. The uprising was brought to a brutal end as the government suspended constitutional guarantees, imposed a curfew, and sent in the army. Order was restored, but not before hundreds had been killed, as soldiers fired without asking questions.

Even with the trauma of the riots, Pérez reaffirmed his commitment to the economic plan. The country fell into deep recession and he ran into problems with his own party, but he stood firm and, as the program progressed, signs of economic recovery appeared. Public finances were put in order, and the deficit was reduced. A 53 percent growth in non-oil exports took place in 1989 as the government weaned the country off its oil habit. In 1990, Venezuela got an unexpected boost from the Persian Gulf Crisis with an extra US$4 billion in oil income. Instead of easing off, Pérez kept up the push toward a free-market economy – difficult to swallow for people who had lived under protectionist regimes for decades.

Hoping to play on continuing public unrest over Pérez's economic measures, military insurgents mounted two coup attempts in 1992. The first was in February, with the most visible leader, Commandant Hugo Chávez Frías; the other, in November, by a disorganized group of Air Force rebels. Neither mustered the anticipated support from the masses, who were still licking their wounds from the 1989 riots that had not brought change, but loss of property and lives.

On May 20, 1993 Pérez was indicted by the Supreme Court for alleged embezzlement and/or misuse of 250 million bolívars (then worth around US$7 million). On May 21, the Senate suspended him from office pending the outcome of his trial and, in June, elected Ramón José Velásquez as interim president until Pérez's term ended in February 1994. Pérez was convicted, and served two years confined to his house. Another president involved in extramarital liaisons, Pérez subsequently left his wife to take up with his mistress, Cecila Matos. New charges were later pressed against the two for having secret accounts where the absconded funds were supposedly funneled.

From one crisis to another

In January, 1994, focus shifted from political to financial woes when Banco Latino, Venezuela's second-largest bank, closed. Four days' later, the government took it over. Huge injections of funds to shore up other banks on shaky ground and assure customers all came to nothing. When the dust settled at the end of 1995, the number of financial institutions had been reduced by a third. Commercial banks that

---

LEFT: the Paseo de los Próceres, a monument to Venezuela's heroes, in Caracas.
RIGHT: modern politician: Irene Sáez went from being Miss Universe to 1998 presidential candidate.

failed represented 46 percent of total deposits. By May 1994 alone, estimates were that it had already cost Fogade (the national deposit guarantee fund) the equivalent of 132 percent of Venezuela's oil income for that year.

Rafael Caldera, president from 1969 to 1974, won re-election, taking office in February 1994 aged 78. Despite initial optimism, the country was sent reeling and investor confidence plummeted with his policies: suspension of economic guarantees, 66 percent devaluation of the bolívar, exchange controls, return of price controls, and a 1,000 percent increase overnight in gasoline prices.

A brief respite and renewed enthusiasm came with the "Petroleum Opening," initiated with the formation of strategic associations in 1994 and, in 1996, with the genuine opening through the public auction of marginal fields; this brought US$245 million in additional revenue. It marked the first time since nationalization two decades' earlier that foreign companies were allowed to search for Venezuelan oil.

On April 22, 1996, control measures were lifted. Prices soared. Coupled with continuing monstrous internal debt and minimal reduction of bloated government payrolls, inflation hit 103 percent in 1996. Meanwhile, the value of the bolívar continued on a downhill slide.

Although a new economic plan, privatizations, and the sale of many properties inherited during the banking crisis, were initially viewed as steps in the right direction, Caldera's economic plan did not achieve its desired effects. A budget based on high projections for oil prices (which never materialized but instead hit historic lows), coupled with a failure to reduce bureaucracy and its costs were all major factors that led to a grave economic crisis. By 1997 an incredible 90.5 percent of the population were living below the poverty level (67.8 percent of whom were considered to be living in extreme poverty) according to official statistics.

A hint of dictatorship

This situation resulted in a political vacuum just waiting to be filled. Fed up Venezuelans responded hungrily to the "revolution" proposed by the charismatic candidate for presidency in the 1998 elections, Hugo Chávez Frías. The 1989 coup leader was back.

Chávez told every group what they wanted to hear, promising the poor land and homes, workers increased wages, and industry a stimulation of investment. He won by a landslide.

Eighteen months later, his focus remained on political issues while Venezuela wallowed in the worst depression of recent history. Despite raking in the highest oil revenues ever, the economy was sinking, unemployment was growing, social reform had stalled, and crime had begun to spiral. Chávez was also developing a close friendship with Fidel Castro,

After approval of a new constitution for his "Bolivian Republic of Venezuela," Chávez ordered "megaelections" in July 2000 to relegitimize his presidency and won 59 percent of the vote to secure a new 6-year term.

Unfortunately, despite an enormous windfall from the quadrupling in price of Venezuela's oil, it quickly became apparent that the populist president would be unable to deliver on election promises. Certainly be brought inflation levels down to the lowest levels for over 20 years, and within the 1999 Constitution raised the status of women and indigenous peoples while attempting to break the former stranglehold of political parties, give social security benefits to all workers and increase state powers to protect food interests, land reform, tourism, and the fair distribution of wealth.

However, with more than a hint of the dictator, Chávez also managed to concentrate power in his own hands, take over much of the management of the economy, dominate the national media, increase the political role of the armed forces, and appoint friends and allies into top state and commercial positions. Closer to home, he alienated the US, Venezuela's main trading partner, not least by accusing it of "fighting terror with terror" after September 11, 2001.

Despite spending enormous sums of public money to reduce inflation and foreign debts and on implementing his Plan Bolívar 2000, his "revolution" has had little or negative impact on the lives of ordinary citizens, over 85 percent of whom still live below the poverty level. His initial worthy aim to reform PDVSA (Petroleos de Venezuela S.A.), which he had denounced as a "state within a state" siphoning petrodollars from the poor, has been completely mismanaged by sabotaging the company's effective business strategy and replacing experienced board members with yes-men. This led to the devaluation of the bolívar, a huge decrease in foreign investment (not helped by September 11 and a global recession), and finally a coup on April 12, 2002. Chávez has tried to court the opposition since being reinstated two days' later, but faces a very uncertain future. ❏

LEFT: LA gear in Caracas.

A Society Divided

Venezuela enjoyed many years of democratic rule dominated by two parties, COPEI (the Christian Democrats) and the social democratic AD (Democratic Action). Their decades in power came to an end in the late 1990s with the emergence of one man who has completely changed the political life of Venezuela, Hugo Chávez Frías.

As a paratroop commander, Chávez led an unsuccessful coup attempt in 1992. He said he was protesting at the system of power-sharing and patronage typical of the political parties, and accused them of corruption and of wasting the huge oil revenues from which Venezuela had benefited since the 1960s. After the failure of the coup, Chávez was imprisoned for two years, but he continued to enjoy great popularity, and used this to start a political movement.

Chávez's message struck home with the millions of poor Venezuelan's who felt left out of political life. In 1998, he swept to power as president and leader of what he called the "Bolivarian Revolution", named after the 19th-century independence hero Simón Bolívar.

After his election, President Chávez's first step was to change the country's Constitution, with the aim of bringing those who felt excluded into the political process. In 1999, the new Constitution was approved in a plebiscite, and Venezuela became a "Bolivarian Republic." In order to cement the gains of what he called his "peaceful revolution," the grassroots Bolivarian Movement was strengthened, with the intention of creating organizations throughout the country who would promote change and set concrete tasks for the government to achieve.

Confident that he still enjoyed widespread support, Chávez then stood down as president and called fresh elections. Once again he won handsomely, and it seemed that his plans for widespread change were unstoppable. In 2001 however, the divisions within Venezuelan society came to the fore again. COPEI and AD began to reorganize and present a more coherent opposition. Business leaders and landowners reacted strongly against President Chávez's proposals to take over what he called "unproductive" estates and businesses. The long-established trade unions also fought back against the government's attempts to set up new, more controllable labor organizations.

Early in 2002, this conflict spilled over into the streets. There were an increasing number of anti- and pro-government demonstrations in Caracas and the other main cities. In April 2002, more than 40 people were killed in the capital, and shortly afterward President Chávez was toppled from power. Parts of the army and the business sector took over the government, and announced that the "Bolivarian Revolution" was over.

Their new government lasted less than two days. Large sections of the armed forces remained loyal to Chávez, and more than a million people came

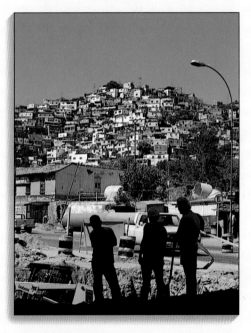

down from the poor neighborhoods of the capital to demonstrate their support for him. He was soon reinstated, and his opponents sent into exile or arrested. After the revolt, however, it was plain that President Chávez would have to try to find ways of healing the divisions within Venezuelan society. Government and opposition set up a joint commission to look into how to reconcile the interests of different sectors on behalf of the country as a whole. President Chávez adopted a more conciliatory tone in his speeches, and stressed his willingness to serve the entire nation. But the split between the poor and the better off remains wide in Venezuela, and the possibility of further unrest and instability continues. ❑

RIGHT: continuing the urban sprawl.

THE VENEZUELANS

The country's people are predominantly young and urban. Can they preserve their traditions against the pervasive culture of the United States?

To casual visitors, Venezuelans seem to import culture wholesale from the United States. There is little evidence of Venezuelan history in the public buildings; few signs of the indigenous cultures so prominent elsewhere in Latin America. Instead, Venezuelan radios blare a steady output of rock and reggae. Young people sport designer jeans and T-shirts with slogans in English. The impression is of a place trying hard to be like southern Florida but which has managed only to approximate the climate.

This attraction to the United States is even reflected in sport, as Venezuela is the only country on the South American continent where baseball is more popular than soccer.

All this may lead one to ask – where is the real Venezuela? The answer is, this is it: an overwhelmingly young, urbanized society, with a dwindling middle class whose eyes are constantly fixed northward; a country in permanent, frantic motion, eating fast food and drinking its coffee from disposable plastic cups; a country that has lived through a debauch of fabulous wealth which it can't quite believe is over, despite the cold shower of austerity doled out in recent years.

City folks, country ways

Yet this Americanization of Venezuelan society is a relatively recent occurrence. Indeed, few of the world's countries have changed so much in such a short time as Venezuela, thanks to the discovery of oil. From a poor, isolated, agricultural nation that was the fiefdom of successive dictators, it was transformed within the space of a few decades into the consumerist, high-tech society that visitors see now: one with a democratic government and the trappings – if not always the benefits – of development.

PRECEDING PAGES: folk musicians in the Andes; vendors at the Caracas bus terminal.
LEFT: a face in the country.
RIGHT: a businessman wearing the *liqui-liqui* – traditional Venezuelan dress.

It has all happened so quickly that Venezuelan society is still endeavoring to keep up with the changes – leading to an often bewildering mix of traditional and modern traits.

Venezuela today is the most urbanized nation in Latin America, with 87 percent of its 24 million people living in a handful of big cities.

Yet Venezuelans persist in a surprisingly rural lifestyle. They rise early, often before dawn, and are usually required to be at their desks by 8am. Workers take 2 hours off at midday, during which time they are more than likely to return home for lunch. This routine may be logical for rural workers in order to avoid the midday sun, but in a city the size of Caracas or Maracaibo it creates four traffic jams a day instead of two.

And while Venezuelans are surrounded by high technology, they sometimes display a surprising lack of sophistication: with the largest cell phone per capita ratio in Latin America, the telephone is an instrument to which many people are still unaccustomed and telephone callers may be regarded with suspicion unless they are known personally.

Facing up to change

Obviously, Venezuela hasn't quite shaken off its long history as a poor farming country largely isolated from the outside world. Only a few generations ago, it was a nation with a small population, few roads, and little national coherence.

This meant that Venezuela developed as a fragmented rural country with strong regional

> **TRAVEL BY MULE**
>
> As recently as 1945, the journey from Caracas to the German immigrant town of Colonia Tovar (a distance of only 38 km/23 miles) had to be made on muleback.

tile roofs" had all but vanished. The city's shape reflected the new Venezuelan society: a high-tech heart of glass skyscrapers; luxury apartments of the burgeoning suburbs; and a ring of slums for the growing number of Venezuelans unable to get a slice of the country's wealth.

Adolescent nation

Venezuela is a young country: some 32 percent of Venezuelans are under 14 years old, with just 4.7 percent over the age of 65. As a result, Venezuelan culture is decidedly

identities. Everything was upset when oil wealth hit in the 1920s. Agriculture was no longer important, and there was massive migration from the country to the cities. During the period from 1936 to 1971, the rural-to-urban population ratio turned around completely: a quarter of Venezuela's people lived in cities during the 1930s, but by the 1970s that proportion had changed to three-quarters.

The velocity of change was nowhere more evident than in the capital city, Caracas. In 1945, Caracas had a quarter of a million inhabitants and only a few buildings more than two stories tall. Three decades later, the population had increased sevenfold, and the "city of red

youth-orientated, as reflected in advertising and in the national passions for sport, beauty contests, and other youthful pursuits.

At the same time, Venezuela has become a much more cosmopolitan nation. The vast majority of Venezuelans are *mestizos* – people whose descent mingles the blood of Spanish settlers with the indigenous peoples or African slaves.

But after World War II, a wave of immigrants arrived from Europe and other parts of Latin America; Venezuela's last military dictatorships encouraged them to come in search of opportunities. Between 1948 and 1959, an estimated 412,500 immigrants entered

Venezuela, an almost indigestible number for a country that had fewer than 5 million inhabitants in the early 1950s.

The large number of first-generation Venezuelans has given rise to ethnic stereotypes: the Spanish taxi driver, usually a Galician *(Gallego)*; the Portuguese grocery store or bakery owner; and the Italian car mechanic.

As well as Europeans, a large number of Chinese, and people from Middle Eastern countries, there are recent immigrants from nearby Latin American countries – especially Colombia, Ecuador, and Peru. They came during the oil boom to work as laborers and domestics.

to one) but their influence is great. A small group of North American families have settled in Venezuela and founded successful businesses or industrial conglomerates. One case in point is the Phelps family, which owns Radio Caracas Televisión station and Aereotuy airlines.

The Americans who have come to Venezuela have, on the whole, been technocrats – oil industry engineers or executives with the multinationals. All have come to further their own interests but have nonetheless made contributions in terms of technology, science, and culture. The late patriarch of the Phelps family, William Phelps, for example, was an

Blacks from Trinidad, Guyana, and other Caribbean countries also arrived at that time. Many of the poorer immigrants have returned home since the recent economic crisis hit, but a large number have stayed to raise families and take on Venezuelan citizenship.

Yankees, stay here!

As for North Americans, their numbers are few (European immigrants outnumber them by 50

ornithologist who wrote the definitive guide to Venezuelan birds. His widow, Kathy Deery Phelps, is an author, philanthropist, and ardent environmentalist.

Perhaps as a result, there is little in the way of resentment toward foreigners. The word *musiu*, a corruption of the French *monsieur*, which refers to a light-skinned foreigner, is not an insult. Similarly, Venezuela is racially tolerant, with marriage between *mestizos*, blacks, and whites commonplace.

The only exception to this open-mindedness is the attitude toward the Colombians, Venezuela's poorer neighbors to the west, who have entered the country in large numbers, often

FAR LEFT: farmer in the Andean region of Mérida.
LEFT: native Guajira woman in Maracaibo.
ABOVE: a big grin on Isla Margarita.
RIGHT: Caracas vice.

illegally, since the oil boom days. Because the Colombians are generally acknowledged as hard workers and even their poor have usually benefitted from formal education, they are viewed with suspicion by poor Venezuelans, who see them as people who steal their jobs.

Defining "Venezuelan"

So, after all this, what are Venezuelans really like? Today's citizen might still be anyone; a barefoot cowboy in the *llanos*; a store-owner in Caracas recently immigrated from Portugal; a high-powered oil industry executive in Maracaibo; or a Yanomami Indian in the

Amazon basin whose lifestyle has not changed a great deal from that of his forebears living thousands of years ago.

In general, Venezuelan society is unusually open, friendly, and informal. Spanish speakers are sometimes surprised to note how quickly – often immediately – Venezuelans discard the polite *Usted* form of address and use the more familiar *tú*. To some, this is an excess of familiarity, behavior that borders on disrespect – especially when carried a step further, with men and women alike being addressed by people they have never even met before as "*mi amor*" (my love) – or some other equally affectionate greeting.

Venezuelans may seem exceedingly polite and unfailingly generous or hopelessly frivolous and maddeningly inconsistent. Friendships are struck up quickly but rarely last; people seem unwilling to take any relationship beyond the superficial level. On the other hand, someone with whom you have only a fleeting acquaintance will greet you effusively, as if you were a long-lost friend. Even among young Venezuelans who have been educated abroad or foreigners who have married into local families, deep-rooted cultural distinctions can be difficult to understand or overcome.

Superficial lifestyles

Unlike their southern neighbors the Argentines, who tend to psychoanalyze every conceivable issue, Venezuelans are little given to self-examination – a fact that may explain the surprising lack of literature about the country itself. Conversations often remain on the anecdotal level and people seem more comfortable with humor than serious topics.

Some Latin Americans regard Venezuela as a *nouveau riche* society where the prevailing norm is money without good taste. Others admire it for having maintained a democratic government during a period when almost every other South American nation was ruled by a military dictator.

Perhaps the dominant aspect of the Venezuelan mindset is its transitory view of life. Marriage, business, career, and even family are all regarded as short-term concerns which could be here today, gone tomorrow. Venezuelans who invest in a business, for example, usually do so with the intention of making a quick profit and then selling out – something akin to buying a lottery ticket.

Women's role

Although Venezuela shares the cult of machismo with other Latin American countries, Venezuelan women have managed to achieve a place in society that would be the envy of their sisters in many developed nations. The first woman cabinet minister was named in 1968; the first female presidential candidate, Ismenia Villalba of the Unión Republicana Democrática, stood for election in 1988; and, in 1996, Cecilia Sosa Gómez became the first female elected to the position of chief magistrate of Venezuela's Supreme Court.

Women business executives, medical doctors, judges, engineers, and architects abound; in some professions, such as law, women actually outnumber men in the current graduating classes. The push for sexual equality has been accomplished without the help of any nationwide women's organization or any cohesive feminist movement. Some writers believe their success in a male-dominated society has been due to their non-confrontational – and therefore non-threatening – approach.

Foreign feminists find it bizarre that this apparent success sits alongside such traits as a national obsession with traditional beauty

street crime. She was re-elected to a second term with a landslide victory of more than 90 percent of the vote, and was a presidential candidate in the 1998 elections.

At least part of the progress of Venezuelan women has been due to necessity. In Venezuelan society, infidelity is widepread and men often have entire second families. Many women have learned not to count on their husbands as a steady source of income.

Because of the high incidence of promiscuity, infrequent use of birth control, the absence of legal abortions, and the proliferation of men who refuse to take any responsibility for

contests and cosmetics *(see Pop Culture Paradise, pages 71–5)*. Venezuela's professional women maintain a high sense of glamor, playing up their femininity much more than their North American or European counterparts.

Proving that glamor and brains can mix, former Miss Universe, Irene Sáez, was elected mayor of the Caracas municipality of Chacao. Her winning looks surely didn't hurt in gaining a few votes. However, she quickly demonstrated an ability for fast, effective, and creative ways of handling everything from traffic to

LEFT: Piaroa elders in Amazonas.
ABOVE: *llaneros* (cowboys) strut their stuff.

EXTENDED FAMILY LIFE

Divorce, which was legalized in Venezuela in 1909, has become a fixture of family life. Most people approaching their forties are on their second marriage; men often refer to "my first marriage" as if that were a normal phase in life. All this has given rise to a disjointed family structure in which half-brothers, step-parents, and in-laws coexist (at times even under the same roof) in a manner that is often baffling to outsiders. Moreover, with the difficult economic situation of recent years, not only are unmarried children not "leaving the nest" but many married couples unable to afford rent or mortgages are moving in with their parents.

paternity outside of marriage, single women – very often girls under 16 – with one or more children to support alone make up a huge portion of the poorer sectors of society.

Problem case for the Pope

On the whole, Venezuelans are not a religious people, with the exception of the western Andean region, where the Catholic faith has strong roots. In general, the church is regarded as a traditional but somewhat irrelevant institution, its role largely ceremonial. Church attendance is so low that, before the visit of Pope John Paul II in 1985, the Venezuelan Catholic

Remnants of traditional culture

The US cultural invasion of recent years doesn't mean that the centuries-old Venezuelan culture has been completely wiped out. You just have to look a little harder for it.

Music is a good place to start. Venezuela is an eminently musical country, in which singing comes as naturally as breathing, and everyone seems to be able to carry a tune. On trips to the beach or at parties, someone will inevitably produce a *cuatro* (the traditional four-stringed instrument, similar to a ukelele) and the singing will begin. Aided by a few good rums, even the shyest Venezuelan will begin to improvise

Bishops' Conference began a public relations campaign with the slogan: "The Pope wants to be your friend."

Statistics released by the conference showed that while more than 90 percent of the population claims to be Catholic, only 20 percent attend church regularly. There is, however, fervent devotion by many to figures such as Dr José Gregorio Hernández, a turn-of-the-20th-century physician who dedicated his life to helping the poor and who has been postulated for sainthood. There are also numerous bizarre cults: perhaps the most popular of these is dedicated to María Lionza and combines elements of Catholicism with witchcraft.

lyrics in the *contrapunto* style which has its origins in the *llanos*.

Among the best traditional artists are the singing group Un Solo Pueblo (One Single People), who have become something of an institution during the past three decades and have even incorporated their children into the group. More than "folk singers," they are serious students of the different trends in Venezuelan traditional music and go to some length to explain it at concerts, detailing the names of the villages where the songs were collected and their particular significance.

Un Solo Pueblo presents the wide variety of Venezuela's traditional music: the plaintive country music of the *llanos*, with its nasal vocals and whimsical lyrics; the complex rhythms and exuberant dances of the *tambores* or drums of the Afro-Venezuelans in Barlovento and along the rest of the Caribbean coast; the gentle, nostalgic waltzes of the Andes; and the English-lyric calypsos of the Guayana Region, the legacy of the Caribbean blacks who worked in Venezuela's gold rush during the 19th century.

Venezuelans also excel in classical music. One of the country's most accomplished instrumentalists is guitarist Alirio Díaz, who has also served as Venezuela's ambassador to Italy. Caracas alone has four symphony orchestras, and cities throughout the interior have municipal orchestras and youth symphony programs.

Contemporary artists

In the plastic arts, Venezuela has produced some outstanding modern painters and sculptors. Jesús Soto, of Ciudad Bolívar, is responsible for much of the monumental art that graces the new buildings in Caracas, including the entrance to the Teresa Carreño Theater and the Chacaíto subway station. Other noted painters include Jacobo Borges and Héctor Poleo.

One of Venezuela's greatest men of letters was Arturo Uslar Pietri, a towering figure who was both a chronicler of contemporary Venezuelan events and an active participant in them until his death in 2001. The winner of international literary awards, Uslar Pietri was a novelist, a historian, a cabinet minister, and a television commentator, among other things. He is remembered for urging Venezuelan governments, in the 1930s, to "sow the petroleum" – that is, to invest the tremendous income from the country's principal export in productive enterprises. Uslar Pietri is held in great esteem for his literary output, which includes *La Visita en El Tiempo* ("The Visit in Time"), winner of Spain's Prince of Asturias literary prize in 1991.

Looking to the future

The idea of Venezuela as a country bursting with natural wealth but lacking in human resources is common, particularly in other Latin American nations. The reality, however, is changing, as a generation of Venezuelans educated abroad take the helm of government, the private sector, and the professions. They have returned with professional skills and a new style of management that is helping business and industry to modernize. Many were beneficiaries of a government scholarship program that, during the 1970s and early 1980s, sent some 40,000 Venezuelans abroad to study (the program still continues on a smaller scale). Others who did not benefit from such scholarships also had the opportunity to travel and study abroad during the "boom years."

Yet although many Venezuelans have lived or studied abroad, few have emigrated perma-

nently and, unlike other Latin Americans, few express the desire to do so. Shortly after the February 1989 riots, there was a move among first generation Venezuelans – sons and daughters of Spaniards, Portuguese, and Italians – to obtain the passports of their parents' countries in preparation for a return to their land of origin. However, only a small number actually went through with emigration.

Despite their frustrations with corrupt politicians and inefficient public services, Venezuelans love their country and recognize its potential. Although their gaze may be distracted by the latest North American cultural totems, their feet remain firmly fixed on home soil. ❑

LEFT: dominoes for the boys, by Sinamaica Lagoon, near Maracaibo.
RIGHT: rooster and shades.

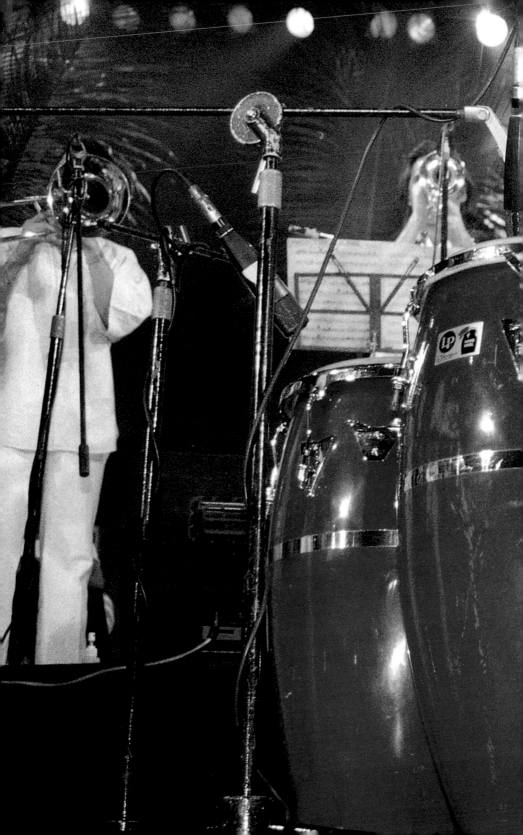

POP CULTURE PARADISE

Pop entertainment is big business in Venezuela, launching
many top performers onto the world stage

Take a disproportionately young audience fascinated with looks, music, and TV, and mix it with the world of pop culture (which, incidentally, grew up in an oil-rich environment that provided the disposable income to indulge in these fascinations) and you have Venezuela, where life becomes a show, and the show becomes an integral part of most of the population's lifestyle.

Pop culture paradise

Venezuela has produced a great number of well-known pop singers, and its television soap operas *(telenovelas)* are breaking records in Europe and the United States. Actress María Conchita Alonso appeared in a number of American movies, including *Moscow on the Hudson*, but she got her start as a beauty queen in Venezuela. The Caribbean's unchallenged "Devil of Salsa" is Venezuelan Oscar d'León, who has been shaking it up on stage for several decades.

South America's single most successful soap opera so far has been *Cristal*, a Venezuelan production that interrupted work and social schedules in half a dozen neighboring countries. *Farándula*, as the world of pop entertainment is called here, is serious business.

But those who claim Venezuela leads the continent in pop culture shortchange the nation. The sphere of influence extends far beyond South America. When the soap opera *Cristal* aired in Spain, it was one of the most popular TV series ever shown there; another 7 million Spaniards saw Venezuela's second most successful soap opera, *La Dama de Rosa*. Both shows broke ratings records in Italy.

Several Venezuelan singers, including José Luis Rodríguez, sell records in the United States

where they record in both English and Spanish and are wildly popular, especially with North America's burgeoning Hispanic population.

Geographically, Venezuela has everything needed to be a *farándula* heaven. Its proximity to Caribbean islands and countries long known as music spots has transformed it into

the gathering place for performers from the whole region. They find larger audiences in Caracas and it costs far less for a Dominican singer to travel to Venezuela in search of fame and fortune than it does to head straight for Miami, the world's undeclared capital of Spanish-language pop music.

Afro-Caribbean roots

The wild salsa, merengue, rumba, reggae, and calypso beats that find their way into Venezuela's infectious melodies and rhythms are pure Caribbean; much of this hip-gyrating music and dancing betrays African roots – intrinsic in Venezuelan music.

PRECEDING PAGES: belting out the rhythm in a Caracas night spot.
LEFT: Venezuela's soap operas have a following far beyond South America.
RIGHT: Eileen Abad, one of the country's many reigning soap queens.

Pop singer Yordano and the band Adrenalina Caribe claim they were influenced by Cuban *Nueva Trova* performers such as Silvio Rodríguez and Pablo Milanés, whose dark jazzy ballads with political themes talk of social inequality, the Latin American identity, and regional integration.

A nation of addicts

But Venezuela's success may have less to do with its location on the globe than with its fascination with "the tube." When it comes to television, at least 83 percent of Venezuelans own a set, and those who don't generally live in the jungle or outback areas where transmissions won't reach. Even the humblest shacks in slum developments have television antennas popping up on their roofs; upscale neighborhoods are easily identified by a plethora of satellite dishes; and even places as remote as Santa Elena de Uarién – by the Brazilian border in Bolívar state – have DirecTV delivering steady transmission of channels from around the world. Some 98 percent of families in Caracas have access to at least one TV set. One is likewise hard-pressed to find any but the most luxurious restaurants or bars that don't have numerous televisions mounted to assure customers a

VENEZUELAN CINEMA ON SHOW TO THE WORLD

In December 1994, "Venezuela: Forty Years of Cinema, 1950–90" debuted in The Museum of Modern Art of New York, the first exhibition in the US to present the rich achievement of Venezuelan cinema. A subsequent tour of the exhibit included bookings at The Carnegie Museum of Art (Pittsburgh), Cinemathèque Quebequoise (Montreal), The Cleveland Museum of Art, Museum of Fine Arts (Boston), Pacific Cinema (Vancouver), and the National Gallery (Washington DC), among others. Highlighted were works by three of Venezuela's best-known movie makers, including the internationally acclaimed documentaries of Margot Benacerraf (*Araya* stands among the first major social documentaries in Latin America, twice awarded at Cannes); the dramas of Román Chalbaud; and the visually expressive, experimental movies of Diego Risquez. At the domestic box office, smash hits such as *Macú, The Policeman's Wife* (Solveig Hoogesteijn, 1987) outsold even some Hollywood "blockbusters." The movie remained 83 weeks in Caracas cinemas and 228 weeks in national exhibition, with the second-highest attendance ever. However, in recent years Venezuelan cinema has not received much critical acclaim abroad and the domestic film industry has been completely overshadowed by the boom in TV production.

steady fix. All this provides a wonderland for television advertisers and a dream come true for performers in need of exposure.

Publications are also able to cash in on the craze. Any newsstand has magazines dedicated to the pop entertainment industry, aimed at satisfying the eager craving of gossip-hungry readers with the latest scandals, alleged loves, sexual preferences, and infidelities of Venezuelan music, movie, and television stars. Keeping abreast with entertainment developments is not a pastime, it is an addiction.

People on the street discuss the latest adventures of current soap stars such as Eileen Abad,

other aspects of everyday life that Venezuelans face have been dominant themes in commercial movies. However, commercial success has still been limited to the domestic market and the economic recession beginning in the 1980s and the financial crisis and political uncertainty of the 1990s greatly slowed the momentum.

Farándula financial empire

If a performer makes it in Venezuela, his or her success is almost guaranteed and a ticket to Miami isn't far off. Some may argue that Venezuelans are not necessarily more talented than their counterparts in nearby nations but

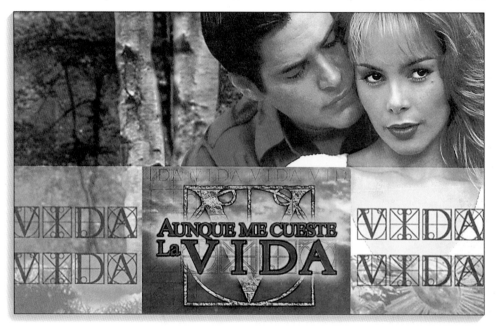

Rosalinda Serfaty, or Miguel de León as if they were intimate friends, and chat about the goings-on in the latest episodes of current programs as if they were real life.

The big screen

Although their movie industry is fledgling, Venezuelan directors already have a number of documentaries and feature films which have garnered some critical acclaim outside the country. Passion, struggles of life in the *barrios*, and

LEFT: glued to the box.
ABOVE: *Aunque me Cueste La Vida* ("Though It May Cost Me My Life"), a top-rating soap opera.

they receive an invaluable amount of promotion thanks to bountiful coffers in Caracas and the local record company's US links. Part of this promotion stems from the incestuous relationship that the recording monopoly, Sonorodven, has with the music video firm Video Rodven and TV station Venevisión. The trio is owned by the Cisneros Group, which also has a major chunk of the Galaxy consortium and DirecTV Internacional.

Sonorodven artists are advertised extensively on TV, and *telenovela* songs (guaranteed hits) are performed by Sonorodven musicians. Rudy Escala's recording of *Cristal*'s theme song was hummed in homes on three continents, and Jorge

Rigó's *telenovela* songs have overshadowed his other music to such an extent that he has become irreversibly identified as a soap singer.

Although actors can make it without singing, singers are obliged to take a role or two in local soap operas; *telenovela* work is detailed in recording contracts. Sometimes the TV fame supersedes the music and aspiring singers such as Guillermo Dávila became better known as leading men than musicians. "El Puma," Jose Luis Rodríguez, began his now stellar singing career as a soap opera leading man; it was his role in the historical soap opera *Estefanía*, not his tropical music, that pushed him to fame.

and exposed, dangling rhinestone earrings and spike heels, and you can be sure she's on her way to work – as a bank teller or perhaps a legal secretary.

Fashion is likewise a matter of great national pride in Venezuela, with a number of designers attaining international fame. These include Carolina Herrera (with both *haute couture* and fragrances), Angel Sánchez (whose gowns traditionally grace Miss Venezuela winners), Mayela Camacho (whose streamlined *prêt-à-porter* outfits line the most fashionable outlets), and Dorita Vera (with show-stopping bathing suits), among others.

It is rare that a musician makes it big unless signed to the Sonorodven label. Conversely, artists may sign with the label then be pushed into the wings, blocked from performing or recording by iron-clad contracts like those that restricted movie stars during the Golden Age of Hollywood in the 1930s and 1940s.

Dressing for success

In Venezuela, looks count. Although female executives are likely to be in an elegantly cut designer suit, for the majority of working women, dressing for success means the tighter the better. You see a woman slinking down the street in a skin-tight mini, plenty of cleavage,

Women have an additional path to fame in Venezuela: by means of winning a beauty contest. Annually, Miss Venezuela is virtually guaranteed an acting and/or singing career if she shows even the remotest amount of talent. Those who don't make it into feature films often make it into the advertisements that precede movies. Enterprising Venezuelans have made a business out of beauty; a Caracas "Miss" Academy has groomed four Miss Universes, five Miss Worlds and many runners-up, and there is also a website (www.missvenezuela.com) for would-be contestants. *Venezolanos* are among the highest per capita consumers of cosmetics and personal-care products.

A recent phenomenon has been beauty as a stepping stone to politics. Irene Sáez, a former Miss Universe (1981), entered the political ring in 1992, vying for mayorship of the prestigious and very populous Chacao municipality in Caracas – and won. Although looks and a familiar face probably didn't hurt in vote getting, the true test was in action. She founded a police force lauded for efficiency, friendliness, helpfulness, and honesty. For the first time in years, municipal taxes were collected and put to work for the community. Abandoned parks were rescued, streets repaired, sidewalk vendors evicted, and community events organized.

The startling difference earned Sáez re-election in 1995 with an astonishing 96 percent of the vote. She lost her bid for the presidency in 1998, but became Governor of Nueva Esparta State. Similarly, during the same period, Yvonne Attas changed roles from a popular soap opera star of the 1970s to that of mayor of Baruta – another huge Caracas municipality. With the same strategy, no sooner had the votes been counted than she set about effectively attacking problems and implementing improvements – winning as dedicated a following in real life as she had on TV.

A feminist's nightmare

In many countries, beauty contests are being downplayed as women's rights advance. Not in Venezuela. The Miss pageant has weathered feminism with barely a scratch. Here, beauty opens doors. Every aspiring model knows that entering the Miss Venezuela pageant can do much to boost her career.

How do women become Miss Venezuela contestants? It's not something they simply sign up for. First of all, they must be "discovered." Chances improve dramatically if a woman is from a prominent family and enrolled in a top Caracas modeling agency. While the candidates are officially representatives for districts or states throughout the country, in truth, recruiting in the interior is almost non-existent. Most are "discovered" in Caracas and are simply assigned to represent a given area after having passed muster. For example, the winner of the 1998 Miss Venezuela title, Lucbel Carolina Indriago Pinto, won as the representative of

Delta Amacuro, but is a Valencia (Carabobo state) native and resident. This has caused problems at times in local interviews when the candidate for a certain zone clearly knows nothing about the place she is representing.

Once past the first hurdle of selection, she must then survive Osmel Souza's Miss Academy (which is not cheap, and she has to foot the bill – but they all willingly pay for tuition and brace themselves for the strict regimen with the glitter of a Miss crown in their eyes).

Souza's goal is turning out not just another pretty face, but a woman with that certain something that guarantees winning. He plays

the roles of talent scout, agent, trainer, image-maker, fund-raiser, producer, and, when necessary, whip-cracker.

As the song goes, you're never fully dressed without a smile. Teeth a little discolored or crooked? Nose not exactly like a button? It's no secret that cosmetic orthodontia and plastic surgery are all part of the beauty game. One Venezuelan magazine noted that "before smelling the sweet aroma of success, the majority of the participants have breathed the ether of anesthesia."

Clearly – regardless of gender – vanity and Venezuela have rather more in common than just the letter V. ❑

LEFT: backstage at the Miss Venezuela pageant.
RIGHT: a happy winner.

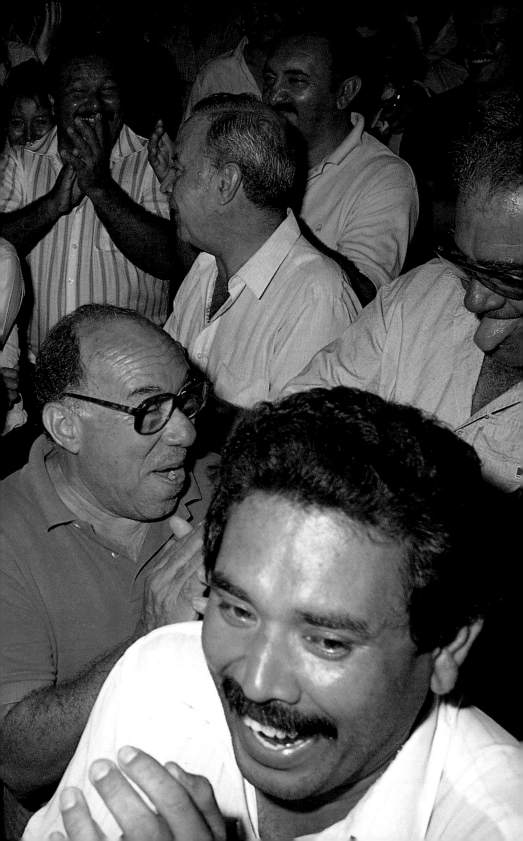

FIESTAS

The true colors of Venezuela are revealed at fiesta time.
Even religious festivals show how this nation loves to party

The least mentioned, but most unmissable events to be enjoyed by those exploring the distinct regions of the Venezuelan countryside are the great number of colorful and varied folkloric and religious festivals taking place throughout the year. Drawing on the nation's rich ancestry, which blends indigenous, European, African, and Caribbean cultures, Venezuela's fiestas have been spiced by diverse elements.

Most celebrations are linked with Catholic saints or other dates of religious significance, but the acts often seem more like pagan rites than anything remotely related to the church. Lively music, free-flowing liquor, sensual dancing, devils, and men dressed as women are common components.

Despite appearances, most participants are involved in the rituals as payment for solemn religious promises with a self-imposed commitment for years or even their lifetime. Whether observers get into the significance or not doesn't matter: the fiestas are entertaining, providing yet another view of Venezuela's multi-faceted personality.

Time to be merry

The Christmas season has the greatest number and diversity of festivals.

The Fiesta de los Pastores began in the village of Aguas Calientes in Carabobo state at least a century ago, and the tradition soon spread to the nearby town of San Joaquín and to El Limón in Aragua state. Each community has added its own touches to the celebration, which is based on the re-enactment of the *pastores* (shepherds) bringing news of the birth of Christ, their search for Him, and their jubilant dancing after finding Him.

Half of the main participants – all paying religious promises and all male – are the *pastores*, with skirts of long colored streamers worn over slacks, hats decorated with flowers, bows, and

more streamers, and a "musical instrument" – a long pole with loosely attached bottle caps to jingle when pounded on the ground as they sing and dance. The other half are *pastorcillas* (shepherdesses,) complete with well-padded frilly blouses and full make-up. The complex series of dance patterns is performed before the

creche from dusk until the wee hours of the morning, led by the *cachero*, who is adorned with streamers and bows, and has a set of horns in hand to keep his people in line.

Events start at dusk in Aguas Calientes. The most serious of the three fiestas, usually on the first Saturday in December, it includes an impressive candlelit procession prior to the dancing, with many people inching forward painfully on their knees before the image of baby Jesus. At El Limón on the second Saturday of December, women are allowed to dance and the fiesta is less traditional. Midnight Mass on December 24 starts events in San Joaquín: a theatrical performance in the church follows.

PRECEDING PAGES: applauding fireworks at a fiesta.
LEFT AND RIGHT: jesters and high camp at *Carnaval*.

The commemoration on December 28 of the *santos inocentes*, the innocent children killed by Herod, is celebrated throughout the country, with children donning old clothes and masks and generally having free rein. The event is also known as the Fiesta de Locos.

Formal celebrations take place in Aguas Blancas (Portuguesa) with *locos* and *locaínas* carrying out a military-type ceremony and dancing with small children to bless them. In Sanare (Lara), along with acts of buffoonery, *Zaragozas* dancers with distinctive masks and colorful costumes perform with children in their arms before a painting of the historic massacre. With its own character, but the same motive, is the Fiesta del Mono in Caicara de Maturín. This dance has indigenous roots adapted to honor the *Santos Inocentes*. Most celebrants wear monkey masks and everyone joins in the dancing.

The black saint

In the Andes, acts for the *Santos Inocentes* are often combined with those for San Benito, a black saint, whose following is concentrated in the area circling Lake Maracaibo. On December 29, in Mucuchíes (Mérida), men and boys with blackened faces and bright-colored satin costumes dance before the saint, before firing

black-powder rifles and homemade shotguns with wild abandon! Just up the road, in Timotes, the *negros, indios,* and *vasallos de San Benito* all dance in the street at once; the *negros* with blackened skin and grass skirts; *indios* with bronzed skin, war paint and feather headdresses; and the *vasallos* (vassals) in elegant white outfits adorned with long ribbon streamers and wearing glittering crowns, do their maypole-type dance – very colorful!

Paraujano Indians in Zulia's Sinamaica Lagoon dedicate their fiesta to San Benito alone. They parade around the lagoon on December 27, dancing on the prows of their launches and carring images of the saint.

PARTY TIME

Keep in mind that Venezuelans are as "relaxed" about starting hours for their fiestas as they are for every other aspect of life. Sometimes more so. After all, in the small villages, what else is there to do? Thus, elements of the celebrations often occur in different stages spread over a whole day with long breaks in between to eat, drink, socialize – and make the party last longer. Most of the celebrations tend to start at about 10am, usually by the main church and/or in the plaza.

In remote communities, the festivals are the social highlight of the year. Ice cream and snow cone vendors turn out en masse and there's always a beer stand.

Communities with predominately African roots, from El Moján down to Borbures and Gibraltar on the eastern shore of the lake, bring out their traditional drums to honor San Benito with processions with his image, dancing, and the beating of drums from December 27–31.

A day or two before New Year's Eve, effigies of the *año viejo* (old year) are seen along rural roads and city streets in many parts of the country. Representing the ills of the past year, on the night of the 31st they are ceremoniously set aflame. On Easter Sunday, similar effigies, these labeled Judas (though lately used to represent unpopular politicians with stinging

lights, painted decorations, and music, turning the neighborhood into a spectacular scene.

Pesebres also take part in the Paradura del Niño (January 1 to February 2), "stealing" baby Jesus from the *pesebre*, searching for Him, then celebrating when He is found.

In the big cities, these holiday customs have mostly been replaced with more hedonistic fiestas. The main event is Christmas Eve – *Noche Buena*, with a huge family feast (*see Food, pages 89–95*), and ever-present music and dancing. Christmas Day is primarily for going to the beach or visiting friends. New Year's Eve celebrations depend more on per-

epitaphs read as they burn), are given the same treatment, with the *Quema de Judas*.

Christmas festivities

All through the Christmas season, many families set up elaborate *pesebres* (nativity scenes) in their homes – or outside for all to enjoy. Residents of the Táchira town of San Pedro del Río set them up all through the streets. In Carora (Lara), one neighborhood near Calle Torrellas pulls out all the stops with *pesebres*, colored

sonal taste than tradition – some spend the evening at home with family and friends, while others head for the big hotels which always host an all-out party with champagne toasts at midnight. On Christmas Eve and New Year's Eve fireworks light up the skyline for hours.

At the Romería de los Pastores ("shepherds' pilgrimage"), on January 6 in San Miguel de Boconó in Trujillo, you will see more folkloric and religious events in one day than anywhere else in the country, including *pastores* (devotees of San Benito) dancing to African-style drums (in a different style to the *pastores* of Carabobo and Aragua states), religious processions, *mamarrochos* (boys dressed as

LEFT: dancers honoring San Benito in Mucuchíes.
ABOVE: drummers at San Benito celebration, Timotes.
RIGHT: dancing at the Romería de los Pastores.

women), devils, the Three Kings on horseback, and more masks than you can imagine: and that's just for starters.

Every year, on February 2, Nuestra Señora de la Candelaria is honored in La Parroquia (just south of Mérida in Mérida state) with a colorful ceremony and dance by costumed males dancing to pay promises.

Carnival and calypso

Carnival, the last fling before Lent – and known here as *Carnaval* – is celebrated with tremen-

Guanare, in the western state of Portuguesa, is known for its fertile crops, but in recent years its *Carnaval* has grown to outstrip those in any other part of the country, with spectacular floats and costumes, numerous *banda-shows* and some 100,000 visitors converging on this otherwise sleepy farm town for the fiesta.

Common throughout eastern Venezuela at this time are folkloric celebrations such as the dance of La Burriquita and El Pájaro Guarandol, in which a man dressed as a bird acts out a popular legend.

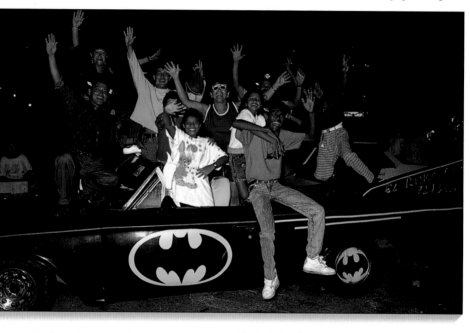

dous enthusiasm in some of the most unlikely places. Carúpano (Sucre), which is frankly dead at any other time of year, springs to life with people flooding in from all over the country for the big party by the beach. El Callao, a tiny gold town in Bolívar state, is another surprising venue for a big party – especially when the main part of the celebration involves calypso music and devil masks.

Calypso arrived with gold miners from Trinidad and the French and British Antilles who came during the mid 19th-century gold rush and stayed. The tradition of devil masks has resulted in intense competition for the most original creations.

Holy Week

At Catholic churches in every corner of the country, there are processions with images representing the Passion of Christ during Semana Santa – Holy Week – mainly from the Wednesday to Good Friday. In Caracas, one of the most awesome acts of faith is on Wednesday, when tens of thousands turn out to honor the 400-year-old image El Nazareno de San Pablo, the most venerated holy image in the city. People wearing purple robes, with offerings of orchids, form immense lines from 3am–9pm to pay homage in the Basilica of Santa Teresa.

Processions of *Nazarenes*, garbed in purple robes, and live Passion plays are seen in many parts of the Andes between Wednesday and Friday. In Ureña (Táchira) on Good Friday, dozens of groups, each with a person carrying a heavy wooden cross, make their way up Avenida 1° de Mayo to "Calvary," stopping at adorned stations of the cross along the way to pray. Same town, but different location, at about 9.30am at the church of the Sagrada Familia, costumed participants re-enact Christ's sentencing and also march to Calvary.

However, there are three places which outshine the rest for their superb, ambitious, well done *Pasión Viviente* – live Passion plays. One is La Parroquia (Mérida), with a week-long presentation, mostly taking place in or in front of the church (main days Thursday and Friday) about 7.30pm. Caripito (Monagas) has become the focal point for a week-long Passion play, one of the most ambitious in Venezuela, with hundreds taking part. The scene for most of the presentations is a hillside on the edge of town, which makes for a perfect natural amphitheater. Tostos (Trujillo) is the third place, with a Good Friday drama that attracts hundreds of visitors to the picturesque mountain village.

Corpus Christi – the ninth Thursday after Maundy Thursday – is the day for devil dancers or *diablos danzantes (see pages 84–5)*.

Flowers and feasts

Traditional celebrations for Cruz de Mayo are held every Saturday in May in private homes, with special altars set up for the cross, decorated with candles and flowers. Friends are invited to join in the singing of the rosary, dancing to the rhythm of *tambores* (African-style drums made from hollow logs) and more social aspects with everyone bringing food to share.

On the Fiesta de San Isidro (May 15 in Tostos, Trujillo; the Sunday closest to the date in Tabay, Mérida) farmers take oxen, their yokes decorated with spring blossom and garden produce, along to the church for blessing. In Tabay, there's a procession with a figure dressed as the saint.

The main annual event for communities with African roots, all along the central coast (with Curiepe in Miranda of special note), is the Fiesta de San Juan Bautista, June 23–4. A particular friend of the blacks, he is "baptized"

in the sea or river and fêted with sensual dancing to the *tambores* and abundant *aguardiente* (potent sugar cane liquor) or rum.

The Parranda de San Pedro, June 29 in Guatire and Guarenas (Miranda), relates to the legend of a slave, María Ignacia, who promised the saint she would dance throughout his feast day if he cured her daughter, Rosa, who was near death. The girl was cured and María Ignacia kept her promise. A man plays the part of María, carrying a doll representing Rosa, accompanied by black-faced fellow slaves.

Feasts of patron saints are celebrated across the country, in Valle del Espíritu Santo,

Margarita (the Virgen del Valle, September 8); Maracaibo (La Chinita, November 18); and San Cristóbal, Táchira (San Sebastián, January 20). Nuestra Señora de Coromoto, the patron of Venezuela, is fêted on September 11 in Chachopo (Mérida) with the Indios Cospes depicting the Virgin's appearance to their chief and his subsequent acceptance of the faith.

The night-long dance of the *turas* on September 23–4 in Mapararí (Falcón) is a celebration with indigenous-agrarian roots for the Virgen de Mercedes, while the Negros de San Jerónimo, men with blackened faces who dance for the saint every September 30, are found only in Santo Domingo (Mérida). ❏

LEFT: high times with the batmobile.
RIGHT: dancing to the *tambores* at Choroní.

DANCING WITH THE DEVILS

The pounding of drums, rattle of maracas, jangling of bells, and dancing men in masks paint a vivid scene of the diablos danzantes

On Corpus Christi, *diablos danzantes* (devil dancers) don grotesque masks, colorful costumes, and take to the streets of several towns along the coast. Hardly a frivolity, the event's participants are members of confraternities dedicated to the Eucharist, who dance to pay solemn religious promises (such as petitions for divine intervention or gratitude for cures), made for life or a specific period.

Active dance groups are concentrated on Venezuela's central coast. Since participants are principally black, many people assume the tradition has African roots. In fact, the rites have been practised in Europe since the Middle Ages (antecedents date back to the feast of Natalis Calicis, recorded since the 5th century), and were brought to this continent by the conquistadores as a means of spreading Christianity. The Spanish ritual adopted elements from indigenous peoples, and later from African slaves, but it has retained the same common thread for five centuries: use of the Eucharist and symbolic figures representing acts of submission of evil or heresy to Christian doctrine.

Performances by *diablos danzantes*, each group with distinct costumes but enacting basically the same rites, can be seen in San Francisco de Yare, Naiguatá, Patanemo, Turiamo, Cata, Cuyagua, Chuao, and Ocumare de la Costa.

▷ **INITIATION RITES**
As an act of submission, inititates into Turiamo's confraternity advance to the church on their knees to whisper their promise into the priest's ear.

△ **HANGING LOOSE**
Rather than face masks, many groups of devils wear their masks hanging loosely on the end of transparent fabric covering the head.

◁ **FEARSOME BEASTS**
The masks of Naiguatá's devils usually represent fantastic animals, based on the belief that the devil often appears in the form of an animal.

△ **SHE DEVIL**
Confraternities are usually male only, but in Yare, one woman, *La Capataz*, is annually elected by the brotherhood and permitted to wear a devil mask.

DEVIL MASKS HIT THE MARKET

In 1948, when Manuel Sanoja was just 10 years old, he joined the rank of the *diablos danzantes* of San Francisco de Yare. Even then, when he made his first mask to participate in the dancing, Sanoja's exceptional artistic talent was evident, with a very particular style making his creations immediately identifiable. Many other devil dancers, fascinated by his masks, contracted him to make theirs too.

The impressive quality of his work won the admiration both of the general public as well as of the savvy merchants of original Venezuelan crafts, who recognized the masks' commercial potential. As a result, the masks have provided Sanoja's livelihood for half a century, and nowadays family members help out in his workshop (tel: 583 929 191) to keep up with the enormous demand both at home and abroad. Sanoja even had the unlikely distinction of making the mask worn by Carolina Herrera as her "typical Venezuelan dress" when she won the Miss Universe title in 1984!

△ **EARLY COMMITMENT**
Very often, a father will commit his sons to the confraternity, with the promise to dance from an early age to protect them from possible future harm.

◁ **COLORFUL COSTUMES**
In Naiguatá, the devil dancers are distinguished by their very large masks, their colorful, hand-painted clothing, and by the wearing of many bells.

VENEZUELAN CUISINE

If deep-fried ants don't take your fancy, then don't worry – the
variety of Venezuelan cuisine ensures that there's something for everyone

One word describes the Venezuelan palate: eclectic. Due to the country's fertile farm land and warm tropical waters it enjoys an abundance of beef and a great variety of seafood, freshwater fish, fruits, and vegetables. Its distinctive regional specialties reflect a mix of foreign influences and local traditions. One can savor anything from a exquisite mango *mousse* or exotic Thai delicacies in the capital, to stewed capybara and cheese made from water buffalo milk in the *llanos* to piranha and deep-fried ants in Amazonas.

Not by bread alone

For most Venezuelans, the staff of life is not bread but a flattened, fist-size ball of fried or baked corn or wheat flour dough called an *arepa*. As pervasive as the *tortilla* in Mexico, the cheap and filling *arepas* are eaten in great quantities by the country's poor, but they also turn up in smaller, daintier versions in the bread baskets of fine restaurants, where diners slice them in halves and slather them with *natilla*, a cross between sour cream and butter.

Seldom are *arepas* eaten plain. Usually they are slit and part of the inside is scooped out to form a pocket that's stuffed with virtually anything imaginable. Favorite fillings include *reina pepiada* (chicken salad with sliced avocado), *carne mechada* (shredded beef), *ensalada de atún* (tuna salad), *diablitos* (canned deviled ham), or simply grated *queso amarillo* (yellow cheese). At breakfast, a popular filling is *perico*, eggs scrambled with tomato and onion.

The *arepa* accompanies Venezuela's national dish, *pabellón criollo*. This large, tasty dish comprises shredded beef spiced with onions, green pepper, tomato, *cilantro* (coriander), and garlic, a mound of white rice, a scoop of *caraotas negras* (black beans), and strips of fried plantain. With demand frequently outstripping national supply, black beans are often imported,

mainly from Chile. It has been suggested that this is the reason Venezuelan politicians traditionally maintain such good relations with this southern neighbor. *Pabellón* is not eaten on any particular occasion; rather it is part of the daily diet of many working-class Venezuelans and a standard on many restaurant menus.

On Isla Margarita, *pabellón* has a distinct local flavor, with flaked fish flavored with onion, peppers and tomato taking the place of shredded beef.

Arepas, as with *pabellón*, vary from region to region. For example, in the Andes, particularly in Mérida, the standard variety is made with wheat flour rather than corn meal, and looks more like a stiff pancake.

The most traditional "bread" of all, however, is *casabe* (with a strong wheat taste). Eaten by indigenous peoples since long before colonists arrived, it continues as their staple, and also is made throughout the interior. *Casabe* is made of grated bitter yucca root which has had its

---

PRECEDING PAGES: a piscine platter.
LEFT: chef at the Avila Hotel, Caracas.
RIGHT: hard at work in a country kitchen.

toxic juice squeezed out, before being toasted, then moistened and formed into large rounds – *tortas* (cakes) some 60 cm/24 inches in diameter – and "baked" on a hot griddle until dry and crispy. There is a thick version (about 1 cm or ⅜ inch) and a thin one – *galleta* (cracker). A sweet variation is *naiboa*, a thick round, about a quarter of the usual size, and with raw brown sugar pressed into the surface.

A flavorful tidbit is the *tequeño*, white cheese wrapped in thin pastry dough and deep fried. *Tequeños* may be served as *pasapalos* (hors d'oeuvres) or eaten as a snack. *Hallaquitas* are common accompaniments to grilled meat.

grated sweet corn. *Cachapas* are usually folded in half with a slab of local cheese such as *queso guayanés* or *queso de mano* inside.

Empanadas are deep-fried cornmeal turnovers filled with cheese, meat, fish, or black beans. Meanwhile, the Andean version (like their style of *arepas*, relying on wheat flour rather than cornmeal) is the *pastelito* – usually round, with a delicate pastry stuffed with anything available, from cheese to smoked trout.

Surf and turf

For main courses, the country produces fine meats, fish, and shellfish. Beef is mainly pro-

Made with a dough of white cornmeal, they are like a mini-*tamale* (another cornmeal snack popular in other Andean countries) – but without stuffing. The most common form is with cornmeal only, but sometimes bits of sweet pepper, *chicharrón* (fried pork rind), or cheese are mixed in the dough. They are wrapped in corn husks and boiled. The firm, hot mush inside is subsequently sliced and doused with *guasacaca*, a typical sauce used in many dishes, with a base of a variety of ingredients, including fresh coriander and parsley leaves, avocado, onion, oil, vinegar, and garlic.

Another Venezuelan standard is the *cachapa*, a thick, slightly sweet pancake made with

duced in the *llanos* (central plains) and southern Zulia state. Menus feature cuts such as *punta trasera* (rump steak), *solomo* (chuck), and *lomito* (tenderloin). The *parrilla criolla* (mixed grill with beef and sausage) or *parrilla argentina* (with intestines also added) are regular favorites among serious meat eaters.

Andean lakes and streams are abundantly stocked with *trucha* (trout), which is farmed for export, too. Fishermen along the 3,000-km (1,800-mile) coast of Venezuela haul in *pargo* (red snapper), *dorado,* and shellfish, including clams and oysters. Shrimp are also plentiful in many coastal areas. You may be disappointed though, at the scarcity of lobster and conch –

Venezuelan fishermen spirit this bounty away to the resorts of Aruba where they fetch a far higher price.

Fruit paradise

Tropical Venezuela offers a cornucopia of fresh foods that remain key parts of the diet despite the increasing presence of multinational processed-food companies. Widely available fruits make succulent seasonal treats for visitors from colder climes. Street vendors sell amazing watermelon-sized *lechosa* (papaya), mangos, *guayaba* (guava), *guanábana* (custard apple), *zapote* (sapodilla plum), *níspero* (the crabapple-like fruit of the medlar tree), oranges, melons, pineapples, and strawberries.

You might also see vendors with carts full of what look like green ping-pong balls. They are *mamones*. Venezuelans buy them by the bag-ful, peel off the skin and suck on the pale pink flesh that clings to the pit. Some fruits go by names unfamiliar in other Spanish-speaking lands: passion fruit is called *parchita* rather than *maracuyá*, watermelon is *patilla* rather than *sandía*, and limes are *limones* (literally, lemons). Avocado is *aguacate* instead of *palta*.

Fresh juices are a thirst-quenching alternative to soft drinks. On a hot day, sip a tart, refreshing *limonada frappe* (limeade with crushed ice) or a *papelón con limón* (raw brown sugar dissolved in water with a squeeze of lime). Street vendors do big business with *jugo de caña*, pale green sugar cane juice, and also coconut juice drunk straight from the shell (*coco frío*). Just about any fruit can be whipped into a *jugo* (juice), *batido* (frothed with ice), or *merengada* (with milk).

You'll find every kind of banana – from the stubby sweet *cambur*, ready for eating, to the large, starchy *plátano* (plantain) for frying. A favorite snack is crisply fried, lightly salted plantain chips called *tostones*.

Holiday dining

Food takes on a special significance during the Christmas season, when bosses throw parties for employees featuring *pan de jamón* (ham rolls), and families gather for home-cooked feasts. The most cherished holiday food is the *hallaca*. This packet of cornmeal dough is bursting with a filling of chicken, pork, and beef flavored with the following ingredients: green pepper, onion, garlic, tomatoes, capers, sugar, cumin, black pepper, parsley, pork fat, olive oil, almonds, raisins, and green olives. Each *hallaca* is lovingly wrapped in banana leaves and steamed (the leaves are not eaten). Needless to say, the preparation takes hours, even days.

This festive dish supposedly has humble origins; it is said to have been created by servants recycling the jumble of scraps from the master's table. Yet *hallaca* has grown so

SWEET FANCIES

Many Venezuelans have a sweet tooth. Ever popular are *churros*, crispy fried batter tubes sprinkled with sugar and usually served with thick hot chocolate. Dunking is allowed. Flan *(quesillo)*, puddings, cakes, ice cream, coconut, candies, and other goodies are also craved, but the distinctive Venezuelan dessert is a dreamy sponge cake doused in coconut cream called *bienmesabe*. That translates as "tastes good to me," and to say it's rich is a colossal understatement! Note that when preparing fruit juices, a scoop or two of sugar is added, so if you don't like it too sweet, ask for *muy poco azúcar* (very little sugar) or *sin azúcar* (without sugar).

dear to Venezuelans that exceptions were made during the era of import restrictions for such key ingredients as olives, and when supplies ran short or grew too pricey, people took to the streets and staged protests.

Local tastes

Because Venezuela is a large country, with many varied zones, distinctive regional cuisines have evolved. In coastal areas and on Margarita Island, you'll find various *hervidos de pescado* (fish soups). A favorite is *sancocho* (fish stew), a steaming brew with large chunks of fish, pumpkin, root vegetables, and tomatoes.

("typical food"), a dinner of rainbow trout. But although this trout is intimately associated with Mérida, it is not in fact native to the Andes. The Venezuelan government imported the fish from Europe and the United States between 1938 and 1941, and now several trout hatcheries outside Mérida enjoy a thriving export business.

The *llanos* and southern Zulia are beef country. Since grass-fed tropical beef has little fat, it is often larded by making small cuts that are filled with bacon or pork fat. One recipe calls for filling a tough roast with large whole carrots and onions, plus bacon or pork and garlic. As the joint cooks, it may swell to

Consomé de chipi chipi is a thin broth laced with tiny clams that is reputed to be an aphrodisiac. *La tortuga marina* (sea turtle) is a delicacy, but the species is endangered. Conservationists also advise avoiding *pastel de morrocoy*, a pie made from land turtle. In Lara and Falcón states, *chivo en coco* (goat in coconut milk) is a specialty.

Home cooking is popular in the Andean region. The small white potatoes are remarkably sweet, and the home-made cheese fried in cubes is not to be missed. Sausages and cured meats are sold by the roadside in many villages.

When the Pope visited Mérida, the Andean capital, in 1985, he was treated to *comida típica*

double its original size and when carved is a surprisingly tender mesh of meat and vegetables.

In the Amazon region, indigenous groups fish, catch turtles, and hunt tapirs, monkeys, and birds – but not parrots, whose meat is considered too tough. Markets in Amazonian towns may offer unusual meat such as peccary (wild pig) and venison. Deep-fried ants are considered a delicacy – especially the large winged ones known as *culonas* (big bottoms). At the market in Puerto Ayacucho, you can buy bottles of a sauce, *katara*, made from the liquid of yucca, hot peppers, and the heads of *bachacos* (a large, leaf-cutter ant with massive mandibles), said to have aphrodisiac powers.

Locally harvested cashew nuts are sold along the roadsides between Puerto La Cruz and Ciudad Bolívar. *Palmito* (palm hearts) are a mainstream delicacy from Delta Amacuro, but conservationists advise against eating *palmito* since harvesting the crop kills the trees.

Foreign influences

Although fried ants have not exactly caught on in Caracas, the impact of foreign cultures is obvious in restaurants of the capital. A sizeable Italian community ensures that pasta is a standard and well-prepared dish. If you see *pasticho* on the menu, that's lasagne. The Italian fruit bread *panettone* is all the rage at Christmas.

The Spanish influence shows up in the prevalence of *paella*, *tortilla española* (omelet with potatoes) and other Iberian specialties. Venezuelans prefer *paella a la valenciana* over other Spanish variations. French pastries, Swiss chocolates, and Dutch cheeses are sold at delicatessens, and North America's pizzas, burgers, and fries are becoming all too prominent.

While chains such as Tropiburger, Burger King, McDonald's, and Wendy's dish up standard American-style fast food, the multitude of curbside mobile hamburger and hot dog (*hamburguesa* and *perro caliente*) stands have a style of their own. *De rigueur* toppings for hot dogs are grated cabbage, crushed potato chips, and chopped onions – all slathered with ketchup, mayonnaise, pink sauce, and mustard. Hamburgers may have microscopic beef patties, but they make up for this by adding a fried egg, a slice of cheese and ham or bacon, avocado, tomato, and lettuce, plus the toppings and sauces used on hot dogs.

Creole restaurants, *areperas*, hamburger chains, and the ubiquitous *pollo en brasas* (spit-roasted chicken) are interspersed with eateries devoted to virtually every international cuisine. And although the present economy dictates that big splurges at restaurants are less frequent, 30 percent of the population still eats outside the home at least once a day.

After lunch there's a siesta, so *caraqueños* can enjoy a hearty noontime meal with a few

hours to sleep it off before returning to work. Many restaurants close after lunch, and do not reopen for dinner until 8pm, but then carry on serving until midnight.

> ## RESTAURANT HEAVEN
>
> According to the National Restaurant Owners' Association, Caracas has more restaurants per capita than any other city in Latin America.

Coffee worshipers

More than just a drink, coffee is an integral part of the lifestyle in Venezuela. Rich, aromatic, and always fresh, each *café* is brewed to order – Venezuelans would never dream of letting a pot languish on a heater. They enjoy coffee throughout the day: big milky cups at breakfast, small heavily

sugared shots from stand-up counters for breaks and glasses of cappuccino smothered in whipped cream late at night. Coffee comes in a dozen ways, and if you simply ask for *café*, the waiter won't know what you want. You must specify the size and exact degree of strength you desire.

Here's how you do it. Size is easy: *pequeño* (small) or *grande* (large). On the street, coffee is served in plastic cups without handles. A *pequeño* is the size of a large thimble; a *grande* is close to a *demitasse*. Venezuelans usually drink their coffee well-sugared – with a large cup you'll get at least two packets of sugar. It is specifying the coffee strength that takes a

LEFT: a colonial-style restaurant near Mérida.
RIGHT: warming up *arepas*.

little savvy. A black coffee is a *negro* – a small one, using the Spanish diminutive suffix, a *negrito*. A watered-down black coffee, about the closest thing to North American coffee, is a *guayoyo*. Coffee that's half milk, which Venezuelans often drink at breakfast but almost never after a meal, is a *café con leche*. Order by asking for a *con leche grande* or *con leche pequeño*. It's not necessary to say "*café*".

Coffee with only a spot of milk is called a *marrón* (brown): you would order a *marrón grande* or a *marróncito*. Coffee that's somewhere in between a *con leche* and a *marrón* is a *marrón claro* (light brown).

A taste for alcohol

In contrast to coffee, there are few choices when it comes to brands of beer. Venezuela's best-selling *cerveza* (by a wide margin) is Polar, which for several years has been exported with the gimmick of using refrigerated containers to ensure freshness. Other beers are; Nacional Regional, produced in Zulia with primarily local distribution; Polar Negra and Nacional Stout – dark, malty beers; Solera, a light beer (not in calories, just taste); and Brahma Chopp, which was introduced from Brazil and is produced at a local brewery.

On a hot day, ask for a *cerveza bien fría*, meaning you want it just short of frozen.

Throughout Venezuela's heady oil-boom days, the country is said to have consumed the highest per capita quantity of fine Scotch whiskey in the world. Waiters at society parties would carry trays of nothing but premium Scotch and guests would choose their favorite brand. At restaurants, hosts would order bottles placed at the center of the table with mixers and diners would help themselves.

During the import restrictions of the 1980s, the best restaurants managed to smuggle it in – at a price. Although the exorbitant cost (then, as now, imports averaged US$25–50 a bottle) prompted many to switch to rum, this was only temporary. With taste buds attuned to Scotch, either something else in the budget had to give, or people condescended to drink cheaper brands of whiskey, nationally produced under license, many of which are quite good.

Venezuelans drink rum with cola, almost any fruit juice (a favorite, and delicious, is *ron con parchita*, rum with passion fruit), *aguaquina* (tonic water), or with Angostura bitters (which were invented in the Orinoco port city of Angostura, now known as Ciudad Bolívar), on ice with fresh lime slices.

Rarely do Venezuelans choose clear drinks such as vodka and gin, nor are they noted wine connoisseurs, although, through an agreement with Chile to eliminate duty, wines from that country are reasonably priced. Venezuela's beer giant, Polar, has even entered wine making, with amazing results, earning top awards in European competitions for its whites and brut, under the Viñas de Altagracia and Pomar trademarks, respectively.

As with food, there are different regional spirits. *Llaneros* are known to swill the potent, clear *aguardiente*, made from sugar cane, until they slide out of their saddles. To brace them against the chilly air, *andinos* whip up *calentado*, hot brown sugar water spiked with the anise-flavored liquor, *miche*.

After a hard night, when Venezuelans groan "*Tengo un ratón*" (slang for "I have a hangover"), they don't take aspirin. There is only one cure – a steaming bowl of *mondongo* (tripe soup). If you're up early on a weekend morning, you'll probably detect its unmistakable aroma mingling with the scent of coffee. ❑

LEFT: a hearty buffet lunch at Hato Doña Bárbara in the *llanos*.

Cacao – Brown Gold

Long before the early European explorers arrived in Latin America, indigenous inhabitants were putting cacao to many uses: as a basic element in their diet, as a cosmetic, in their religious practices, as a medicine, and even as currency. The first known cultivation of cacao in Venezuela took place in the land south of Lake Maracaibo and in the western foothills of the Andes. Dominican priests introduced it to the northeast coast in 1580.

In 1600, the Province of Venezuela began exporting small quantities of cacao to Spain, making this country the first to export the product to Europe. By 1683, exportation had increased dramatically, with its price reaching the all-time high achieved during the colonial period. From that date, however, production decreased, mainly because of the wars of the Spanish Empire against other European powers, which reduced inter-colonial navigation. Nevertheless, topping the list of Venezuela's riches in the 17th century, cacao boosted the country's foreign commerce and brought in a quantity of gold, prompting the development of a monetary economy. This in turn led to the strengthening of a criollo social class caustically dubbed by the lower classes as *"Los Grandes Cacaos."*

By the mid-1700s, Venezuela was the world's largest cacao producer, a supremacy it maintained for more than 70 years, until its wars of independence left agriculture in ruins. By 1831, coffee had taken over as the country's top export, and even leather surpassed cacao in export importance.

In 1901, cacao moved back into second spot in export volume (after coffee) and, by 1915, production surpassed 20,000 tons annually. Ten years later, annual output reached 23,000 tons, the highest figure ever up until that date. Just when it looked as though the industry was on a steady climb, the rapid and surprising development of African cacao destabilized the international market from 1930–45, with a dramatic drop in prices; and in 1933 a cyclone devastated the cacao plantations in the eastern part of the country, reducing production by 90 percent. Many plantations were abandoned.

Today, a major effort is being mounted to improve productivity since Venezuela's cacao is still

RIGHT: chocolate delight – cacao beans recently extracted from the pods.

regarded as the most aromatic and flavorful in the world. One company leading Venezuela's comeback is Chocolates El Rey, founded in 1929. Although principally a supplier of chocolate (made wholly from Venezuelan cacao) to the food industry domestically and abroad, it has also enjoyed success in the mass consumption market.

El Rey reports that while Venezuela's northeast and central zones have long been traditional sources for cacao, production in these areas is beginning to decline. Emerging as new prime sources are Barinas (where El Rey has installed its own plantation) and southern Zulia – the original growing areas in pre-Hispanic times.

One of El Rey's customers is Chocolatier La Praline. Belgian born and trained, Ludo Gillis set up shop in Caracas to be near the best cacao in the world. Although La Praline's premium bonbons are sold through its factory outlet and several select stores, it principally supplies customers such as the Hotel Tamanaco Inter-Continental, Caracas Hilton, and Marriott.

A further testimony to their quality, in Chantal Coady's *The Chocolate Companion: A Connoisseur's Guide to the World's Finest Chocolates*, La Praline is the only maker from Latin America included and its bonbons are even rated above those of Godiva, the chocolate supplier for the Belgian Royal Household. ❑

SPECTATOR SPORTS

*Even when it comes to "spectator" sports, Venezuelans are lively
participants, cheering, dancing, and having a great time as they watch*

The principal spectator sports favored by Venezuelans are baseball, basketball, bullfighting, and betting. Some might argue that the latter is technically horse racing, but it is not so much the horses or the challenge, but the fever for trying to win "The Big One" that appeals to 99 percent of Venezuelan fans.

Baseball is king

No question about it, baseball is the king of spectator sports in Venezuela. While soccer holds this honor in other South American countries, baseball firmly took root here as a favorite decades ago.

Unlikely as it sounds, this development was related to petroleum. When US oil companies came to Venezuela in the early 1900s, their personnel brought the game with them. Initially played only in the oil camps, baseball's popularity took off, especially in the 1940s when professional winter leagues were started.

Eventually, teams were built up throughout the country with North American support. As the level of play started to improve each year, major league teams began regularly scouting here and started giving opportunities to promising Venezuelans to compete for positions in *Las Grandes Ligas* ("The Big Leagues").

Extensive coverage in local newspapers of games in the US season and the performance of Venezuelans playing for these teams, has further contributed to enthusiasm for the sport.

The first great Venezuelan player in the majors, Alfonso "Chico" Carrasquel, earned the starting shortstop position for the Chicago White Sox in 1950. His success was the inspiration for thousands of Venezuelan kids to spend hours on dusty diamonds throughout the country, dreaming of the day they too would wear a major league uniform.

An idol with whom Venezuelan kids can more easily identify than adult stars is Kenji

García Sonofuku. In 1998, this 16-year-old infielder from Caracas signed a one-year deal with the New York Mets for a tidy $1.64 million to initiate in the minors. Another national idol is Luís Sojo, who in 2000 dramatically helped the New York Yankees in their 26th World Series title with his ninth-inning hit.

The most remarkable Venezuelan player to date has been Hall-of-Famer Luís Aparicio, with an 18-year career. Some of his records as shortstop are still in place. More recently, the home-run tally of Andrés *El Gato* ("the cat") Galarraga (Atlanta Braves), with a major-league career which started in 1984, and the fielding of Omar Vizquel (Cleveland Indians), winner of multiple "Golden Glove" awards, have been principal subjects of headlines in the Venezuelan national media.

The local professional league season runs from October through January. Being the off-season for US baseball, Venezuelan teams hire several US players from AA or AAA teams

---

PRECEDING PAGES: thumping a home run.
LEFT: Omar Vizquel, star of the US Cleveland Indians.
RIGHT: fan and mascot.

(many go on to stardom after honing their skills here.) Well-known players such as Dave Parker and Darryl Strawberry have played in the Venezuelan league; as did Pat Borobers, named "Most Valuable Player" in the 1992 World Series.

This "winter league" consists of eight teams organized in two divisions: the *Leones* of Caracas, the *Navegantes de Magallanes* from Valencia, *Tiburones* of La Guaira, *Cardenales* from Barquisimeto, *Tigres* of Maracay, *Aguilas* of Maracaibo, *Petroleros* from Cabimas, and *Caribes* of Puerto La Cruz.

The games draw huge crowds of loyal and raucous fans, who dance to their own bands and wave home-made banners. Even those who do not make it to the ballpark follow their favorites via television, radio, and the newspapers.

Perennial rivals

Although each team has its *fanáticos* (fans), nothing compares with the passion evoked by the traditional rivalry between the *Magallanes* and *Leones*. Precisely how this started is not clear. However, in most people's opinion, the *Navegantes de Magallanes* have the largest and most rabid following of any team in the country.

One reason might be that the team has moved around over the past 50 years, picking up fans

GAME FOR SOME BALL?

If you would like to combine some beach time with a little Latin American winter ball, make the trip to Puerto La Cruz – about 4 hours by car from Caracas – which has some of the country's liveliest resorts and a busy baseball season. There is also plenty of action in the capital, where the atmosphere is terrific for baseball – the lights are good, the fields are in solid shape and the fans are lively. For people passing through Caracas during the winter season, which begins in mid-October and finishes at the end of January, it is relatively easy to secure game tickets to see the Caracas or La Guaira teams in action. Just check the *Daily Journal* for the baseball schedule.

in each location. It started in Caracas. With a change of name, the team was sold and sent to the eastern part of the country, playing "home games" in three or four different cities. It then got the name *Magallanes* back and was sold to the city of Valencia (quite literally being owned by the city government – in itself unique), where it has remained.

Lively games

Leones–Magallanes encounters are a sight to behold. In Caracas, the experience begins with jostling crowds lined up hours ahead of game in time to obtain the precious tickets for the 20,000-seat stadium of Universidad Central.

The first couple of innings are relatively tranquil. But "relatively tranquil" in Venezuelan terms would translate as "rowdy" in most other countries, with yelling, screaming, and dancing being performed passionately. By the third inning, the countless numbers of cold beers that have been downed start taking effect and anything can happen – from fights to hecklers being sent flying.

For this reason, security is very tight throughout the stadium in both Caracas and Valencia. Attack dogs are placed on the field together with armed guards near the end of the games to prevent fans from entering the field.

acknowledges recognition if a new record is set. To add a bit of flair, when hands go up, plastic cups of beer that are being held invariably go sailing into the crowds.

Summer basketball

Like baseball, the season for basketball is opposite to that of the US professional league, in this case starting in early March and ending with the play-off finals in early July. And, in the same manner, during their off-season many pros from up north join Venezuelan teams.

The professional basketball league is composed of eight teams: two in Caracas *(Coco-*

Another diversion at these contests is "the wave." This nowadays popular crowd show consists of fans in one vertical section of the stands simultaneously rising to their feet, lifting their arms aloft, then lowering them and sitting down in one long sinuous movement. The motion has to be passed on to those in the adjacent seats, until "the wave" has gone completely around the stadium; then it circulates again and again. The scoreboard indicates the old record for the amount of minutes "the wave" takes to go around the stadium and

drilos and *Panteras)*, and one team each in Maracaibo *(Gaiteros)*, Valencia *(Trotamundos)*, Barquisimeto *(Bravos)*, Maracay *(Toros)*, Puerto La Cruz *(Marinos)*, and Porlamar *(Guaiqueries)*. Most games are televised.

La fiesta brava: bullfighting

All major Venezuelan cities have bullrings. Valencia's Plaza Monumental is the second-largest in the Americas, surpassed only by the ring in Mexico City; and, in San Cristóbal, the capital of Táchira, top international bullfighters perform during the very popular annual festival in February in honor of the city's patron saint, San Sebastián.

LEFT: the "wave" makes the round.
ABOVE: a bullfight in Maracay.

Maracay is considered the real cradle and capital of bullfighting in Venezuela, having produced the country's biggest stars. Its beautiful Moorish-style ring, La Maestranza, is also called the Plaza de Toros César Girón, named after one of the city's and nation's greatest bullfighters. The most important contests take place during the annual fair for the city's patron saint, San José, in March.

Bullfights in Caracas are held in the Plaza de Toros Nuevo Circo on Sunday afternoons during the November to March season. Local newspapers have exact dates and times. The bullring is on Avenida Lecuna, one block east of Avenida Fuerzas Armadas. Because of the huge crowds and non-existent parking at Caracas' bullring, the best way to get there is by the subway, with the La Hoyada station just a block to the west.

SIT IN THE SHADE

Seats for bullfights are sold as "*sol*" (sun) and "*sombra*" (shade). Since fights take place in the hottest part of the day it's worth paying extra for *sombra* seats, which are a lot more comfortable.

alternatives to man versus beast (with no weapons or killing of animals involved), which are enormously popular in rural areas.

The contest consists of a massive bull being set free down a long, narrow chute (the *manga* or "sleeve"), with about a half dozen contestants (called *coleadores*) on horseback racing behind him.

Each contestant tries to earn points by grabbing the bull's tail, single-handedly throwing him down, and then keeping him on the ground for a given

period, for which points are earned: *toros coleados* is definitely not a sport for the faint-hearted.

Some of the fancier *mangas* actually have stands but, generally, one simply climbs up on the bordering rails, beer in hand, to cheer on the fearless contenders.

Tweaking the tail

While conventional bullfights tend to draw many elite fans and are replete with pageantry and spectators outfitted in elegant "typical" Spanish-style dress meant to be noticed, the *toros coleados* are totally unpretentious, macho

The sport of kings

Caracas has an excellent racetrack, La Rinconada, located at the south end of Autopista del Valle. (There is a Metrobus connection between El Valle and La Rinconada, which costs about 50 US cents each way.) On Saturday and Sunday, there are 12 races (1–6pm). Along with the regular grandstands, there is the more select

"Section B," which offers a view of both paddocks and where men are required to wear jacket and tie (ladies must also be suitably dressed). In the upper tiers, there is an elegant restaurant for members only.

This scenario is repeated at the tracks in Valencia (located near the bullring, with races on Friday and Saturday) and Maracaibo (races on Wednesday). It should be noted that "Maracaibo's" track was moved some years ago to a much more spacious site on the other side of Lake Maracaibo, in Santa Rita, a short distance east of the pay station for the Rafael Urdaneta Bridge crossing the lake.

Betting on the ponies

There are undoubtedly some people who attend, or otherwise follow the races, because of their interest in a particular horse or simply the joy of watching the sleek animals run. But for 99 percent of the Venezuelan public, the weekly races mean one thing: a chance to pick a winning ticket and strike it rich.

Venezuelans are enthusiastic gamblers (not only on horses, but lotteries, and every other game of chance) and visitors will find it hard not to catch the fever. In addition to a wide variety of bets made at the track windows, there is the popular off-track system called "5 y 6." This consists of attempting to pick at least five winners of Sunday's last six races. Official "5 y 6" betting locations are found not only all over Caracas, but across the country, usually identified by a sign out front: "Sellado de 5 y 6," indicating their agents are authorized to officially stamp – *sellar* – them for validity.

Although Sunday mornings are usually rather lazy times, these places are jammed with people intensely reviewing the various weekly horse racing publications (available at newsstands), pull-outs from the newspapers, and last-minute scratch sheets, as they fill out their *cuadros* (official betting forms) to have them validated before the 11am deadline.

Soccer second

Although there are certain sectors (the strongly Portuguese, Italian, and Spanish communities) and areas (above all the Andean state of Táchira whose influence comes from Colombia) where

soccer has a large following, *fútbol*, as it is known in Spanish, is universally acknowledged to be greatly overshadowed by baseball in popularity. However, this would have to be qualified with… "except during World Cup."

Venezuelans, who at any other time are completely indifferent to the sport, inexplicably become rabid soccer fans – painting their faces in team colors, waving banners for their favorite team from car windows, and taking part in horn-honking caravans each time "their team" wins a game (particularly if, against the odds, they defeat or even score a goal against rival neighbors, Colombia or Brazil).

Every soda-pop and beer producer puts out special cans allusive to the World Cup. Banks and stores offer promotions with the chance to win all-inclusive packages to final matches, and so forth. For all except the most elegant specialty restaurants and bars, it would be unheard of (or commercial suicide) not to install large-screen TVs and offer "World Cup Specials" to coincide with the games.

However, in typical Venezuelan fashion, when the final match is played, those who were adamantly rooting for the losing team, join in celebrating for the victor – with just as much fervor. After all, why would someone miss out on a party over a silly game? ❏

LEFT: La Rinconada race track in Caracas.
RIGHT: a jockey weighs in.

PARTICIPANT SPORTS

Blame it on the sun. In Venezuela, active participation in
sports – and outdoor activities in general – is a national passion

When a climate offers almost permanent "shorts" weather, you can dive, sail, run, climb, cycle, or take part in just about any other sort of outdoor sport on any day of the year. And in Venezuela the people do just that.

Going up?

In Caracas, ascending "El Avila," the capital's impressive mountainous backdrop, has assumed the character of a sacred rite. Particularly on weekends, thousands of *caraqueños*, along with a large assortment of tourists, make their pilgrimage.

Although referred to as "El Avila," this is not just one mountain, but part of an 88-km (53-mile) long section of the coastal range in Parque Nacional El Avila, with trails of every degree of difficulty. As much a social experience as a form of exercise, the young don their best leisurewear and there is lively interchange among participants.

A popular route for casual hikers begins in Altamira just beyond Tarzilandia Restaurant (located near the end of Avenida San Juan Bosco, on the 10th Transversal), and leads to Sabas Nieves, a park-like grassy area about 40 minutes into the trail. In recent years, weekend crowds converging on this departure point have become so enormous that parked cars line every street for many blocks; a police presence is needed to keep the flow of traffic moving, and neighborhood associations regularly mount noisy protests over the huge influx of hiking fanatics who jam their otherwise tranquil residential zones.

Those wanting to ascend "El Avila" without exerting themselves can take the cable car from Maripérez for the 12-minute ride to the summit, where the Humboldt Hotel (due to re-open 2002/3) has outstanding views of Caracas.

LEFT: landing a huge *dorado* fish, off the coast of La Guaira, takes skill and not a little strength.
RIGHT: a gentle stroll in the Parque Nacional El Avila, overlooking Caracas.

An excellent three-volume pocket-sized compendium (*Los Caminos del Avila*, by Paul and Jocelyne Rouche in Spanish, published by Oscar Todtmann Editors) is available in local bookstores. This is a detailed step-by-step guide to 34 trails, with corresponding maps, and photographs of local flora, fauna, and landmarks.

On the run

Joggers, on the other hand, flock to Parque del Este (with a subway station at its entrance and a measured 2,500-meter (2,750-yard) loop around the park) every day of the week. Answering the sizeable demand, the park even opens for joggers at 5–8am on Monday (a day when it is otherwise closed for maintenance) and provides a safe and pleasant place for early morning workouts.

Every Sunday, three principal Caracas roads are closed to vehicular traffic from 6am–1pm so they can be used for runners, walkers, cyclists, skateboarders, and roller-bladers. These are: the Cota Mil, between the exits for

Avenida Baralt and El Marqués; Paseo Colón from just west of Plaza Venezuela to the Teatro Teresa Carreño; and Avenida Río de Janeiro, between Calle Veracruz and Avenida Jalisco, in Las Mercedes.

In the interior, Mérida is the prime target for hikers and climbers, offering a full range of options. In Parque Nacional Sierra Nevada experienced guides are available for anything from trekking from Los Pueblos del Sur to the plains state of Barinas, to scaling the glaciers of the country's highest peaks.

The gathering spot in Mérida for climbers and hikers is Calle 24, in front of the cable

car station. Here, half a dozen or more businesses focus on organizing climbs, providing registered guides, and renting and selling equipment. Talking to fellow travelers is a good way to get recommendations.

Take to the skies

Many mountainous areas with easy access are ideal for parasailing and hang-gliding, locally referred to as *parapente* and *ícaro*. Avid Venezuelan followers are estimated in the thousands and every year more and more aficionados from abroad come to try the best sites, with the year-round warm climate a definite plus.

Among the most popular sites are: in the Caracas area, Oripoto, and Picacho de Galipán; in Aragua, El Jarillo, Loma Lisa (by La Victoria), and Placivel (30 minutes from La Victoria via Colonia Tovar); El Morro (in the Puerto La Cruz-Barcelona area); Anzoátegui and Humocaro in Lara; and, near the city of Mérida, La Trampa, Cerro Negro, Las González, and Loma Redonda.

Surfing and windsurfing

Although Playa Los Angeles, the favorite spot for surfers, was demolished by the storms in December 1999, there are still many other destinations to choose from. Heading east from Caracas, Chirimena (east of Higuerote in Miranda state) is a popular spot.

In Aragua, after the beautiful drive through Henri Pittier National Park to Cata, continue east to Cuyagua – considered Venezuela's best surfing beach. Meanwhile, surfers visiting Margarita head directly for Playa Parguita.

Rated among the top places in the world for windsurfing is Playa El Yaque, near Margarita Island's airport. (Waters off the neighboring island of Coche are also gaining popularity.)

Although not as widely publicized, windsurfing fanatics consider Adícora, on the west coast of Falcón's Paraguaná Peninsula, a prime location on a par with El Yaque. Also offering excellent conditions in Sucre state is Araya, at the tip of the peninsula of the same name (ferry service available from Cumaná; road access from Cariaco).

All of the principal windsurfing destinations have lodging directed specifically at windsurfers, including places for board and sail storage. They also offer lessons, and (except for Araya) rent equipment.

Those looking more for easy riding than for challenges enjoy windsurfing in Morrocoy National Park (Falcón), gliding between Chichiriviche shore and nearby keys.

Gone fishing

The quality and diversity of fishing in this country is renowned. Indeed, it has been known as a paradise for billfish alone for more than 30 years in international circles. And fishing for delicious yellowfin tuna on the La Guaira Bank (less than an hour off the East Coast from El Caribe) is rated first choice in the world; from January through March catches of up to 20 a day are common.

After the tuna, the most sought-after species are: Atlantic blue marlin, white marlin, Atlantic sailfish, and swordfish. From February through April, grand slams (catching a blue and a white marlin, and a sailfish all in the same day) are more frequent than at any other time of the year.

Average white marlin on the La Guaira Bank are 45–68 kg (100–150 lbs), sailfish 27–68 kg (60–150 lbs), and blue marlin 55–159 kg (120–350 lbs), but catches can be much bigger: a recent record was a 545-kg (1,200-pound) blue.

Smaller but equally feisty game fish (all year) include wahoo, barracuda, bonito, and the colorful (chartreuse with blue dots) dolphin

Roques has been relatively recent, but word spread rapidly of large schools being common, most averaging about 1.8 kg (4 lbs), which is considered exceptional anywhere, and some more than 4.5 kg (10 lbs). Fishing is good here all year, but best in May, followed by June through September. Aereotuy airlines is the main operator, offering assorted packages through travel agencies. Another option is La Tortuga island, northwest of Barcelona, a virgin fishing destination where barracuda is the star.

Laguna de Tacarigua (at Río Chico) is the main location for tarpon, although the Gulf of Paria is another good spot.

(locally known as *dorado* and not to be confused with porpoises, which frequently put on a ringside show, along with occasional whales).

Standard policy for sport fishing is catch-and-release (although a few *dorado*, tuna, peacock bass, and certain others can be kept).

Bonefishing in the flats of Los Roques Archipelago (a 35-minute flight from Maiquetía) has international fame. Fly fishing and light tackle are standard methods while wading the miles of firm, shallow flats is favored by the lightning-fast fighters. Their "discovery" in Los

LEFT: windsurfing in Morrocoy National Park.
ABOVE: keeping dry – landsurfing on Isla de Coche.

TOP SPOT FOR FISHING

In a report in the magazine *Salt Water Sportsman* on the world's best fishing grounds, just for one period alone, in its February through March summary, Venezuela is listed as the first choice anywhere for Atlantic blue marlin, white marlin, yellowfin tuna, bonefish, and swordfish; it was given second place for Atlantic sailfish and tarpon.

Especially convenient for foreign anglers flying in to Maiquetía, Venezuela's principal deep-sea fishing grounds are located just northeast of there on the La Guaira Bank, less than an hour off the coast from Caraballeda (30 minutes east of the airport), where great quantities of billfish cruise the waters feeding on migrating tuna.

The *Salt Water Sportsman* rates Venezuela as "No. One" for the period July and August (though locals say that the biggest fish are more active December through May), while the remaining months carry a recommendation of No. Two on the globe. Tarpon average 3–5 kg (8–10 lbs), although catches of 13–27 kg (30–60 lbs) are frequent, with even the occasional 70-kg (150-lb) whopper. Snook, another popular game fish, the best being bagged February through April, averages 1–3 kg (3–5 lbs), but 14 kg (30 lbs) is also possible.

TICKLE A TROUT

The trout season in Venezuela is from March 15 to September 30. Travel agencies can handle getting the required permit.

ary and February) 100 strikes a day are not uncommon, whereas in Amazonas there are fewer strikes but record sizes are much more likely. Payara, a fierce fighting fish with two huge razor-sharp lower teeth, is usually found in the same areas as *pavón*. Nevertheless, the biggest catches often tend to come from fast-moving rapids.

Clubs and racquets

Participation in golf and racquet sports in Venezuela is rather limited because of the lack

The Andes is the top place for trout fishing, principally in the glacial lakes of the *páramo* (roughly the area between Santo Domingo and Tabay) of Mérida.

Throughout Venezuela there is great fishing for peacock bass (known locally as *pavón*), with its notoriously explosive strike and, pound for pound, considered the toughest-fighting freshwater game fish anywhere. Among favorite sites are Camatagua reservoir (Aragua), Guri reservoir (Bolívar), the Alto Ventuari and Casiquiare watersheds (Amazonas), and Cinaruco and Capanaparo rivers in the heart of Apure's plains.

Reservoirs are usually easier to get to. But, along the Cinaruco River (best fished in Janu-

of public facilities in the country. Public golf courses are non-existent. There are some excellent courses, but these are all within expensive country clubs. Although access is sometimes available for guests at luxury hotels, this of course results in their use being restricted from the outset to the minority of travelers spending big bucks for lodging.

There are a few public tennis courts, but any worth using by serious players are found exclusively in private clubs or at some top-of-the-range hotels; the same circumstances apply for racquetball or squash.

Most of the top-class hotels have "Sports Clubs", which allow non-guests to use tennis courts, swimming pools, gymnasiums, saunas, lockers, and other such facilities (depending on the hotel) upon payment of a membership fee.

On two wheels

In rural areas in particular, bicycles are considered "the people's transportation" and cycling is very popular as a sport. Competitions are frequent for all age and fitness levels and two annual events draw international participants: La Vuelta de Táchira (a killer competition in this Andean state held in February) and the Vuelta de Venezuela (a cross-country contest held in late August or early September).

along with a proliferation of community teams. There is even a Venezuelan equivalent to Little League: Los Criollitos.

Soccer likewise has its company and community teams. Basketball tends to be limited more to pick-up games.

Bowling

Being an indoor sport and very disciplined, traditional bowling has never really caught on in Venezuela. But *bolas criollas* – similar to bowls but usually played on a bare dirt surface (not necessarily smooth and in a space of any chosen size) – is very popular, especially in the

The combination of friendly climate and a wide variety of landscapes has also begun attracting great numbers of mountain bikers from around the globe seeking challenging, yet beautiful destinations, although bicycle rental is sometimes difficult away from the many adventure operators in Mérida.

Ball games

Out of baseball, basketball and soccer, baseball is the most popular participant ball game, with nearly every company having its own team.

LEFT: mountain biking in Mérida state.
ABOVE: *bolas criollas* on a sunny afternoon.

interior of the country. *Bolas criollas* is considered a great occasion for men to meet up and have some beers with their buddies.

Two teams of four are formed, one using red, grapefruit-sized wooden balls, the other green ones. A small target ball, known as the *mingo*, is tossed out a short distance, and then players take turns trying to lob their ball as close as they can to it. To liven things up, if the opposition's balls are blocking the target, a player can always decide to blast the offending balls out of the way with a mighty direct hit. Add this to the usual cheering and heckling over close measurements, and what you get is a raucous and fun sport that anyone can play. ❏

BENEATH THE WAVES

The great number and variety of dive sites along the coast and around hundreds of offshore islands provide options for amateurs and professionals alike

On land, there's no denying that Venezuela offers it all to the tourist and explorer, from pristine beaches to the Andes mountain range and Amazon jungle. But for the adventurous snorkeler or scuba diver, there is a whole new world of life and breathtaking beauty to explore underwater.

Several of Venezuela's diving sites rate right up there among the top forms of marine viewing available in the Caribbean. *Aficionados* are beginning to discover that parts of the Venezuelan coastline can hold their own with Bonaire and the Cayman islands – considered two of the top diving sites in the world. The news hasn't caught on, and Venezuelan diving remains a diamond in the rough, with few tourists taking the time to discover its virgin offerings.

Anyone with a mask and snorkel can enjoy the underwater life in Venezuela, but scuba diving can be dangerous if the right precautions aren't taken and, for emergencies, there are now 14 decompression chambers in Venezuela. Among the most strategically located are in La Guaira and Puerto Cabello, and two (at the Petróleos de Venezuela facility in Lagunillas in Zulia state and at the Navy hospital in Arrecife, on *El Litoral*, a short distance west of Catia La Mar) are available 24 hours a day. Moreover, there is a US-trained doctor in Caracas (René Guilliod, tel: 212 963 5114) who is a specialist in the medical problems of divers.

Choosing a site

Unlike many other Caribbean destinations, Venezuela's long coastline offers a whole range of diving areas, giving divers the opportunity to discover new marine life each time they enter the water. In addition to the underwater flora and fauna, divers can also explore the remnants of sunken ships, some of which have been lying on the seabed since the 17th century.

There are three marine-based national parks in Venezuela, all ideal for different types of

LEFT: among the coral on the Caribbean coast.
RIGHT: ready to take the plunge.

diving: Los Roques National Park covers a group of more than 350 tiny islands just off the northern Venezuelan coast; Morrocoy National Park is located in the state of Falcón, on the country's western coast; and Mochima National Park is located in the Puerto La Cruz/ Barcelona area.

As well as the marine-based national parks, there are hundreds of potential sites scattered along Venezuela's coasts. Although it's possible to dive directly from the shoreline, the best underwater life is found around the plethora of islands a little way off the coast. This means that divers must make arrangements to get to the islands by boat – and back to shore again!

The following are currently considered the most exciting dive spots in Venezuela.

Chichiriviche de la Costa

The bay at Chichiriviche de la Costa, west of Caracas, has a pleasant beach for non-diving companions, as well as opportunities for snorkeling, scuba diving and skin diving. While there are two routes from Caracas – via Antímano-La Yaguara-El Junquito, then heading north to the coast just before Colonia Tovar; and via Maiquetía-Catia La Mar – the latter is the more advisable route because of the extremely poor condition of the other alternative, which is only passable with a four-wheel-drive vehicle. However, whichever route you take, a 4x4 vehicle is advisable if the weather forecast threatens even a hint of rain. There are various

CLOSE TO CARACAS

One of the closest dive sites to Caracas, Chichiriviche de la Costa is a perfect place for divers to spot large groupers, angelfish, and an occasional sea turtle.

posadas (lodgings) in the coastal village catering specifically to the needs of divers.

In Chichiriviche, a coral wall along the sides of the bay drops to a depth of 45 meters (145 ft), then a sandy slope continues down to 90 meters (290 ft). The somewhat rocky bottom gives divers the opportunity to glimpse rock- and crevice-dwelling marine life, while the shallow bay is home to, among other creatures, an array of brilliantly colorful tropical fish, octopus, and seahorses.

Although good diving and decent snorkeling can normally be expected in Chichiriviche, you should be aware that the clarity of the water is at times limited.

Puerto Cabello

Farther to the west of Caracas, and about a 25-minute ride from the city of Valencia, is Puerto Cabello. Although this town is mainly known as an industrial port and a stopping-off point for container ships, it's possible to find some good diving on outlying islands. Isla Larga and Isla del Faro are the major diving sites here, although the latter is more suited for snorkelers since the maximum depth around the island is only about 15 meters (50 ft).

The waters off Isla Larga are also home to two ships sunk – both World War II cargo ships. The rear of one boat sticks out of the water just off the island, while the prow is on the bottom at a depth of about 20 meters (65 ft). A coral wall has formed around the hull, giving an added dimension to the dive. In addition to the sting rays that can be seen roaming the sandy ocean floor, many sponges, barracuda, lobsters, crabs, and coral have taken over the hull of the 50-meter (165-ft) boat.

Another favorite dive spot, Islas Las Aves (Islands of the Birds), is accessible by private yacht or charters from Tucacas (arrangements can be made via the Submatur dive shop, established in 1972, tel: 242 83 0082/0598, tel/fax; 242 83 1051, e-mail: submaturmorrocoy@cantv.net). One of the main reasons for its popularity is the presence of no less than an entire fleet of 16 sunken 17th-century war ships, which lie only 3–4 meters (10–13 ft) below the surface, making it possible for not just divers, but even snorkelers to visit them when the water is calm.

Morrocoy National Park

A 3½ hour drive west from Caracas, Morrocoy is considered the best area for beginners. The water is especially clear and divers can only go down to around 20 meters (70 ft). The sandy sea bottom is comfortable and less intimidating than the rocky bottoms found at places such as Chichiriviche de la Costa and the islands in the Puerto La Cruz area. In addition, the water temperatures off Morrocoy are almost always warm so that a full wet-suit is not necessary.

Diving facilities in Morrocoy are provided by the long-time union of boatmen operating from both Tucacas and Chichiriviche. They offer a very reliable and regular shuttle service to all the islands, with posted prices for the round trip and pick-up at the hour you designate (even if you camp there overnight). Alternatively, you can contract them for full-day exclusive use.

The sandy sea bottom is home to many species of coral, sea fans, and sponges, all of which are growing out of the ocean bed. Because of the clarity of the water, excellent snorkeling can generally be found within a short swim of these islands' shores. It's easy to spot brightly colored angel fish, trumpet fish, needlefish, and an occasional barracuda – and

("Little Farallón") are nothing more than a couple of big rocks sticking up out of the ocean. But the adjacent waters teem with a marvelous variety of marine flora and fauna.

Farallón is actually the tip of an underwater mountain and is equipped with a lighthouse at its peak, which stands only 30 meters (100 ft) above the surface. The area is located on the continental shelf, where the ocean bottom begins a gradual drop off to a depth of more than 400 meters (1,300 ft).

Among other attractions, an 8-meter (26-ft) long subaquatic tunnel approximately 27 meters (80 ft) below the surface of Faralloncito

all in water as shallow as 3 meters (10 ft). Night diving is a special attraction at Morrocoy. A swoop with an underwater flashlight can often reveal otherwise unseen colorful coral and nocturnal creatures that emerge to feed when the sun goes down.

Higuerote

To the east of Caracas and about a 90-minute boat ride from the town of Higuerote (covering approximately 50 km/30 miles) lies Farallón Centinela. It and its partner, Faralloncito

is home to sharks, big groupers, large schools of barracuda, and many queen angelfish.

The plethora of sea creatures that frequent the waters of Farallón mean that divers rarely have a clue as to what might float up from the ocean depths, and there have even been reports of whale sharks in the area. It is apparently more likely to see these creatures here than anywhere else in the country.

The boat ride to Farallón can be a rather hair-raising experience. But the incredible diving at the other end makes it all worthwhile. However, it's worth noting that since strong currents are the norm, only experienced divers should take to the water here.

LEFT: tube sponges.
ABOVE: pink anemones.

Puerto La Cruz

Farther east – about five hours' drive from Caracas – lie the islands off Puerto La Cruz and Barcelona, included within Mochima National Park, where there is some excellent deep-water diving. Unlike Morrocoy, divers in this area can reach depths as great as 45 meters (150 ft). The currents in this region can be extremely strong, and the water can be very cold, so full-body wet-suits are mandatory for divers in this area.

Roques archipelago, La Orchila, and the little-known Los Frailes and Los Testigos are definitely not to be missed.

Divers who have visited Los Roques come back raving about the strikingly beautiful marine life at Gran Roque, which includes sharks, barracuda, jacks, spotted rays, black margates, and the soft coral that inhabit the archipelago. There are also several caves at depths around 25–30 meters (80–100 ft), which leave underwater photographers spellbound.

> **FAVORED WATERS**
>
> La Tortuga, about 80 km/48 miles off the coast northwest of Puerto La Cruz, is favored for its under-water wall and clear water, with a great abundance and variety of corals, crustaceans, and fish.

Those who make the effort will be enthralled to see the greatest variety of anemones anywhere in the world. Anemones are prevalent in the Puerto La Cruz area because they thrive in the rocky terrain that exists here. Divers have also reported seeing dolphins and an occasional whale. It's advisable to go to this area between July and November, when underwater visibility is at its very best.

More distant isles

Although they are more difficult to reach, for those underwater enthusiasts wanting an experience of a lifetime – one that rivals diving in Bonaire and the Cayman Islands – Los

Although commercial airlines generally don't allow divers to bring full tanks aboard, with the recent development of the tourist industry on Los Roques there are now compressors available there. Moreover, most of the boats providing tourist services also have their own compressors.

Isla La Orchila is even more difficult to get to, since it is a Venezuelan military and government retreat. Although civilians are rarely allowed to visit, diving groups are sometimes invited for long weekends – which turn out to be unforgettable experiences. Since relatively few divers visit the virgin waters of La Orchila, they are teeming with life. Divers have reported spotting huge lobsters, moray eels, manta rays, large groupers, and schools of hundreds of different fish species.

Preserving the underwater world

It's safe to say that the environment has not yet come to the political forefront in this developing country. Nevertheless, some Venezuelans in the diving community are working assiduously to make sure its pristine marine areas remain that way.

Because they are classified as national parks, technically speaking the waters of Morrocoy, Los Roques, and Mochima are off-limits to Guardsmen or *Inparques* personnel to adequately patrol the vast areas that make up the marine national parks.

Environmental damage is also done by irresponsible boat owners who decide to dock on the coral reef itself. Many boaters drop their huge anchors overboard without any forethought, not realizing that they could be killing entire colonies of coral. Scuba divers and snorkelers in Venezuela are often unaware that even the slightest contact can kill the vegetation. Students of local diving and snorkeling schools are taught never to touch anything when underwater. ❑

spear fishermen. Unfortunately, a large number of poaching spear fishermen don't think twice about obtaining fish illegally at the expense of the underwater habitat. On rare occasions, a spear fisherman gets caught in the act and is reported to the authorities (the National Guard). However, it's highly unusual for a violator to be severely punished, so the financial incentives outweigh the risks.

Part of the problem is the current state of the Venezuelan economy. Budgetary cuts mean that that there are simply not enough National

LEFT: a school of fish in Morrocoy National Park.
ABOVE: coral in the Aves de Sotavento archipelago.

DIVING ASSOCIATIONS

A couple of the *posadas* in Chichiriviche de la Costa which are specifically directed toward divers are:

La Cotua
Tel: 241 72 2284
E-mail: nany@ubiculo.net

La Quilla
Tel: 212 945 0551
Fax: 212 944 4023

Though it is not their specialty, **Posada El Montero** (tel/fax: 212 862 0436), which has a larger installation and wider range of services, might also be a good bet. They can arrange snorkeling and diving with local operators.

PLACES

*A detailed guide to the entire country, with principal sites
clearly cross-referenced by number to the maps*

To explore Venezuela is easily accomplished: the highway system is considered the best in South America, and scheduled commercial airlines service every part of the country. Moreover, since most of the population doesn't own a vehicle, there is plentiful and inexpensive public transportation in every part of the country.

Caracas is the "first encounter" for most travelers, being the capital and just across the coastal mountains from the country's principal international and national airport of Maiquetía. Spread out in a narrow, high valley, with a spring-like climate year-round and a beautiful backdrop of El Avila National Park, it offers a wide range of cultural attractions, restaurants, stores, top-class hotels, parks, and an excellent subway system. However, like any large city, it also suffers from traffic congestion, has areas of obvious poverty, and increasing levels of street crime.

But it is the Venezuela outside Caracas that most travelers come to see. A key attraction is its 3,000 km (1,800 miles) of Caribbean coastline. The most luxurious resorts are found east of Caracas, including Venezuela's most popular tourist destination, Isla Margarita. Another "hot spot" is Los Roques Archipelago National Park, a 45-minute flight north from Maiquetía. Less developed is the coastline to the west, where the most popular beach areas are those near Playa Colombia in Henri Pittier National Park, and the islands and cays of Morrocoy National Park.

Second in popularity is the Andean region, with the state and city of Mérida being the principal targets. The city is proud of having the world's longest and highest cable car, providing a close-up view of the country's tallest peaks. Picturesque mountain villages seem like scenes from past centuries and proudly conserve age-old traditions.

The arid northwest offers everything from the internationally acclaimed colonial architecture in Falcón's capital of Coro to adjacent sand dunes and the oil-rich state of Zulia.

Venezuela's richest farmlands are in the midwestern plains; while the central plains of Apure and Barinas, referred to simply as the *llanos*, are Venezuela's Wild West, with sprawling cattle ranches, fiercely independent cowboys, and opportunities for birding.

The "last frontiers" of the Guayana Region comprise nearly half of the national territory. Here, the sparce population is primarily indigenous and the scenery is spectacular; it includes the huge delta of the Orinoco River and magnificent *tepuyes* (mesas of rock billions of years old) topped by unique lifeforms. These sights have inspired works such as Sir Arthur Conan Doyle's *The Lost World*. ❑

PRECEDING PAGES: a holiday weekend in Choroní; siesta hour in the *llanos*; a young mule train leader in the Sierra Nevada de Mérida.
LEFT: Checkpoint Carlos in Los Aleros, the reproduction of a typical pre-1950s Mérida village.

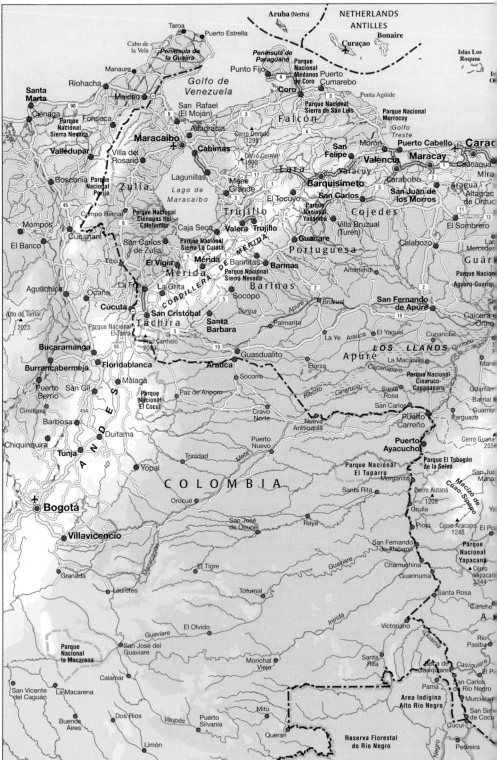

Aruba (Neths)   NETHERLANDS
ANTILLES
Bonaire
Curaçao

Islas Los
Roques

Is
O

Taroa
Puerto Estrella
Cabo de
la Vela
Península de
la Guajira

Península de
Paraguané
Punto Fijo
Parque
Nacional
Médanos
de Coro
Puerto
Cumarebo

Manaure

**Golfo de
Venezuela**

Coro

Punta Agüide

Ríohacha

Maicao

San Rafael
(El Moján)

Parque Nacional
Sierra de San Luis

Parque Nacional
Morrocoy
**Santa
Marta**

Ciénaga
Fonseca

Altagracia

Cerro Dorado
1295

Falcón

**Golfo
Treste**

Morón
Puerto Cabello
Cara
Parque
Nacional
Sierra Nevada

Maracaibo

Cabimas

Cerro Cerrón
1990

**San
Felipe**

Valencia
Maracay

Valledupar
Villa del
Rosario

Lagunillas

Lago de
Maracaibo

Mene
Grande

Lara
Yaracuy
Carabobo
Caucagua
Mira

Bosconia
Parque
Nacional
Perijá

Zulia

El Tocuyo
Barquisimeto

**San Carlos
de los Morros**
Aragua
Altagrac
de Orduc

Campo Bernal

Parque Nacional
Ciénagas del
Catatumbo

Caja Seca

Parque
Nacional
Yacambú

Cojedes
Parque Nacion
11
13
El Sombrero

Mompós

Curumaní

San Carlos
de Zulia

Valera **Trujillo**

Villa Bruzual
(Turén)

Guanare

Calabozo

La
Mercedes

El Banco

Parque Nacional
Sierra La Culata

Portuguesa

Guár

Tibú

El Vigía
Mérida
Barinitas
Barinas

Arismendi

Parque Nacion
Aguaro-Guariqu

Aguachica

Ocaña

La Fría

Mérida
Parque Nacional
Sierra Nevada

Barinas

**San Fernando
de Apure**

Alto de Tamar
2023

La Grita

Socopó

Suripá
Apure
Bruzual

19

Caicara
Orino

Cúcuta

San Cristóbal

**Santa
Bárbara**

Palmarito

La Ye
Arauca
El Yaguel
Cunariche

S
Ori

Parque Nacional
El Tamá
Río Carmelo
2031

19

Guasdualito

Apure
LOS LLANOS
La Macanilla

Mani

Bucaramanga

55

Floridablanca

Arauca

Socorro

Etorza
Capanaparo
Parque Nacional
Cinaruco-
Capanaparo

Guanlan

Burrancabermeja

Málaga

Paz de Aripora

Riecito
Cinaruco
Santa
Rosa

Barrial

Puerto
Berrio
San Gil

Parque
Nacional
El Cocuy

Cravo
Norte

San Carlos

**Puerto
Carreño**

Guamu
Parguaza

Cimitarra
45A

Nueva
Anttioquia

Barbosa
Duitama

Puerto
Nuevo
**Puerto
Ayacucho**
Cerro Guana
255

Chiquinquirá

Tunja

Yopal

Trinidad
Meta

Parque El Tobogán
de la Selva

San Jua
Mana

Morganito

Bogotá

**A
N
D
E
S**

COLOMBIA

Orocué

Santa Rita

Cerro Autana
1208
Grulla

Macizo de
Cúao-Sipapo

Ye

Villavicencio

San José
de Ocuné

Raya

San Fernando
de Atabapo

Piojo
Cerro Aracapo
1248
El Po

Granada

Chamuchina

Parque
Nacional
Yapacana
Cerro
Yapacan
1344

El Tigre
Guaviare

Guarinuma

Laureles

Totumal

Santa Rosa

Cariche

Inirida

Victoriano

A

El Olvido

Guaviare

Morichal
Viejo

Santa
Rita

Rio
Pasiba

Parque
Nacional
la Macarena

San José del
Guaviare

Bota del
Casiquiare
Casiquiare
El P

Calamar

Pamá
San Carlos
de Río Negro
Murcielag

San Vicente
del Caguán
La Macarena

Mitú

Area Indígena
Alto Río Negro

San Sim
de Cocu

Buenos
Aires

Dos Rios

Puerto
Silvania

Cucui

Limón
Vaupés
Querari
**Reserva Florestal
do Rio Negro**

Pedreira

CARIBBEAN SEA

ST VINCENT AND
THE GRENADINES

Venezuela

0   100 km
0   100 miles

N

St George's   GRENADA

Isla La
Blanquilla

Isla de
Margarita

Islas Los
Testigos

Tobago

Isla La
Tortuga

Nueva Esparta

Punta de   **Porlamar**
Piedras   Carúpano

Parque Nacional
Península de Paría

**Port of
Spain**   Toco

**TRINIDAD
AND
TOBAGO**

Sangre Grande

Cumaná   **S u c r e**
Puerto La Cruz   Parque Nacional
Barcelona   Mochima

Parque
Nacional
Turuépano

Güiria
Golfo de Paría
Punta Campana

Trinidad

San Fernando

9

Clarines   El Caribe

Caripito

Maturín   Pedernales

Onoto   16   13

Guamal

M o n a g a s

Parque
Nacional
Mariusa

A T L A N T I C

O C E A N

Zaraza

Anaco

San José
de Guanipa   Temblador

Tucupita

Misión San Francisco
de Guayo

15

El Tigre   Chaguaramas
10   15

D e l t a
A m a c u r o

San José de
Amacuro

A n z o á t e g u i

(Puerto)   (San Félix)
Ordaz   **Ciudad Guayana**

La Ceiba

Morawhanna

Zuata

Soledad   **Upata**

Campamento
Río Grande

Requeña

**Ciudad
Bolívar**   19   Villa Lola

Port Kaituma

Mapire   La Carolina   La Ceiba   El Cogollar

El Miamo

Bochinche

19   Máripa

La Esperanza   Embalse
de Gurí   El Manteco

El Callao

Tumeremo

Arakaka   Marlborough

Cerro Mato
1863   Cerro El Trueno
1839

La Quina

Purgatorio

Fairfield

Las Trincheras   Hato
Bucaral   La Paragua

Cuyuni
Maipuru   Aurora

Georgetown

San José
de Nicháre   La Vergareña   Sabanita

El Dorado   La Reforma

*Meseta
de Icutú*   Entre Ríos   Caño Negro

B o l í v a r

Triana   Peters
Mine

Bartica

Sierra de Maigualida   Caura

Gualquinima-
tepuí   **Auyán-
tepuí**

Wareipa

Las Claritas   Kamarang   **G U Y A N A**

Cerro
Corobo
1904   Paranaquire   Cerro Pialma
1703   Parupa

P
A
R
Q
U
E

Iboribo

Ituni   Omal

Cerro Daku
1790   Tanimiña

Campetoy   Urimán

N a c i o n a l

C a n a i m a

10   Monte Roraima
2810   Mahdia

Cacuri   Ganacoco-
jidi   Aripichi   Wonkén   Santa Elena
de Uairén   Orinduik

Kurupukari

Junglaven   Sarisariñama-jidi
2500   *Meseta
de Ichún*   Mahigía

El Paulí   Área
Indígena
Raposa
Serra do Sul

Apoteri   **SURINAM**

Mawishiña
Jamacare   Catisimiña   Cerro Kirikíri
1312

Içabarú   Milagre   Annai   Kumaka

Parque Nacional
Ouida Marahuaca   **S**
E
R
R
A   **P**
A
R
A
C   Santa Cruz   Pirara   Lucie

Cerro Ouida
2232   **A**   Tepequém   Uraricoera   174   Lethem

Las Esmeralda   **Parque**

n a s   **Parque**   **Boa Vista**   Dadanawa   Aishalton

Nacional

Mavaca   Cerro Delgado
Chabaud   Mucajaí
1047

Aratitiyope-tepuí   **Parima-**   **Indígena**
1690   Mayabi-teri

Tapirapecó   Jaya-teri   Caracaraí   Bilaku

Sierra de Unturán   Aratabi-teri   **Y a n o m a m i**   Vista Alegre

Akave-teri

Cerro Tamacuari
2340   **B R A Z I L**

Novo
Paraíso   Moderna

San José
de Ahaua   174

CARACAS

Glass-walled office buildings tower over the few remaining colonial structures in central Caracas, while makeshift slums form an ever-expanding ring around the nation's capital

Caracas

W hen conquistador Diego de Losada founded Caracas on July 25, 1567, he thought he had found an ideal location. The city would lie in a narrow valley with refreshing breezes, few mosquitos, and days that were sunny and warm – but never too hot – all year round. Naturally, de Losada did not dream of the explosive growth the city has seen in recent decades. He certainly did not foresee that more than 5 million people would one day squeeze into the farming hamlet named for the fierce Caracas Indians. Today, Caracas is a city with growing pains. Shanty towns spread up the slopes of the mountains boxing in this glitzy, glittering city. For the most part, the solution to overcrowding has been to build vertically, making Caracas the high-rise capital of South America. Except for the crumbling streets of La Pastora neighborhood and historic buildings surrounding Plaza Bolívar, visible signs of the past are gone.

Backwater to a chaotic capital

Caracas was never an important Spanish viceroyalty and Venezuela did not have the gold, the sophisticated Indian civilizations, or even the strategic importance of some other South American countries. Because of this rather pale history, *caraqueños* (as the city's inhabitants are called) worship the modern. In the boom years of the 1970s and early 1980s their petroleum wealth gave them enough money to follow the philosophy of buying new rather than repairing or restoring the old.

Colonial Caracas is difficult to imagine, looking at the Caracas of today. The Guaire River is still there, now murky and controlled within concrete-lined channels, but you'd have to strip away highways, flatten the skyscrapers, and insert farm fields and palm trees before you come close to picturing the original city. If the task requires too much imagination, you can always head downtown to the Concejo Municipal, the town hall, and take a look at the 18th-century painting of *Nuestra Señora de Caracas* (Our Lady of Caracas) hanging there. Much of the canvas is occupied by the white-clad virgin, but tucked into the center bottom of the painting is the city of Santiago de León de Caracas, as it was known in the 18th century: nothing more than a collection of adobe houses with red tile roofs and courtyards. While Lima was filled with mansions for Spanish viceroys, Quito was graced by more than 80 colonial churches, and Potosí basked in the wealth of its silver mines, Caracas was a small malaria-ridden outpost where nothing happened except for the occasional earthquake or pirate raid.

As recently as a century ago Caracas was still a plain dotted with trees, farmers' fields and one-story whitewashed houses. The tallest structure was the

PRECEDING PAGES: a panoramic view of central Caracas. **LEFT:** visiting musicians in the park. **BELOW:** jammed traffic gives way to a mobile market.

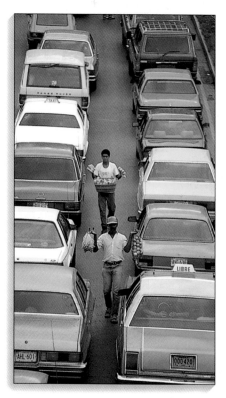

Central Caracas

500 m
500 yds

Map on page 130

cathedral spire. In 1955 the population of Caracas hit 1 million, although it wasn't until 1958 that the first building of more than six stories was completed, the Centro Simón Bolívar. Now, skyscrapers fill the valley and the population is unofficially five times greater, which explains why the city's reservoirs are inadequate and water is rationed in the dry season, why its highways are bumper-to-bumper, and parking – let alone walking – is a definite challenge.

Superb subway

One exception to flagging public services is the Caracas Metro (subway), the best friend of tourists wishing to explore the city. The subway opened in 1983 following a year of public education advertisements aimed at teaching normally unrestrained *caraqueños* that graffiti, pushing, yelling, eating, and a long list of other infractions would not be permitted. Against all expectations, the campaign was a success. The Metro is clean, quiet, and efficient – astonishingly different from the above-ground scene of undisciplined commuters and the sometimes uncooperative drivers.

Since its inauguration, the French-built subway has extended its original east–west line and added two north–south lines, as well as complementary Metro-bus feeder lines that service areas well beyond subway coverage, connecting with given Metro stations, and with tickets good for both a bus and subway ride.

Although a raging success, the Metro could never accommodate the city's entire demand for public transportation. That is why, above ground, Caracas is complete chaos. Streets are jammed with slow, fume-spewing buses, honking minibuses (known as *por puestos*), and tens of thousands of taxi-cabs, along with the private vehicles of any *caraqueño* with the need to drive in the city.

BELOW: an example of the Caracas Metro's impressive art collection.

ART IN THE METRO

Almost everyone visiting Caracas has noticed some of the artwork located under or above ground at the stations of the capital's subway, but normally without realizing the extent of the Metro's "collection."

More than three dozen major works decorate the stations, with the list of their creators a virtual "Who's Who in Venezuelan Artists": Héctor Poleo, Harry Abend, Marisol Escobar, Carlos Cruz Diez, Jesús Soto, Lya Bermúdez, Rafael Barrios, Gego, Mercedes Pardo, Francisco Narváez, Alejandro Otero, Enrico Armas, Max Pedemonte, Beatriz Blanco, and many others.

Most of the art inside the stations is beyond the turn-stiles. This means that you have to buy a maximum-price one-ride ticket to see it, but also that one ticket will let you observe the great majority, getting off the train to view the art at each station and re-boarding without leaving the station and having to pay again. If you want to see the outdoor art, you will have to pay to re-enter the system.

You can save time and money with multi-ride Metro tickets (*multiabono* – just for the subway, or *Ida y Vuelta* – round-trip destination tickets.) They can be purchased at many newsstands and stores bearing a large "M" sign near Metro stops as well as in each station.

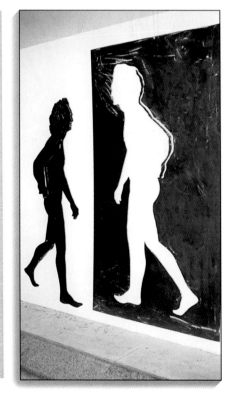

There are more than one million vehicles competing for space in Caracas.

And, like Los Angeles in the US – another car-loving city built in a basin – air pollution is a problem, especially with the lack of any emissions controls and the use of leaded gasoline.

According to statistics, more than 40 percent of Caracas residents spend at least 2 hours in cars and buses every day, not because they travel long distances to work, but because of traffic congestion. Another 37 percent commute for at least an hour.

Unplanned expansion

There are no easy solutions to the city's problems. Already overtaxed, Caracas is still growing. Immigration to the city continues, fuelled by poor Peruvians, Ecuadorians, Colombians, and other South Americans who find it easier to buy visas or forged papers to enter Venezuela than to continue north to the United States. The homeless and the mentally ill sleep on cardboard in store doorways. And Caracas' sidewalks are clogged by street vendors offering everything from strawberries to shoulder pads.

Even so, experienced South American travelers will find the Venezuelan capital empty of the abject poverty rampant in other countries. There are fewer beggars and panhandlers. The shanty towns of the poor are not built of discarded cardboard and tin sheets but of cement and clay blocks; some squatter neighborhoods (*barrios* or *ranchos*) even have running water, electricity, and sewage systems. Still, millions of *caraqueños* live in poverty and are surrounded by crime.

The Caracas workday begins long before dawn. For the poor, this is due to the long lines and time-consuming transfers for public transportation. However, even residents of exclusive suburban apartments and those with private vehicles start filling the freeways at sun-up to drop the kids off at school and join the *cola* – the daily traffic jams at peak hours – from 6–9.30am, 11.30am–2.30pm, 4.30–8.30pm, and most hours in between.

Trying to keep their heads above water in the face of continually rising costs and decreasing real income, lower and middle class *caraqueños* now inevitably have something going on the side to bring in extra money, with secretaries often selling cosmetics or jewelry to colleagues, executives doing some free-lance consulting, and technicians offering repair services on evenings and weekends.

Colonial Caracas

Although Caracas prides itself on being a modern metropolis, if one looks hard, there are still some historic corners. The best place to begin exploring the city is the colonial center, **Plaza Bolívar ❶**. In a country where nearly every city and town has a plaza named after independence leader Simón Bolívar, it is some honor to be the original Plaza Bolívar.

Towering centenary trees shade the equestrian statue of the Liberator at the plaza's center. Children chase pigeons around its edges, the disabled hawk lottery tickets, and camera-wielding tourists snap photos. Aged *caraqueños* sit on shady benches and reminisce about the days when Caracas was a smaller and considerably quieter capital.

Just as Plaza Bolívar is a hub of activity now, it was the scene of spy rendez-vous, political forums, concerts, public executions, markets, and even bullfights in past centuries. The plaza is flanked by Venezuela's symbols of power: the cat-edral, Palacio Arzobispal, Concejo Municipal, Capitolio Nacional where Con-gress meets, and the so-called Casa Amarilla, which houses the Foreign Ministry.

Map on page 130

The **Casa Amarilla** ❷ is one of the oldest buildings in the city, reconstructed in 1689 on the foundation of an earthquake-damaged structure dating to 1610. It formerly served as presidential palace and residence, and even for a while as the royal prison. Among various stories relating to the origin of its name is that when Gen. Guzmán Blanco became president, he had it painted the color of his political party, yellow (*amarillo* in Spanish).

It is a curious *caraqueño* custom, a holdover from colonial days, to identify addresses not by street or number but by their location between corners that each bear a nickname. Many corners have logical names – having been named for a long-standing building or activity there, but others are frivolous or linked to now-forgotten anecdotes. "Hospital," self-explanatory, was the name of the corner where medical treatment was dispensed; "Pelota" (Ball) is the corner where ball games were once played; "Pele el Ojo" (Keep Your Eye Peeled) was once a seedy part of town; but few remember how names such as "Cola de Pato" (Duck Tail) or "Aguacatico" (Little Avocado) made their way onto the Caracas scene.

The **Catedral** ❸, at the northeast corner of the plaza, is known as La Torre ("the tower") in recognition of the church spire's former lofty status. Although rebuilt after earthquakes, and modified to accommodate new architectural styles over the centuries, the cathedral is modest by Latin American standards. But its

BELOW: pigeons and polaroids in the Plaza Bolívar.

collection of religious art is outstanding. The painting of Christ's Resurrection is said to be a Rubens donated by a French admiral who escaped harm during a storm off the coast of Venezuela. The unfinished *Last Supper* is a work by beloved Venezuelan painter Arturo Michelena, and *Purgatorio* by Cristóbal Rojas is a haunting canvas. The crucifix in the church is a model of the cross Columbus took to the Dominican Republic in 1514; the copy was given to Venezuelan Cardinal José Alí Lebrún during a visit by Pope John Paul II.

A side chapel in the cathedral is dedicated to the Bolívar family. Here, under a Moorish ceiling painted to represent the Holy Trinity, lie the remains of the Liberator's wife and parents. Twelve years after his death, Simón Bolívar's remains were brought from Colombia and interred in the chapel. They were moved to the Panteón Nacional in 1876.

At the south side of the cathedral is the **Museo Sacro** ❹ (closed Mon; token admission fee), the former convent, which has been restored to highlight its vintage architecture and to provide a space for rotating art exhibitions and even a popular café.

The **Palacio Arzobispal** ❺, more than 350 years old and remodeled yet again in recent years, is one of the few structures in the plaza to have survived earthquake damage. From 1637 to 1803 it was the bishop's residence before it was upgraded to its present status as the home of the archbishop. Next door is the **Concejo Municipal** ❻, a structure that may have had more functions than any other building in the downtown area. The original building, a seminary dedicated to Santa Rosa of Lima, was the only higher education facility for young men in the whole of Caracas. Severely damaged in the earthquake of 1641, it was formally reinaugurated, after major reconstruction, in 1696. In 1725, the Spanish

Plaza Bolívar is home to Edificio La Fancia, a gold lover's paradise that houses floor after floor of tiny jewelry stores. Some of their designs incorporate the now hard-to-find Margarita pearls and Venezuelan gemstones.

BELOW: a friendly disagreement.

king Felipe V ordered it to be renamed the Royal University, a center for learning open only to young men with the proper lineage and Christian morals. In the structure's chapel, a holdover from the building's religious origins, Venezuela's Declaration of Independence was written. It was not until 1870 that the complex became the seat of the city government. Rebuilt and modified, much of the present building dates only from the turn of the 20th century.

The little-known **Museo de Caracas** (Mon–Fri 10.30am–noon, 2.30–4.30pm; Sat, Sun, hols till 5pm; free), hidden away in the Concejo Municipal (facing Plaza Bolívar), houses some half-dozen scale-models of central Caracas created by architect Ruth Neumann depicting how it looked in different periods of its history – not only the buildings, but figures in appropriate costume, transportation, wares of street merchants, and such like. The museum also contains a marvelous collection of miniatures created by Raúl Santana, depicting every aspect of early life in Venezuela. Between these two lovingly made displays, one can visualize Caracas (and Venezuela) of the past. As a bonus, there is also an ample representation of the works of Venezuelan painter Emilio Boggio (1857–1920).

Gobernación, the headquarters of the Distrito Federal government, has an art gallery on the first floor with frequent exhibits, but no fixed hours.

Map on page 130

Convent turned Capitol

The gold-domed building by the southwest corner of Plaza Bolívar is the **Capitolio Nacional ❼**, or Congress building. When the rabidly anti-Catholic Antonio Guzmán Blanco, one of Venezuela's string of 19th-century dictators, outlawed all convents – declaring they were incompatible with the ideals of a

LEFT: golden dome: Capitolio Nacional. **BELOW:** tropical Gothic at Santa Capilla.

liberal and advanced society, the exiled included the nuns from the Concepción convent that was once located on this spot. The building was leveled and the new Legislative Palace, built in an amazing 114 days, opened in 1874. The main building of the Federal Palace was completed four years later, but the gold dome was not added until 1890.

TIP

Visitors are welcome to enter the Capitolio Nacional to admire its art, but photography is not permitted.

The walls and ceilings of this **Federal Palace** (open daily 9am–12.30pm, 3–5pm) are covered with patriotic works by Venezuelan artists, including *Tovar y Tovar*, whose scene of the Independence War's decisive Battle of Carabobo was painted in sections in Paris then shipped to Venezuela to be fitted into the building's cupola. Here, too, is Peruvian artist Gil de Castro's famous painting of Bolívar standing on an orange and black checked floor.

The black marble box displayed in the Capitolio holds the gold key to the urn containing the Liberator's remains in the **Panteón Nacional ❽** (Tues–Fri 9am–noon, 2–5pm, from 10am on weekends and hols; free), the national monument half a dozen blocks directly north of the cathedral. Guarded around the clock, the Panteón is the mausoleum for Venezuela's most venerated heroes. An ideal time to visit the Panteón is just before it closes, when guards parade through the building.

The **Biblioteca Nacional** (National Library; Mon–Fri 9am–5pm; free) faces the Panteón. Along with expected books, it has an exposition salon with rotating in-depth shows (such as one on the science, art, and culture related to the Orinoco River), and another hall used as the **Centro de Fotografía de Conac** (Tues–Sat; free).

Although he died alone and penniless, shunned by fellow Venezuelans, Simón Bolívar is today one of the continent's most revered heroes. Two blocks east

BELOW: inside the Bolívar museum.

from the Capitolio, between the corners of San Jacinto and Traposos, are the **Museo Bolivariano** , with a permanent display of memorabilia relating to Bolívar himself and to the most important Venezuelan families of the Bolivarian era, and the neighboring **Casa Natal** ⑩ (both open Tues–Fri 9am–noon, 2–5pm, Sat–Sun 10am–1pm, 2–5pm; free). The latter is the reconstructed house (now a museum) where the Liberator was born to María Concepción Palacios y Blanco and Don Juan Vicente de Bolívar, a wealthy businessman 32 years her senior. When Don Juan Vicente died at 70, he left a young widow with four children, Simón being the youngest.

The house remained in the Bolívar family until 1806. Sold by heirs, it passed through numerous hands and fell into disrepair. In 1911 it was purchased through private donations and ceded to the nation to create a museum honoring Bolívar. In the patio of the Casa Natal is the stone font where he was baptized.

Fighting talk

It was not far from the Casa Natal that the Liberator met one of the biggest challenges to his campaign to free Venezuela from Spanish rule. Painter Tito Salas has captured in oil the moment when Bolívar, on the plaza at the corner of San Jacinto, addressed the priests and people who had claimed that an 1812 earthquake that destroyed the plaza was God's message to him to stop his seditious talk. "If Nature opposes us, we will fight against her and we will make her obey us," Bolívar exclaimed. The famous quote is recorded here in huge letters on one side of the building.

Several blocks to the south is the **Teatro Municipal** ⑪ (Oeste 8, at the corner of Municipal), inaugurated in the late 19th century, and whose restoration after years of neglect was completed in 1998. However, despite looking much smarter now, from a security point of view its location is far from ideal for attracting culture vultures.

On the corner of El Chorro stands the headquarters of the H.L. Boulton Company, a huge travel agency that deals in myriad other services. A modern high-rise has replaced the original one-story building. However, neither its history nor that of the country has been forgotten. On the 11th floor, the **Museo Fundación John Boulton** ⑫ (Mon–Fri 8am–noon, 1–5pm; free), with an outstanding collection, built up by the family over a period of more than 150 years. It includes colonial furnishing and art, china and pottery, paintings by renowned artists, the largest collection of memorabilia relating to Simón Bolívar in the world, original books from the Boulton Company since its foundation in the early 1820s, and an extensive microfilm and document library on economic and historical themes.

Although some way from other principal tourist attractions, if you have a vehicle at your disposal, you might take a quick detour to visit **Los Próceres** (Avenida Los Próceres, Autopista El Valle, exit: Los Próceres). These formal gardens were laid out in the 1950s by dictator Marcos Pérez Jiménez as part of one of the most opulent officers' clubs in the world. At their southern extreme are two towering marble pillars with the names of Venezuela's *próceres* – heroes –

Map on page 130

The Panteón Nacional: the resting place for Venezuela's great Liberator.

BELOW: the Casa Natal, Bolívar's birthplace, overshadowed by the modern city.

carved into them. A guard of honor in colonial-style uniforms keeps vigilance. On July 5 (Independence Day) there is a colorful parade with attendance by the president and an immense Venezuelan flag is hung between the two pillars.

Slum renovation

A few blocks west of the Casa Natal is the city's most misnamed neighborhood, **El Silencio**. Even the oldest *caraqueños* don't remember a time when the title was appropriate for the traffic-clogged area, noisy with sidewalk vendors.

Years ago, this neighborhood, which had degenerated into miserable slums, was designated as the guinea pig in the city's boldest experiment in urban planning. Buildings were razed and replaced with Venezuela's first urban renewal project. Completed in 1943, the El Silencio *bloques* are low-rise apartment buildings, designed by architect Carlos Raúl Villanueva. Although the overall excellent design and handsome details such as the distinct stone doorways are still evident, lack of maintenance and the low socio-economic make-up of the area have contributed to its increasingly seedy appearance.

Venezuela was the first colony to proclaim independence from Spain, on July 5 1811. The annual parade on this day along the Paseo de Los Próceres is a colorful event.

Far away from the eastside neighborhoods of the rich, here is the **Palacio de Miraflores** ⑬, once one of the most opulent homes in the country, constructed by former president General Joaquín Crespo in the 1880s. Unfortunately, in the eight years it took to build the mansion, Crespo died in battle. Since the early 20th century, when the government purchased the building, Miraflores has been used by every president as a work-place. It is decorated with European tapestries, damasks, and French and Italian furniture.

BELOW: Bolívar's words after the 1812 earthquake.

Atop a steep hill to the west of El Silencio is the oldest park in Caracas, **El Calvario** ⑭, built in the 1870s. Named for the Stations of the Cross once found

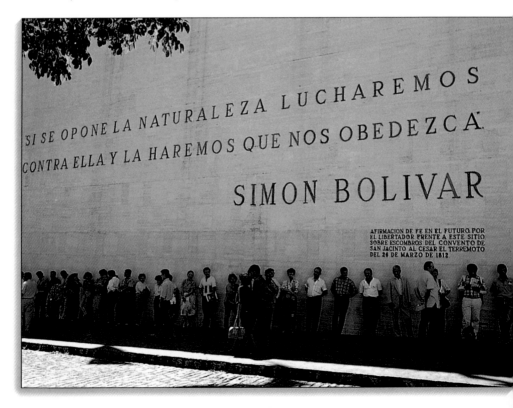

at its summit, this was once a gathering spot for pilgrims who, with lighted candles in hand, followed paths up the hill past the crosses that marked each station. The one cross that survives is in a museum. Although it appears in many guidebooks, the park is not safe to enjoy any more, singly or in groups, by day or night, because of the dangerous slum area of tin-roofed brick homes – the 23 de Enero *barrio* in the Catia area – immediately behind it.

Map on page 130

Museum mecca

Most museums, galleries, and parks (which have entrance gates) are closed on Monday. At the few that charge admission, the entry fee is usually less than US$1, used more as a means of controlling entry than for income.

One of the city's most outstanding museums is the **Quinta de Anauco Museo de Arte Colonial** ⓯ (Tues–Fri 9–11.30am, 2–4.30pm; Sat, Sun, hols 10am–5pm; closed Carnival Tues, Thur & Fri of Easter, May 1, Dec 20–Jan 10; token admission fee), a restored coffee *hacienda* converted into a showpiece of colonial art and furniture. On Avenida Panteón in San Bernardino, this house, with Andalusian and Moorish touches, was built in 1797 by a well-connected military official. The owner fled to Curaçao with others loyal to the Spanish Crown during the revolution, and the house was confiscated and rented to the Marqués del Toro, a friend and collaborator of Simón Bolívar. A bust of Del Toro sits amid the orchids and citrus trees in the tropical garden. Bolívar was a frequent guest at the house, which he loved for its view, and he spent his last night in Caracas here before heading to Colombia, where he died.

Within several blocks to the south and east of the Bellas Artes subway station is the largest concentration of museums and cultural centers in Venezuela.

BELOW: Caracas has a wide-ranging cultural scene.

To the south is the mega-complex urban renewal project of **Parque Central**. It was designed to solve the deficit of downtown housing, office space, and modern stores, and is a city in itself, complete with a school, its own Catholic parish, and all other services. It has seven 44-story apartment towers; two 225-meter (740-ft) high office towers (offices of the Tourism Ministry, Corpoturismo, are in the west tower); more than 40,000 sq. meters (47,850 sq. yards) of commercial space; and three museums:

● **Museo de los Niños** ⓰ (at the west end; Wed–Sun 9am–noon, 2–5pm; admission fee). This is an outstanding, privately operated, hands-on children's museum with participative displays over five levels on all aspects of the physical sciences, biology, communications, and ecology; the museum is very crowded with families on weekends. There is also a huge center that focuses on science and technology, complete with rocket simulators.

● **Museo de Arte Contemporáneo de Caracas Sofía Imber** ⓱ (Tues–Sun; free). In the eastern extreme of Parque Central, this internationally acclaimed museum has changing exhibitions and a permanent collection that features Venezuela's finest contemporary artists, including Marisol, Carlos Cruz Diez, Alejandro Otero, and Jesús Soto, along with many others. It also has one of the finest collections of the works of Pablo Picasso in Latin America and works by Chagall, Matisse, Braque, Leger, Fernando Botero, and Henry Moore, among other famous names. There is a café, which serves salads, in its sculpture garden, and an extensive library.

● **Museo del Teclado** (Keyboard Museum; Wed–Sun 9am–noon, 2–4pm; token admission fee). This museum has a wide array of exhibits, mostly of antique musical instruments, and also puts on weekend concerts.

BELOW: trips to the theater are popular with *caraqueños*.

A short distance to the west of Parque Central, on Avenida Bolívar, is the **Museo de la Estampa y del Diseño Carlos Cruz Díez** (daily; free), with exhibits of works of its renowned namesake plus other design themes.

Fine Arts district

Diagonally from Parque Central, in front of the Caracas Hilton, is the *Bellas Artes* (Fine Arts) area. Its focal point is the **Teatro Teresa Carreño** ⓲, a vast complex with two main halls, including the headquarters of the national theater, national symphony orchestra, and the contemporary dance troupe, Danzahoy. Guided tours lasting an hour are given several times a day, for a small fee.

Next to the TTC is the home of the avant-garde Rajatabla theater troupe, the **Ateneo de Caracas** ⓳, a venue for stage presentations, film festivals, and concerts. It also houses two art galleries, a restaurant, and a huge bookstore. Behind you'll find the **Museo de Ciencias Naturales** (closed Mon), a science museum with free admission to the general exhibition halls plus free weekly lectures by experts on different themes relating to the natural sciences.

Facing the science museum is the classical-style **Galería de Arte Nacional** ⓴ (closed Mon; free), which exclusively features works of Venezuelan artists, and also houses the Cinemateca Nacional – the national film library, with an ample program of classic, art, and foreign movies (for programming, call 02 576 1491). Behind is the ultra-modern **Museo de Bellas Artes** (closed Mon; free), which offers changing displays of art from around the world. Both museums were the work of Carlos Raúl Villanueva, who also directed El Silencio's rebirth.

The **Universidad Central de Venezuela** ㉑, or simply UCV (three blocks south of Plaza Venezuela, with the Jardín Botánico providing a buffer from the

Maps, pages 130 & 142

BELOW: guitar lesson on the Sabana Grande Boulevard.

Francisco Fajardo freeway), is another master work of Villanueva, who managed to incorporate into the design four large colored-glass windows, four frescos, 10 major sculptures and 49 murals, among other works of art. Its construction took from 1945–57. While maintenance has not been perfect, the integration of art and function in the campus presents an interesting documentary of what, in its time, made headlines on an international level. It is still considered one of the most important architectural complexes in Venezuela.

Open-air "mall"

Many of the poor in Caracas live in small hillside shanties called ranchos.

Except for the wealthy, who live in large homes *(quintas)* surrounded by walled-in grounds with exuberant flowers, mango trees, and bougainvillea, and the poor, who live in hillside shanties, most *caraqueños* live in skyscrapers. Yet, despite being high above ground, *caraqueños* haven't lost their farming roots. Vines trail down the sides of buildings, bright flowers spring from window planters, and, inside apartments, potted plants thrive in the tropical climate.

But Caracas is not all high-rise concrete jungle. The biggest outdoor gathering place for pedestrian fun is **Sabana Grande** ㉒, a car-free boulevard that stretches 2 km (1 mile) from **Plaza Venezuela** ㉓ to the Chacaíto subway station, the latter unmistakably marked by a giant yellow kinetic sculpture of acclaimed Venezuelan artist Jesús Soto. Clothing and shoe boutiques, perfume stores, bookstores, and outdoor cafés line one side of the sidewalk while street vendors lay out their goods on tables and plastic sheets on the other.

There may be discount clothing and tacky home decorations, but there are also sturdy hammocks, finely crafted avant-garde jewelry and fashionable shoes mixed among the untaxed sales items. Buyers are young couples strolling hand-

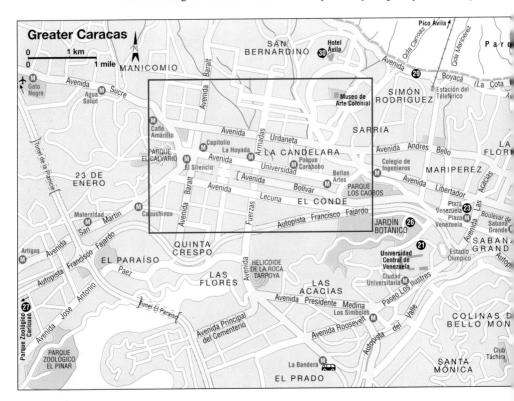

in-hand; families out for ice cream, businessmen who stop at Sabana Grande's bars for a cold Polar beer or shot of Pampero rum after work, and fashion-conscious women in mini-skirts and stiletto heels, who come here to be seen.

A favorite among the many sidewalk cafés grouped at the west end of the boulevard is the **Gran Café**. Cappuccinos compete with more traditional coffee and elaborate ice-cream concoctions, while guitarists and Andean pipe players vie for attention and tips. This is also the haunt of betting enthusiasts seeking updates on the popular *5 y 6* horse-racing cards. Some customers lounge for hours, discussing politics or the economic situation, or simply watching the passing parade of people, while other tables are occupied by chess aficionados.

With a bit of everything, Sabana Grande also has abundant upscale lodging, such as Hotel Lincoln Suites, Hotel President, and the enormous Gran Meliá-Caracas Hotel, Suites, and Conference Center – just blocks from the "hot sheets" hotels, as they are known by gringos in the city, with rooms available at hourly rates used for on-the-sly romantic encounters and as the workplace of prostitutes who fill the zone by night.

For handicrafts, you should check out **Artesanía Venezolana**, across from the Plaza Venezuela fountain at the western edge of the pedestrian mall. If you visit here at night, note that despite being very pretty with its multicolored lights, the zone undergoes a distinct change of atmosphere after dark – when it is best viewed while driving by, with car doors locked.

While pedestrian traffic in the Sabana Grande mall runs all day and most of the night, there is nearly as much activity underground. The Metro line runs directly below the boulevard, with stops at Plaza Venezuela, the mall's end – Chacaíto – and an intermediate station, Sabana Grande.

Map on pages 142–3

BELOW: playing chess on the Sabana Grande.

Shopping paradise

If your preferences lean more toward shopping malls, you won't be disappointed. A few blocks east of Chacaíto is the sophisticated **Centro Lido**, with stores, offices, and the luxury Hotel Centro Lido. The newest on the scene is the **Centro Sambil**, on Avenida Libertador in Chacao. Said to be the largest in Latin America, it has 550 stores and opening hours that have proved very popular: 10am–9pm Mon–Sat, and 1–7pm Sun and holidays. This is exceptional in Venezuela, where even in malls, stores usually close at 7pm, and always on Sundays and holidays – the only times most working people can shop.

Not far off is the **Centro Plaza ㉔**, on Avenida Francisco de Miranda, two blocks east of the Altamira Metro. En route from the subway, take time to stop at **Centro de Arte La Estancia** (closed Mon), in the restored 18th-century La Floresta coffee *hacienda*. The focus here is on three-dimensional and graphic design, photography, and artistic alternatives to objects in common use. You can also go on a guided tour of the *hacienda*'s beautiful gardens.

Along with its shopping and cultural activities, the district of Altamira–La Castellana–Los Palos Grandes has some of the city's best restaurants and excellent accommodations.

Crossing over to the south side of the Francisco Fajardo freeway, shopping areas include **Centro Comercial Ciudad Tamanaco**, better known as CCCT, and one of the capital's most exclusive collections of boutiques. Mixed in with the designer stores and hair salons are ice-cream parlors, movie theaters and bistros.

A few blocks away from CCCT and the highrating Eurobuilding Hotel and Suites is **Las Mercedes ㉕**, an upscale district known for its huge selection of excellent restaurants and nightspots, as well as for its stores. It also has the largest concentration of private art galleries in Caracas. Sunday, when galleries open 11am–2pm, is a good day to visit, with many artists and art-circle personalities present.

At the eastern extreme of this sector, facing the grand dame of Caracas lodging, the luxury **Hotel Tamanaco Inter-Continental**, another popular shopping option among moneyed *caraqueños* is the **Centro Comercial Paseo Las Mercedes**, an older but still elegant shopping mall (which also houses the upscale Hotel Paseo Las Mercedes). Among its stores and restaurants, hidden back in the La Cuadra section by the exit to the car park, is a store run by the **Audubon Society**, which sells books specializing in birds and natural history, as well as native crafts. You can sign up here for the society's own ecotourism excursions (which do not just feature birding).

The trendiest spot for exploring on foot is **El Hatillo** (with Metrobus connection from the Altamira station), on the southern outskirts of Caracas. The streets surrounding its tree-filled plaza (complete with a pair of resident sloths) and the colonial church, are filled with the workshops of local artists and craftsmen; unusual boutiques; antique shops and art galleries; Hannsi – the most comprehensive shop for Venezuelan crafts in the country; and some of the best restaurants and coffeehouses in the metropolitan area, from traditional *criollo* to Japanese, Swiss, and American fare.

BELOW: La Hoyada Market: one of many to be found in Caracas.

Saturday night fever

Although there are many good places for music and dancing scattered throughout eastern Caracas, the most popular area – because of the great variety and the upscale clientele (who flock there in droves to see and be seen) – is Las Mercedes. This is also one of the safest parts of town for night action.

Caraqueños unwind in a big way, especially on weekends when all kinds of live music is available, from *mariachi* bands (street musicians who wander round the streets and plazas improvising tunes) to Latin jazz, salsa, and rock; check www.planetaurbe.com for details of the most exciting forthcoming events. Discos don't start to fill until nearly midnight (and don't slow down until near dawn). Here, energetic couples take control of the dance floor while illicit trysts take place in the shadows. These clubs are so dark that doormen must lead patrons to their seats with flashlights. Some only allow couples; others allow groups regardless of gender, but single women may be refused entry.

However, if you have never seen Caribbean dancing, don't miss this golden opportunity to dress up (at many, men must wear jacket and tie). Venezuelans take their music seriously and their dancing is amazing, although the volume may make you wish you had brought ear plugs. Alternatively, if you want a quiet evening, the city abounds with cozy jazz bars and excellent restaurants, serving food from around the world, to suit all tastes and budgets.

The great outdoors

Despite the capital's growth, numerous beautiful green spaces have been reserved to give harried *caraqueños* oases of calm and contact with nature. **Parque Los Caobos**, planted with the mahogany, or *caobo*, trees that inspired

TIP

Take plenty of money if you go to a disco in Caracas. On weekends, in particular, clubs often require *consumo mínimo* ("minimum consumption"), which means that single drinks, soft drinks, and wine by the glass are not available.

BELOW: late nights at L'Attico bar and restaurant.

BELOW: children fooling around in a fountain in Parque Los Caobos.

its name, is a huge park located behind the Museo de Bellas Artes. Sunday is the busiest day of the week, with families out in force, joggers, kids on bicycles and roller blades, games of softball and soccer, and clusters of friends practising karate or dance moves.

Across the highway from the south side of Parque Los Caobos, prefacing the entrance to the Universidad Central de Venezuela, is the **Jardín Botánico** (no picnicking allowed) – magnificent botanical gardens with more than 150,000 examples of over 2,200 species, a herbarium, and orchid greenhouses.

For a more cozy setting, try the tiny park called **Los Chorros** (end of Avenida Cachimbo; closed Mon; token entrance fee; no pets) tucked against Caracas's northern hillside with a waterfall and stream running through its wooded setting (swimming is allowed). Although it is pretty year-round, Los Chorros is home to ferocious mosquitos during the rainy season (May–Oct), so come prepared with plenty of repellent.

The city's biggest and best zoo is the **Parque Zoológico Caricuao** (closed Mon; token admission fee; Zoológico Metro stop is a block from the entrance), which occupies part of an old coffee *hacienda*. Opened in 1977, the Caricuao Zoo has hundreds of animals in natural uncaged habitats, as well as a petting zoo that allows children to get close to domestic animals. As well as the animals, the zoo is a great place to head for to rest from the hustle of the city, and is crisscrossed with paths and walkways. You may also read about the El Pinar Zoo, but neither its maintenance nor its location can compete with Caricuao.

There is also a zoo in the huge **Parque del Este** (Tues–Sun; Mon 5–8am for joggers only; token admission fee; no bicycles or roller skates allowed), which was designed by Brazilian landscape architect Robert Burle Marx, with a subway stop of the same name at the northern entrance. Delights here include grassy areas for picnicking and games, paths for strolling or jogging, a lagoon with pedal boats for rental, and a replica of Christopher Columbus's ship, the *Santa María*.

The **Planetario Humboldt** (Sat, Sun, hols; half-hour programs shown hourly 1–4pm; token admission fee) is also located in the park, along with a bandstand where free concerts and other performances are offered on weekends. An overhead walkway at the park's eastern edge links this beautiful park up with the grounds of the **Museo de Transporte** (Wed–Sun; token admission fee).

Lofty landmark

Parque Nacional El Avila, comprising some 88 km (55 miles) of the coastal mountain range separating Caracas from the Caribbean Sea, forms the city's impressive northern backdrop. On sunny days, fluffy clouds cap the peaks. Dark clouds gathering above them signal the inevitability of the drenching rain that floods city streets in minutes, mercilessly pounding the pavement and pedestrians until, just as quickly, it stops and the sun returns.

In the foothills of El Avila is **Avenida Boyacá** which runs along the 1,000-meter (3,280-ft) mark – or the "Cota Mil," as the avenue is also known in Spanish – above which no houses may be built. Specia iewing areas, or *miradores*, where motorists can pull off the road, offer a anoramic view over the city. On Sunday, the avenue is completely closed to raffic between 6am and 1pm to allow joggers, cyclists, and roller skaters to use ts full expanse in safety. Numerous marked trails can also be followed to xplore its upper reaches (*see Participant Sports, pages 105–109*).

You can see the lines and stations of the *teleférico* (cable car) leading from the Maripérez section of town to the mountain-top **Hotel Humboldt**. The cable ar has been inoperative for most of the past two decades – as has the other line, vhich runs between the coast and hotel. As a result, the Humboldt Hotel, built t the summit of Mount Avila by dictator Marcos Pérez Jiménez in the 1950s and irtually inaccessible without the cable car, was turned into a giant and highly isible white elephant. However, in February 2001, after a multi-million dollar enovation, the cable car service from Maripérez to the summit was reopened nd there are plans to reopen the refurbished hotel, possibly as a new casino, in 002 or 2003. This has raised concerns about sufficient protection of the park's ropical bio-diversity as record numbers of visitors flock back to Caracas's fore-most tourist attraction.

Hotel Avila 30, despite being at the base rather than in the park itself, is a vell-loved landmark. Built with the riches of the Rockefeller family from North America half a century ago, the hotel has been well-maintained. While nowadays it is overshadowed in popularity by the luxury hotels in the heart of the city's shopping and restaurant districts, it is still sought out by many for its cool, tranquil atmosphere in a residential setting, with fair prices as an added ›onus. Furthermore, there is no more romantic outdoor swimming pool in the ›ity than that of the Avila, surrounded by cool, tropical foliage. ❑

Map on pages 142–3

Epiphytic bromeliads cling to the trees in Parque Nacional El Avila.

BELOW: the open spaces of the Parque del Este.

Colonia Tovar

A cool mountain breeze wafts into the restaurant where blond, blue-eyed, German-speaking waiters serve sauerkraut and *wienerschnitzel*. After a meal washed down with a stein of beer, diners might stroll along the steep streets before returning to their mountain cabins. But this is not Bavaria but Colonia Tovar, a mountain village near Caracas, first settled by German immigrants, which has maintained many of its traditions during years of total isolation.

Venezuela's 19th-century War of Independence stripped the countryside of its slave workers and farmers. To ease the labor shortage, immigration laws were rewritten to entice European farmers. In 1843, 145 men, 96 women and 117 children from the Black Forest community of Kaiserstuhl made the ocean crossing to Venezuela where they had agreed to farm virgin land owned by a wealthy creole named Martín Tovar. Smallpox aboard the ship claimed 70 lives and put the vessel

in quarantine when it finally reached Venezuela. After 40 days of isolation, the confused colonists were allowed on shore near Choroní, down the coast west of La Guaira.

But news of the disease had spread and there was no welcoming committee, no fanfare, not even transportation. Accompanied by their own priest, tailor, teacher, druggist, carpenter, printer, and blacksmith, the colonists trudged 30 km (20 miles) up the mountains to Tovar's lands, burdened by their farm implements, fruit trees, seeds, and the barley that would make their beer.

A second boatload of Germans arrived soon after but Venezuela's cold reception of the first immigrants was never forgotten. The ill-will was further fueled when the Germans were told they would need signed permission from the government bureaucrats each time they wanted to leave the town. In response to this demand, the colonists set up the most closed community the country had ever seen.

Isolated, Colonia Tovar residents recreated the Black Forest community they had left. They ate German-style sausages, drank home-produced beer, kept traditional customs, and married their blond-haired children off to one another. Venezuela's many 19th-century conflicts passed them by and for more than a century they survived, excluded and excluding, in the cool, sunny clime of their highland home.

But with the end of World War II came the fad for outdoor treks, which lured Venezuelans to the peaceful town. Robust walkers made 9-hour weekend trips from Caracas, 30 km (18 miles) away, while those with less stamina mounted mules to explore the hills surrounding the Humboldt Valley. Many stayed in the Hotel Selva Negra (Black Forest Hotel), which dates from 1937. They drank coffee grown by the colonists, ate barley bread, and bought bouquets of flowers grown in fields around the town. Gradually, Colonia Tovar's walls of isolation crumbled.

With the arrival of a paved highway in 1963 came regular visitors who bought baskets of strawberries and blackberries, handcrafted cuckoo clocks, and local beer. With the outside contact, the German language began to disappear. There is still a majority of fair-skinned, light-haired residents but their grandchildren have dark hair and Spanish names, and the once typical Black Forest costumes are now worn mostly to please tourists.

Seen from a distance, Tovar buildings look as if they have been culled from the pages of a European magazine. Although nearly all appear to have traditional *fachwerk* construction, on closer inspection one sees that while some of the older structures, (such as the beautiful Muhstall Café and general store), are indeed made with massive numbered beams and freshly whitewashed plaster, most of the newer buildings have plain, smooth walls with "beams" painted on the surface. Somehow, even when we know this, we can forgive the trick, because the *trompe l'oeil* was done to create a harmonious visual aspect to maintain the Germanic image.

The summary of development glosses over the details of the progress of "La Colonia" from 1843 to the present, with residents not given due credit for their tenacity. Aside from problems caused by an outbreak of smallpox when they arrived, the settlers quickly discovered that promises of basic shelter, some animals, and cleared farmland awaiting them when they arrived were falsehoods. Thus, the struggle for survival began from day one.

Even after they had established farms to provide for their own needs and as a source of income, the extremely difficult journey to markets and the negligible ability to communicate in Spanish proved to be great obstacles for commerce. They persisted, but until the paved highway was built, daily life was hard.

It took 120 years, but that single factor, the new highway, opened the way for easy, two-way traffic, and marked the turning point for the village. Marketing of its products rose dramatically and tourism boomed, to the extent that today Colonia Tovar enjoys the highest per capita income in Venezuela.

The village – inspiration for the fictional town in Isabel Allende's contemporary bestseller, *Eva Luna* – is a curious and anachronistic escape from Caracas. Travelers winding their way up from the smoggy capital see palm trees and pines side by side. By day, the air is brisk but at night it gets downright cold. The streets are steep but good for

strolling. At the main plaza is the L-shaped Catholic church, drawn from the plans of a chapel in Germany. The interior is simple, its most valuable possession an organ made by a local craftsman. On the bell tower you can see inscriptions in German.

Behind the church is one of the three mills (two for corn, one for coffee) of the original six still in existence in the colony. Walk downhill on the main roadway from the church to see the cemetery, hidden among pine trees at the side of the road. The graves of the first German immigrants are marked by checkerboard patterns of ceramic tiles. Burials continue in the old-style, with lines of black-clad mourners following the pallbearers – all on foot – down the hill from the church and into the graveyard.

Fine local potters and woodworkers display their goods in stores around the town. Hot breads, bowls of fruit or glasses of strawberry juice sold at outdoor cafés and kiosks sustain visitors until they work up an appetite for German sausage and *strudel* – always washed down with a beer. ❏

LEFT AND RIGHT: descendants of the original German immigrants still live in the same village in the Andes.

EL LITORAL

Map on pages 152–3

In December 1999, nature's fury left a path of devastation along Venezuela's central coast. With the most popular beaches destroyed by storms, more distant options have filled the gap

Caracas

For years, stressed out residents of Venezuela's cities flocked to the beaches of the central coast, popularly referred to as simply El Litoral (the littoral). With the verdant mountain chain of El Avila National Park as a backdrop and the Caribbean Sea gently lapping against the shoreline, this was an ideal nearby getaway. As a result, numerous resorts and vacation properties were developed, along with permanent housing in the seaside towns.

Disaster strikes

However, the same Mother Nature who lovingly created this appealing destination did an about-face in mid-December 1999, venting her rage on the coast. Torrential rains turned mountain streams into swollen rivers surging down ravines, picking up ancient trees, giant boulders, and tons of earth as they rushed to the sea. Workers' homes, luxury condominiums, and businesses were indiscriminantly leveled on the way. From the north, the shores were furiously pounded by high seas, which wreaked further havoc on this paradise destination.

The loss was tremendous. Due to the enormous number of unregistered residents inhabiting densely packed slums built in the most vulnerable areas, the exact death count will never be known. Estimates ran as high as 50,000, with possibly 300,000 people left homeless. The economic loss to the country was calculated at some US$10 billion, and thousands were left without work as businesses simply disappeared.

Aid poured in from sympathizers at home and abroad, while President Chávez promised to "turn tragedy into opportunity" and rebuild the affected zone. In addition, a plan was to be launched for population redistribution from the overcrowded coast by relocating refuges in sparsely inhabited areas in the country's interior.

The only visible sign of action was the clearing of the coastal highway (people literally digging with pick and shovel to salvage what they could) and the re-opening of international air and maritime ports. Frustrated members of the public began to wonder what had happened to all the money in the aid coffers.

It took several months for the redevelopment and restoration of the local infrastructure and commerce to begin and for the people of El Litoral to rebuild their lives. In Spring 2002, many beaches and hotels were still closed and understandably this stretch of coastline does not attract many international visitors.

It remains to be seen whether the government will successfully deal with flood control issues and at the same time provide suitable accommodations and re-establish El Litoral as the weekend playground of Caracas.

LEFT: Todasana beach.
BELOW: clearing the devastation.

History erased

One of the most heavily damaged areas was unfortunately also the most historic: **La Guaira ❶**. Founded in 1589, it was chosen as the site of the country's principal port due to its proximity to Caracas (20 km/12 miles), although now it is overshadowed by Puerto Cabello (in Carabobo State) which handles 77 percent of Venezuela's commercial traffic. Many buildings dated back to the 18th and 19th centuries. While the modern port suffered only minor problems, a good number of the adjacent vintage buildings were damaged beyond repair.

A notable survivor was the beautiful **Casa Guipuzcoana ❷**, erected in 1734 by the Basque Guipuzcoana Company. Because of its location, in the sector most far-removed from the river passing through La Guaira, the building was not hit by the full force of the slides. Mud reached a depth of several meters along the front, but its thick walls and doors resisted entry. Not so lucky were the former 19th-century headquarters of the Boulton Company, Catedral de La Guaira, and Ermita de Carmen, along with the colonial homes in the main streets parallel to the river, which provided a natural pathway for the avalanche of water and debris.

Even less fortunate were many highlights of El Litoral located in **Macuto ❸**. Its swimming beach, the Plaza de Palomas, the 19th-century presidential vacation residence (La Guzmania), the Museo Armando Reverón (former home of one of the country's most renowned impressionist painters), and nearly all of the popular waterfront restaurants and hotels were partially or totally destroyed.

The large *balneario* (bathing beach development) of **Camurí Chico**, a short distance east of Macuto, and nearly every other beach between La Guaira and Naiguatá were left covered by a thick blanket of debris and mud.

The most upscale sector of the coast, the resorts of **Caraballeda ❹** (inland) and **El Caribe ❺** (close to the beach), 20 km (12 miles) east of La Guaira, has started to come back to life, but tourism is restricted by the fact that its two luxury hotels, the **Macuto Sheraton Resort** and **Hotel Gran Carib**, are indefinitely closed for repairs, and the beach clubs of Playa Azul, Puerto Azul, and Tanaguarenes were badly affected. It will take years for the infrastructure of this part of the coastline to be totally rebuilt.

Refreshing jungle juice for sale on the beach.

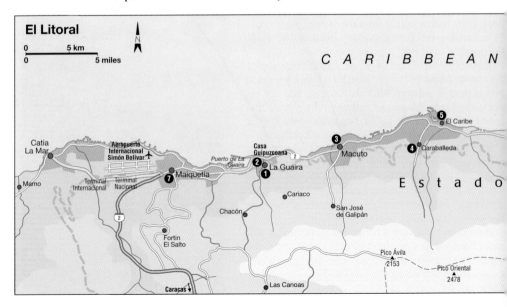

Map below

A changing coastline

Though the beaches in the 80-km (50-mile) stretch between La Guaira and **Los Caracas** ❻ all but disappeared, those along the 43 km (27 miles) from Los Caracas to Chuspa, if anything got better! In a lucky twist of fate, they were spared from the flooding from the mountains, the buildings were largely unaffected and beaches were left wider and prettier than ever.

The main problem here has always been access, which is still only by dirt road. Mud slides which closed many sections of the route were removed and in dry weather, normal city cars can use the tracks providing care is taken, although a four-wheel-drive vehicle is advisable for both comfort and peace of mind. Hopefully, the fact that the beaches of **Osma, Oritapo, Todasana, La Sabana, Caruao,** and **Chuspa** are now the prime recreational destinations of El Litoral will prompt authorities finally to pave this road.

If you are planning to return to the capital after this excursion, the easiest route to take (all paved) is via Higuerote–Caucagua–Guarenas–Caracas, a drive of about 90 minutes. You can also use this route to bypass the areas affected by the tragedy and work in visits to the beaches of Higuerote and Chirimena in Miranda state en route.

Western beaches

On reaching the coast from Caracas, taking the westbound road, you almost immediately pass the terminals of **Aeropuerto Simón Bolívar** in **Maiquetía** ❼, the principal airport serving Caracas and Venezuela. The beaches here were spared from significant harm, but have never been as popular as those in the east.

Facilities of the *balneario* installed years ago at **Catia La Mar** have been virtually abandoned, and the area is plagued by pollution and insecurity.

The main destinations of beach-goers heading in this direction are various private clubs and tourism developments, such as **Marina Grande**, **Oricao**, and **Shangri-la**, which have blocked off sections of beach, limiting access to members or those paying an entry fee for day use. In addition, access by road to these developments is not easy. Thus, for the vast majority, visiting beaches of El Litoral means following the coastal road eastbound from Maiquetía. ❏

La Sabana beach, along the eastbound unpaved coastal road, is accessible only to those with 4x4 vehicles.

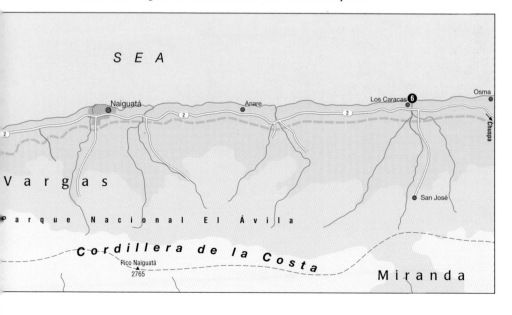

LOS ROQUES

Take warm, shallow waters and beautiful reefs, then add mangroves and the blue Caribbean Sea. The result: an idyllic setting in this conveniently located archipelago

Map on page 156

Caracas

A corner of paradise is how the majority of visitors describe the **Archipelago of Los Roques**, lying approximately 128 km (80 miles) north of Maiquetía. With some 40 islands and cays *(cayos)* large enough to bear names (and more than 300 others only emerging during low tide), pristine white sand beaches, and crystalline waters that converge subtly with the sky in one glorious azure sweep, Los Roques is rapidly becoming one of the country's most popular tourist destinations.

Although the steady flow of visitors has predictably had an effect on the archipelago as a haven for a small population of fishermen, Los Roques remains relatively tranquil and unspoiled. This is partly due to fairly restricted access to tourists, who can reach the islands only by small planes or private yachts and sailboats, and partly because Los Roques has been protected as a national park since 1972. The archipelago covers an area of more than 225,000 hectares (556,000 acres), making it one of the Caribbean's largest marine preserves.

Wildlife sanctuary

While the archipelago bakes under a blazing sun all day, at night it is caressed by cooling trade winds that keep annoying insects at bay. Most of the *cayos* are low, their pure white sands barely rising above the surface of the turquoise and emerald waters. A few have rocky outcroppings. Clumps of mangrove trees, cacti, and seagrass add splotches of green to an arid landscape that is home to iguanas and lizards. Marine turtles lumber ashore to lay their eggs.

Over the years, many names in the archipelago have changed due to fishermen writing phonetic spellings on their charts. North East Cay is now **Nordisquí ❶**, Sailors Cay is **Selesquí ❷**, Domus Cay became Dos Mosquises and is now **Cayo Estación Sur ❸**.

Seabirds are abundant, both nesting and migratory species, including frigate birds, boobies, terns, pelicans, and herons. The tiny western island, **Selesquí**, has the largest bird population, earning it the nickname "Cayo Bobo Negro" (Black Booby Cay). Flocks of gulls nest on **Francisquí ❹** (Cayo Francés).

Snorkelers and divers will be delighted by the shoals of rainbow-colored parrot fish, royal-blue angelfish, puffy porcupine fish, and slender trumpet fish. There are mollusks, sponges, sea urchins, and many colorful varieties of coral, including gorgonia, brain, and fire. Occasionally you will see a barracuda or moray eel.

The islands of Los Roques have been known to humans for centuries, but because they have no fresh water, it is only recently that they have supported a permanent settlement.

LEFT: despite a steady flow of visitors, the islands are still unspoiled. **BELOW:** pelican patrol.

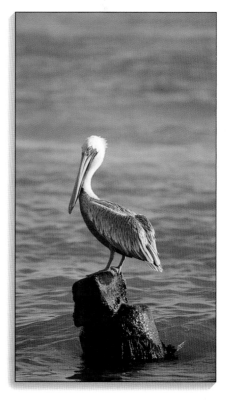

Long ago, the archipelago may have held some mystical significance. Prehispanic ceramics, possibly used in sacred or magical ceremonies, have been found on four of the islands. Cayo Estación Sur has yielded a number of squat human figurines, including a man with "donut" eyes and women with tiny arms and hands and large rectangular heads that have been pricked or incised. More recently, Los Roques has been a secret haven for Venezuelan sun-worshipers, who fly in by private plane for a day's amusement or sail their yachts over for a long weekend.

In the 1980s, when the Venezuelan currency crashed and the country imposed import restrictions, *contrabandistas* (contraband runners) found Los Roques to be a convenient stopping-off place. Restaurateurs in Caracas had a secret pipeline from the Caribbean for obtaining duty-free liquor, crystal, and fine china.

A prize catch: lobsters are usually spirited away to top restaurants on nearby Aruba, where they command a high price.

Foreign invasion

Today, Los Roques are being discovered by sailors and sport fishermen from abroad. The islands are reputed to offer some of the world's best bonefishing *(see Participant Sports, pages 105–109)*. Aeroejecutivos, Aereotuy, and Chapi Air are among the local companies now offering regular flights, usually sold as all-inclusive packages. But take note, even the "all-inclusive" packages do not usually include the 14.5 percent sales tax or the National Parks Institute entrance fee for Los Roques that everyone has to pay (the equivalent of about US$7 per person for residents and Venezuelans, US$15 for non-residents).

The only permanent settlement is on **Gran Roque ❺**, the biggest island. At 3 km (2 miles) long and scarcely more than 1 km (½-mile) wide, that is none too big. It has the only paved airstrip in Los Roques. All of the more than 60 *posadas*

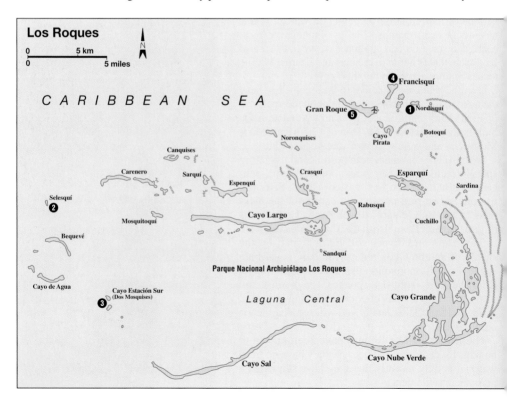

Los Roques

0 — 5 km
0 — 5 miles

N

CARIBBEAN SEA

❹ Francisquí

Gran Roque ❺

❶ Nordisquí

Noronquises

Cayo Pirata

Botoquí

Canquises

Carenero

Sarquí

Crasquí

Esparquí

Espenquí

Sardina

Selesquí ❷

Rabusquí

Mosquitoquí

Cayo Largo

Cuchillo

Bequevé

Sandquí

Cayo de Agua

Parque Nacional Archipiélago Los Roques

Cayo Estación Sur (Dos Mosquises) ❸

Laguna Central

Cayo Grande

Cayo Nube Verde

Cayo Sal

which have flourished to accommodate tourists are located here. Unfortunately, because of the new-found popularity, prices have soared, but, unless you plan to do extensive diving, fishing, or sun-worshiping, day tours are a viable and less costly alternative (averaging about US$120–150 per person). The economy of *roqueños* is based on fishing, with wooden boats beached on the sand and nearby hungry pelicans dive-bombing fish in the shallows. Everything except fish is imported from the mainland. There's a desalinization plant, but the navy sometimes has to supply fresh water.

Fishermen haul in *pargo* (red snapper), *mero* (grouper), lobster, and shellfish. For fish their main market is La Guaira, but most catches of lobster, crab, and queen conch have been spirited away to restaurants in Aruba, where they fetch a higher price. From time to time, moratoriums on the harvest of queen conch have been instituted to preserve their waning numbers. On Gran Roque, the favored dish is *sancocho de pescado* (fish soup). *Consomé de chipi-chipi* is also popular; the little clams that go into this pot are said to be an aphrodisiac. They're found mainly around the island of Crasqui.

Biological research

Researchers at the marine biological station run by the **Fundación Científica Los Roques** on **Cayo Estación Sur** have been trying to farm lobster and crab, which are being overfished. So far the lobster experiment has failed, but the crab project shows promise. The foundation also studies marine turtles and investigates other ecological issues, supported by grants from government and industry. Courses in marine ecology are open to small numbers of qualified students. The navy helped build the laboratory, and there's a dirt landing strip. ❑

Map on page 156

TIP

The beaches of Los Roques are shadeless. This, combined with the high degree of reflected sun from the water and white sand, make the wearing of sun block, a hat, and sunglasses imperative.

BELOW: Gran Roque Pueblo – the only permanent settlement on the archipelago.

EL ORIENTE

The entire northeastern sector of the country, referred to simply as "El Oriente," spells beach resorts to Venezuelans, but also offers historic sites and ecotourism

Map on pages 162–3

Caracas

For *caraqueños* given a weekend, or *puente* (long weekend, literally "bridge," or longer vacation period), it goes without saying that the destination for most sun worshipers is El Oriente – the east coast.

Tambores and cacao

Barlovento, meaning windward, applies to the eastern third of Miranda state, from Cabo Codera to Boca de Uchire. Fed by many rivers and receiving steady moisture-carrying trade winds, it is one of the few areas along Venezuela's coast to be lush and green all year long.

When the Spaniards first came to Venezuela they imported cacao plants and large numbers of African slaves to work the huge *haciendas* (farm estates). The crop would become a principal source of the country's wealth for nearly three centuries. But, during the long War of Independence fought in the early part of the 1800s, plantations were abandoned as men took to the battlefield. After the war, with the abolition of slavery, working the huge plantations was impossible. The *gran cacaos* ("big cacaos"), as the rich plantation owners were called, disappeared. But the former slaves remained and, in their isolated setting, maintained the purity of their African race, conserved their cultural traditions, and continued to tend the cacao.

Along with cacao trees, one of the most distinctive plants seen growing among the lush tropical foliage along this route, between **Caucagua** and **El Guapo**, is the heliconia, a member of the bird-of-paradise plant family with beautiful, brilliant red flowers edged in pale green. These flowers (cut), as well as rooted orchids and bromeliads, are sold along the roadside.

Not much has changed since slavery was abolished. The population is largely black. Cacao trees with their pink, orange, and deep red pods growing directly out of the trunks flourish in the luxuriant environment. All along the pavement and on concrete patios, nuts from the cacao pods are spread out in the sun to dry.

The African-style drums of Barlovento – called *tambores*, and made from hollow logs – and the sensual dance performed to their beat, are well known, particularly for their role in the Fiesta of San Juan Bautista; St John the Baptist is especially revered by people with African roots, and his festival (June 23–24) is a great occasion.

Curiepe ❶ is famous for its all-out celebration in honor of San Juan Bautista, which attracts a great numbers of visitors. The saint's effigy is baptized in the river. Then, to the sound of the drums, and with celebrants downing copious amounts of rum and *aguardiente*, everyone dances to the *tambores* throughout the night.

PRECEDING PAGES: Playa Colorada, between Puerto La Cruz and Cumaná. **LEFT:** a leap in the deep. **BELOW:** jewelry on sale at Puerto La Cruz.

Not far away from Curiepe is the tiny mountain village of **Birongo ❷**, considered the "magic capital of Venezuela" and renowned for having the most powerful *brujos* (witches) in the country. They can cast and remove spells, make predictions, and perform other "works" for those who come to ask for their help – and a surprising number do come, from every social and economic group, and from far and wide.

Parque Nacional Laguna de Tacarigua is a breeding ground for crocodiles.

Barlovento's beaches

The main towns in Barlovento are **Higuerote ❸** and **Río Chico ❹**, both about 90 minutes by road from Caracas. The towns themselves have virtually nothing to offer in the way of "attractions," but no matter. What people come for are the beaches. Those in Higuerote are characterized by murky water, owing to sediment from a nearby river, which *guacucos* (small clams) obviously adore, because they are plentiful. Gathering *guacucos* to cook up in a rich broth on the beach is a ritual among visitors to these shores.

If you are more interested in crystal-clear water than you are in clam-gathering, then you should make your way farther north to the beaches of **Buche Island** (to which there is shuttle boat service), **Puerto Francés**, or **Chirimena**; the latter is favored by surfers because of its powerful waves.

The best beaches at Río Chico border Los Canales (natural canals connecting with the sea, and a key place for the development of vacation property), such as Playa Cocada. To the east is the town of **Tacarigua de la Laguna ❺**, entry point to **Parque Nacional Laguna de Tacarigua**. This national park has a 30-km (18-mile) long lagoon bordered by mangroves. It is rich in birds and fish (attracting sport fishermen for tarpon and snook), and is a breeding ground for

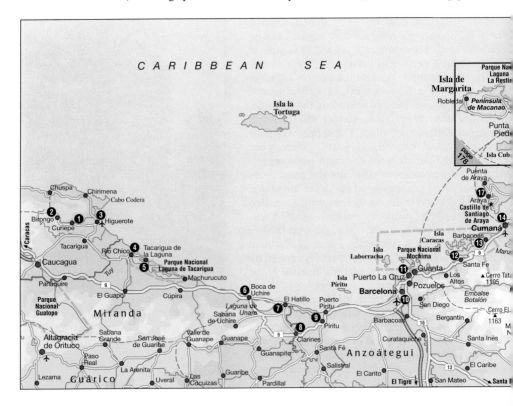

crocodiles. It also has 30 km (18 miles) of pristine sandy, palm-lined Caribbean beach on the outer banks. In the channel between the sea and the lagoon, fishermen toss out their circular nets. Close by, roseate spoonbills, scarlet ibis, and herons feed.

Thousands of these colorful birds put on a show every day at dusk as they come home to roost, completely covering one of the large clusters of mangroves inside the lagoon. Arrangements can be made with fishermen at the mouth of Laguna de Tacarigua, by the park ranger's station, to watch the return of these huge flocks of birds to a single spot in the late afternoon. Unfortunately, because of the descending darkness, it is almost impossible to photograph this "show."

Since the area's designation as a national park in 1974, no building has been allowed within its borders. However, **Club Miami** at the west end and the **Club Managua Caribe** at the east end, which were both there before park status was declared, were allowed to remain. Staying at either of them is by reservation only, since both operate on the basis of all-inclusive packages. Club Miami is accessible only by boat (this service is included in the package), while the Managua Caribe can be reached by land. Both are in excellent locations, but have suffered from a certain amount of deterioration.

One of many coastal shrines decorated with shells.

No vehicular traffic at all is allowed on the beach since it is an egg-laying area for marine turtles. Boatmen in Tacarigua can be hired to take visitors to the beach or the lagoon.

Boca de Uchire ❻, at the western extreme of **Laguna de Unare**, is littoraly lovely. Driving east along the outer bank, after passing a string of rustic beach houses, there are wide bands of secluded coves. The highway now runs all the

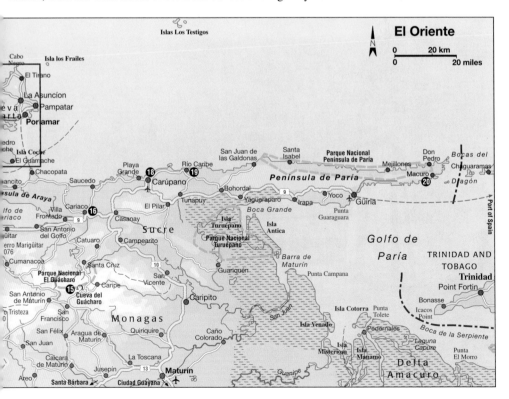

way between Boca de Uchire and **El Hatillo** ❼, making it possible to explore the beaches, little fishing villages, and lodges which stretch along the full length of the sandbar; however, the condition of the highway is deplorable.

Colonial temples

It is worth a quick detour to **Clarines** ❽ to see its 18th-century church and the surrounding streets, where the town's colonial heritage is eminently visible.

Píritu ❾ and its seaside neighbor, **Puerto Píritu**, lie 16 km (10 miles) farther east. The focal point of Píritu is its church, in a commanding hilltop location. Dating from the mid-1700s, the exterior is plain and fortress-like, but inside, it harbors ornate colonial altarpieces. The focus of the port town is the beach, one of the prettiest in El Oriente, bordered by seafood restaurants. From a dock at the west end, boatmen will take you on the 40-minute ride to **Las Isletas**, two small islands with sandy beaches.

All along the highway by Píritu, there are roadside stands where artisans sell local crafts: hand-carved wooden platters and rustic, bent-wood furniture.

Petroleum port and tourist mecca

The main destinations in El Oriente are Barcelona and Puerto La Cruz in Anzoátegui, which are about 4½ hours' driving from Caracas under normal conditions. The state is a major source of petroleum; after Zulia, it is the largest producer of oil in the country, and has three huge refineries, two of them in Puerto La Cruz; the giant Jose Complejo Criogénico de Oriente, with an important orimulsion fossil fuel energy project, is just west of Barcelona. These areas are also major magnets for tourists.

One of the main harvests from the Laguna de Unare is shrimp, available simply prepared in the modest restaurants at the eastern extreme of the outer banks, or in the multitude of dining spots along the old highway by the south shore.

BELOW: colonial mannequins in the Museo de Anzoátegui.

Barcelona is the capital of the state, and the site of the airport. As well as having a handsome colonial zone, it is the location of the mega tourism project, Complejo Turístico El Morro. The two areas of historic interest in the capital center on the three main plazas: Bolívar, Miranda, and Boyacá. The first two, on Avenida 5 de Julio, are adjacent, and facing them is **Casa Fuerte**, the ruins of the Convent of San Francisco – outfitted with cannons and used by Republican troops during the War of Independence as a fort to defend Barcelona. In a fierce battle on April 7, 1817, Casa Fuerte was destroyed by Royalists, who massacred everyone there. It has been preserved as it was, a memorial to the event.

Plaza Boyacá, the original square of Barcelona when it was founded in 1671, is surrounded by colonial buildings, many dating from the 1600s. The **cathedral** was built between 1748 and 1773, but work was set back in 1766 by a major earthquake that destroyed part of the building. This is a surprisingly picturesque zone, and a strong contrast with the newer – and frankly unattractive – downtown area that you have to pass through to reach it. The **Museo de Anzoátegui** (Mon–Fri 8am–noon, 2–5pm; Sat & Sun 9am–3pm; free), in the oldest existing house in the city, built in 1671 and handsomely restored, now serves as Barcelona's historical museum.

El Morro tourist project

Between Barcelona and Puerto La Cruz, a turn-off leads to the huge **El Morro** tourism complex and beaches. One of the first places you see when you make this turn is the **Centro Comercial Plaza Mayor**, striking for its design based on the colorful architecture typical of the historic waterfront area of Willemstad, capital of the former Dutch Caribbean colony of Curaçao.

Map on pages 162–3

BELOW: fishermen set out.

Avenida Principal of Lecherías is another commercial zone where the entire avenue is lined with small shopping centers and many restaurants.

The El Morro project was initiated in 1971 to accommodate 60,000 tourists in single-family homes, condominiums, and hotels. It is constructed on a maze of canals that provide boat access to the sea from every building. Among the most ambitious projects in the complex is the **Golden Rainbow Maremares Resort and Spa** (a huge luxury compound with various lagoon-sized pools, a golf course, and so on). Even if you do not stay in one of the resort's top-class hotels, it is worth a detour to admire its planning and architecture along with the world-class marina.

Continuing past the tourist complex, the main coastal beach area of Puerto La Cruz and Barcelona – consisting of Playa Cangrejo, Playa de Lecherías, and Playa Mansa – is on the isthmus to El Morro. Outdoor restaurants do a brisk trade, serving meals to hungry sun worshipers.

Paseo Colón: action around the clock

Although **Puerto La Cruz** ⓫ came into being in the late 17th century, you will find no trace of the old town. Shiny new and geared toward tourism, the focal point is **Paseo Colón**, a waterfront boulevard jammed with hotels, restaurants, bars, nightclubs, and stores on the south side; and a beach bordered by a wide pedestrian walkway lined with seafood restaurants, outdoor cafés, and local artisans selling their wares on the other.

Even though the long, palm-lined beach bordering Paseo Colón looks appealing and offers great opportunities for shelling (murex, long-tailed spindles, cone shells, turret, and augers are so plentiful they are practically regarded

BELOW: Caribbean sunset.

as "garbage" shells), the water is too polluted for safe swimming. But don't be disheartened: lying off shore are the island beaches of **Parque Nacional Mochima**. Explosub, operating out of the Maremares resort, is one of the companies that offer a variety of packages on yachts with visits to several islands.

The "anchors" on Paseo Colón are the **Hotel Hesperia Puerto La Cruz** (still the only luxury hotel on this strip and the only hotel right on the beach), the **Hotel Rasil Puerto La Cruz**, and the ferry terminal (for trips to Margarita) on the west end. With only 12 blocks between these two hotels, and the great concentration of dining, drinking, sleeping, and shopping places, it is hardly surprising that the boulevard is busy with visitors and residents day and night. Directions for finding recommended spots are not really necessary, and neither are maps, because everything you want can be found right here.

Island fun: shelling and diving

From Puerto La Cruz, the best option for transfers to the beaches of **Parque Nacional Mochima** is with the well-organized and reliable boatmen's union, Transtupaco, located at the east end of Paseo Colón. It runs shuttle services to **Playa El Faro** on Isla Chimana del Sur, and to **Playas Puinare** (good diving) and **El Saco** (good shelling) on Chimana Grande; there are departures all morning to Chimana Grande, with return trips from 4–5pm, as well as special boats for deep-sea fishing and diving trips. Just east of town, at Pamatacualito, shuttle boats go to **Isla de Plata** and **Isla de Monos**, also good for diving.

From **Playa Arapito**, *peñeros* (the traditional wooden fishing boats) are available to take you to La Piscina and Isla Arapo, a popular diving site. From **Mochima** (about 45 km/30 miles east of Puerto La Cruz), shuttle boats go to

Map on pages 162–3

TIP

Some of the best *empanadas* (cornmeal turnovers) you will find in Venezuela are made fresh and sold at a string of stands at the west end of the ferry terminal at Puerto La Cruz. With the local style of thin dough, they are light, crispy, and not at all greasy.

BELOW: luxury boats at Puerto La Cruz.

Playas Careñero, Tacuarumo, and Coral (all of which are good for beach-combing for shells); to Playas La Cruz, La Playuela, and Las Cuicas (all on the Península de Manaure); and to Playas Blanca, Cautaro, and Cautarito, where access is only by sea.

"Route of the Sun"

Playa Arapito: a long white sweep of sand, edged with palms, with mountains forming the backdrop.

Beyond its insular part, the Mochima national park also includes a continental stretch between Puerto La Cruz and Cumaná, aptly referred to as the "**Route of the Sun**", one of the most scenic coastal highways in the country. The steep, winding route is cut into the sides and along the base of steep mountains that plunge dramatically to the shoreline. Rounding each curve, you are presented with yet another beautiful vista of rugged coast with pounding waves, or coves harboring beaches rimmed with palm trees. The arid, rocky hills that are covered largely with cactus form a stark contrast to the lush seaside valleys snuggled between them.

Although there are appealing beaches along the full length of the route, two of the most famous – and most photographed – are **Playa Arapito** and **Playa Colorada**; the latter is on a small protected crescent bay known for its reddish-colored sand (hence the name).

Making a detour from the highway into **Santa Fe** ⓬ is well worth the effort. It has one of the most spotless beaches in Venezuela (the residents clean it daily), and it has benefitted from a successful grass-roots effort to establish a network of family-style tourist lodging, all right on the beach. For dining, stop at the handsome open-sided, waterfront restaurant, **Club Nautico "Santa Fe,"** where jumbo shrimp are a specialty.

BELOW: Spanish ramparts at San Antonio de la Eminencia fortress, Cumaná.

As you approach the turn-off for the fishing village of **Mochima**, the road climbs Cerro Aceite Castillo and you get a spectacular view of the islands of Mochima National Park. Take the clearly marked side road down into the village for access to the docks, where boatmen will pounce on you to offer transfers to the islands. More than a dozen modest *posadas* are located in Mochima.

There are numerous places all along this route where local *artesanía* (handicrafts) can be purchased directly from the creators at stands set up by the roadside. Near **Barbacoas** ⑬, you can buy traditional black-faced rag dolls, beautiful delicate bird cages made with thin reeds, and hand-carved replica sailboats. If you are interested in boat building, watch for craftsmen at work using age-old techniques.

Cumaná: South America's oldest city

The first view on approaching **Cumaná** ⑭ via Avenida Universidad is the long public beach, Balneario Los Uveros, with a number of small, basic beachside hotels and several upscale offers at its west end. Near the eastern end of the avenue, opposite the Sucre campus of Universidad de Oriente, is the **Museo del Mar** (daily 8.30–11.30am, 2.30–5.30pm; token entry fee), although the museum is threatened with closure. Displays range from typical boats to old-time diving equipment, shells, and a preserved example of a coelacanth, the "fossil fish," which was long believed extinct; it has a modest-size aquarium.

Cumaná, nicknamed "First-born of the Continent," was the first Spanish settlement on the continent of South America. It endured a turbulent first century of existence and was established by Franciscan friars in 1515. After destruction through indigenous attacks, Cumaná was re-established by Gonzalo de Ocampo

Map on pages 162–3

BELOW: handmade dolls at Barbacoas.

in 1521. However, faced with continual assaults by Cumanagoto Indians, the fledgling city would fall several times until, in 1569, Diego Fernández de Serpa established the city that survives today. Fortifications have been of primary importance in the history of Cumaná. First they protected against attacking Caribe and Cumanagoto Indians, and subsequently against assaults by English, Dutch, and French pirates and slave traders.

The most visible landmark is the imposing **Castillo de San Antonio de la Eminencia**, majestically overlooking the city and coastal waters from Cumaná's highest point (daily 9am–noon, 3–5pm; free). The first fort on this site was erected in 1660. An earthquake in 1684 destroyed it and most of Cumaná, but by 1686 a new fort had been built. In 1853, another earthquake left the fort in ruins. Dictator General Cipriano Castro had it rebuilt in the early 1900s, but once again nature prevailed and, in 1929, yet another earthquake, this time joined by a tidal wave, left the fort (and many other buildings) in ruins. It has since been restored and is now open to the public. Beside it is the attractive new **Museo de Arte Contemporáneo**.

Down the hill is the **Castillo de Santa María de la Cabeza**, a fortress constructed between 1669–73 to give residents a closer refuge than La Eminencia when pirates attacked. Entrance is through the **Iglesia de Santa Inés**. First constructed in 1637, this church, like most of Cumaná, was destroyed and rebuilt five times between 1637 and 1929. Several blocks south is the former **Convento de San Francisco**, location of the first school on the continent. It is due to human neglect rather than the forces of nature, however, that this historic landmark now stands abandoned. In the streets surrounding the nearby **Plaza Bolívar** are the state's tourism office (Mon–Fri 8am–noon, 2–4pm) and the

BELOW: Iglesia de Santa Inés, erected in 1929 in the colonial zone of Cumaná.

Casa Andrés Eloy Blanco (Mon–Fri 8.30am–noon, 2.30–6pm, Sat 9am–noon; free), birthplace of the revered, early 20th-century Venezuelan poet, and now a museum. Also of interest is the **Ateneo de Cumaná** (Mon–Fri 8am–noon, 2–5pm; free), where art and musical presentations take place.

In the center of town, an inviting park borders the Manzanares River and is the site of the **Museo Gran Marisical de Ayacucho** (Tues–Fri 8.45–11.30am, 3.34–6.30pm; free), with a mix of historical exhibits and artifacts.

To get a better feel for the people and soul of the city, visit the **market** by the fishing port on Avenida Los Manglares. From 5am to noon, the place hums with activity as shoppers come to buy fresh produce and handicrafts such as Cumaná's famous *cuatros*, the four-stringed instrument most closely associated with Venezuelan folk music, and, of course, to stop at the rows of tables where cheerful women prepare fried fish, *arepas*, and other tasty delights.

From the nearby marine terminal, you can catch ferries to Isla Margarita and to the Araya Peninsula, just across the Gulf of Cariaco (which provides most of the sardines consumed in Venezuela).

Venezuela's largest cave

Many visitors to Cumaná fit in a side trip to the **Cueva del Guácharo** ⓲ (tours 8am–3pm; admission fee); it lies about 90 minutes to the south in Monagas state near **Caripe**. The cavern is home to the nocturnal, fruit-eating *guácharo*, or oil bird, and is renowned for being Venezuela's largest and best cave, with an extension of more than 10 km (6 miles). Information about the cave first emerged on a widespread basis in the writings of German naturalist Alexander von Humboldt *(see page 173)* after his visit there in 1799. You can enter the cave only on guided tours with park guards. Nothing may be taken in – no flashlights, cameras, or purses. Guides lead you using only a kerosene lamp. You will not be able to see the birds, only hear them. Incidentally, the town of Caripe has many excellent *posadas* and cabins, and places to stay on working farms.

From hot springs to a colonial fort

Continuing eastward, distinct among the usual *balnearios* are swimming areas with hot springs. These include the **Núcleo Integral Turístico Recreacional Cachamaure**, along the coastal highway near San Antonio del Golfo, the **Balneario Los Cocoteros** and **Poza Cristal**. The last two are reached via Cariaco-Casanay (about 8 km/5 miles from the turn).

Cariaco ⓰, the second oldest town on the continent, is the point of departure for the highway along the Península de Araya. The route, with startlingly beautiful desert landscapes, solitary beaches, and excellent shelling, leads to **Araya** ⓱, at the western tip of the peninsula (where the Cumaná–Isla Margarita ferry also stops). After passing the eerie-looking salt-evaporation lagoons with brilliant lilac-colored water bordered by a ring of glistening salt crystals, you will find a gorgeous expanse of beach (with outstanding windsurfing off shore), the giant Ensal plant (the source of most of the country's salt), and the imposing ruins of the **Castillo de Santiago de Araya**.

Map on pages 162–3

The mouth of Cueva del Guácharo: the path inside is often muddy because of an internal stream, so wear old shoes.

BELOW: statue in Plaza del Indio, Cumaná.

Map
on pages
162–3

The fort, begun in 1618, was the most important and costliest construction of the colonial era. There were tremendous difficulties in building it, due to the lack of drinking water or land suitable for growing crops, meaning all supplies had to be shipped from the mainland. In addition, the salt ate through the workers' shoes, and the sun was so brutal that work could be done only at night.

A hurricane in 1726 turned the salt lake into a gulf, ruining the beds. With the tremendously expensive upkeep, especially when the salt was no longer a factor, the Spanish abandoned the fort in 1762, after blowing it up so it wouldn't fall into enemy hands. The haunting ruins beg to be explored and photographed.

The far east

Carúpano ⑱ has little to draw tourists – except during **Carnaval** when visitors flock to the town for its lively celebration *(see Fiestas, pages 79–83)* – but it is important as a commercial center for agriculture and fishing; its port houses large tuna fleets, which supply several onshore canneries. Over 70 percent of the country's cacao crop is exported from here to Europe and Japan. Continuing eastward along the coast, the waters are filled with fishing fleet launches, there are boatyards, and gutted fish hangs out to dry in the sun along the roadsides.

Although principally a fishing village, **Río Caribe** ⑲ has a pretty beach, various pleasant lodgings, and attractive tree-shaded streets lined with old houses. This is also the exit point for **Playa Medina**, one of the most beautiful beaches in Venezuela. En route, you pass through the village of **San Francisco de Chacaracual**, with houses and fences painted every color of the rainbow.

Densely forested mountains form the lush green backdrop for the spectacular Playa Medina. Lined with a thick grove of palm trees nearly to the water's

BELOW: view of Playa Medina, reputedly one of the most beautiful beaches in Venezuela.

edge (providing welcome shade), it has an outstanding tourism infrastructure. There is an immaculate beach, controlled parking, and inviting food stands; the latter are operated on a concession basis under strict controls, despite their quaint appearance in open-sided thatch-roofed huts *(bohios)*. Fried fish, *arepas*, and *orejones* (sweet, deep-fried pastries) are all prepared fresh as you wait. There is also a group of cottages, built with earthen walls painted in rich earth tones, offered for tourists in packages with lodging, meals, open bar, excursions, beach services, and transfer to and from Carúpano airport. Contact Corpomedina in Carúpano, tel: 094-31 1341/31 1361/31 5241/ 31 3917 for details of these and other attractive lodgings in the area. You can also continue from here to other pristine beaches farther east, including **Playa Puipuy** and **San Juan de los Galdonas**, some 80 km (50 miles) from Carúpano.

Although the route along the Península de Paria to Güiria doesn't offer any specific "tourist attractions," it is a pretty drive, with the verdant mountains of the **Parque Nacional Península de Paria** to the north and glimpses of the Gulf of Paria to the south.

Of great historical importance to Venezuela but not worth the effort of getting there, is **Macuro** ⑳, near the tip of the peninsula. The village is famous as it is believed to be the sole place where Christopher Columbus set foot on the mainland of South America. ❑

Von Humboldt

Simón Bolívar described Von Humboldt as "the true discoverer of America because his work has produced more benefit to our people than that of all the conquistadores." Praise indeed from the Liberator of the Americas. But how did this wealthy Prussian minerologist come to play such a vital role in the history of the continent?

Von Humboldt was born in Berlin in 1769. As a young man he studied botany, chemistry, astronomy, and mineralogy and at the age of 27, he received a legacy large enough to finance a scientific expedition. With his companion Aimé Bonpland, Humboldt set off for Venezuela. They were the first non-Spanish scientists to be permitted to visit South America since Charles de la Condamine in 1735.

After passing through the valleys of Caracas and Lake Valencia, he proceeded through the *llanos* to Amazonas in 1800. His goal there was to prove that the Brazo Casiquiare was the natural canal which united the hydrographic basins of the Amazon and Orinoco rivers. The route from the present-day Puerto Ayacucho followed the Orinoco, Atabapo, Guiania, and Negro rivers as far as the junction with Brazil and Colombia; returning via San Carlos de Río Negro, Brazo Casiquiare; then to Tamatama and La Esmeralda. From there, he headed east via the Orinoco to its delta, then north toward Cumaná.

En route, Humboldt explored Venezuela's largest cave, which would later bear his name: "Monumento Natural Alejandro de Humboldt" (more popularly known as "Cueva del Guácharo" after the colony of *guácharo* – oil birds – that inhabit one of the chambers). He was the first to classify the *guácharo*, indicating this word in old Castillian means one who sobs or laments continually. Although known by early Spanish explorers, and indigenous residents long before, it wasn't until Humboldt's writings were published in Paris in 1814 that the cave became widely known.

RIGHT: the young Humboldt. At 27 he received a legacy enabling him to finance his research.

More than just an adventurer, Humboldt was an astute observer. His detailed accounts painted a vivid picture of the countryside, and of the lives of indigenous peoples encountered in the Amazonas region.

Humboldt's achivements seem endless. His *Essays on the Geography of Plants* were pioneering studies of the relationship between a region's geography and its flora and fauna. He claimed another first by listing many of the indigenous species: vanilla, avocado, yucca, maize, and manioc, among others.

Off the west coast of the continent, he studied the oceanic current, which was subsequently named after him; his work on isotherms and isobars laid the foundation for the science of climatology.

Humboldt's admirers were many: Goethe, a close friend, referred to him as a man who "overwhelms one with intellectual treasure," and Charles Darwin, who was inspired by Humboldt's *Relation Historique* and by his earlier journey to Tenerife in the Canary Islands, called him "the parent of a grand progeny of scientific travelers." ❑

ISLA MARGARITA

*North of the Venezuelan mainland, this sun-kissed island,
where pearls the size of eggs were once found, is now a beach
resort drawing tourists from all over the world*

Map on page 178

Caracas

Venezuelans – inveterate shoppers – have long flocked to Isla Margarita on weekends and vacations because its duty-free status makes it an inexpensive spot to buy imported cheeses, perfumes, liquors, electronic goods, and clothing. Foreigners may dish out bolívars for beautiful hammocks, baskets, and pottery but their main bargain is the beach – miles and miles of it. Since the mid-1980s, it has become the Caribbean's budget destination for Europeans and North Americans who want to enjoy sun and surf without seriously denting their wallets. But Margarita and its sister islands offer a great many other delights besides sun, sand, and shopping.

Pearl jam

Margarita, as well as the tinier islands of Coche and Cubagua off its coast, had strong ties with the fierce Caribe native peoples and the peaceful Arawaks and Guaiquerís before the Spanish conquest. The Caribes were relentless warriors who gave their name to the hurricane-besieged Caribbean. Despite their conquering ways, the Caribes too fell victim to an even more ruthless foe: the Europeans. Reports of the pearls worn by the Paria Peninsula natives immediately aroused interest. Less than a year after his provocative find, Cristóbal de la Guerra and Pedro Alfonso Niño discovered the source: the pearl beds off the island of Cubagua. The "Pearl Rush" was on as word spread. Before the end of 1500, some 50 fortune hunters had arrived, and it wasn't long before pirates began raiding the island – prompting the construction of forts that still stand today. Because of the great decline of the beds, pearl fishing was banned in 1962 and is now permitted only in season (Jan–Apr) every other year.

In 1529, Coche produced 373 kg (820 lbs) of pearls a month. They were to influence European fashion and, in 1589, Caracas town council authorized their use as money, a practice which continued into the 1700s.

First stop: Porlamar

Visitors reach the island by ferries departing from Puerto La Cruz and Cumaná to the town of **Punta de Piedras**, or they fly into the Gen. Santiago Mariño Airport. Either way, one of the first landmarks spotted are the two rounded mountain peaks officially named the Tetas de María Guevara (María Guevara's breasts). Some say María Guevara was a 19th-century independence movement heroine, others that she was a local madame well known to sailors who docked here. The first destination for most visitors is usually **Porlamar ❶**. Founded on March 25, 1536, this once-quiet fishing town is now a dynamic city with some 200,000 residents, wide boulevards, fine restaurants

PRECEDING PAGES: fishing boats at Puerto Fermín. **LEFT:** Playa La Galera, near Juan Griego. **BELOW:** colonial clock tower in La Asunción.

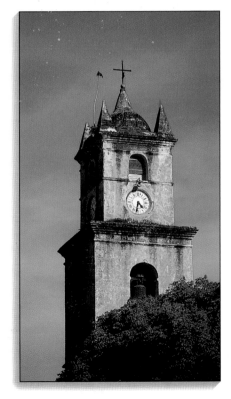

and hotels, and an active nightlife. The city's original name was Puerto de la Mar, but, in true Venezuelan style, the words were run together and shortened.

Porlamar lives on tourism and commerce, and streets such as Avenida Santiago Mariño and Avenida 4 de Mayo, are filled with stores that sell everything from French perfume to locally produced T-shirts – along with a great concentration of restaurants, bars, and downtown hotels.

A pleasant departure from the relentlessly commercial nature of downtown Porlamar is the **Museo de Arte Contemporáneo Francisco Narváez** (open daily; free) on Calle Díaz. Named for the Margarita-born sculptor, its main exhibit hall contains a permanent collection of his works, while additional rooms have rotating shows by other Venezuelan artists. Elsewhere on the island Francisco Narváez's creations can be seen next to the cathedral in La Asunción and around the fountain at the **Hotel Bella Vista**.

Colonial treasures

Northeast of Porlamar is the town of **Pampatar** ❷, where the **Castillo de San Carlos Borromeo** (Mon–Sat, 8am–noon, 3–5pm; free) was the island's most important pirate defense. The present fort, constructed in 1664–84, was built on the site of the original one, which was destroyed in 1662 when the city was burned by the Dutch. During the War of Independence, Spanish soldiers fleeing the fort tried to blow it up, but revolutionary troops discovered the 635 kg (1,400 lbs) of explosive powder hidden in the complex. The fort has been restored and is open to the public.

Facing the fort is the **Iglesia del Santísimo Cristo del Buen Viaje** (Church of the Most Holy Christ of the Good Voyage). The external stairway to the bell

TIP

It is prohibited to take more than one case per person of any one type of liquor out of the island. Custom officers will confiscate any excess. The stores are still duty-free but no longer tax exempt: an 8 percent sales tax is added to every purchase, but this is still less than the mainland where there is 14.5 percent sales tax.

Isla de Margarita

0   5 km
0   5 miles

N

CARIBBEAN SEA

Cabo Negro
Manzanillo
Playa El Humo
Playa Manzanillo
Playa El Agua
Playa Puerto Cruz
El Agua
Playa Caribe
Playa Parguito
Pedro González
El Tirano
Playa La Galera
Playa El Tirano
Playa Juangriego
Juangriego
Paraguachi
Playa El Cardón
Punta de Tigre
Santa Ana
Playa La Carmela
Playa El Tunal
Playa La Auyama
El Maguey
Punta Maria Libre
El Cercado
Tacarigua
La Fuente
Punta de la Pared
El Tunal
El Saco
Ensenada La Guardia
La Asunción
Playa Guacuco
Robledal
San Francisco
Playa La Restinga
Parque Nacional Cerro El Copey
Pampatar
Boca del Pozo
Península de Macanao
Playa La Guardia
San Juan Bautista
Los Robles
Punta Arenas
Punta Arenas
Mangillo
Boca del Río
La Guardia
El Valle del Espíritu Santo
Porlamar
Playa Punta Arenas
Barrancas
Parque Nacional Laguna La Restinga
Villa Rosa
El Morro
Bahía de Mangle
Nueva Esparta
Los Bagres
Isla de Margarita
Aeroporto Internacional General Santiago Mariño
Laguna de las Maritas
Punta de Piedras
El Yaque
La Isleta
Playa El Yaque
Punta Mosquito
Los Agodones
Punta Mangle
Nueva Cádiz
Isla Cubagua
Isla Coche
El Bichar
San Pedro de Coche
Güinima
El Guamache
Puerto La Cruz
Cumaná
Chacopata

Map
on page
178

ower is a distinctive feature seen in most of Margarita's churches, but in only one or two in the rest of Venezuela. Sailors claim that the crucifix over the altar was brought on a passing ship that found itself unable to lift anchor until this religious article was left behind. At **Playa Pampatar**, the local beach, visitors can watch the grizzled fishermen take out their boats. These same fishermen can point out the way to **Cueva El Bufón**, an underwater cave that is popular with divers. Locals say this is where pirates hid their loot.

Near the church is the former Casa de la Aduana (Pampatar's customs house), which now serves as the headquarters for FONDENE (Fund for the Development of Nueva Esparta State). Constructed in 1863, it has been restored and houses a permanent exhibition of art (Mon–Fri). Overlooking Playa Pampatar is another 17th-century defense, **Fortín Santiago de La Caranta**.

Between Porlamar and Pampatar is **Los Robles ❸** (also known as El Pilar). Inside the town's colonial church is the solid gold statue of the Virgin of Pilar, sent to the colony in 1504 by Spanish queen Juana La Loca, Isabella's daughter. The state's tourism office (Mon–Fri 8.30am–12.30pm, 2–5pm; tel: 09 562 3222/3638; email: corpotur@enlared.net) is inside the Centro Artesanal Gilberto Menchini, Calle Jóvito Villalba, as you enter Los Robles.

Warding off pirates: the Castillo de San Carlos Borromeo, Pampatar.

Vintage capital

Since its foundation in 1565, **La Asunción ❹** has been Isla Margarita's strategic center. It was placed just far enough inland to make it both more inaccessible to pirates and more difficult for the rebellious Caribe Indians to attack. Today, it is the political seat of Nueva Esparta state, consisting of the islands of Margarita, Coche, and Cubagua.

BELOW: colonial defenses at Pampatar fortress.

Little more than a century after Captain Pedro González Cervantes de Albornoz founded La Asunción, the **Castillo de Santa Rosa** (Mon–Sat 8am–noon, 3–5pm; donation) was built to guard the town. The scene of important battles, it was here that the pregnant 16-year-old wife of Juan Bautista Arismendi, a well-known hero of the War of Independence, was held hostage. A plaque marks the cell where she gave birth to a daughter who died in the fortress. Luisa Cáceres de Arismendi survived and was later reunited with her husband.

In front of La Asunción's Plaza Bolívar is the **Catedral de Nuestra Señora de la Asunción**, the oldest church in Venezuela. Construction began in 1571 but it wasn't until 46 years later that it was completed. Diagonally across from the church is the **Museo y Biblioteca Nueva Cádiz** (Tues–Sun; free), the seat of government in colonial times, now housing exhibits ranging from pre-Columbian artifacts to model ships.

On the main road northwest of La Asunción lies **Santa Ana ⑤**. The simple church on the main plaza is where, on May 6, 1816, Simón Bolívar signed the decree abandoning the war and proclaimed the formation of the Third Republic. The so-called Assembly of Notables met at the church and formally recognized Bolívar as Supreme Chief of Venezuela and its armies.

The bell tower of La Asunción's cathedral is the only one still standing in Venezuela that was built in the 16th century.

Sunsets, skiffs, and seafood

If a piña colada at a seaside café at sunset sounds appealing, then **Juan Griego ⑥** should not be missed. On the north coast, on one of the island's prettiest bays, with clean waters, brightly colored fishing skiffs, and explosive sunsets, this fishing village also has various restaurants along the waterfront, predictably specializing in seafood. Perhaps the best place for sunset viewing is from the

BELOW: Margarita Hilton on Playa Moreno, between Porlamar and Pampatar.

hilltop landmark, **Fortín de La Galera**. Spanish general Pablo Morillo slaughtered the patriot forces here when he retook Juan Griego from the independence army in 1817. Behind the fort is the **Laguna de Los Mártires** (Martyrs' Lagoon) where the waters are said to have turned red with the blood of 200 political prisoners executed by Morillo.

At the **cemetery** is the headstone of James Towers English, an Irish Legion commander who died far from his homeland while helping Venezuelan independence forces in 1819. English was contracted by Bolívar to organize an expeditionary force to fight in the war against Spain. During a battle in Margarita, the young officer died of a cerebral hemorrhage but his troops went on to fight in the Battle of Carabobo in 1821, the decisive victory in the Venezuelan revolution (see History section, page 37).

Map on page 178

Beloved Virgin

The island's most renowned religious spot is in **El Valle del Espíritu Santo ❼**, home of the **Santuario de la Virgen del Valle**, the chapel guarding the image of the patron saint of Margarita and all of eastern Venezuela. According to the legend a Guaiquerí Indian found the beautiful image of the virgin in the Piache Cave located in a hillside above the town.

An ornate pink and white neo-Gothic chapel was built by the town's main plaza to house the revered image. There is always a steady stream of admirers visiting the chapel, but during the week surrounding her feast day, September 8, thousands of pilgrims come from all parts of the country to pay homage to the Virgin. On this occasion, she is usually dressed in an elegant gown covered with daisies – *margaritas* in Spanish – and a gold crown.

Pelican on board. Margarita's fishing boats traditionally have "eyes" painted on their prows to guide them safely home.

BELOW: Margarita is famous for its handicrafts.

HANDICRAFT HEAVEN

For anyone interested in traditional crafts, Margarita is ripe for exploration. Not to be missed is a visit to Taller de Artesanía Así con las Manos, Tierra, Agua y Fuego (open daily; small fee) just a short distance west of Juan Griego on the coastal highway. Clearly visible on the left side of the road, it is a combination museum, artisan community, and craft shop in one, unlike anything else in Venezuela. A large store, jammed to the rafters with every kind of local craft, is closest to the highway, but the truly fascinating part is behind it: something of an artisan's vision of a vintage Venezuelan village, including shops and a church, in a dozen or so hand-built *bahareque* (mud-walled) structures joined by paths in a desert garden setting. Some contain only memorabilia to create the spirit of the place, others also sell crafts (largely produced by local artists working on the premises).

El Cercado, just outside La Asunción, is famous for its ceramics; while to the southeast of Juan Griego, Los Millanes is known for its hand-rolled cigars. In addition, Tacarigua has a reputation for its *chinohorros* (lacy, open-work hammocks), Pedrogonzález, for its *mapires* (hand-woven pocket-style purses in every size), and Atamo, east of La Asunción, for its sturdy *mara* baskets.

It is traditional to leave gifts for the Virgin, either when asking favors, or in thanks for those granted. Sometimes these are things of great worth, others are simply a symbolic representation associated with the favor. For this reason, you see license plates (to protect the driver), graduation diplomas and trophies (thanks for help in attaining these goals), and wedding bouquets (for a successful marriage). In matters of health, *milagros* (charms in the shape of an arm, leg, and so on, which make reference to the part of the body affected) of gold or silver are the usual offering. The degree of devotion to this Virgin is obvious in the **Museo Diocesano** (Tues–Sat 9am–noon, 2–5pm; Sun 9am–1pm; free) adjacent to the chapel, created to hold the incredible volume of offerings that have been left over the years. The display has to be seen to be believed. Nearby is the **Casa Natal Santiago Mariño** (open daily; free), recently restored birthplace of one of the most important heroes of the independence.

Arid peninsula

Travelers who have exhausted the island's eastern attractions can cross the 18-km (11-mile) isthmus to the western **Península de Macanao**, the largely uninhabited arid terrain that locals call "the other island." As would be expected, cactus dominates the landscape, but to soften its harshness puts on seasonal shows of color as the low-lying prickly pear variety bursts into bloom with large yellow flowers, and bright red fruit adorns the tall spiked columns of the *cardón* cactus.

The peninsula is inked to the rest of Margarita by a bridge at the mouth of Bahía de Mangle, and residents of **Boca del Río ❽** – the peninsula's largest town – live from the proceeds of commercial fishing. Here, and in some of the smaller towns, there are shipyards where you can watch construction of the small boats called *peñeros*.

BELOW: the dry Macanao Peninsula.

The main attraction for visitors to Boca del Río is the **Museo Marino de Margarita** (Tues–Sun 9am–5pm; free), a project of the Universidad de Oriente. The museum has seven rooms focusing on the sea in general, and also on corals, sea turtles, marine mammals, boats and ships, traditional fishing methods, and a marine inventory of the area. Guided tours are available in both English and Spanish. In large tanks located outside, the university is experimentally raising shrimp, marine turtles, and various species of fish.

Boca del Río is close to one of Margarita's main tourist attractions, the **Parque Nacional Laguna La Restinga ❾** (open daily; admission fee). A boatmen's union, operating from the dock behind the park guards' office, has the concession to carry visitors on tours through the 100 sq. km (38 sq. miles) of lagoon, and canals cut through the dense growth of mangroves that ring it. Price is based on a flat fee per round trip per boat.

Depending on the season and the time of day, you can see a wide variety of water birds, including flamingoes, herons, scarlet ibis, gulls, pelicans, cormorants, and magnificent frigatebirds. While passing through the canals, watch for colonies of oysters clinging to the aerial roots of mangroves. The park is about 40 km (25 miles) from Porlamar, but tourists without transportation are warned that although get-ing there is easy, getting back can be tough. It's best to hire a taxi and agree a ime for the driver to return and pick you up, or else to go with an organized tour.

Playa La Restinga ⑩, on a 23-km (14-miles) long barrier reef bordering he lagoon, is covered with finely crushed fossils over its full length. This magnificent Caribbean beach, rather than the lagoon, is the target of most local visitors. Near the docking area informal restaurants serve freshly fried fish and other simple fare.

Sandy shores

Although Margarita is a treasure chest of history, most visitors are more interested in the sun. To satisfy them there are dozens of beaches, each with its own character; palm trees help to increase the amount of shade. The beach closest to he airport is **Playa El Yaque**, which has acquired international fame for its outstanding conditions for windsurfing, with a steady breeze in the afternoons and safe shallow waters. This is where Margarita's windsurfing competitions are held. Stores offering equipment rental and lessons abound. The most popular east coast beaches, reached from the route indicated for Pampatar-Manzanillo, from south to north, are: Guacuco, El Tirano, Parguito, and El Agua.

Development projects have marred the appeal of **Playa Guacuco**, which these days seems to be more popular with locals than with tourists; still, it has a fine sandy, if narrow, beach. When the surf comes in during the late afternoon, the water rises to the line of the palm trees that shade the beach. **Playa Tirano** (in Puerto Fermín), the least-frequented of this group, has a southern backdrop of picturesque peaks. The village offers several pretty *posadas*, and pleasant restaurants dot the waterfront drive.

Map on page 178

TIP

Watch for the endemic Margarita yellow-headed parrot *(cotorra margariteña)*, often seen feeding in bushes on side roads penetrating the center of the Macanao Peninsula from its western beach road.

BELOW: touring the mangrove swamps of La Restinga.

Windsurfing at Playa El Yaque: most local lodgings have space for board and sail storage.

The most popular beach in Margarita is **Playa El Agua**, with its soft waves (but a powerful undertow), and everything from walk-in sushi bars to informal seafood restaurants, which often put on live Caribbean music to entertain diners. Although palm trees shade the eateries, natural shade is at a minimum close to the water. Beach-chairs and awnings *(toldos)* are available for rent.

Just as windsurfers have their beach, so do surfing fanatics. **Playa Parguito** has the island's highest breakers thanks to an offshore shelf of rocks. This is a pretty beach next to Playa El Agua, with a handful of food kiosks and palm and sea grape trees. Bring sandals or deck shoes because pebbles, not sand, dominate the beach. Because of Playa Parguito's location, farthest from the road, it is never too crowded.

North shore beaches

A number of new hotels and vacation properties have recently been built on or near key beaches. One example is a huge luxury hotel, Isla Bonita, which has appeared on **Playa Puerto Cruz**, a long, curving, golden sandy beach extending along a bay between two rocky hills. Some of the hotels have attempted to close off parts of these public beaches for their private use.

At the base of the mountain pass that joins the towns of Pedro González and Manzanillo, is **Playa Puerto Viejo**. The beach can be reached on foot by walking to the far northeastern end of Playa Puerto Cruz, scaling a small rocky hill and descending. Although this is a narrow strip of sand, the surf is calm and the water is shallow – heightening its appeal for swimmers and children. It's best to pack a picnic and plenty to drink because all that's guaranteed here is soft sand, clear Caribbean water and shady coconut trees.

BELOW: even the pirates like Spanish *tascas* (bars).
RIGHT: the Caribbean beckons.

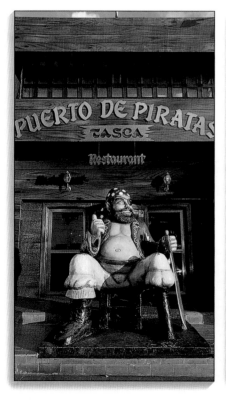

Map on page 178

Playa Pedrogonzález (also known as Playa Zaragoza) is picturesque with its well-preserved traditional-style beachfront homes and wide sandy beach. With the buildings facing a wide promenade (and the sea) shaded by sea grapes and dotted with several small sidewalk cafés, it is more geared toward those seeking relaxation than action. However, if it is action you are looking for, the newest "in" spot is nearby **Playa Caribe** – as crowded by night as by day thanks to a string of lively bars and restaurants with live music.

The pearl islands

At the beginning of the 16th century, it was not Margarita but the tiny islands of **Cubagua** and **Coche** that were the focus of attention thanks to their rich offshore beds of pearl-bearing oysters.The settlement established on Cubagua in 1500 was destroyed by an earthquake and tidal wave in 1541. Except for a few fishermen's shacks and a research station, there has been no redevelopment of the island. Coche was not as affected by the 1541 quake and has several small villages along with a pair of small hotels. With its new free-port status, more growth is sure to come. Many Margarita travel agencies offer day tours by boat (with lunch, bar, and snorkeling) to Coche and Cubagua. There is also a car/passenger ferry service between Punta de Piedras and San Pedro de Coche.

Far-flung day tours

Several companies offer day tours from Margarita to capture tourists who fly directly into the island with charters. Among these are trips to La Blanquilla Island (off the eastern shore of Margarita); Canaima, Kavac, and Uruyén in Parque Nacional Canaima in Bolívar; and to Delta Amacuro. ❏

Because of the scarcity of natural water sources on Margarita, a pipeline was installed from the mainland that carries fresh water to the thirsty island. But there is not enough water, and shortages are often a problem.

BELOW: islanders strumming up a storm.

EXPLORE VENEZUELA'S COASTLINE

With attractions such as coral cays and mangrove swamps, the country's beaches are much more than places for lying around and soaking up the sun

With its 3,000 km (1,800 miles) of Caribbean coast, an island state where tourism based on sun and surf is the principal livelihood, three superb marine parks, and year-round summer climate, it is little wonder that Venezuela is still thought of primarily as a beach holiday destination, both for its own citizens and for visitors from around the world.

NATURAL ATTRACTIONS

Unlike most Caribbean neighbors, whose beaches are essentially the same, the great variety of Venezuela's beaches is a bonus. Those on the east, near the Paria Peninsula, enjoy a backdrop of mountains blanketed with tropical forest and shorelines bordered by swaying palm trees. Waters off Margarita Island's southern shore and the east coast of the Paraguaná Peninsula offer world-class windsurfing. Los Roques Archipelago presents a menu of incredible diving, pristine beaches, and bonefishing rated the most highly in the world. The dramatic, twisted rock islands of Mochima National Park and the sandy cays of Morrocoy National Park beyond intricate, mangrove-lined canals have both dramatic landscapes and fascinating wildlife. Beyond that, nearly a dozen colonial forts can be visited, installed along the coast to ward off pirates. Likewise many areas, such as Cuare Wildlife Refuge and Laguna de Tacarigua National Park harbor a wealth of species to delight bird watchers. And, to satisfy those who may just want a relaxing holiday, a full range of lodging is available, from small cozy inns to luxury mega-resorts with all the trimmings.

△ **SWEEPING BAY**
After a drive through the Henri Pittier National Park, plunge into the clear waters off Puerto Colombia's beautiful Playa Grande.

▽ **GIFTS GALORE**
The booming tourist industry on Margarita Island has opened the doors of opportunity for entre-preneurs, large and small.

△ **NET PROFITS**
Worrying where their next meal is coming from is not a problem for fishermen of the central coast.

▷ **CRYSTALLINE SEA**
There is no natural shade o Los Roques, so most visitors explore the beache from the comfort of a boat.

△ **WAVING THE FLAG**
Cayo Sombrero is the most popular of over a dozen inviting cays in Morrocoy National Park.

▽ **STRESS RELIEF**
A hammock swinging gently between the palms provides total relaxation to even the most hyperactive types.

▷ **ROCKY PERCH**
Pelicans, boobies, herons, cormorants, flamingos, frigate birds, and scarlet ibis are just some of the many bird species that can be seen all along the country's coast.

EASTERN FISHING FOCUS

Most visitors may have more leisurely pursuits in mind, but Venezuela's warm Caribbean waters also support a large fishing industry. The principal commercial fishing areas are in the east, especially in Sucre. The Gulf of Cariaco produces most of the sardines consumed in Venezuela, with processing plants in Cumaná and Marigüitar. This zone is also abundant with mollusks and crustaceans, including shrimps, crabs, mussels, and various types of small clams. Large-scale fishing fleets based in Cumaná take advantage of the quantity of tuna in the open sea, and several large tuna canneries have set up in the area around Carupano. Fishermen on the Gulf of Paria find shrimp, marine catfish, mullet, and weakfish to be the most viable commercially, while many lobster and conch are caught off Los Roques Archipelago.

WEST COAST STATES

The West's natural areas – from cloud forests to island beaches and sand dunes – are superb, and colonial history lives on in fascinating cities such as Puerto Cabello and Coro

Map on page 192

I f you want to get to know the northwestern states properly, set aside at least a week. Leave Caracas via the *Autopista Central*, a modern super-highway that winds south then west to the agro-industrial city of Maracay. From Maracay you can head north across the mountains, through the magnificent cloud forest of Parque Nacional Henri Pittier, to glorious palm-fringed beaches.

Alternatively, you can go via the Lago de Valencia, to the important industrial center of Valencia. North from that city is the thriving port town of Puerto Cabello, with its two colonial forts. To the northwest are the islands of Parque Nacional Morrocoy, home to many water birds and a paradise for snorkelers and divers. From there, you can continue northwest to Coro, with its renowned colonial zone, and, just outside the town, sand dunes. The Península de Paraguaná is dotted with cacti and windswept beaches. The Sierra de San Luís offers beautiful caves and quaint mountain villages where age-old indigenous rites are maintained.

Westbound on the Autopista Central

If your destination is Maracay, Valencia, or points farther west, you can get there quickly on the *autopista*, which is now a toll road. However, taking a detour at the La Victoria exit can lead you to various interesting attractions. A little past the toll booth, turning left on the old Carretera Panamericana (Pan American highway) takes you to **La Victoria ❶**. Although not a major tourist center, there are still things to see here, including the **colonial church** on Calle Candelaria facing Plaza Ribas; a gigantic, handsome military fort, the **Cuartel Marinao Montilla** (open to the public on weekends); the pretty tree-filled **Parque La Victoria** (closed Mon), with the restored station for the long-gone railroad that ran between La Guaira–Caracas–Valencia; and the colonial chapel, **Capilla de Nuestra Señora de la Candelaria** facing Plaza Bolívar.

Continuing west on the main avenue, watch for the sign indicating the turn for **Colonia Tovar ❷** *(see pages 148–9)*. *Caraqueños* usually go there via El Junquito, being a shorter drive from the capital, but this route is infinitely more picturesque, climbing up the mountains on a steep twisting route.

Staying on the Pan American Highway, you will pass **San Mateo ❸**. Nearby is the former *hacienda* of Simón Bolívar's family – a sugar, coffee, and cacao plantation founded in 1593. Bolívar was born in Caracas, but spent much of his childhood here. The family home is now a military museum (labeled **Ingenio Bolívar** outside). The *hacienda*'s sugar mill, across the road, has been restored, housing the **Museo de Caña de Azúcar** (Sugar Cane Museum; both museums open Tues–Sun 9am–noon, 2–5pm; token admission fee.)

PRECEDING PAGES: the beach at Golfo Triste.
LEFT: colonial charm at Choroní.
BELOW: strutting flamingos at the Cuare Wildlife Refuge.

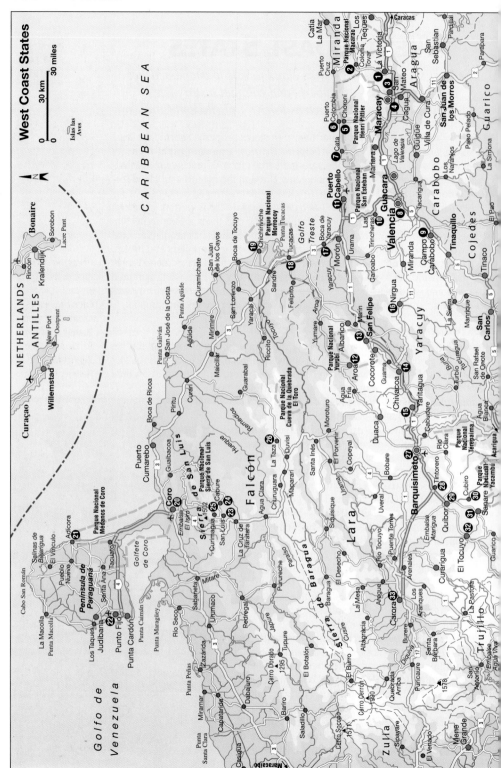

The Garden City

Maracay ❹ is the modern capital of Aragua state. The fortunes of this region have always been made from agriculture: coffee, cacao, indigo, cotton, and tobacco. It earned its sobriquet, however, from its abundance of green spaces.

Dictator Juan Vicente Gómez (in power 1908–35) governed the country from Maracay from 1912 until his death. He is largely responsible for making the city what it is today, leaving a legacy of beautiful architecture and parks. Most are concentrated along Avenida Las Delicias (which leads to Choroní/Puerto Colombia) and Avenida 19 de Abril, both of which are home to most of Maracay's best hotels. At the far end is the compact **Zoológico Las Delicias** (closed Mon; token admission fee), originally Gómez's country house and personal zoo.

Gómez began Venezuela's first commercial air service – to Maracay, Maracaibo, and Ciudad Bolívar. In honor of Maracay being the birthplace of Venezuela's military aviation in 1936, the country's only **Museo Aeronáutico** (irregular hours, usually open weekends; free) is found here, by the intersection of Avenida Las Delicias and 19 de Abril. Opposite it is the Complejo Cultural Santos Michelena with the excellent **Museo de Arte Contemporáneo de Maracay Mario Abreu** and the **Casa de la Cultura** (Tues–Sun; free), along with schools of music and art, and a public library.

Within a few blocks, down Avenida 19 de Abril, is the beautiful Moorish-style **bullring** (known both as La Maestranza and Plaza de Toros César Girón), conceived by Carlos Raúl Villanueva, who designed several landmark buildings in Caracas *(see page 141)*. Nearby is the Ateneo de Maracay, with a schedule of events posted outside. Other main attractions surround the main squares along Avenida Bolívar. Around Plaza Girardot (with a monument in honor of American volunteer soldiers in the War of Independence) are the colonial **Cathedral**, the **Museo de Historia**, **Museo de Arqueología** (with an extensive collection of indigenous artifacts and skeletons in burial urns from local digs), and the **Instituto de Antropología e Historia del Estado de Aragua** – three museums all under the same roof (Tues–Fri 8am–noon, Sat–Sun 9am–1pm; free). On the eastern side of the plaza is the **Sanctuary of Madre María de San José** (Tues–Sun 8.30–11.30am, 2.30–5pm), who was beatified in 1995. Venezuelans flock to see the sarcophagus of the country's only saint.

The **Plaza Bolívar** is the largest and perhaps most beautiful square of this name in Venezuela. Behind it is the art deco Teatro de la Opera, one of the best theaters in the country.

Natural wonderland

Two routes from Maracay cross the mountains to the coast, both with continual hairpin turns. Because of this, while the distance is short (about 50 km/30 miles), it takes at least 90 minutes, but the gorgeous scenery compensates. The 107,800-hectare (266,400-acre) site was set aside in 1937 as Venezuela's first national park. Initially named for its Rancho Grande cloud forest, it was renamed **Parque Nacional Henri Pittier** in 1953 to honor the Swiss botanist who classified 30,000 Venezuelan plants and promoted the national park system.

Map on page 192

TIP

Be sure to check out the Centro Cultural Higuaraya Capanaparo at the base of Maracay's bull ring. Run by Maruja Da Silva for over two decades, it has a shop jammed with native crafts, classes in the arts, cultural presentations and a reference library.

BELOW: Parque Nacional Henri Pittier.

The abundance and variety of fauna and flora is awesome in its life zones, which range from dry forest and xerophytic lands to cloud forests. The highest mountains in the park rise to about 1,280 meters (4,200 ft). Portachuelo Pass, a V-shaped dip in the terrain, is a migratory route for insects and birds. Mammals, reptiles, and amphibians abound, but the stars of fauna, with more than 500 species found here, are birds.

From Maracay, heading north on Avenida Las Delicias by the zoo takes you past the city's fanciest lodging, Hotel Pipo Internacional, with the park entrance just beyond. Almost immediately is **Las Cocuizas Recreational Area** (closed Mon; token admission fee) with river swimming and picnic areas.

Protection from pirates

A few kilometers before the coast is a pretty village of traditional colonial houses. This is **Choroní ❺**, once at the heart of a rich cacao-growing region, with its great *haciendas* worked by slave labor. In colonial times, Dutch and Spanish merchant ships plied the coast. The journey was fraught with danger as pirates stalked these waters and sometimes ventured ashore. That is why Choroní, like Cata and many other towns, was built well back from the sea, to afford some protection from the marauders.

Puerto Colombia ❻, the port for Choroní, is right on the water, with its fleet of brightly painted wooden boats moored in a little river flowing into the sea. A string of small bars and informal restaurants lines the waterfront.

The swimming beach, **Playa Grande**, is just east of Puerto Colombia, wrapped around a bay lined with coconut trees and a few open-air snack bars. Several local beaches are reached only from the sea, by fishing boat from Puerto Colombia. Fishermen offer transfers from the port.

The only way to progress farther west overland is to return by the same route to Maracay and take the Cata road back across the cloud forest, passing the Rancho Grande research station in the Henri Pittier National Park. But, for the beach, continue to **Cata ❼**. Except for two ugly apartment towers at the near end (which can be easily blocked out of photos taken from the ridge above), it is one of the most picturesque beaches in the country. The village of Cata lies a short distance inland. Cata is a swimmer's beach, while **Cuyagua**, 13 km (8 miles) to the east is considered one of the best in Venezuela for surfing.

The populations of these coastal villages are predominantly composed of descendants of African slaves who were brought here to work the cacao plantations. They have maintained three important traditions which combine Catholicism, folklore, and paganism: devil dancers (in Cata, Ocumare de la Costa, and Chuao) who perform on the feast of Corpus Christi; Cruz de Mayo celebrations; and sensual dancing to *tambores* (African-style drums made from hollow tree trunks) *(see Fiestas and Devil Dancers, pages 79–85).*

If planning a trip to the beaches near Choroní, with access only by sea, prepare yourself for inflation. The transfer that used to cost a few dollars (before the popularity surge of Puerto Colombia) now starts at about US$50–60.

Endemic birds in the Parque Nacional Henri Pittier include the handsome fruit-eater, the blood-eared parakeet, and the helmeted curassow. You might also see a harpy eagle, a white tipped quetzal, and flocks of lilac-tailed parrotlets.

BELOW: Choroní fisherman.

Early indigenous presence

Back in Maracay, if you head west, skirting Lago de Valencia, you'll arrive at Carabobo's capital, **Valencia ❽**. Some 4,000 years ago, the area was settled by various indigenous groups. Archeologists have unearthed ceramics and other evidence of early Indian cultures, and fossils of mastodons and other animals. Many are in the anthropological museums of Valencia and Maracay. But, for evidence of ancient indigenous presence *in situ*, visit **Parque Piedras Pintadas**, between Guacara and Vigirima, where scores of petroglyphs cover the hillside. Do not explore the park alone – there have been many hold-ups of lone visitors recently.

Manufacturing capital

Valencia has grown into Venezuela's third-largest city, despite its troubled history. Less than a decade after its founding in 1555, it was nearly destroyed by the invading forces of Lope de Aguirre, the barbaric conquistador on a quest to find El Dorado *(see page 30)*. The city was later attacked by Caribe Indians, sacked by French pirates, and devastated in the earthquake of 1812. Although the decisive Battle of Carabobo took place near Valencia, in 1826 it became the first city to resist Simón Bolívar's Gran Colombia campaign. An assembly held here declared Venezuela a sovereign state and, for a brief time, the city was its captial.

Now, Valencia is principally known as Venezuela's manufacturing capital. In 1948, when the government declared no further industry could be installed in Caracas (and existing factories were moved), Carabobo's leaders took advantage of the opportunity (and the city's excellent location) to launch the development of an industrial zone that now has more than 900 companies, ranging from vehicle assembly plants to food manufacturers.

If you want a coconut in Choroní all you have to do is learn to climb a palm tree.

BELOW: a *hacienda* near Maracay.

TIP

Every Friday, Valencia's *El Carabobeño* newspaper publishes a page on art and culture, listing a weekly schedule of events for the city's theaters, museums, galleries, concert halls, parks, etc, as well as including a list of principal restaurants.

BELOW: the arch guarding the eternal flame of the unknown soldier at Campo Carabobo.

History and culture in Valencia

Valencia has a great deal of historical and cultural interest. In the El Viñedo neighborhood there are several important private art galleries, including the **Galería de Arte Ascaso** (Mon–Fri 8am–noon, 2–6pm; Sat–Sun 10am–2pm; free). Opposite is the open-air Parque de Escultura Andrés Pérez Mujica, with dozens of sculptures by top Venezuelan artists. Continuing the artistic theme, there are two sites dedicated to one of Valencia's most imortant modern artists – the Centro Cultural Braulio Salazar (Paseo Cabriales; irregular hours) and the Sala de Exposiciones Braulio Salazar (Avenida Andrés Eloy Blanco; open daily; free).

Avenida Bolívar Norte (to the north of the center, between Avenida Cedeño and the Guaparo Redoma) is best known for its plethora of restaurants, but here you also find the **Ateneo de Valencia ⓐ** (Mon–Fri 8am–noon, 2–6pm; Sat–Sun 11am–5pm; free), home of the prestigious annual Salón Michelena, as well as exhibitions and stage productions.

Historic attractions are concentrated near the **Plaza Bolívar**. These include the colonial **Cathedral ⓑ**, home to a statue of the Virgen del Socorro in a bejeweled gown. In 1910, this became the first statue in Venezuela to be crowned – with the Pope's permission – in recognition of the many favors granted by the Virgin.

General José Antonio Páez, who forged a formidable army of *llaneros* (plainsmen) and served as Venezuela's first president, lived here for a time. His former home, **Casa Páez ⓒ** (Tues–Fri 9am–noon, 3–6pm; Sat–Sun 9am–2pm; free), has a patio with murals (depicting nine battles in which he fought), restored rooms, and a former subterranean prison used during Gómez's dictatorship.

Another area of focus is around Plaza Sucre. On one side, the **Capitolio ⓓ** (Sat, Sun, hols 10am–2pm; free), a former convent (built in 1722) and the

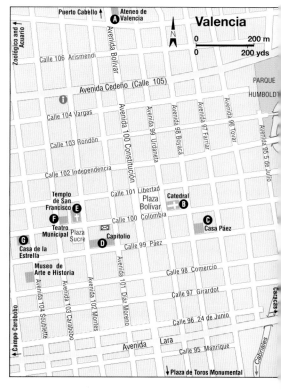

current headquarters of Carabobo's state government, has enjoyed recent restoration. Facing it are the **Templo de San Francisco** ❸ (site of the call in 1826 for Venezuela's separation from Bolívar's Gran Colombia) and the restored **Teatro Municipal** ❻, built in 1892 and apparently designed to emulate the Paris Opera House; it has now been declared a national monument. On Avenida Soublette, the **Casa de la Estrella** ❼ is of interest only for its historical significance: this is where the sovereignty of Venezuela was declared in 1830. Two blocks south is the colonial **Casa de los Celis** (Tues–Fri 8am–2pm; Sat, Sun 9am–noon; free), the beautiful former home of the Celis family, and now a history and art museum.

To visit the city's **aquarium** (closed Mon; small admission fee), head west of the center along Avenida Cedeño, follow it to the end, and then turn right.

Valencia's bullring, the **Plaza de Toros Monumental**, has a capacity of 27,000 and is the second largest in the Americas after Mexico City's. Adjacent to it is the Parque Recreacional Sur, site of the **Museo Antropológico** (closed Mon; token admission fee).

Battle memorial

Some 26 km (16 miles) southwest of Valencia lies **Campo Carabobo** ❾, memorial to the Battle of Carabobo (1821), which virtually secured Venezuela's independence from Spain. There are two dramatic monuments: the first is a large arch marking the Tomb of the Unknown Soldier; and the second, commemorating the battle itself, is topped by an equestrian statue of Bolívar. Honor guards in red colonial-style uniforms stand at rigid attention, except during the impressive changing of the guard ceremony which takes place every two hours

Maps pages 192 & 196

BELOW: petroglyph at the Parque Piedras Pintadas

PIEDRAS PINTADAS PARK

Petroglyphs (*piedras pintadas* – literally "painted rocks," although designs are incised) are found in many parts of Venezuela, but there is a great concentration in Carabobo state around Lake Valencia (which was sacred to indigenous inhabitants); the most easily reached are found just east of Valencia, on the Guacara–Vigirima route. Enter Guacara then double back toward the freeway via Plaza Bolívar. The turn-off is 6.6 km (4 miles) north of the point the road passes under the freeway. Here, turn left toward Tronconero then, after a little over 1 km (⅔ mile), make a right at the school. Continue to the end and park at the former museum at the base of the hill of Parque Piedras Pintadas, covered with scores of etched rocks (take chalk to highlight the designs if you plan to take photos).

Some have easily identifiable human or animal forms, but the significance of abstract shapes remains a mystery. Some may be maps, or possibly magical or religious symbols – but their significance, age, and even who created them is unknown. Faces, outlines of feet, spirals, and holes bored in the rocks are among the most common themes. There are more on the hill, including a line of upright stones, one with "points" bored in to it that is seemingly a trail marker.

from 6am–6pm. A road to the west leads to the *mirador* (viewing site), shaped like a massive inverted pyramid, overlooking the battleground. Inside, there is an audio-visual presentation (with an English version) detailing the historic confrontation.

Gateway to the sea

Heading north from Valencia toward Puerto Cabello, you will pass the exit for **Las Trincheras** , site of Centro Termas Las Trincheras, the second-hottest thermal springs in the world (98°C/208.4°F). It now has a 120-room hotel, giant pools fed by the springs, saunas, steam baths, and naturally heated mud.

Hot baths at Las Trincheras.

Once through **Taborda**, with its shoulder-to-shoulder stands selling shark turnovers, *arepitas dulces* (puffy fried circles of sweetened white cornmeal dough with aniseed), fresh fried fish, iced coconuts, and other such snacks, you reach the coast road, with the giant state-owned oil refinery to the west and the large natural port of Puerto Cabello to the east.

Following the highway toward the port city, at the western edge of Puerto Cabello is a large hill topped by **Fortín Solano**. Financed by the Guipuzcoana Company and finished in 1770, it was the last colonial fort to be built in Venezuela. Take the San Esteban exit, then stick to the street closest to the hill. A large portal on the right marks the entrance via a steep winding road.

Some 7 km (4 miles) farther south – via part of what used to be the route of the colonial Camino Real between Valencia and the coast – you come to **San Esteban**. In the early days, this was a favorite spot for German merchants of the port to live because of its cooler, healthier climate; explaining the surprising number of large (although some now a bit neglected) 19th-century mansions constructed by them.

BELOW: Fortín Solano, Puerto Cabello.

From the parking area at the end of the road, continue on foot on the old trail, which passes a large petroglyph with the only known example in Venezuela showing a person in a boat, as well as a colonial era Spanish bridge at Paso Hondo.

Map on page 192

Port with a past

Puerto Cabello ⑪ has been an important harbor since its foundation in the mid-1500s; it now handles 77 percent of Venezuela's commercial traffic. Almost from the start, the port was plagued by pirates who tried to intercept Spanish galleons loaded with gold and other riches. After a time, Dutch merchants gained a foothold. Cacao, coffee, indigo, and cotton crops moved from Venezuela to the nearby Dutch islands via Puerto Cabello. The Spanish government promised a group of powerful Basque merchants a virtual monopoly if they squelched the Dutch competition. The group formed the Guipuzcoana Company in 1728, and erected **Castillo Libertador** (aka Fortín San Felipe) at the harbor entrance. They also set up warehouses, stimulating the local economy, but they were despised by the local people. After nearly six decades, the company met its demise and the headquarters became the customs house, known as the **Casa Guipuzcoana**, now a library, cultural center, and offices. It overlooks the **Plaza Monumento El Aguila**, with a statue dedicated to ten North Americans who were executed by royalists in 1806, while fighting in Venezuela's War of Independence.

Fortín San Felipe was the only independent defense unit in Venezuela country never taken by force. Following defeat at the Battle of Carabobo, Spanish troops retreated here and managed to hold out for two years. In the 1900s, the fort was put to grim use by the dictator Gómez, who had his political enemies chained in the dungeons.

BELOW: Iglesia El Rosario at Puerto Cabello.

The entire historic section of town, facing the fort and **Paseo Malecón**, the waterfront boulevard, recently underwent a complete restoration. This not only rescued dozens of fading architectural gems, but has also given impetus to a number of pleasant new restaurants and stores; artists have once again set up their easels, and families take leisurely strolls along the streets to admire the distinctive architecture.

Calle de los Lanceros is named for General Antonio Páez, who took a victory ride down this road with his lancers after retaking Puerto Cabello from the Spaniards in 1823. The second-story walkway over Calle de los Lanceros extends from the rear of the **Museo de Historia Colonial**. Above its entrance on the next street to the south is the most beautiful of the "flying" balconies which characterize the port's vintage buildings. At the end of this street is the **Iglesia El Rosario**, dating from 1780, with the only existing wooden bell tower of the era in Venezuela.

Eastern beaches

Puerto Cabello is hot throughout the year, which makes the seashore especially enticing, although beaches located to the west of the city, including Playa Blanca, should be avoided as they are polluted and notoriously unsafe for tourists. Beaches east of town include **Quizandal**, which has a snack bar and is jammed on weekends.

More beautiful and less hectic is **Isla Larga**, an island reached by a ride of 15 minutes in shuttle boats departing from Quizandal. There are two underwater wrecks for divers and snorkelers to explore, and you can camp on the white sand beach. Vendors sell snacks, but there are no bathrooms or other facilities.

Patanemo Bay, about 12 km (7 miles) from Puerto Cabello, is a wide half-moon beach, fringed by coconut palms, that is very popular on weekends.

Heading inland

The main attractions of Yaracuy state are located along four distinct routes:

● **Route 1**: From the Caribbean coastal highway, via Morón-Marín-Aroa-Duaca.

The highlight of this first route is **Aroa ⑫**, or, more specifically, the **Parque Bolivariano Minas de Aroa**. This features buildings associated with a now-defunct copper mine, dozens of sculptures by Venezuelan artists, various recreational areas, and an English cemetery. The area was purchased by the Venezuelan government in 1957, and then passed on to Yaracuy in 1972, when it was developed as a park. Because English settlers in Aroa were Protestant, burial in the Catholic cemetery was forbidden, thus, an English cemetery was established. Here, you can admire gravestones from past centuries with the inscriptions written in English.

● **Route 2**: From Marín, follow the low road to San Felipe, continuing on via Guama, Yaritagua, and Barquisimeto.

San Felipe ⑬, the state capital, is the first stop. For an insight into times past, visit **San Felipe "El Fuerte"** (Tues–Sun; token admission fee), an historic archeo-

BELOW: works of art in Minas de Aroa Park.

logical park and museum. As well as more than 100 species of trees, the 10-hectare (25-acre) park has ruins of the formerly glorious city leveled by an earthquake in 1812. Museum exhibits relate the historic, social, and economic evolution of the city. You should also stop at the striking modern **Cathedral** on Plaza Bolívar; then head for the north edge of town where you'll find the **Parque Nacional Yurubí** and **Parque Leonor Bernabó**, with swimming pools, picnic shelters, and playgrounds (both closed Mon; token admission fee). On the outskirts of San Felipe are the **Parque de la Exótica Flora Tropical** (Tues–Sun 10am–5pm for tours; admission fee), which claims to be the largest garden of exotic tropical flowers in Latin America, with hundreds of showy species protected by trees. The adjacent **Misión Nuestra Señora del Carmen** was reconstructed in the original style on ruins of an 18th-century Capuchin mission and houses a chapel, museum, and restaurants (open until 11pm).

Next, **Chivacoa ⑭** is the entry point for the **Monumento Natural María Lionza**, whose mountains are the birthplace of important rivers as well as of the mystical cult of María Lionza *(see below)*.

In **Yaritagua ⑮**, a beautiful stone neo-classical building (dating from 1861) has been converted into the **Centro Turístico Los Carrascosa** (Carrera 8 at Calle 19; open daily 7am–7pm; free), which includes a museum, a conference center, and a *posada* with top-quality rooms, piano bar, and restaurant. Along the highway are attractive *Aldeas Artesanales* (craft villages) created by the state's tourism board: Guama (basketry), Camunare Blanco (ceramics), Paseo Artesanal José Antonio Páez (naïf art sculptures), La Casona (varied crafts).

● **Route 3**: This circuit enters Yaracuy via Valencia–La Encrucijada–Montalbán in Carabobo, continuing via Nirgua–Chivacoa–Yaritagua.

Map on page 192

CULT OF MARIA LIONZA

Based on the legend of an Indian princess who became the Goddess of Nature, María Lionza (popularly referred to as *La Reina* – the queen) is the central figure of a cult combining Catholicism, nature worship, and paganism that is followed by hundreds of thousands of Venezuelans.

María Lionza always has Negro Felipe and the Indian chief Guaicaipuro by her side (this group is known as "Las Tres Potencias" – the three powers). They are served by many "courts" that seemingly exclude no one – from Catholic saints and African tribal gods to Hitler, Cleopatra, Spanish Queen Isabel, Simón Bolívar, John F. Kennedy, and the Pope, to name just a few.

In 1960, Inparques created the Monumento Natural María Lionza, a 117-sq. km (45-sq. mile) mountain park south of the town of Chivacoa in Yaracuy state. Two of the most important sites in the area are Sorte and Quivallo, where followers perform rites before commencing their pilgrimage up the hill. They allow non-believers to observe discreetly, but discourage them from passing beyond a certain point on the mountain (the higher, the more sacred).

On holidays and long weekends, thousands of followers flock to this site – definitely *not* a recommended time for the casual visitor.

BELOW: a typical hand-built country house, using only natural materials.

Near **Nirgua** , about 10km/6 miles south of town, you can explore the ruins of the San Vicente fortress. This was built in 1577 to protect gold (said to be the first found in this part of the New World) extracted from the Buría Mines prior to its shipment to Spain. Parque Embalse Cumaripa (closed Mon; token admission fee), just before the Chivacoa interchange, is a 14-hectare (35-acre) park along the reservoir's eastern shore.

● **Route 4:** The most impressive way to penetrate the state is on the Yaracuy River, via the Caribbean coast at **Boca de Yaracuy** (from where boat excursions are run). Minutes from the highway, you enter another magical world, traversing narrow channels lined with mangroves and tall trees where silence is broken only by the sounds of animals. Eventually, the river widens to form several huge lagoons, which teem with fish and are rich in wildlife.

Parque Nacional Morrocoy

A little more than three hours' drive from Caracas, via Valencia then west on the coast road, is **Parque Nacional Morrocoy** in Falcón state; it was created in 1974 to protect mangroves, sea-bird rookeries, and coral reefs. Once lined with nothing but coconut plantations and seaside shacks, the approach road is now bordered by waterfront condos. The park is a paradise for snorkelers and birders, though sadly the fragile ecosystems are increasingly threatened by the onslaught of tourism. There are about 30 *cayos* (reef-formed islands), some quite large with palm trees and mangroves, others low-lying with white sand. The mangroves are nesting grounds for frigate birds. The two main points of access to the park are Tucacas and Chichiriviche. (There is also an entrance with marinas, a coast guard station, and several *posadas*, but this is mainly used by people with boats.)

BELOW: enjoying the mangrove islands in Morrocoy National Park.

Map
on page
192

Tucacas ⓲ guards the eastern edge of the park. In the early 18th century, it was a thriving port for Dutch merchants who traded goods with nearby islands. It later fell on hard times, but the tourist boom has once again revived it. Local boatmen run a well-organized, dependable service, both here and at Chichiriviche, offering a shuttle service to the islands and *cayos* for a fixed fee. When they drop you off, it is wise to agree a specific pick-up time. The tariff per round-trip boat ride depends upon distance, with a higher fee if you plan to camp overnight.

Camping is allowed in Morrocoy National Park, but is strictly controlled to reduce environmental impact. It is allowed on just four cays. You must first call the National Parks Institute, Inparques, at their toll-free number (tel: 800-84 847) to request a permit and make a reservation. No fires are allowed (cooking must be done with gas units). The park camping fee is about US$2 per person per night, payable at the Banco Union in Tucacas.

Gateway to the northern cays

It is 37 km (22 miles) north from Tucacas to **Chichiriviche** ⓳, gateway to Morrocoy's northern cays. A bonus en-route is that the 12-km (7-mile) causeway into town passes through **Refugio de Fauna Silvestre de Cuare** (the Cuare Wildlife Refuge), which abuts the national park. Its protected, mangrove-lined, shallow salt flats serve as a major feeding ground for brilliant scarlet ibis, roseate spoonbills, numerous species of herons, cormorants, boobies, pelicans, egrets, hawks, hummingbirds, and a population of some 20,000 southern Caribbean flamingoes, who come from Bonaire to feed. Chichiriviche is fast developing, with vacation accommodations rising out of the mud flats.

At home in the mangrove swamps: the magnificent frigate bird.

BELOW: loading up bananas at Tucacas.

Efforts are now being made to conserve the glyphs on the wall at Cueva del Indio, Cuare Wildlife Refuge.

Distinct options

There are many caves in the park and wildlife refuge in the large coral sandstone promontory, **Cerro Chichiriviche**, between Tucacas and Chichiriviche. But two popular options to visit, despite their names, are not caves at all. **Cueva del Indio** (Cave of the Indian) is a high stone wall completely covered with petroglyphs created by Indians who inhabited the area long ago. Thanks to the efforts of the conservationist group FUDENA, in cooperation with Inparques, a pier and boardwalk have been installed to facilitate access (boatmen offer a shuttle service from Chichiriviche), protect the mangroves from trampling, and assure that damage is not inflicted on the glyphs. **Cueva de la Virgen**, a cove with rock walls, viewed from the water, has particular significance to local fishermen who place religious statues and offerings here to protect them while at sea.

Key to the northern cays

There are seven main cays in the northern part of Morrocoy National Park. **Cayo Muerto**, just offshore, has an outpost of the Environment Ministry. A short distance to the north is **Cayo Sal**, with its salt lagoon in the center. The farthest is coral-ringed **Cayo Borracho** to the north, a favorite for campers and scuba divers. **Cayo Peraza** is another coral-ringed beauty. The tiniest, **Cayo Pelón** (Bald Cay), is a treeless desert island only about 50 meters (162 ft) long. **Cayo Pescadores**, as the name implies, is favored by fishermen. One of the most distant – and the most popular cays for sun-worshipers – is **Cayo Sombrero**. The central lagoon attracts a family crowd, who splash in the shallow waters and pitch brightly colored tents among the palms. Vendors sell snacks on Sombrero, but take plenty of provisions, including mosquito repellant, when you visit any of the cays.

BELOW:
untouched cays
near Chichiriviche.

Colonial elegance

The next stop on this West Coast route is the colonial city of **Coro** , the first capital of the Province of Venezuela. Santa Ana de Coro, one of the earliest settlements in South America, was founded by Juan de Ampiés in 1527. In a rare event for the conquest era, he was welcomed by the local chief, Manaure. Ampiés maintained peace with the Indians by dealing fairly with them and shielding them from the slave raids that were common on the coast at that time. Sadly, this unusual harmony was short lived. In succeeding years, a series of German governors, interested only in finding gold, used Coro as a base for their expeditions. They ruled by exploitation, and the Indians fled.

Coro began to flourish in the 18th century, becoming the supplier for the islands of Bonaire and Curaçao, 104 km (65 miles) away. Agricultural produce and animals were shipped from La Vela de Coro, east of the capital. The Venezuelan flag was planted for the first time on August 3, 1806, at La Vela, by Francisco de Miranda. The tricolor flew over the San Pedro Fort, now gone, but a monument remains. By the shore here is the former customs house *(Aduana)*, which now houses a marine research center; in front is a statue of a girl in typical Dutch dress, recalling the important trade links of the 1700s with the Dutch islands.

Worthwhile is a stop at the little village of **Taratara**, a short distance before Coro (exit to the north). Most of its houses are colorfully painted with creative designs and at its small museum you can usually arrange for one of the local children to lead you on a walk of about 40 minutes to the sea, passing through a dry gorge whose walls are embedded with fossilized seashells. A great variety of birds and lizards can be observed on this walk, and at the beach there is an unusual grouping of petroglyphs.

Between La Vela and Coro, along the Intercomunal, is the Jardín Xerófito. This garden contains a large collection of xerophytic plants from all over the world. Even when the gardens are open, the gates are kept closed to prevent goats from wandering in and munching on the plants.

BELOW: the sand dunes of Coro.

Coro's colonial treasures

Careful conservation of the streetscapes of Coro's colonial zone in a nearly pristine state earned Falcón's capital designation by UNESCO as a World Patrimony City. A short stroll down Calle Zamora will make it clear that this honor is well-deserved. Beautifully maintained buildings line the cobblestone streets extending west and south from the hub, **Plaza San Clemente**, with its early 18th-century chapel and wooden cross, which was supposedly carved from the tree under which Ampiés met Chief Manaure.

Iglesia de San Francisco in Coro.

Situated just east of the plaza is the 19th-century **Iglesia de San Francisco**. But it is the former convent (built in 1620) next door which is of principal interest to visitors. It now houses the **Museo Diocesano Lucas Guillermo Castillo** (Tues–Sat 9am–noon, 3–6pm; Sun 9am–1pm; token admission fee), with a marvelous and handsomely displayed collection of religious, colonial, and decorative art.

The **Casa del Sol** (House of the Sun), on the street across from San Clemente chapel, got its name from a sun design above its door. Built in the 17th century, the house has served variously as a private residence, a monastery, and a college. Today it houses public offices.

On the corner beside the chapel, heading west on Zamora, is **El Balcón de los Arcaya**, one of the few two-story buildings in Coro. It was built by a Spanish nobleman in the late 17th century, and was bought approximately 100 years later by Don Ignacio Luis Díaz de Arcaya, remaining in his family's possession to the present day. The name comes from this and the distinctive balcony which runs along two sides of the house. Some years back, the house was restored and converted into the **Museo de Cerámica Histórica y Loza Popular** (Museum of Historic Ceramics and China; Tues–Sat 9am–noon, 3–6pm; Sun 9am–1pm; token admission fee). Among the exhibits is a room that has pre-Hispanic ceramics (uncovered by the anthropologist J.M. Cruxent) juxtaposed with pieces still being created by local potters.

BELOW: Casa de las Ventanas de Hierro in Coro.

Farther down Zamora is the **Casa de las Ventanas de Hierro** (House of the Iron Windows; Tues–Sat 9am–noon, 3–6pm, Sun 9am–1pm), most admired for its beautiful baroque doorway, although the name comes from the wrought-iron window grilles, imported from Seville at a time when the local people used only wood.

Next door is the **Casa del Tesoro** (Treasure House; Mon–Sat 9am–6pm; Sun 9am–3pm), which belonged to prominent Bishop Mariano Talavera y Garcés, a relative of the patriot Josefa Camejo. It was rumored to have a secret tunnel and years of digging finally produced one 8 meters (26 ft) underground, but none of the eponymous treasure was ever recovered. Neither the House of the Iron Windows nor the Treasure House is open to the public.

Coro's **Cathedral** (facing the Plaza Bolívar) was one of the first churches built in Venezuela; it was founded in 1583. Built like a fortress, the cathedral's tall tower has gun slits, and indeed it served many times as a fort during the pirate attacks that occurred with regularity in the 16th century. The citizens prepared for these frequent onslaughts as best they could, and the wealthiest built secret caches or tunnels to conceal their riches. Even today there are tales of mysterious tunnels stuffed with hidden treasure.

Two blocks from the cathedral, on Paseo Talavera, is the **Museo de Arte Contemporáneo de Coro** (Tues–Sat 9am–12.30pm, 3–7.30pm; Sun 9am–4pm; free), the former home/store of the Senior family of Curaçao, well-known Jewish merchants. Through the impulse of the founder of Caracas' contemporary art museum (MACCSI), Sofía Imber, it reopened as the Coro art museum in 1988. Exceptional works by Picasso, Botero, Bracque, and others from the MACCSI's permanent collection have traveled here for shows.

Coro has long had a significant Sephardic Jewish population. The Dutch islands were a haven for Jews fleeing the Inquisition in Spain and, when Venezuela's War of Independence erupted, they offered support to the new republic and were among the first to trade with the rebels. The Venezuelan government's guarantee of freedom of worship attracted many Jews to the Coro area at the beginning of the 19th century. A Jewish cemetery is said to be the oldest still in use on the continent. It is sometimes possible to arrange a guided tour (tel: 520436/511446).

Paraguaná Peninsula

Coro, which means "wind" in Arawak, is capital of the country's driest state. The city is located at the base of the isthmus joining the **Península de Paraguaná** to the mainland. It's a fitting name, for the continual east winds have formed shifting *médanos* (sand dunes), the tallest of which reach heights of more than 25 meters (82 ft). To protect the dunes, a strip 30 km (18 miles) long by 5 km

Map on page 192

BELOW: an isolated farm on the Paraguaná Peninsula.

(3 miles) wide, encompassing the isthmus plus a section of the continental coast, has been designated as the **Parque Nacional Los Médanos de Coro**.

The peninsula, originally an island, became linked over time to the mainland by a long isthmus of sand. Pirates took refuge in this desolate landscape of cactus to plan their attacks and even today tourists should be wary as there have been reports of muggings away from the populous areas. Today there are said to be more goats than people here. In the rural eastern part, goat herding is a common livelihood. The people sell goat's milk cheese, and *dulce de leche coriano* (goat's milk fudge). *Chivo en coco* (goat in coconut sauce) is a specialty served in restaurants throughout the region. There are also cottage industries producing traditional leather work, pottery, and furniture carved from cactus wood. The 815-meter (2,670-ft) mountain and natural monument, **Cerro Santa Ana**, in the center of the peninsula, is its highest point.

Adícora ㉑ is at the edge of a protected bay on the east coast. While this keeps the wave action down, the continual high winds, along with tradewinds that are strongest from January through September, make the waters excellent for windsurfing. It's no longer a secret, and fans of this sport come from around the world to test their skill. The colorful houses by the waterfront show early Dutch influence in architectural details such as finials on gable ends, window grilles with pedestals and decorated caps, and shutters painted in contrasting colors. There are some half dozen *posadas* to accommodate visitors.

The northern extreme of the peninsula is a wilderness of cactus and salt beds. **Cabo San Ramón** is a cape where pelicans dive and fishermen cast their nets beneath the rocky cliffs. In contrast to the rest of the peninsula, the western side is modern and developed, thanks to the oil refineries that opened in 1947.

The solitary, non-swimming beaches of the isthmus offer good shelling, especially for the abundant tiny winged scallops.

BELOW: the Posada El Duende, on the outskirts of Cabure.

Map on page 192

Today, **Punto Fijo** ㉒, having grown along with the refineries, has a population of over 120,000 people, making it the largest city in Falcón state. Unlike the eastern beaches, the ones on this side offer light breezes and calm waters. Those at **Villa Marina** and **Punta El Pico**, formerly contaminated, have been cleaned up, but be warned: there is no shade, and the sun can be fierce.

Mountain backdrop

The mountains south of Coro pertain to the **Sierra de San Luis**. Whether approaching them from the north or south, en route you pass through desert landscapes where xerophytic species are the only plant life seen. But, as you climb the mountains, the vegetation changes progressively from cacti to dry forests to lush cloud forests. On clear days, from the road ascending the north side, there is a dazzling view of the coast, and sometimes even as far as the island of Aruba. The limestone mountains contain more than 1,000 caverns and sinkholes, plus numerous underground rivers which spew forth their waters along the north slope.

Because of its importance as a source of water for Falcón's arid coastal towns (as well as filling **Embalse El Isiro**, a reservoir that is excellent for fishing), 20,000 hectares (49,500 acres) of the Sierra de San Luis were decreed a national park in 1987. The area's many different habitats, along with its function as a corridor for migratory birds, contribute to this being a good area for birding. Of particular note are three easily accessible areas: Cerro Galicia (the range's highest point at 1,500 meters/4,900 ft), El Haitón, and La Uria. The land around Posada El Duende, on the outskirts of Cabure, also shelters many species. The important mountain towns and villages of **San Luis** ㉓, **Cabure** ㉔, and **Curimagua** ㉕ are grouped roughly in a triangle, in an area primarily involved with coffee growing.

In the villages of **Mapararí** and El Tural, descendants of early indigenous inhabitants maintain the tradition of an ancient agrarian rite, the *Baile de Las Turas*, celebrated September 23–24, with dancing all night around an altar decorated with sugar cane stalks and ears of corn to give thanks for the harvest.

Guácharos and an underground river

La Taza ㉖ is the jumping-off place for the **Parque Nacional Cueva de la Quebrada El Toro**, best known for its three caverns which are among the largest in the country. In the dry season, it is sometimes possible to drive from La Taza to the park, but if there has been any rain a four-wheel-drive vehicle is essential. You can contract locals to drive you there if you do not have a 4x4. The caves can be visited only with the park's personnel. Flashlights and photography are permitted.

The second cave is the most interesting, with night-flying, fruit-eating *guácharos* (oil birds) and the largest subterranean river in Venezuela. This is narrow and shallow up to the part occupied by the birds, but then broadens to fill the entire width of the passageway at the end of this chamber. A small boat is necessary for further exploration. Deeper within the cave, the river forms two great reservoirs. ❑

BELOW: the breathtaking view across to the coast while ascending the north side of the Sierra de San Luis.

LARA

*Since pre-Hispanic times, Lara has been the
principal crossroads for travel and commerce in the
central western region of Venezuela*

Map
on page
192

Despite the barren look of its dominant desert landscapes, Lara grows most
of the nation's produce and has one of the largest wholesale markets in
South America, which supplies all of Venezuela, as well as many
Caribbean destinations. Sold through this market are 85 percent of the grains,
75 percent of the rapidly perishable vegetables, and 60 percent of all other produce consumed in Venezuela. Lara has 80 percent of the country's largest sugar
cane growers and has proved to be ideal for growing both table and wine grapes.

This market is located in **Barquisimeto** ㉗, the capital of Lara, one of the
oldest cities in Venezuela. Barquisimeto was founded in 1552 and is now the
fourth-largest city in the country. The city is within four to five hours by road
from the main cities of Caracas, Maracaibo, Valencia, and Maracay, and the
hub for travel to the western plains and Andean states.

Capital attractions

The principal attractions in Barquisimeto are focused around the **Plaza Bolívar**
(between Carreras 16 and 17, and Calles 25 and 26). At its southwest corner is
the Iglesia de la Concepción. The original 16th-century church was destroyed,
along with most of the city, by an earthquake in 1812, but it was later rebuilt.
A block farther south is the **Museo de Barquisimeto**
(token admission fee), with exhibits ranging from art
to archeology. Two blocks north, the **Teatro Juarez**
puts on a variety of live presentations.

Two blocks east of Plaza Bolívar is **Plaza Lara**. On
the south side is the **Iglesia de San Francisco**, erected
in 1865 and Barquisimeto's cathedral until dedication
of the current modern one (Carrera 26, between Calles
20 and 29). **The Centro de Historia Larense** (Mon–
Fri 9am–noon, 3–6pm; Sat, Sun and hols 10am–5pm;
free), on the square's east side, is also worth a visit. It
has a large collection of antiques and miscellaneous
memorabilia. Also in the square is the **Ateneo de
Barquisimeto**, a popular venue for everything from
art shows to classic films.

The **Parque Zoológico y Botánico Miguel Romero
Antoni** (also known as **Parque Bararida**; closed
Mon; token admission fee), on Avenida Los Abogados
at Calle 15, is a refreshing oasis with many shade trees
and a compact yet well-stocked zoo. You can also
escape the city streets in **Parque del Este José María
Ochoa Pile** (closed Mon); you'll find this just past
Redoma Las Trinitarias, on Avenida Libertador Este,
unmissable with its giant Carlos Cruz Diez sculpture,
Homage to the Rising Sun.

The principal restaurants and modern malls in
Barquisimeto are on or around Avenida Lara, between
Paseo Los Leones and Avenida Vargas.

LEFT: the dramatic
landscape of the
Lara region.
BELOW: one of
the instrument
makers for which
the area is famous.

*Reproductions of
indigenous-style
pottery from the
Quíbor area.*

Western attractions

The main attractions outside Barquisimeto lie within about an hour's drive to the west, via the road from the Obelisco traffic circle which is clearly marked for Carora/Quíbor. About 15 minutes out of town, the highway splits: one route heads toward Carora (an hour directly west of the capital), while the other runs southwest toward Quíbor, Sanare, and El Tocuyo.

From either road, just past the split there is access to **Tintorero** ㉘, renowned for its weavers. Many homes bear signs announcing the sale of hand-woven goods. Before 2pm on weekdays or noon on Saturdays, visitors can also watch the weavers at work. Several families there also specialize in ceramics.

Southwestern route

Long before explorers arrived, the **Quíbor** ㉙ area was settled by indigenous tribes dedicated to farming and with a well-developed ceramics tradition. Under-scoring Quíbor's past, opposite the Iglesia de Nuestra Señora de Altagracia (beside the Plaza Bolívar, at Calle Pedro León Torres and Avenida 8) is the site of a famous dig in an Indian cemetery. You can visit the **Museo Arqueológico de Quíbor** (Tues–Fri 9am–noon, 2.30–6pm; token admission fee), one block south of the church, to see some of the artifacts and skeletons discovered at various local digs. If time allows, walk nine blocks north to see the ornate 17th century chapel, **La Ermita de Nuestra Señora de Altagracia**.

On entering Quíbor, signs indicate a southern bypass (lined with crafts stands) which will take you up winding roads away from the desert and into fertile verdant hills dotted with farms. You come first to **Cubiro** ㉚, whose main attraction is **Las Lomas**, above the town. With its summit usually in the clouds

BELOW: a weaver's
workshop in
Tintorero.

it can be quite cool, but visitors wrapped in sweaters flock there at weekends to rent horses or picnic in the velvety meadows.

Beyond Cubiro is **Sanare ③**. Things worth seeing here include El Cerrito, a small restored colonial zone at the southern edge of town, and, a short distance farther south, the **Parque Nacional Yacambú**, with lush cloud forests and abundant birds (attracting numerous bird watchers). Surrounded by mountains in the interior of the country, it is surprising to learn that **El Tocuyo ③** is one of the oldest towns in South America, founded on December 7, 1545. Furthermore, from 1546 until 1577, it was capital of the Province.

El Tocuyo is also known as the "Cradle of Folklore." One of its best known celebrations (June 13) is the Tamunangue, a seven-part dance preceded by a mock battle with sturdy sticks called *garrotes,* initially a form of martial art. In the earthquake of 1950, most of El Tocuyo's seven colonial temples and magnificent vintage homes were leveled. Its principal church, **Iglesia de Nuestra Señora de la Concepción**, was severely damaged, but was rebuilt by the government. Its colonial altar-pieces somehow went unharmed, and are gems.

Colonial Carora

The best-kept secret of **Carora ③** is its marvelous colonial district. Following the principal westbound avenue, at the main intersection (signs indicate Maracaibo north, Trujillo south) continue straight for seven blocks. Turn right onto Calle San Juan, which is lined with handsomely restored homes and leads to the plaza and 17th-century **Iglesia San Juan Bautista**. In contrast to this church's restrained design is the handsome baroque **Capilla del Calvario**, built in 1787, at the end of the southbound street bordering the plaza. ❑

Map on page 192

TIP

Tours of Bodegas Pomar winery, Carora, whose wines and champagnes have gained international acclaim, are available for groups with advance reservations, tel: (252) 21 2191.

BELOW: Carora's beautiful colonial zone.

NORTHERN ZULIA

The city of Maracaibo, northern Zulia, is the hub of the nation's oil industry. Its inhabitants also lead a startling mixture of modern and traditional life styles

Map on page 218

Caracas

For newcomers, the strongest initial impressions of northern Zulia are the large presence of indigenous women in traditional native dress, the forest of oil derricks in Lake Maracaibo, and the perpetually hot, sunny climate. Nicknamed *La Tierra del Sol Amada* – "the land of the beloved sun" – the average year-round temperature is 28° C (82° F). Those used to cooler climes may melt at first, unless they follow the lead of the locals. By dawn, residents are on their way to work and markets are a beehive of activity. But, being neither mad dogs nor Englishmen, they do not go out in the midday sun: instead they take a long break until around 3–4pm for a leisurely lunch at home or with friends in one of the many excellent restaurants, then enjoy a snooze, or head for a park. They then restart their activities once the heat of the day has passed.

Oil capital

To most of the world, mention of Venezuela conjures up one image: oil. And **Maracaibo ❶**, rather than being known just as the capital of Zulia state, is considered "capital" of the nation's petroleum industry.

Although Lake Maracaibo separates the capital from the oil fields along the eastern shore, the city of Maracaibo is the seat of power of the industry. Modern high-rise towers, filled with offices of the oil companies and those providing complementary goods or services, as well as plush urbanizations populated by oil company executives, each attest to the effect of petroleum wealth on the city.

In pre-oil days, Maracaibo's geographical position contributed to its development as a transit point for voyages across the Atlantic – with the lake also providing a shipping link between the Andean states and the coast for important products such as coffee. With silver, gold, and other riches from across the continent also loaded in Maracaibo, the city was a frequent target for pirates. In the 1800s, brisk trade between Venezuela and the nearby Dutch islands boosted Maracaibo's commerce. However, it was the announcement by the entrepreneurs at the Barrosos No. 2 oil well on December 14, 1922 of the wealth that lay below its surface that changed the course of Venezuela's history.

Viewing the oil derricks

The huge deposits along the northwestern shores of Lake Maracaibo lie principally below the water's surface, thus you see only grasshopper pumps and an occasional derrick on land. To view those in the lake, there are access roads to the dike bordering the lakeshore from the oil towns such as **Tía Juana ❷** and **Lagunillas ❸**. Your best bet is to enlist the ser-

PRECEDING PAGES: fish for dinner. **LEFT:** entering the mouth that feeds you. **BELOW:** a Guajira woman.

vices of local taxi drivers who know the best access routes. The visual impact of the forest of derricks covering the lake surface etches a graphic impression of the vast liquid wealth being extracted, that no words can equal. However, taking photos of the derricks is illegal for security reasons – so if you see a National Guardsman approaching, stash your camera.

Access to Maracaibo from the east is via the **Rafael Urdaneta Bridge**, the longest pre-stressed concrete span in the world, 8 km (5 miles) long and 50 meters (164 ft) above the water at its highest point to permit easy passage by giant oil tankers. It crosses **Lake Maracaibo ❹**, the largest lake in South America, at the neck of water between the lake and the Gulf of Venezuela in the Caribbean Sea. Just east of the bridge is the **Hipódromo de Santa Rita**, Maracaibo's horse-racing track (races Wed, from 5.30pm; free entry; *see pages 102-3*).

Feisty residents

Despite the presence of oil, fishing is still a source of income on Lake Maracaibo.

The oil boom shaped the city and its people. Maybe it's the heat or the hard labor required to sweat out a living in the oil fields or on the region's cattle ranches, but something toughens the *maracuchos*, as local residents are known. Easily identifiable by a mile-a-minute way of speaking, a *maracucho* man would think nothing of walking into a Caracas bar wearing a hand-lettered T-shirt bearing a politically sensitive message. And nobody is likely to bother him too much either. *Maracucho* machismo is the stuff of legends.

BELOW: Sunday service at Maracaibo Cathedral.

Reshaped city

Government coffers loaded with oil money bank-rolled urban development based on the notion that "modern is best." In a controversial move, most of

Maracaibo's oldest neighborhood, **El Saladillo**, was razed to make way for a seven-block-long park and pedestrian boulevard, **Paseo Las Ciencias**.
An attack on tradition provoked public ire over the move. The wrecking ball leveled a great concentration of the unusual Maracaibo-style houses characterized by marked Dutch influence, with tall windows and doors, elaborate designs applied to the facades, and vivid contrasting colors. But even more than the buildings themselves, was the loss of the heart of one of the two rival districts claiming to be birthplace of the *gaita*, the traditional music of the *maracuchos* (who maintain this destruction killed the city's "spirit").

Originally, the *gaita* had lyrics with a pious theme, dedicated to various saints, but the prevalent form now is a popular (some would say profane) adaptation which is political, humorous, and totally irreverent – no topic or person is sacred. Lively verses are sung to music typified by the use of the *furruco* and metal *charrasca*. The first makes a distinctive deep sound produced by rhythmically stroking a pole fastened to the head of a drum; and the latter is a rhythm instrument looking like a metal grater, played with a small rod.

Paseo de Las Ciencias, filled with trees, benches, and sculptures by Venezuelan artists, extends from the **Plaza Bolívar ❶** to the church dedicated to Zulia's patron saint, the **Basílica de Nuestra Señora de Chiquinquirá ❷**. This is where you will find the main historic sites of Maracaibo.

Beginning at Plaza Bolívar, unmistakable with its statue to The Liberator in the center, the restored colonial **Cathedral ❸** is home to the highly venerated Black Christ of Maracaibo, a statue dating from the 16th century. Two blocks behind it stands the **Capilla de Santa Ana ❹**, a colonial chapel with a fabulous *mudéjar* (moorish-style) ceiling and handsome vintage altar-piece. Diagonally

Maps:
Area 218
City 220

The season for gaitas is considered to be October 15 to February 2. But due to the increasing popularity of the music, it is now heard all year long in Zulia, and Caracas clubs and restaurants import the best-known gaita groups during the Christmas season.

BELOW: colors of Maracaibo's Santa Lucía district.

across from the chapel is the **Mercado de los Guajiros** . Next to the cathedral are the **Casa de Gobierno** , state government headquarters in an impressive early 19th-century building with two-story arcade, and the **Casa de la Capitulación** or Casa Morales. The latter was the home of the last Spanish Captain General in the city, Francisco Tomás Morales. The Casa Morales is now the only remaining residential colonial building in Maracaibo. The Treaty of Capitulation was signed here by Spanish forces defeated in the 1823 battle of Lake Maracaibo. It is now a museum (Mon–Fri; free). Its neighbor, the **Teatro Baralt** , was reopened in 1998 after years of restoration.

Behind the theater is the **Calle de la Tradición** (its real name is Calle Carabobo or Calle 94), a restoration of the few houses of the old Saladillo neighborhood that escaped demolition. Many have been turned into small stores. The focal point is **El Zaguán**, a restaurant-garden-café that hosts live entertainment.

On the other side of the *paseo* in the Concejo Municipal (city hall) is the **Museo de Artes Gráficas** (Tues–Sat; free). A block south, the Iglesia de San Francisco stands at the entrance to Plaza Baralt.

Markets past and present

At the far end of this store-lined plaza is the **Centro de Arte de Maracaibo Lia Bermúdez** (open daily; free). The huge structure entered into service in 1928 as the city's principal market. For the last 20 years it has been through hard times. Ambitious plans for restoration were initiated, and sometimes completed, but always lacked a clear vision of the ultimate purpose. Success finally came when a private group of artists and cultural activists petitioned the governor to convert it into an arts center honoring one of Maracaibo's most famous sculptors.

Although at street level many of the commercial buildings lining Plaza Baralt have been "modernized" (for the worse), if one looks hard, especially above the store fronts, there are many interesting architectural details, ranging from Herculean pillars to the head of the messenger Mercury.

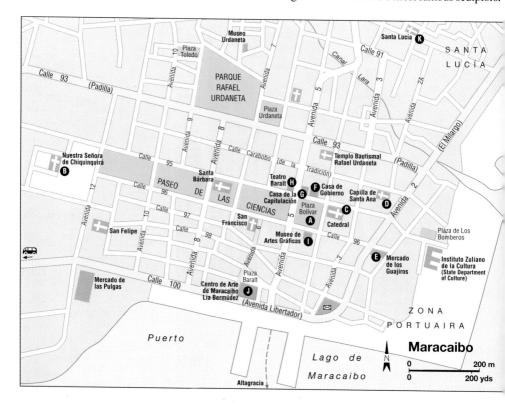

Map
on page
220

The result was the creation of a foundation with representatives from the private and public sector. The beautiful center now houses galleries, a large theater, conference rooms, a museum, an art and bookstore, and a cafeteria; dynamic programing makes it one of the city's most important cultural centers.

Opposite the art center is Maracaibo's **Mercado de las Pulgas**, or flea market. It is at once fascinating and a study in utter chaos: jammed together under the roof and outside a huge warehouse and outside are hundreds of stands, tables, plastic sheets spread out on the ground – all piled high with every imaginable type of goods. Music blares, hawkers scream offers, and bargain hunters push and shove through the narrow aisles. Most of the vendors are Guajira and Paraujana Indian women in their traditional flowing *mantas* (a floor-length, loose caftan-like dress). The market operates daily, but Saturdays are busiest.

Back to the *paseo*, the basilica, at its western end, appears to have an ornately sculptured facade. Closer inspection reveals these are all painted on. The same *trompe-l'oeil* technique is used in its elaborate interior. The focal point, however, is the tiny image of the Virgin of Chiquinquirá, affectionately known as *La Chinita* (the pebble). Legend has it that the Virgin's image miraculously appeared on a board that had floated to shore on the lake and was taken home by a local woman. *La Chinita*'s feast day, November 18, is celebrated with a week of processions, bullfights and music.

Other Maracaibo attractions

Some half dozen blocks north of the historic zone is the Santa Lucía district. Getting its name from the **Iglesia de Santa Lucia** at its hub, this is the rival area of the old El Saladillo neighborhood. It also claims to be birthplace of the

A local maracucho *fast-food treat is* patecones. *This is a sandwich, but one in which bread is replaced with fat slices of green (i.e. starchy, not sweet) plantain that have been pounded to pancake thickness and deep fried until crisp on the outside, tender on the inside.*

BELOW: religious icons outside the cathedral.

gaita and has Maracaibo-style architecture. Some houses by the church have been restored, but most need a dose of loving care. Principal commercial streets are Avenida 5 de Julio and Avenida Bella Vista, lined with modern shopping malls and the city's most popular restaurants. Important venues for cultural events include the **Centro de Bellas Artes** (Mon–Fri 9am–noon; Sat 8am– 12.30pm; free) and the **Museo de Arte Contemporáneo del Zulia** (MACZUL), the second-largest contemporary art museum in Latin America.

The colonial fort on Isla de San Carlos.

Northern side trips

Heading north toward the Guajira Peninsula via the road for El Moján (San Rafael on some maps), you encounter the ambitious **Complejo Científico, Cultural y Turístico Simón Bolívar** (closed Mon; token admission fee), which has a planetarium, anthropological museum, health museum, a park with an artificial lake (boats can be rented and there is a huge playground area), horse-back riding, picnic areas, and a soda fountain. There is also live music on weekends.

El Moján ❺ is the departure point for shuttle boats to **Isla de San Carlos** ❻ (with a stop at Isla Taos). A photogenic **colonial fort** on its southern point is the dominant feature of the island; with well-informed guides providing a tour. A long, wide stretch of sandy, shadeless beach extends northward.

Indigenous homeland

BELOW: the *palafitos* of Sinamaica Lagoon.

Continuing northward from El Moján, after crossing the El Limón bridge, at **Sinamaica** ❼ follow signs to the *muelle* (dock) at Puerto Cuervito, where the indigenous Paraujano offer boat tours to the **Laguna de Sinamaica** ❽. The traditional construction of the Paraujanos (meaning the water or boat people) is

Map on page 218

a one-room *palafito*, built independently on piles in the lagoon, with thatched roofs and walls made of *esteras* – reed mats lashed together. All movement between houses and to the shore is by boat. It was this same type of dwelling that prompted Amerigo Vespucci in 1499 to call the area *Venezuela* – "little Venice" – because it reminded him of his Italian hometown.

In Maracaibo, it is impossible for most people to differentiate between the Guajiro and the Paraujano since their most identifiable trademark is the *manta* worn by the women of both groups (the Paraujano copied the style from the Guajiro). However, in their homelands, one knows immediately which is which. The Paraujano are sedentary, living on the water, and depending primarily on fishing for their livelihood. The Guajiro, on the other hand, are nomadic, erecting temporary houses, and moving freely between the border lands of Venezuela and Colombia with their herds of goats and cattle.

Los Filudos ❾, just beyond Paraguaipoa, 32 km (20 miles) north of Sinamaica, is the site of the **Guajiro market** (Saturdays and Mondays are usually the busiest days). It's not geared toward tourists, so don't expect to find indigenous crafts here, although their finely woven hats and amulets are plentiful. This is where fresh produce and livestock, piles of animal hides, medicinal herbs, and kitchen equipment and other utilitarian items are sold. It is also one of the few places outside the wild upper Guajira Peninsula where you see Guajiro men in traditional *guayucos* (a cross between a diaper and short sarong) and hear practically nothing except their native language. Go early to the market, since it is active only in the cool morning hours.

The National Guard warns against going farther north than Paraguaipoa because of dangerous border problems and drug-trafficking. ❑

The Guajiros are fiercely independent. They simply ignore any governmental attempts to control their cross-border movements or make them get cédulas *(national ID cards); they are Guajiros and they move about as they please.*

BELOW: the Guajiro market.

THE ANDES

With its principal peaks soaring to breathtaking heights, the Venezuelan Andes present a dramatic surprise in a predominantly lowland, tropical country

Map on page 228

Caracas

Logically, a visit to the Andes promises some distinct contrasts to Venezuela's sun-drenched beaches, Amazon rainforests, or the great central plains. And, even within the the the Andes themselves, visitors will be surprised at the great variety in climate, landscapes, lifestyles, folkloric customs, and much more. However, just looking at the landscapes alone – from tropical forests and coffee plantations in the foothills to barren high moors, glacial, lakes, and snow-capped peaks – gives you a clue that a trip through these mountains is likely to be a highly rewarding experience.

Regular commercial flights go from Caracas and other major cities to key destinations including Valera, Mérida, Santo Domingo (servicing Táchira's capital of San Cristóbal), and San Antonio de Táchira; or you can take a bus. But you should go by car to fully savor this beautiful region, to be able to stop to inspect fragile orchids growing alongside the road, sample smoked trout at a roadside stand, and to walk through the cobblestone streets of a remote colonial village.

PRECEDING PAGES: mule trains through the mist. **LEFT:** a roadside ice grinder. **BELOW:** the rooftops of Mérida.

Take the scenic route

The most scenic route through the Venezuelan Andes can be enjoyed by taking the westbound exit for Biscucuy in Trujillo state from Guanare in Portuguesa.

The road almost immediately begins to climb, passing through a major coffee-growing region as it winds through the mountains toward **Boconó ❶**.

Slopes are covered with coffee plants shaded by towering "mother trees," nearly every house has a large patio for drying harvested beans in the sun, and the air is redolent with the aroma of toasting coffee.

Boconó was dubbed "The Garden of Venezuela" by Simón Bolívar for its variety of flora. Today, the name more fittingly applies because of the multitude of farms blanketing surrounding hills.

Worth seeking out downtown, half a block north of Plaza Bolívar, is **La Vieja Casa** (closed Tues and 3–7pm daily), a delightful restaurant and museum. Following the main downhill street, past the front of the church, you'll find the **Museo Trapiche de Los Clavos** (Tues–Sun; 8am–noon, 2–5pm; token entry fee). This restored 19th-century sugar mill contains three museums (coffee, brown sugar, and botanic) as well as offering cultural events.

The best places for local crafts are at the **Centro de Acopio Artesanal** (Tues–Sun, 8am–4pm; free) located within the farmer's market, and also the **Centro de Servicios Campesinos Tiscachic**, three blocks north on the last street before the bridge as you leave town. This artisan cooperative with reasonable prices sells some unusual stone-polished black pottery made by the Briceño family, and particularly

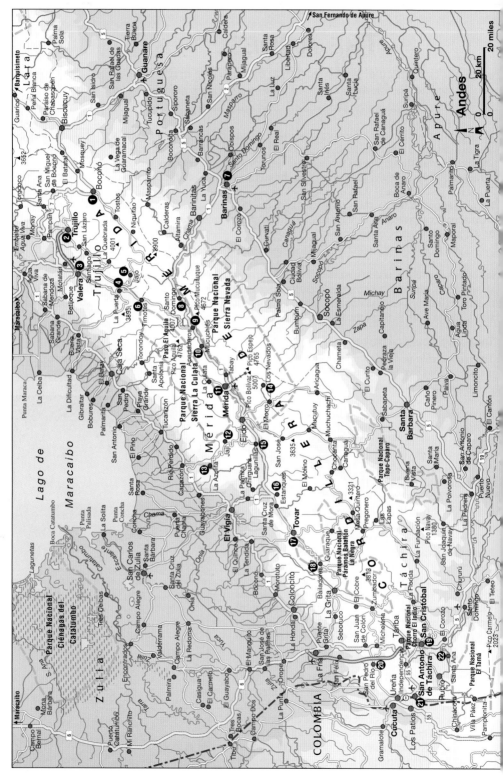

outstanding carved wood *arte popular* (naïf art) sculptures; Trujillo's most famous artist of this genre, Rafaela Baroni, lives in Boconó.

There are several interesting villages en route to Valera: **San Miguel de Boconó** is worth a visit. It has a polychrome altar-piece in its colonial church and a singular annual festival on January 6, with more fascinating folkloric and religious ceremonies on one day than you will see elsewhere in Venezuela. It is also worth stopping off at **Santa Ana**, with pretty traditional streetscapes, and **Burbusay**, which has another outstanding altar-piece in its 18th-century church.

Map on page 228

Heading south

Detouring to the south takes you to **Trujillo ❷**. Once you have passed through **Plazuela**, the state's capital and a restored colonial zone, then battled your way through Trujillo's shopping area to the Centro, exploring is easy as there are only two main streets: Independencia (one-way southbound) and Bolívar (one-way northbound). Various handsome colonial structures, including the 17th-century **Cathedral**, are by the Plaza Bolívar.

South of town, you can visit the 46-meter (150-ft) tall image of the Virgen de la Paz overlooking Trujillo (an internal elevator goes to the top). And farther south is the pristine 17th-century village of **San Lázaro**. You can continue on a good unpaved road along the mountain crests to Santiago, La Quebrada, and on to **Valera ❸**. This is the state's largest and most economically important city – although it has little to interest tourists. **Motatán**, 12 km (7 miles) north of Valera, has hot springs at Hotel Hidrotermal San Rafael. Detour west from Valera for **Isnotú**, best known as birthplace of Dr José Gregorio Hernández, founder of bacteriology in Venezuela and postulated for sainthood for his philanthropic labors attending the poor.

To take the alternate southbound "fast route" to the cities of Mérida or San Antonio del Táchira through the tropical lowlands and cattle country bordering Lake Maracaibo, continue west past Isnotú and Betijoque to join Highway 1 (taking the turn-off at El Vigía for Mérida).

Before **La Puerta ❹**, known as the "gateway to the Andes", landscapes are pretty; beyond it, they are spectacular, as you pass through soaring mountains with terraced fields and ancient houses with pounded-earth walls, where farmers still work the land with wooden plows pulled by oxen. **Jajó ❺** (37 km/22 miles east of La Puerta) is a thoroughly picturesque colonial village.

Mérida

Mérida state is known as *el techo de Venezuela* – "the roof of Venezuela" – with the country's highest peaks permanently capped by snow.

The people of this often harsh Andean terrain are hardworking, resourceful, and religious, and Mérida is an enclave of tradition. Peasant farmers eke out a living on steep terraced plots. Villages with Indian names are strategically located about a day's mule trek apart. Often these settlements are little more than clusters of crooked, red-roofed, single-story houses built flush against the narrow road.

TIP

Comfortable daytime temperatures tend to prevail all year long in Trujillo. However, at night or if it is particularly rainy it can turn chilly.

BELOW: stand selling local produce.

As you continue toward the city of Mérida, the state's capital, the route is never boring – with views or hairpin turns, switchbacks, and a few sheer drop-offs. The Transandean Highway traces part of the trail Simón Bolívar braved on his campaign to liberate Nueva Granada (Colombia).

The first stop in Mérida state is **Timotes** , legendary among trout fishermen. Casting for brown and rainbow trout is a popular sport in the streams and lagoons all over Mérida.

Some 45 km (28 miles) from Timotes, you'll reach the freezing **Paso El Aguila** (Eagle Pass), just below **Pico Aguila**. This is the highest point in the Venezuelan highway system, at an elevation of 4,000 meters (13,125 ft). Bolívar and his troops marched through the pass in 1813 on the Admirable Campaign that concluded with his triumphant entry into Caracas.

If you aren't prepared for the chill, you may want to stop at a roadside stand to purchase a *ruana*, the woolen poncho of the region. The most distinctive style is made of double-sided cloth – one side red, the other blue.

Barren beauty

The area above the treeline – from about 3,500 meters (11,500 ft) – is called the *páramo* (high moor). The Venezuelan expression "to end up in the *páramo*" is used to describe someone at death's door. Life is hard here, for the climate is cold, windy, and wet. Little grows at these altitudes, but it is not all bleak. The poverty is not as widespread as in the Andean regions elsewhere in South America. And the terrain has its own eerie beauty. If you visit in October, you will see the *frailejón* at the height of its flowering period. This plant has fuzzy leaves and usually yellow flowers that grow on tall stems up to 2 meters (6 ft) high.

The trout season is mid-March through September. Permits are available (weekdays only) from the Ministerio de Agricultura y Cría in Mérida or the Oficina Nacional de Pesca of the MAC in Caracas.

BELOW: walking in the Andean foothills in Mérida state.

Map on page 228

One particularly unusual type can be seen at the beginning of the road from Paso El Aguila, via the quaint farm village of **Piñango**. These look more like trees with thick trunks formed of layer after layer of dead leaves, some of which are up to 200 years old. Another, the *frailejón morado* (purple *frailejón*) is well known for its medicinal benefits.

Andinos have numerous ingenious uses for *frailejones*. They wrap home-churned butter in one type to impart a delicate flavor and stuff another type in mattresses. They fry the pith of the stems of yet a third kind for munching.

Birders will find the *páramo* a rewarding challenge. Mérida harbors nearly 600 species of bird. In the rainy season, from May through October, when the wildflowers bloom, the high plain positively buzzes with hummingbirds; the *frailejones* attract the bearded helmetcrest.

Friar's delight

The Transandean Highway winds through the *páramo* to Apartaderos. From there you can backtrack, along the road to **Barinas** ❼, to visit the famous **Hotel Los Frailes** (Friars Hotel). Probably the most attractive and popular resort in Mérida, the hotel is built on the site of a 17th-century monastery and offers comfortable rooms with wooden beams set around a cobblestone courtyard with a fountain. If you ask in advance, you can hire horses to ride across the *páramo*. The hotel offers a fine, rather elegant restaurant. Even if you find no room at the inn (reservations must be made well in advance), be sure to visit the dark, cozy bar where a fire roars in the hearth. Try one of the local drinks, such as *calentado*, a toddy with the anise liqueur *miche*, brown sugar, and hot water; or *ponche andino*, with warm milk, *miche*, brandy, and cinnamon.

The frailejón *is considered the symbol of the* páramo. *Some 45 varieties of these "tall friars" grow here.*

BELOW: mountain village near Mérida.

If you decide to go for a hike behind Los Frailes, be wary of the "killer llamas" kept in one of the fields. Many people have suffered aggressive attacks from these "cuddly" animals, apparently triggered by the males' jealousy of anyone entering their territory.

Returning northwest on the main highway again brings you to the town of **Santo Domingo** ❽, with its trout farm, Truchicultura El Baho. The rare Andean cock-of-the-rock bird can be found in the countryside around Santo Domingo.

Mountain park

The Parque Nacional Sierra Nevada, extending from Santo Domingo to well south of the city of Mérida, includes the Andean ranges of Serranía Nevada de Santo Domingo and Sierra Nevada de Mérida. Besides the mountains, the national park encompasses *páramo* dotted by *frailejones*, pine forests, and some 170 glacial lagoons. The largest, Laguna Mucubají, appears bleak at first but offers an abundance of birds, including the speckled teal, black-chested buzzard-eagle, and the páramo pipit. Snow from Pico Mucuñuque, the highest mountain in the Santo Domingo range, melts into streams that feed the enchanting Laguna Negra, an hour's hike from the park entrance. Laguna Los Patos is a hard, 2.4-km (1½-mile) trek past Laguna Negra. Fishing, camping, and horse-back riding are allowed in areas of the park. Between Pico El Aguila and Apartaderos is the exit for the Observatorio Astronómico Nacional de Llano del Hato (high season, daily 10am–10.30pm; low season Sat 10am–10.30pm, Sun 10am–4.30pm; admission fee). Visitors may view the heavens from this observatory, at 3,600 meters (11,800 ft), with four giant telescopes.

Culinary treats

By the intersection of the Transandean and the Barinas highways lies **Apartaderos** ❾, famous for its cold, cured hams, which hang from the rafters of roadside *charcuterías* (delicatessens). The meat tastes like Italian prosciutto.

BELOW: highway through the Andes.

Cold, smoked sausages are another local specialty, and many Venezuelans wouldn't consider a visit to Mérida complete without bringing home the bacon, so to speak. *Charcuterías* also stock the local white cheese, *queso del páramo*, which is available smoked *(queso ahumado)*.

Many people fry cheese as part of an Andean breakfast that also includes *arepas* made of wheat, rather than cornmeal. Other *charcutería* staples are *mantecada*, sweet bread made with a yellow cornmeal base, and bottles of *miche*.

Map on page 228

Lush valleys

As you descend from the *páramo*, you'll notice sweeping green valleys, fields of yellow mustard, bright and slender carnations (destined for markets around the country), exotic orchids and lilies, and dahlias. Most farms are still small, labor-intensive operations. Farmers grow potatoes, garlic, carrots, onions, and all manner of other vegetables. In the valleys you'll find every kind of fruit tree, including mango, orange, and avocado. Berries are gathered from bushes in the wild as well as cultivated.

Farmers in the area till their fields with wooden plows pulled by oxen, maintaining this is the most efficient, effective, and economical method to deal with smallholdings where the soil is full of rocks, the fields are often steep and narrow, and each property is small. You'll see that fields are divided by stone walls. All this rock was painstakingly pulled from the soil to make the land tillable. The walls serve to define property lines, fence in animals, and act as a depository for rocks that at times seem to "grow" better than the crops. Some of the walls at Apartaderos are said to date back to the time of the Timoto-Cuica Indians, and the fields are still called by their traditional Indian name, *poyos*.

BELOW: harvesting by hand is still the norm in the Andes.

Here and there you will see a large, low circular wall in the middle of a field. These are primitive mills, still in use, where the walls keep animals harnessed to a long pole attached to a central pair of millstones in a circle, which they rotate to grind up the grain.

When the Spanish arrived in the area during the 17th century, they found a civilization of skilled farmers. The native population were growing more than 30 crops, including maize, potatoes, squash, and beans. The *conquistadores* killed many of the men and married the women, so today there are hardly any pure Amerindians. But the indigenous culture has survived in the foods, the folklore, and to a degree, the place names. Most celebrations honoring Catholic saints feature dancing to the beat of drums and *maracas* (typically indigenous) and dressing in costumes with masks. Nearing Mérida city, you'll notice several names with the prefix *mucu*, a native word meaning "place of."

Farther along the Transandean Highway at **San Rafael de Mucuchíes** is a curious little chapel made of thousands of stones. It was pieced together by the enigmatic Juan Félix Sánchez, an artist who was also revered locally as a mystic. He finished the project in 1984, when he was 84 years old. The chapel is actually a small replica of the one Sánchez built at his isolated homestead in El Tisure, high in the mountains. Sánchez was honored with the National Prize for Art when he was 90 years old. While his chapels and carved wood scuptures are best known, it was his beautiful weaving that first brought him fame. He died just short of reaching the century mark.

An Andean breed of dog

The next town, **Mucuchíes** ⑩, has a tidy plaza dominated by a blue and white church, and also features a famous statue of a native boy, Tínjaca, and his dog, Nevado (Snowy). The story goes that Simón Bolívar stayed in the area in 1813 and that his host gave the boy and the dog to El Libertador as a sign of allegiance. Supposedly, they both stayed faithfully by Bolívar's side until they were shot down and killed in battle. The dog Nevado was a Mucuchíes breed – seen usually only in the Andes and the closest thing Venezuela has to a national canine. When fully grown, the dog resembles a Saint Bernard and has a white coat splotched with brown and black.

The Mucuchíes breed was developed in the early 18th century, when Spanish monks established a monastery in the Andes and began raising sheep. They imported Pyrenean mountain dogs from Europe to guard their flocks; the dogs mixed with local mutts to eventually create the Mucuchíes.

Although the Pyrenean mountain dogs were prized for their loyalty, obedience, and strength, Mucuchíes have an added characteristic: ferocity. They are often used as guard dogs on Andean farms. A colorful local celebration for San Benito is held in the town of Mucuchíes on December 29 *(see page 80)*.

Stepping back in time

Along the highway, only about 20 minutes north of the city of Mérida (between Mucuchíes and Tabay), is the popular Los Aleros (daily 8am–6pm; admission fee), the re-creation of a typical Andean village of times past. Visitors go up to the old hilltop settlement in old-time buses to explore the buildings constructed using the traditional pounded earth method; demonstrators in vintage clothing go about their chores just

BELOW: chapel of San Rafael de Mucuchíes.

Map on page 228

as they did in the past, baking bread in a wood-fired oven, arranging type in the print shop, and so on. Live music, a daily wedding, and such like are also part of the fun. This was created by 100 percent private initiative on the part of Alexi Montiel. Due to its success, he subsequently opened another place with the same idea but broader scope, Alexi's Venezuela de Antier, via Jají. Although interesting, both charge expensive admission fees.

Beside Los Aleros is **Delicattesses Catalina** (open daily 8am–6pm) which, in 1993, moved its principal location here from the original outlet on the El Valle–La Culata highway north from the city of Mérida (they now have a smaller shop there and another in the Mercado Principal). Since 1984, this operation of the Ramírez family has become famous for its 100 or so flavors of homemade conserves, plus cakes, smoked trout, and cheeses.

A tranquil place to live

Even the metropolitan state capital of **Mérida** ⓫, which shares the state's name, maintains a tranquil air. It is not a beautiful city, but its setting is spectacular. Located on a high plateau with the Chama River at is base, it is accented by trees draped with Spanish moss, and enjoys a dramatic backdrop of five of the highest peaks in the Venezuelan Andes. Locals call the mountains Las Cinco Aguilas Blancas ("The Five White Eagles"). They are La Corona, La Concha, La Columna, El Toro, and El León. La Corona is actually two peaks, Humboldt and Bonpland, and La Columna comprises Espejo and Bolívar. All are more than 4,700 meters (15,420 ft) high; Bolívar, at just over 5,000 meters (16,400 ft), is the highest.

Over 250,000 people live in Mérida city, including more than 35,000 students who study at the **Universidad de Los Andes** (ULA). The community definitely

An unexpected change in Mérida from the ubiquitous statues of Simón Bolívar.

BELOW: Andean people.

has a university flavor, an intellectual atmosphere, and an animated nightlife (as well as occasional disruptive – and noisy – demonstrations).

Difficult beginning

Mérida may seem a tranquil place today, but its foundation involved scandal and bloodshed. Juan Rodríguez Suárez, an officer who was supposed to be exploring the Sierra Nevada with a party of soldiers in 1558, decided to found a town, which he named after Mérida in Spain. In those days, towns were founded only by royal proclamation, so Rodríguez Suárez found himself in serious trouble. He was branded a criminal, and tried and sentenced to a gruesome death. But sympathizers intervened and helped him flee to Trujillo, where he was granted the first political asylum in the New World.

Rodríguez Suárez had founded Mérida on the site of present-day Lagunillas. Hostile Indians forced the settlers to pack up and move some distance to the east, to a place now known as La Punta. Finally, Juan Maldonado y Ordóñez, the man who had arrested Rodríguez Suárez, established Mérida once and for all at its present site, giving it the grand name, La Ciudad de Santiago de los Caballeros de Mérida. *Caballeros* means gentlemen, and for many years Mérida was known simply as "the gentlemen's city." Even today, Mérida remains perhaps the most polite metropolitan area in Venezuela. *Merideños* tend to be well-mannered, but also reserved and conservative.

In Mérida there is great respect for the Church. When Pope John Paul II first visited the country in 1985, he drew consistently large crowds here. There is also respect for Simón Bolívar. Mérida was the first place to proclaim him *El Libertador* – on May 23, 1813. As an indication of the degree of admiration, up

BELOW: handwoven rugs: an Andean specialty.

Maps, pages 228 & 236

until recently one would have been subject to police reprimand for carrying a large bundle, suitcase, or backpack too close to Bolívar's statue in the plaza.

Not surprisingly, given the setting, *merideños* appreciate nature and sports. Within the city alone they have around 40 parks and gardens. The climate at this altitude (1,645 meters/5,400 ft) is pleasant and moderate. It's usually warm in the daylight hours – from 21–31°C (70–80°F), but at nightfall the mercury drops and it gets nippy – about 5°C (40°F). Siesta hour is a good time to head to one of the city's many parks. **Parque La Isla** features hundreds of orchids, and **Parque Beethoven** has two clocks – one made of flowers and one with wooden soldiers that march to the tune of Beethoven compositions when the hour strikes. The **Parque de las Cinco Repúblicas Ⓐ** (Park of the Five Republics) features a tall white column bearing a bust of Bolívar. When erected in 1842, this was the world's first monument dedicated to *El Libertador*. The park also has soil from each of the five countries that Bolívar emancipated.

Among Mérida's parks, perhaps the best loved is the **Parque Zoológico Chorros de Milla** (8am–6pm; high season, Mon–Sun; low season, Tues–Sun; small admission fee) with its beautiful cascades, pretty gardens, and a small zoo. Local legend says that an Amerindian princess whose lover was murdered by the *conquistadores* cried so hard that her tears turned into the falls. There's a statue of the tragic princess at the park entrance.

Beethoven Platz, in Parque Beethoven, Mérida.

City center

In the heart of Mérida is the peaceful, green **Plaza Bolívar Ⓑ**. On its south side is the **Palacio del Gobierno Ⓒ** (state government headquarters), which has a monumental triptych by painter Ivan Belsky representing the three zones of

BELOW: view over Mérida.

Mérida state, from the steamy lowlands near Lake Maracaibo to the high plain and the Andes. In the formal reception room upstairs is a painting by Jorge Arteago of Bolívar's entrance into Mérida in the Admirable Campaign of 1813. The guards usually let you in to have a look at the triptych, at least if you present some kind of identification.

Along Calle 3 is the **Casa de Cultura Juan Félix Sánchez ⓓ**, named for one of Mérida's most beloved naïf artists. About half a block off the plaza is the Universidad de Los Andes, one of the largest and oldest in Venezuela, founded in 1810 after first opening in 1785 as a seminary. A stained-glass window over the entrance bears the biblical quotation (in Latin): "You cannot hide a city on a mountain." To handle ULA's great growth, its different schools are now scattered all over the city, with the largest part near Chorros de Milla. In the Rectorada (dean's office) of the university is the **Museo Arqueológico ⓔ** (high season: Tues–Fri 8am–noon, 2–6pm, Sat & Sun 3–7pm; small admission fee), with only a small display of artifacts.

On the plaza's Calle 4 side is the long-suffering cathedral. Construction of the massive **Catedral Metropolitana ⓕ** began in 1803, but damage from war and several earthquakes necessitated continuous rebuildings, and the cathedral was completed in its present form only in 1958. The result is an eclectic architectural style. One of the paintings is supposedly of God. Beside the cathedral is the Palacio Arzobispal (Archbishop's Palace).

Located nearby is the **Museo de Arte Colonial ⓖ** (Mon–Fri 8am–noon, 2–6pm; Sat–Sun 9am–1pm; admission fee, but children under 10 free) in the recently restored Casa Juan Antonio Parra (Avenida 4, between Calles 20 and 21). It features religious paintings, furniture, and ceramics.

One block from here, within the Centro Cultural Tulio Febres Cordero (between Avenidas 2 and 3 and Calles 21 and 22) is the **Museo de Arte Moderno ⓗ** (Mon–Fri 9am– noon, 3–7pm; Sat–Sun 10am–5pm; free), with a small but high-quality collection of contemporary works by national artists.

On the side streets near the plaza are a number of colonial houses that have been converted into stores and restaurants. National Monument plaques on their walls give information about the buildings' history.

Food for thought

The many small, typical restaurants downtown serve dishes such as *trucha andina* (trout caught fresh from Andean mountain streams), usually accompanied by the small, sweet white potatoes grown in the area. The Mérida version of *hallacas*, which are *tamal*-like packets of stuffed cornmeal steamed in banana leaves, are also popular. In the rest of Venezuela, *hallacas* are strictly a Christmas food, but in Mérida they are eaten throughout the year and their filling is quite distinct, with potatoes and chickpeas *(garbanzos)* often more dominant than the usual meat base. Other local specialties are *pisca andina*, a soup with potatoes and eggs, and *mondongo* (tripe).

Local drinks include *chicha andina* (the potent Andean beverage made from corn) and hot punches such as *calentado*.

BELOW: statue of the Liberator on Pico Bolívar.

Map on page 236

The large **Mercado Principal** (Mon, Wed–Sat 7am–6pm; Tues and Sun morning only), the city's farmers' market on Avenida Las Américas, is a fascinating place to explore. Garden fresh fruits and vegetables are star attractions, but there is also a bit of everything. In season, look for baskets of sweet *fresas* (strawberries). There are always plenty of bags of *dulces abrillantados*, a chewy, taffy-like candy rolled into balls and coated with colored sugar, giving it the sparkling effect from which it gets its name; and the many small restaurants here serve more substantial fare.

Ice cream with a difference

If you are an ice cream fan with a craving for something a little different, then head straight for **Heladería Coromoto** (Avenida 3 at Calle 29; Tues–Sun, 2–10pm) in front of Plaza El Llano. Owner Manuel Da Silva Oliveira was searching for a new taste sensation when he dreamed up his first exotic – and unusual – flavor, avocado. It took 50 kg (110 lbs) of experimenting to get it right. From there, things blossomed, and in 1991, Oliveira's ice-cream parlor first entered the *Guinness Book of Records* as having more flavors of ice cream than anywhere else in the world – then with nearly 500. At the last count, the figure stood at over 700.

The flavor list takes up the entire back wall. Along with more traditional combinations for the less adventurous, there are definitely unusual options such as pumpkin, ginger, garlic, beet, fried pork rind, fresh trout, and beer. Among the most requested is *pabellón criollo*, a take-off of the national Venezuelan dish of shredded beef, black beans, rice, and plantains. Each day Heladería Coromoto offers a rotating short list (simply for logistics) of 60 flavors.

BELOW: lookout on top of Pico Espejo.

Near the southern extreme of the city, via Avenida Andrés Bello, are two other places worth visiting. **Parque Jardín Acuario** (8am–6pm; daily in high season, Tues–Sun in low season; small admission fee), along with its expected tanks with many species of fish, also has interesting displays with life-size figures depicting various aspects of traditional Andean life of the past. Highlights of the **Museo de Ciencia y Tecnología de Mérida** (just off Andrés Bello, Via Laguna La Rosa, Urb. Las Tapias with signs indicating the turn; 10am–6pm, daily in high season, Tues–Sun in low season; admission fee) include the first robot model in the world of a giant prehistoric elasmosaurus, displays on the Andean cloud forests, and optical phenomena.

After being closed for several years due to serious cable problems, the first three stages of Mérida's teleférico were finally reopened in 1996; the last section was completed in 1999.

Pico Espejo: high-wire adventure

Mérida's *teleférico* (cable car; ascents 7.30am–2pm; high season Tues–Sun; low season Wed–Sun; fee) is the highest and longest (12.5 km/7½ miles) in the world. The cars climb in four stages to the top of **Pico Espejo** (Mirror Peak) at 4,765 meters (15,630 ft), where a large statue of the Virgen de las Nieves (Virgin of the Snows), patron saint of mountaineers, stands with open arms amid the swirling mists. Departure is from **Parque Las Heroínas** ⓙ, at the end of Calle 24.

The area in front of Parque Las Heroínas has also come to be *the* gathering place for those wishing to hike in the mountains, scale the icy peaks, or go parasailing. All of the half dozen or so tour agencies and stores here offer mountaineering equipment for sale or rent, guides, and more.

No matter how warm it is in Mérida, there's always snow on Pico Espejo. Take winter clothing to beat the cold. Most people carry sweaters, ski jackets, and gloves, layering them on as they ascend.

BELOW: cable car to the top of Pico Espejo.

There are four stations along the ascent. The first part of the ride swoops up and over the Río Chama gorge, and soon the entire city of Mérida, on its long narrow plateau, is in view. **La Montana station**, at 2,400 meters (8,000 ft), offers a view of nearly the entire Chama Valley. The station has a little restaurant-bar. The second stop is **La Aguada**, at an elevation of 4,045 meters (13,272 ft). This is the starting point for many easy treks on foot, horseback, or mountain bike – normally down to the base station, or (with a guide) to La Vega and Chorros de las Nieves. Hang gliders also take off from here.

En route to the third station, **Loma Redonda**, at an altitude of 3,400 meters (11,300 ft), you'll be flying over treeless *páramo*. It's here that some people begin to feel a bit light-headed or experience a shortness of breath – symptoms of *soroche* (altitude sickness). There's oxygen at each station, and a doctor at the top. If you start to feel uncomfortable, take it slow. Drinking or eating something may help. Don't hesitate to ask for oxygen if you're getting queasy.

Just a short walk from the Loma Redonda station, past the shrine to the Virgin, you can see the twin lagoons, **Los Anteojos** (The Eyeglasses), shimmering black in the valley. At this level there are usually a number of guides with mules offering to take visitors to **Los Nevados**, a 400-year-old Indian village that's about a 6-hour hike or mule-ride away along a

Map
on page
236

steep, narrow trail. Some 2,000 people live in this agricultural settlement, where potatoes, garlic, wheat, and beans are farmed. Villagers haul their produce by mule to the *teleférico* station and whisk it down to Mérida in the cable cars. With the popularity of Los Nevados, there are now more than half a dozen *posadas* formally operating there, offering basic lodging plus optional meals.

It's cold at the top, the fourth station, but there's a store selling comforting cups of hot chocolate, big slices of cake, and other snacks. The rocky summit of Pico Espejo rises beside the platform, and if the weather isn't too gray or snowy, you can see the glacier on neighboring Pico Bolívar. A fit hiker could reach Bolívar from here in 3–5 hours, but it's a tough journey.

Day tripping

There are several trout farms in the Mérida area that are open to visitors. A few decades ago the government introduced rainbow trout from North America and the industry has flourished. Besides Truchicultura El Baho near Santo Domingo *(see page 232)*, you can visit El Paraíso at **Mucunután**, where big Mucuchíes dogs stand guard over the tanks fed by icy mountain spring water. If you're lucky, you may get to feed the fish from a large bag of nutrient-rich pellets called "trout wheat." When you see how they gobble the stuff up, you'll understand how it takes only a matter of months for the fish to grow to market weight.

Numerous local artisans – particularly wood-carvers – live along the route to Mucunután. They offer their creations at roadside stands or in their homes, with signs identifying the locations.

Via El Valle-La Culata, northbound from Mérida, there are many small stands selling typical Andean snacks and crafts. Another attraction is the **Parque**

BELOW: mists roll in on the mountain village of Jají.

Pueblito Sueños del Abuelo (high season only, 9am–5pm; admission fee), a vintage village in miniature. This drive climbs through pretty wooded hills, with the **Parque Nacional Páramo La Culata** at the end – a favorite for hikers.

Colonial restoration

A popular day trip from Mérida is to the restored colonial village of **Jají** . Buses leave from Mérida, and cab drivers will also negotiate a price to take you there. The 40-km (25-mile) ride northwest offers splendid views, following a winding mountain road washed by streams and waterfalls. The government restoration of Jají was completed in 1971. Houses have traditional wooden grilles on the windows. Almost everything worth seeing is clustered around the plaza with its typical church, souvenir shops, and places where tourists can grab a snack. It's all charming, but sometimes the place is almost overwhelmed by tourists, mostly Venezuelans.

La Azulita ⓭ is a lovely little village near Jají, located in the midst of mountains covered with lush tropical forests, accented by crystalline streams and occasional waterfalls, and abounding with avifauna. The setting serves as a magnet for birders and other nature lovers; as well as a large number of alternative religious and spiritual groups attracted by the consummate peace and serenity of the setting.

Remote villages

Deep in the mountains south of the city of Mérida, are a number of small villages, **Los Pueblos del Sur**, which, because of their isolation appear untouched by time. Access to most is only possible by 4x4, by mule, or on foot; except for Pueblo Nuevo, which is an easy drive by car. All have one or more basic *posadas*. Best known is **Los Nevados** ⓮. Insiders recommend going by road (4–5 hours) with one of the *"Toyoteros"* who gather in the early mornings at Mérida's Plaza Las Heroínas, staying overnight, then returning by mule (4–5 hours) to the third cable car station. You can then descend the rest of the way by that means.

Other routes through the mountains include going from Las González, via Tierra Negra (top spot for paragliding), to San José, the Páramo de San José (with dozens of different species of *frailejones*), Mucutuy, and Mucuchachí; from Estanques via El Molino, Las Mesas, Canaguá and Chacantá; and from Tovar via San Francisco and Guaraque to Mesa Quintero.

Changing landscapes

Once south of the city of Mérida, the mountains change dramatically, with those bordering the highway (which follows the Chama River) dry and scarred with deeply eroded surfaces. You pass the entrances marked for various villages to the north of the highway: **Lagunillas** ⓯ is best known for its Laguna de Urao, from which soda crystals have been "harvested" since long before the arrival of colonizers; and **Chirguará** has a central area with a very photogenic old look, and a surprising xerophytic garden near the entrance to town.

BELOW: dumplings on a street stand.

Map on page 228

From **Estanques** ⓰ southward the landscapes become very tropical. Sugar cane, coffee, and bananas are the important crops. Just beyond this village is the La Victoria *alcabala* (National Guard checkpoint). Right next to it is the beautiful Hacienda La Victoria, originally the focal point of the coffee plantation which commercially produced coffee bearing its name. Several years ago it was restored, with rooms surrounding the huge central patio (formerly used to dry coffee beans) now housing the **Museo de Café** and **Museo de la Inmigración** (9am–6pm; daily in high season, Wed–Sun in low season; admission fee). The first demonstrates history, processes, and implements associated with the cultivation of coffee. The second, with old photos, documents, and personal items, deals with the Europeans who came to this area to work the first coffee plantations.

The road to the right is the old way to the Highway 1 intersection at **El Vigía** (now reached by a new toll freeway from Estanques); to the left the road continues south to Santa Cruz de Mora, **Tovar** ⓱ (the second-largest city in Mérida and heart of coffee and sugar-cane country), and **Bailadores** ⓲, near the border of Táchira state, and best known for its cultivation of strawberries and flowers.

Orchid by the roadside.

Táchira

Outside Bailadores, the highway rises steeply into the mountains and rolls on into Táchira, the home of many Venezuelan dictators. It produced at least five strongmen in the 19th and early 20th century, including perhaps the most notorious of them all, Juan Vicente Gómez. The portraits of various native sons displayed in the bars and homes of Táchira show that some locals are still proud of the mark these *andinos* made on the country.

BELOW: Santo Domingo, in the *páramo* region.

It is an interesting point of conjecture why such an isolated region should yield such a number of dictatorial rulers. One historian suggests that it may be because *tachirenses* possess "deep and unbending patriotism stimulated by their condition of being a frontier people." This may be true but other, perhaps more objective, observers have noted that the Andeans do tend to appoint their cronies to influential positions, thus ensuring a more or less inherited line of power.

Although it receives virtually no promotion, Táchira offers multiple attractions: landscapes ranging from tropical lowlands to *páramos* (high moorland), hot springs, a strong artisan tradition, colorful religious manifestations, and fairs. There is easy road access via the western plains on Highway 5, entering Táchira via Santo Domingo – site of the state's principal airport, and Highway 1, through the tropical lowlands along the eastern edge of Lake Maracaibo, via La Fría and San Juan de Colón; the more scenic approach is by Highway 7, passing through the mountains via La Grita.

Captivating capital

All routes lead to **San Cristóbal** , the capital, and an ideal base from which to explore. San Cristóbal's annual Feria Internacional de San Sebastián, celebrated at the end of January, attracts thousands of visitors who come to enjoy activities including its famous bullfights, the *Vuelta de Táchira* bicycle race (drawing competitors from around the world), and many other sporting events, agricultural exhibits, shows by big-name entertainers, and more.

San Cristóbal's highlights include the Complejo Ferial (between Avenidas España and Universidad), Plaza de Toros Monumental (bullring), Olympic Stadium, Baseball Stadium, and the **Museo Antropológico de Táchira** (Tues–Fri 9am–noon, 3–5.30pm; Sat–Sun, 10am–6pm; free). Its historic zone (Carrera 3, between Calles 3 and 6) has the requisite **Cathedral**, and colonial structures around **Plaza Juan Maldonado Ordóñez y Villaquirán** (honoring San Cristóbal's founder) and **Plaza Rafael Urdaneta**. The architecture of buildings surrounding **Plaza Bolívar** (Avenida 7 at Calle 9) present startling contrasts, with the elegantly ornate traditional design of the Salón de Lectura (cultural foundation, built 1907) on one side and modern Centro Cívico facing the other. Within the civic center is the **Museo de Artes Visuales y del Espacio** (1st floor, Torre B; Mon–Sat 8am–noon, 2–7pm; Sun 8am–1pm; free).

Fascinating architecture

Central San Cristóbal abounds with distinct architectural gems. Many such buildings, with a great variety of styles can be found along Carreras 9 and 10, between Calles 4 and 6: the epitome of the "wedding cake" and art nouveau styles are particularly evident in the elaborately decorated facades of the Universidad Abierto Nacional and its neighbor; a two-story private home with very traditional Spanish styling and whimsical owl sculptures incorporated in its window grilles. Another example worth a closer look is the colorful central doorway (the only part of the facade to have survived) of the former **Hospital Vargas** (Carrera 6, Calle Carabobo).

TIP

Advance reservations are vital for San Cristóbal's Feria Internacional de San Sebastián. Expect to pay "high season" rates – staying in peripheral towns is often a better idea.

BELOW: Iglesia San José in San Cristóbal.

Map on page 228

Three churches display particularly interesting designs: **El Angel**, on Carrera 23 at Pasaje Acueducto, with the huge figure of an angel sculpted in its facade; the Gothic-style **San José**, on Carrera 9 at Calle 8; and **El Santuario**, on Carrera 13 at Calle 13, built with stone blocks in shades of beige, ocher, and muted orange; the blocks of its interior space are painted pink, yellow, and blue).

Western loop

San Pedro del Río has a beautifully restored colonial village; it is always delightful, but more so at Christmas when numerous *pesebres* (Nativity scenes) are erected in the streets. During Easter Week, passion plays and processions take place throughout **Ureña**. Neighboring Aguas Calientes is sought out for its hot springs. **San Antonio de Táchira** ㉑ is the lively commercial border town marking the entry point to Colombia. Some nearby villages are of interest: **Rubio** is noted for its unusual brick church, while **Independencia** and **Libertad** (aka Capacho Viejo and Capacho Nuevo) are famous for ceramics and wood carving.

North and south

Palmira and **Abejales** (above Táriba) are known for split-cane baskets, while the main plaza in **Peribeca** is ringed by craft shops, cafés, and places selling local culinary specialties; there is also a distinctive Alpine-style church. Just above it is **El Topón**, a typical farm village which has been developed as a tourist attraction. Traveling between Páramo, La Negra, and Zumbador, you can enjoy beautiful mountain landscapes and traditional architecture.

The area around **Santa Ana** ㉒, to the south, is an important coffee-growing region, and **La Alquitrana** was the site of Venezuela's first oil well. ❑

TIP

A drive on the road between Zumbador and Michelena should not be missed; it follows the crest of the mountains most of the way and offers spectacular views.

BELOW: mule transport in Táchira.

Oil in Táchira

Although most people assume that Zulia was the birthplace of Venezuela's petroleum industry, this is not the case. La Alquitrana (between Santa Ana and Rubio) holds that honor. Parque la Petrolia now marks the spot where, in 1875, oil began seeping out of the ground on the land of Manuel Antonio Pulido. He obtained mineral rights and formed La Compañia Nacional Minera Petrolia de Táchira. Initially, oil was extracted in buckets from hand-dug pits, but after a trip to Pennsylvania to check out the petroleum industry there, in 1880, Pedro Rincones (an associate of Pulido) shipped back a cable-tool drilling rig to be used instead.

In 1882, a primitive distillation unit was installed and the company also sank its deepest well (42 meters/138 ft). Most of the 15 barrels a day produced were sold in Táchira for lighting. Petrolia remained the nation's only petroleum producer until 1907, when the first important concessions were granted. Its wells were still producing a small amount when its concession ran out in 1934. Some of the ancient artifacts associated with the pioneering company, including the remains of the rudimentary "refinery," are displayed in the attractive 10-hectare (25-acre) park.

THE LLANOS

Map
on page
250

The savannah is beautiful and terrible at the same time; it easily accommodates both beautiful life and atrocious death. The llanos *are terrifying; but this fear does not chill one's heart; it is hot like the great wind of its sunburnt immensity, like the fever from its swamps*

– RÓMULO GALLEGOS, *Doña Bárbara*

The vast, blisteringly hot plains, referred to as *los llanos*, hold a special place in Venezuela's mythology, something akin to the Great Plains of the United States, the pampas in Argentina, and the outback of Australia. Opened up as cattle country in the 19th century, the area became a wild frontier of cowboys and ranchers about which modern Venezuelans still become dewy-eyed.

Taking up fully a third of the country's land mass, the region contains only a minuscule fraction of its population. A single paved highway links the few, widely scattered towns in the southern *llanos*, and hard-bitten *llaneros* (as this Venezuelan breed of cowboy is known) still chase herds on horseback across the plains.

Along with this lingering "Wild West" feel, the *llanos* comprise one of the great wildlife-watching areas of South America. More bird species can be seen here than in the United States and Great Britain combined, and in such abundance that binoculars are hardly necessary. Crocodiles inhabit the lagoons; jaguars prowl its fields (though are rarely sighted by visitors), and, with luck, freshwater porpoises can be spotted in the rivers.

PRECEDING PAGES:
a line-up of *llaneros*
(cowboys).
LEFT: the man with
the golden grin.
BELOW: *llaneros*
rope a steer on
Hato Doña Bárbara.

A macho past

Eleven Spanish families were the initial colonial settlers to move into the *llanos*, introducing the first cattle ranch near the modern town of Calabozo in 1548. The production of leather and salted meat were crucial in colonial Venezuela, and the march of hooves proved unstoppable: 200 years later, more than 130,000 head of cattle roamed the enormous ranches, *hatos,* of the *llanos* while local Indian tribes had all but disappeared.

Despite the economic importance of the *llanos* and the contribution made to the independence struggle (*llanero* troops made up the backbone of Bolívar's army), the area has often aroused mixed emotions in the rest of the country. While its inhabitants were admired for their toughness, honesty, and frontier spirit, they were at first feared as barbaric, then later mocked for their backwoods slowness and lack of sophistication. Their homeland was viewed as a hot and primitive backwater best avoided by civilized folk.

When oil was discovered in Zulia in the 1920s, the country began turning its back on the *llanos*. After all, if Venezuela needed beef, it could be imported just as cheaply from abroad. Suffering from attitudes such as this, the *llanos* stagnated for decades, and only after the oil crisis of the early 1980s did Venezuelans again think of developing the vast resources to the south.

Even so, every country needs the folk memory of a romantic past, and there is a lingering feeling that the *llanos* somehow embody the "real Venezuela." Photographs of the *llanos* still hang in many Venezuelan bars, dignitaries occasionally dress in the typical *llanero* collar of the *liqui-liqui* (traditional *llanos* costume) and, most importantly, the *llanos* provided the setting for the most famous Venezuelan novel: *Doña Bárbara.*

Written by Rómulo Gallegos in 1929, it is a melodramatic and bleakly sexist work about a woman called Bárbara, who is gang-raped when young and learns to dominate and destroy men in revenge. By a mixture of seductiveness, malice, and the threat of witchcraft, she becomes the virtual ruler of the otherwise male-dominated *llanos* – that is, until an upright man from Caracas awakens her long-repressed feminine instincts and finally destroys her.

The novel nicely sums up Venezuelans' ambivalence toward the *llanos.* The hero, Santos Luzardo, finally marries Doña Bárbara's abandoned daughter – thereby bringing the refined elements of the urban dweller together with the raw, natural spirit of the frontier, and ensuring a neat ending.

White-necked heron on the llanos.

Central flatlands

The stereotypical image of the *llanos* – and indeed the principal destination for tourists visiting this region – is that of the sparsely inhabited lands south of the Apure River in the state of the same name. However, the great plains of Venezuela actually include a wide band of land stretching for nearly 1,000 km (600 miles) through the entire mid-section of the country, extending from the base of the Andes all the way to the banks of the Orinoco River, marking the western border of Delta Amacuro.

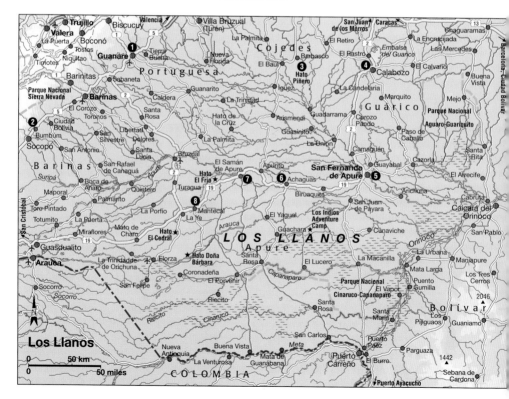

Los Llanos

For geomorphological reasons, the *llanos* are divided into the "western plains" (Portuguesa and Barinas), "central plains" (Guárico and Cojedes), "eastern plains" (Anzoátegui and Monagas), and "southern plains" (Apure).

Map on page 250

Dramatic climate changes

In the wet season (May through November), the lower *llanos* are so flooded that they look like an inland sea. Roughly 80 percent of the land of the southern and central *llanos* is under water. Many sections of even its elevated roads are covered, and cattle have to be driven to outcrops of higher ground to prevent their drowning. The dry season (December through April) is the best time of year to see wildlife, since animals congregate around receding watering holes. With the total absence of rain for nearly six months, one can also see many animals, such as the anaconda (one of the world's largest snakes), trapped to die in the thick mud that remains as the watering holes disappear.

Year round, the heat of the *llanos* is intense – although "winter" (the wet season) is, predictably, much more humid. In both seasons, the desolate plains are hauntingly beautiful.

Routes for visitors

Independent travelers with their own transportation have several routes from which to choose. They can head almost directly south from Caracas via Sombrero and Calabozo to San Fernando de Apure – the capital of Apure state, then west to La Ye through lands that are the epitome of the *llanos* image. For the relatively flat but fertile western section, go west from Caracas via Valencia then to San Carlos, Acarigua, Guanare, and Barinas – the four main towns of the

BELOW: San Juan de Los Morros, gateway to the *llanos*.

The Llaneros

The *llaneros* of Venezuela stand alongside the gauchos of Argentina as the finest horsemen in the history of South America. The true *llaneros* have now all but died out, and their descendants are rapidly shedding *llanero* traditions and dress. But even so, small groups of these tropical cowboys can still be seen on ranches in the plains of Apure and Barinas, rounding up and branding cattle using traditional skills or listening to melancholy *llanero* ballads.

The *llaneros* come from a racial mix dating back some 400 years, combining the blood of Spanish frontiersmen, escaped black slaves, and local Indians. It was during the lawless colonial days that the *llaneros* developed the distinctive customs that can still, on occasion, be seen today: their own working style and a tropical variation on the classic cowboy dress – wooden stirrups, woollen ponchos (often worn in the rain, despite oppressive heat), and straw hats.

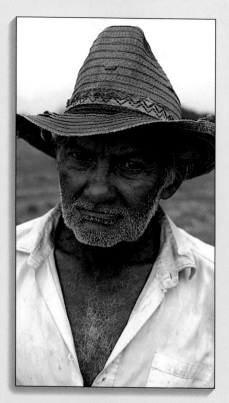

A haunting form of music began to accompany *llanero* ballads, usually about knife fights, sexual conquests, or prowess in breaking horses. In this macho cult, leaders won respect for their skills in the field, and once proven, could demand total loyalty.

The German explorer Alexander von Humboldt was impressed by the *llaneros'* toughness, especially their diet of pure salted meat, but also noted their laziness. "Being always in the saddle, they fancy they cannot make the slightest excursion on foot," he recorded. Despite their abundance, cows were never milked, and during summer, *llaneros* preferred to drink fetid yellow water rather than dig a well.

Even so, the hard-living *llaneros* became a terrifying fighting force during the wars of independence, first on the side of the Spaniards and only later with Bolívar. They made up the backbone of the Liberator's army, fighting without food or pay – instead taking both from the towns and villages they brutally pillaged. *Llaneros* did not even need to be supplied with arms, since they took a fresh supply of lance points from every outcrop of palm trees they found.

In the end, the average *llanero* gained little from his contribution to Venezuela's independence. By law, every *llanero* was given some land as reward – but the small plots proved impossible to work profitably. Wealthy officers were easily able to buy up the smaller lots, and a new landowning class was born. Most families owning *hatos* today are descended from these purchasers.

The rest of the 19th century saw a boom in beef exported to Europe, along with the declining freedom of the *llanero*. However, just as the Venezuelan cowboy began to disappear as part of an identifiable group, writers and intellectuals began to romanticize him as embodying important traits of the "national character" – independence, toughness, and an egalitarian spirit born of living in the wild. It was a mish-mash of values similiar to those being praised in diminishing frontiers as far away as Argentina, Australia, and the US, with the *llanero* standing in contrast to the sickly, Europeanized city-dwellers, cut off from the primal forces of nature. ❏

LEFT: *llanero* gaze.

western and central plains states. From Barinas, travelers can connect with La Ye. If you want to visit the other main town, apart from Calabozo and Sombrero, in the high *llanos*, detour south to El Baúl – extending this drive to Arismendi offers some great opportunities for wildlife watching.

Map on page 250

The western and central plains

The country's richest farmlands are found in the "western plains," particularly in Portuguesa. The area also has its attractions for tourists. In **Guanare ❶**, capital of Portuguesa, for instance, there is the interesting **Museo de los Llanos** (closed Mon; free), which includes in its grounds a *posada* with a western theme and, a short distance to the west of Guanare, the impressive **Templo Votivo Nacional a la Virgen de Coromoto**, the monumental national sanctuary and highly revered pilgrimage site honoring Venezuela's patron saint, which was formally dedicated by the Pope during his visit in 1995.

Barinas has various groupings of petroglyphs located near **Bumbúm ❷** and, recently, river rafting has also become popular here too – not just for the white-knuckle exhilaration of the activity, but because those taking part can also enjoy the observation of abundant wildlife in the calmer stretches.

One of the highlights for visitors to Cojedes is **Hato Piñero ❸**, east of **El Baúl**, the pioneer in Venezuela of the ranches installing tourist facilities. In fact, this was an outgrowth of the Branger family's 80,000-hectare (200,000-acre) cattle ranch, which had functioned since 1953 as a private wildlife refuge for the recovery of endangered species and the conservation of those that abound on their land; in 1982 a biological station was set up to facilitate the work of researchers studying the flora and fauna of the zone.

TIP

While in Guanare, be sure to stop at the Basilica dedicated to the Virgin of Coromoto (facing the Plaza Bolívar) to admire its beautiful 18th-century altarpiece and silver tabernacle.

BELOW: round-up time.

The installation of tourism facilities came about in answer to the many requests for a place to stay by avid birders and researchers (the income now goes to support the biological station). With land that includes a variety of life zones more typical of this section of the "high plains" – ranging from hills covered with semi-evergreen forests to wetlands and savannah subject to annual flooding – the variety of fauna is tremendous.

San Juan de los Morros, capital of Guárico state, with its backdrop of a grouping of pink sandstone *morros*, or promontories, from which its name derives, is considered "the gateway to the *llanos*" from the central region. Just minutes from **Calabozo** ❹ is the closest of the "dude" or tourist ranches, in the *llanos*, Chinea Arriba (www.chinea-arriba.com).

Into the wilderness

The city of **San Fernando de Apure** ❺ (pop. 130,000), capital of Apure state, has little appeal. The streets are mostly lined by undistinguished buildings, although one, the old Palacio Barbarito (the old customs building), is worth a look. Hunters at the turn of the 20th century would bring egret feathers they had collected, for export to Europe and the United States. The trade in these feathers was so valuable that it was the cause of ambushes, gun fights, and blood feuds. Locals say that one particularly large shipment of egret feathers actually led to seven deaths.

Adjacent to this building is a *redoma* (traffic circle) with an unusual concrete fountain based on a crocodile motif. And in another nearby traffic circle is a bronze statue of Pedro Camejo, on a rearing mount with spear in hand, one of the most famous *llanero* lancers who fought in the independence struggle,

BELOW: a saddle sale in San Fernando de Apure.

heroically dying at General Páez's feet at the Battle of Carabobo. Ringing the statue are glass containers with samples of earth from various battlefields where he fought around the country. Within sight of the plaza, craftsmen often set up informal stands from the backs of their pick-up trucks, selling a variety of leather goods: new saddles, stirrups, bullwhips, and leather boots. Other stores sell small carvings made from *azabache*, a petrified wood that is like a smooth black stone. Meanwhile, at the Apure River docks, motorboats and *bongos* (big dugout canoes fitted with outboard motors) load up with goods for delivery as far away as Ciudad Bolívar.

When you are traveling between San Fernando de Apure and **La Ye**, small towns such as **Achaguas** ❻ and **El Samán** ❼ begin to appear, each with a "Wild West" atmosphere so strong they feel like a Latino version of old Hollywood movie sets.

In **Mantecal** ❽, the largest settlement en route, unshaven men stand on the unpaved street corners, thumbs hooked in their jeans and cowboy hats cocked at a Clint Eastwood angle. Occasionally a *llanero* will amble by on horseback, or tie up his mount at a roadside post. The image continues in the bars, where everyone is served standing up, and although they would not refuse to serve a woman, there is little doubt these are strictly male domains.

In these steaming rural outposts, people tend to work from 4am to around noon, leaving the afternoon for a long siesta before returning to their labors after the heat of the day. Even the truck drivers stop work then, hitching up their hammocks in the shade beneath their rigs to take a snooze.

Map on page 250

Bracket fungi found in the llanos.

The heart of the *llanos*

Beyond Mantecal, the landscape changes from scrub to the classic Venezuelan savannah. The grassy plains stretch off to the horizon in every direction, and the only trees are perched on occasional isolated hillocks (*metas*), lost in the distance.

Driving through here, it is easy to sympathize with the German scientist Alexander von Humboldt (*see page 173*), who was aghast at the landscape during a journey in the 18th century. "*There is something awful... about the uniform aspect of these steppes,*" he wrote. "*All around us the plains seem to ascend to the sky, and the vast and profound solitude appears like an ocean covered with seaweed. Through the dry mist... the trunks of palm trees are seen from afar, stripped of their foliage and... looking like the masts of ships descried upon the horizon.*"

The road here is elevated for the rainy months. In the early 1970s the Venezuelan government started building dikes (locally called *módulos*) to help control the devastation and to save water for the dry season. These, combined with *préstamos* (artificial lagoons) that were privately installed on the sprawling ranches, provide areas of small, muddy "lakes" adjacent to the highway, and they are utterly teeming with wildlife during the dry season.

On this route, you'll be lucky to see a vehicle every hour, so it is easy to pull over for some wildlife-watching without animals being disturbed by passing

BELOW:
a contemplative local Arauco.

traffic. A great deal can be seen just from the road. White egrets pick among the reeds. Clouds of colorful birds erupt from the watering holes. Crocodiles – known as *babas* – and turtles sun themselves in the mud by the lagoons' shores, although they will disappear in a flash at any noise.

Tourist-friendly ranches

Although independent travel through the *llanos* is possible, most visitors opt to stay at one of the ranches offering tourist packages. Verify the specific dates for the change between high and low season prices before you commit yourself. And booking a week before or a week after can save you considerable cash.

While the ranches of the northern part of the plains previously mentioned are certainly enjoyable, the heart and soul of this region still remains in the *llanos adentro* – the interior of Apure state. Catering to visitors' fascination with the lifestyle of the ranches and the fabulous fauna, various ranches have followed the lead of Hato Piñero in actively working in the area of wildlife conservation. Many places now offer similar packages with lodging, meals, and excursions to observe the flora and fauna (some also specialize in fishing for peacock bass, which abound in its rivers *(see Participant Sports, pages 105–9).*

The best known of these ranches are Hato El Cedral, Hato Doña Bárbara, Los Indios Adventure Camp, Cinaruco Bass Lodge, Campamento Sorocaima, Campamento Ecológica Mata 'e Totumo, and Hato El Frío – which also has a biological station.

One of the attractions of the ranches is being able to see their everyday workings. Early in the morning *llaneros* can be seen rounding up the longhorn cattle around the ranch in the traditional manner, often chasing after them with

BELOW: the *hoatzin* is part of the exotic wildlife of the *llanos*.

lassoes. They also give demonstrations of their extraordinary riding skills, and how to swing cattle to the ground by their tails. Milking cows by hand is another dying tradition that is kept up, even though *llaneros* rarely drank the milk.

Abundant wildlife

Excursions on horseback, by boat, and in trucks especially outfitted for photo safaris are made from all of the *hatos* in the area to observe the astounding variety and quantity of fauna. Birds are a dominant feature, and it is not unusual to ride over a ridge in the farm and see a lagoon full of roseate spoonbills sieving food through their beaks – and then to be able to watch them unmolested for several minutes before they disappear in a graceful cloud.

The *llanos* are also a habitat of the world's largest rodent, the web-footed capybara (known here as the *chigüire*), which is as much at home in the water as on land. The rivers may be infested with piranhas and electric eels, which deliver a nasty shock, so swimming here is not recommended, despite the heat.

Monkeys, such as the red howler and capuchin are frequently seen, as well as deer, but don't count on seeing a wildcat. Although species including pumas, ocelots, and jaguars are found here, most visitors will be lucky even to see tracks in the mud of these human-wary animals.

A stay in the *llanos* turns out to be surprisingly affecting. Along with the heat and barrenness, the extremes of flooding and dryness, there is the serenity of being lulled to sleep by crickets or the distant haunting song of a ranch hand; or watching the activity of birds at dawn or with the background of a brilliant red sunset. Many people find that images from the *llanos* linger in their minds more clearly than recollections of yet another Caribbean beach. ❏

Map on page 250

TIP

Although some ranches receive tourists all year long, the dry season (Dec–Apr) is the best time for wildlife observation, although prices are higher at this time of the year.

BELOW: the capybara, whose numbers are multiplying thanks to their protection on the *hatos*.

THE *LLANOS* – A VENEZUELAN SAFARI

*On huge ranches, where protection of
the countryside is the norm, the abundance of
wildlife on the* llanos *is mind-boggling*

Covering nearly a
third of Venezuela,
from the base of
the Andes in the
west to the delta of
the Orinoco River
in the east, the vast,
plains, or *llanos*,
present a stunning
vista: huge ranches
(hatos) and
enormous expanses of land, but scant human
population. They include the richest farmlands in
the country in the high northwestern plains, yet
even dry grasses struggle to survive in the
lowlands to the south where, during the May
through November rainy season, they take on the
appearance of a huge inland lake. In the other half
of the year, months pass with scarcely a drop of
rain, turning the land rock-hard, and scarring it
with deep cracks.

WILDLIFE HAVENS

Thanks to limited human interference on the
extensive ranches, wildlife abounds. Many of the
hatos, realizing the importance of conserving this
treasure, have become self-designated wildlife
reserves, with strict "no hunting" policies.

Many *hatos* have now established ecotourism
camps as an up-and-coming sideline, complete
with organized excursions by boat, 4x4, or on
horseback, geared specifically toward observation
and photography of the wildlife. Many have
also compiled checklists of fauna
found on their spreads (on most,
numbers of bird species alone
exceed 300.)

Aside from the species
diversity, the quantity
of animals that gathers
around shrinking
water holes during the
dry season is stunning,
making it obvious why the Venezuelan
llanos are a lure for nature lovers.

◁ **MATERNITY WARD**
During the rainy season,
ibises *(shown here)* and
other water birds gather in
huge flocks in tree-top
areas, called *garceros*, to
build their nests.

△ **TURTLE TOTER**
Reptiles abound in *llanos*
rivers and lagoons,
including the *babas*, or
spectacled caiman; the hug
Orinoco crocodile; as well
as several species of turtle.

◁ ROLLING PLAINS
The concentration of huge ranches and lack of urban development on the *llanos* have meant that enormous areas of countryside have remained unspoiled and provide safe haven for rare plant and animal species.

△ OLD WAYS KEEP GOING
Many traditions and working practices on the ranches have changed little over the centuries, such as boiling down sugar cane juice to make a thick, honey-like syrup.

▽ SWIMMERS BEWARE!
Bathers should check before plunging into rivers and lakes here – they might be infested with piranhas, hungry caiman, or the enormous anaconda.

▷ FOR THE BIRDS
Hundreds of bird species live here, including macaws, herons, ibis, storks, vultures, hawks, the highly eccentric hoatzin, and white egrets *(shown here)*.

▽ MEDLEY OF MONKEYS
Various species of monkeys can be found on the *llanos*, including the highly vocal *araguato* – red howler – and the tiny capuchin monkey *(shown here)*.

WHERE ALSO THE BUFFALO ROAM

For the *llaneros* – the tough, independent inhabitants of the *llanos* – the central plains have been synonymous with *hatos* and cattle-raising since colonial times. Some of the ranches have bred cattle that are very resistant to the local climate and environment. Among these ranches, Hato Piñero in Cojedes state has become one of the most prestigious in South America for its work with pure-breds and for crossing breeds as diverse as ones from India and Pakistan, Holstein and Swiss Brown from Europe, and Longhorns – descendants of herds brought over by Spanish colonizers.

In recent years, many *hatos* have even introduced water buffalo, found to be well adapted to the tropical climate and producing a higher yield of meat and milk than traditional cattle. A whole new side industry has been developed on many *hatos*: making world-class mozzarella cheese!

GUAYANA REGION

This region has lured fortune-hunters, inspired great writers, and left explorers and tourists with indelible memories

The entire area to the south and east of the Orinoco River – encompassing the states of Amazonas, Bolívar, and Delta Amacuro – comprises Venezuela's Guayana Region. Despite accounting for nearly 50 percent of the nation's territory, it shelters less than 6 percent of the population – many of whom are indigenous peoples. There are more than a dozen different groups, ranging from those who have had significant contact with *criollos* (people of mixed Spanish-American descent) to others who, because of the remoteness of their homelands, have changed little since the Stone Age.

The region's name comes from its geological base: the Guayana Shield of pre-Cambrian rock, nearly 3 billion years old, among the most ancient on earth. The oldest parts of this formation are concentrated in the entire Gran Sabana region of Bolívar state and in the *tepuyes* of Amazonas.

Without a doubt, the region's most distinctive features are its *tepuyes* – mesas of ancient rock formed through a process of erosion over millennia and towering majestically above the surrounding grasslands or jungle. Those who have explored their summits describe the environment as seeming to be from another place and time, incomparable with anywhere else. And, indeed it is. Isolated from the surrounding land for millions of years, a great percentage of the flora and fauna is endemic, having evolved to adapt to the extremes of temperatures and, in the past, having also faced glaciation. Constant wind and rain have likewise affected the plants and animals, along with creating other-worldly formations.

A great motivation for exploration here by the earliest adventurers and conquistadores was the lure of riches based on the legend of El Dorado: Prince Dorado, a descendant of the Incas fleeing from the Spanish, was believed to have founded a kingdom of great treasures in the city of Manoa, a golden capital located somewhere in this region.

While the Europeans fruitlessly searched for this city, they failed to realize that fabulous treasure was really there – below the ground on which they were walking. The region has proven to be among the world's richest in mineral resources, with enormous reserves of gold, iron, bauxite, diamonds, magnesium, and more. Now, it is valued not just for its minerals, but for its great biodiversity and the role of its vast expanses of virgin rainforests as a supplier of oxygen to the world. Moreover, tapping the power of its mighty rivers, without destroying the water resources, has permitted non-contaminating generation of electricity to assure the progress of the nation.

The Guayana Region's great natural beauty and its diverse attractions has also opened the doors for tourism, letting visitors in on some of the region's secrets. ❏

PRECEDING PAGES: the banks of the Orinoco; the Canaima Lagoon, Gran Sabana.
LEFT: more than a dozen groups of indigenous peoples live in the Guayana Region.

DELTA AMACURO

Map
on page
270

*With the opening of tourist camps in the interior of this watery
wonderland, visitors have a chance to observe its abundant fauna
and learn about its principal inhabitants, the Warao*

Caracas

Delta Amacuro state was first visited by Spanish explorers in 1532, it has thousands of kilometers of "roads," and some 370 km (230 miles) of coastline along the Atlantic Ocean – yet few visitors have had contact with the natural beauties and indigenous inhabitants of this extraordinary environment.

The principal reason for the delta's relative anonymity is the fact that except for roughly 100 km (60 miles) of routes which can be traveled by land vehicles around the capital, Tucupita, the delta's system of "roadways" is all fluvial: hundreds of fingers and arms of the Orinoco River, known as *caños,* which divide the delta into countless humid islands covered with dense foliage.

The state's name comes from the Amacuro River, in its southern sector, which merges its delta with that of the Orinoco.

A great river

For millennia, the world's eighth-largest river, the 2,574 km (1,600 mile) long Orinoco has surged toward the Atlantic, creating some 44 meters (144 ft) of new land each year. There, the exceptionally strong Equatorial Current has forced the mighty river to deposit its load of sediment along the coast, creating one of the world's largest deltas and Venezuela's youngest state (since 1991).

Seventy percent of the national territory and a portion of the Colombian Andes and plains are part of the Orinoco basin, with 2,000 rivers (including 196 of the largest in Venezuela, fed by 530 tributaries) emptying over 1.1 trillion cubic meters (35 trillion cubic ft) of water into the Atlantic Ocean each year.

The Warao

The geography has dictated that since the delta's original inhabitants, the Warao, settled here in prehistoric times, their entire lifestyle has revolved around the water, with the Orinoco considered "The Father of our Land."

Warao means "the boat people" in their language, and from the earliest days of the discovery and conquest of Venezuela, the Warao became famous for their skill as dug-out canoe builders and navigators, being sought after as shipwrights and seamen by explorers from many nations.

The Warao are a fishing society, even though certain fish, such as catfish, are not eaten because of their supposed magical qualities. They have also hunted birds since mythological times, but marsupials, snakes, primates, and carnivores are never eaten. It is only recently that small animals such as agouti and small reptiles such as iguana have been considered acceptable for food. The traditional Warao aversion to hunting larger wild animals is because these are

PRECEDING PAGES:
Warao stilt houses
on the delta.
LEFT: view across
one of the world's
largest deltas.
BELOW: adventurers
take to the water.

considered "people of the forest," with blood like that of man. Eating them would therefore be like cannibalism. These people practised no agriculture before 1860. Now, the root vegetables *ocumo* (taro) and yucca are staples.

The Warao usually live in small extended family groups, but apart from that, their social organization is very weak. According to sociologists, the Warao do not even consider they belong to a nation. However, all speak the same language. There are currently about 24,000 Warao living in Guyana, Suriname, and principally in Delta Amacuro.

The one curious attraction of Tucupita is its cathedral, an amazingly huge and imposing structure considering the small and generally poor population.

Few settlements

Except for small settlements established by missionaries in the interior, only two main towns have developed: Pedernales, at the northeastern extreme, and the capital of Tucupita along its midwestern border.

In the past, **Pedernales ❶**, accessible only by boat or small private plane, enjoyed a great economic boom when oil was exploited on nearby **Cotorra Island ❷**. When the operating firm abandoned the well over three decades ago, the economy tumbled and most of the population departed. However, with the Petroleum Opening initiated in 1994 and the reactivation of the old fields there, Pedernales is once again enjoying a boom as preliminary work is taking place prior to production.

Tourist camps

Although **Tucupita ❸** is easily reached by road, it is hardly a tourist mecca. However, the genuine attraction in the ecotourism sector has been the establishment of some ten tourist camps in the delta's interior.

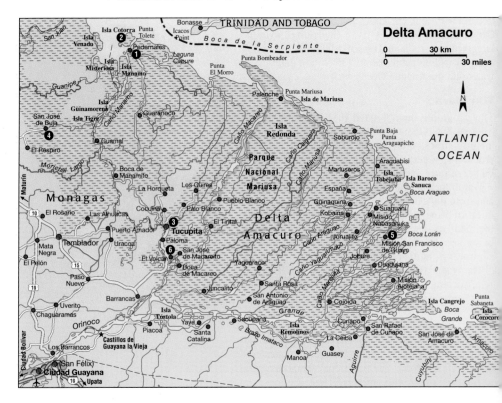

Most are concentrated roughly halfway between the capital and the coast along or near Caño Manamo, the major channel defining the state's western border, which empties into the Atlantic at Pedernales. Previously, tourists were transported by boat from Tucupita. But now, since Tucupita's airport has been out of action for several years, most tourists arrive by plane at Monagas' Maturín airport, from where they are transferred by land to **San José de Buja** ❹ for a fairly short boat via the *caño*, taking them directly to the zone of the main camps. The other camps, mostly clustered around the **Misión San Francisco de Guayo** ❺ near the mid-eastern coast, require a day-long boat ride. The usual departure point is the port of **El Volcán** ❻ near Tucupita.

Regardless of their location or degree of comfort, all the camps try hard to give visitors a feel of life in the delta. They offer boat excursions to visit indigenous communities living in *palafitos* dwellings (built on piles at the water's edge), and a chance to observe the abundant flora and fauna.

Spending several days and nights in this environment is an incomparable experience. Without artificial lighting to interrupt darkness, the night sky comes alive with stars. Without TV, radio, or traffic, city dwellers may have their first encounter with natural silence, broken only by the "night music" of crickets and frogs. As dawn approaches, nature's alarm clocks – howler monkeys, toucans, macaws, and countless other birds – begin sounding their wake-up calls. On excursions, you will be able to observe the uncomplicated manner in which the Warao live in harmony with nature, as well as watch the women weave their beautiful baskets (surprisingly, not a traditional craft) and hammocks from moriche palm fiber and see artisans carving animals from the light, white wood of the Dragon's Blood tree; you can purchase crafts directly from them. ❑

Map on page 270

TIP

Freshly caught river fish, such as *lau-lau*, *morocoto*, and *sábalo*, feature in Tucupita's restaurants and at the tourist camps.

BELOW: a Warao house on the Orinoco delta.

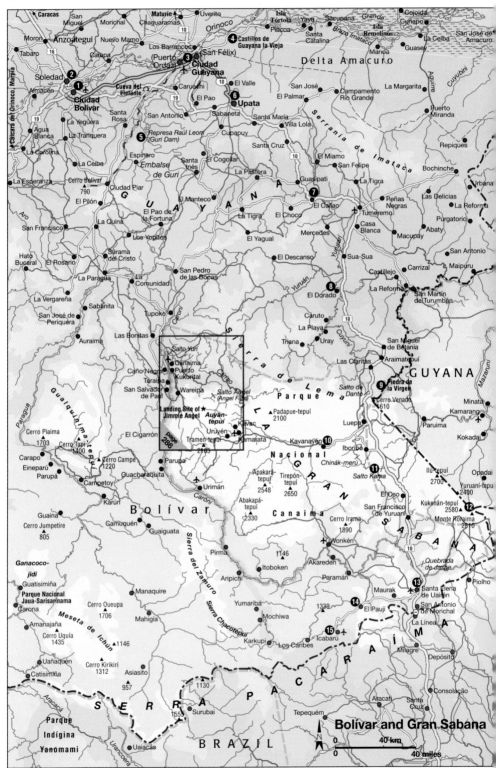

Bolívar and Gran Sabana

NORTHERN BOLÍVAR

*The important cities of Ciudad Guayana and Ciudad Bolívar
are full of surprises for the visitor. But the gold-obsessed
El Dorado is no place for dreamers*

Map
on page
274

Caracas

The Guayana Region's two largest cities, as well as Venezuela's center for heavy industry, are located in the northeast corner of Bolívar state on the banks of the Orinoco River. Ciudad Guayana is the site of giant steel and aluminum plants, while Ciudad Bolívar is of greater historical importance.

Historic capital

The capital of Bolívar state, **Ciudad Bolívar** ❶ is a relaxed colonial city. It was founded in 1764 as Santo Tomé de la Guayana de Angostura – Angostura (meaning "narrows") for short – because its site was chosen at a point where the Orinoco River is less than a mile wide. During the independence struggle, Simón Bolívar used Angostura as a base to regroup after his early defeats.

On February 15, 1819, the Liberator installed the Congress of Angostura and gave his celebrated speech proposing the ideals of a free and united South American federation. Twenty-seven years later, Congress renamed the city in his honor. For the next century, Ciudad Bolívar was the key transhipment point for goods from the interior to markets around the world.

Ciudad Bolívar developed in tandem with its sister city, **Soledad** ❷, across the river, which could be reached by boat. It was only in 1967 that Soledad and Ciudad Bolívar were linked by the Angostura suspension bridge – still the only bridge to cross the Orinoco over its 2,574 km (1,600 miles). It stretches 1,678 meters (5,505 ft), and is 57 meters (187 ft) above the river at its highest point. Small motor launches still ferry passengers between the two banks from early morning to late at night.

A project is in the planning stages – to be carried out on a concession basis – for the construction of a second bridge over the Orinoco, with the crossing point by Puerto Ordaz. It will also include a rail and highway link to a new deep-water port to be constructed on the east coast near Cariaco in Sucre state.

Slow rhythm of life

Today, Ciudad Bolívar is a city of 300,000 people, but it retains the feel of a small town. With an average temperature of 28°C (82°F), the city's residents cherish shade. Traditional homes face the Orinoco and have floor-to-ceiling windows to take advantage of the cool breezes (as well as the view). Commerce grinds to a halt in the heat of the day while people enjoy a siesta. In the evenings, families relax in the shade of an open doorway or stroll by the river. The waterfront remains a hive of activity, with many shops located in the arcade on Paseo Orinoco. Here craftsmen work with precious gems and fashion gold into distinctive brooches shaped like orchids.

PRECEDING PAGES:
the Angostura
Bridge crosses the
Orinoco River.
BELOW: a room
with a view:
Ciudad Bolívar.

Across the street, overlooking the river and bridge, is the viewpoint, **Mirador Angostura Ⓐ**. You can also see the calibrated rock, Piedra del Medio, which shows the depth of the river. Normally the Orinoco is highest in August and lowest in March, at the end of the dry season.

One of the distinctive architectural features in the area near Ciudad Bolívar's Plaza Bolívar is the variety of balconies with ornate wrought- and cast-iron designs.

On Paseo Orinoco, west of the Mirador, is the **Museo de Ciudad Bolívar Ⓑ** (closed Mon; free) where the *Correo del Orinoco* was formerly printed. It circulated from 1818 to 1822 as the government's official newspaper, established by Simón Bolívar and published in English as well as Spanish for the benefit of his British troops. Along with a display of the original printing press are antiquities and works of art donated to the museum. One block east is the restored fortress-like former jail that houses the **Museo Etnográfico de Guayana Ⓒ**, which includes an interesting selection of artifacts from Venezuela's southern indigenous communities; it is also the home of the state's historical archives.

Two blocks up from Paseo Orinoco takes you to the **Plaza Bolívar Ⓓ**, with statues representing the five countries Bolívar liberated – Venezuela, Colombia, Ecuador, Peru, and Bolivia. Bordering the plaza is the **Cathedral Ⓔ**, dedicated to Nuestra Señora de las Nieves (Our Lady of the Snows) – a curious choice, since snow is unknown here. The building was started in 1765, eventually completed in 1840, and restored in 1979.

Across the street is the **Museo Piar Ⓕ** (closed Mon; free), dedicated to Gen. Manuel Piar, who was put to the firing squad against the side wall of the church on October 16, 1817 as a "conspirator and deserter." One of the leaders of the independence struggle, Piar had refused to be subordinate to Bolívar and was accused of encouraging Venezuela's *pardos* (people of mixed blood, as Piar was himself) and slaves to begin their own rebellion.

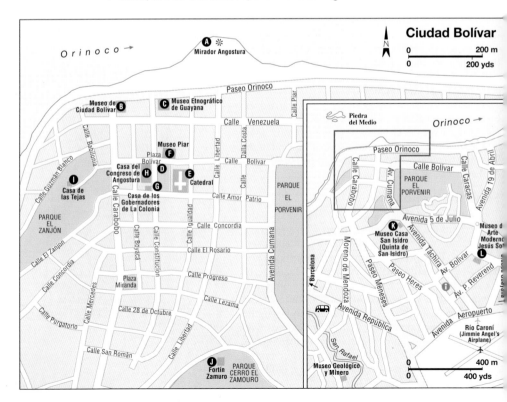

The **Casa de los Gobernadores de La Colonia** , on the west side of the plaza, was built for the Spanish governors and is now the state government's headquarters. The influential Don Manuel Centurión lived here from 1766–77, founding towns and opening the first secondary school.

Next door is the elegant **Casa del Congreso de Angostura** (Tues–Sat 9am–noon, 4–7pm; Sun 9am–noon; free), also built in 1766–77 to house the national school of Guayana. It was later the site of the Congress of Angostura, and now has historical exhibits, art shows and salons for cultural events.

Although Angostura is now known as Ciudad Bolívar, the old name lives on in the world-famous Angostura bitters. A key ingredient in the secret recipe is derived from the bark of a local tree. A mixture of this substance with honey is said to have saved the life of German scientist Alexander von Humboldt in 1800, when he was stricken with a fever following an expedition to the Upper Orinoco.

Solid foundations

Enormous boulders, called *laja*, are found throughout the city, particularly in the old part of town near the waterfront. Since moving them for construction was out of the question, residents have simply worked them into the plans. Thus, one sees entire houses built atop mammoth rocks; there are also buildings which use the giant stones as walls, with boulders protruding into rooms of houses.

An ideal place to see this is in **Parque El Zanjón**, a few blocks west of the plaza via the street on its upper side. Here, all the houses incorporate the *laja* and a path has been defined between them with little pocket gardens planted in their crevices. One such house is a brick one known as **Casa de Tejas** , which was recently restored and is the focal point of the area.

Map on page 276

TIP

Parque El Zanjón offers one of the most picturesque points in the city to take a representative photo, including the aspect of the *laja* and old-style houses, with a backdrop of the Orinoco River and the Angostura Bridge.

BELOW: traditional homes in Ciudad Bolívar, facing the Orinoco River.

Old and new

Some 10 blocks to the south, entered from Paseo Héroes, is **Fortín Zamuro**  (closed Mon; free), named after a vulture because of its site; it is poised on a hilltop overlooking the city. In colonial times a battery occupied this spot. The present fort, erected in 1901, saw military action up to 1903 when Gen. Juan Vicente Gómez waged a victorious battle to end a civil war.

The Museo de Arte Moderno Jesús Soto.

From 1818 to 1819, Bolívar stayed at the Quinta de San Isidro, supposedly penning his address to the Congress of Angostura here. The handsomely restored house, another structure built on *laja*, is now the **Museo Casa San Isidro** (Tues–Sun 9am–noon, 2–5pm; free). On a more contemporary note, the **Museo de Arte Moderno Jesús Soto** (open daily; free) has works by the world-famous kinetic artist. Soto was born in Ciudad Bolívar in 1923.

Mining heartland

The region's two principal iron mines are at El Pao and El Piar, south of Ciudad Guayana. Both are open-pit mines, the latter the entire top of a mountain called Cerro Bolívar. In 1945, an expedition of US Steel geologists found the high-grade ore at Cerro Bolívar. Subsequent exploitation of iron ore here and at El Pao by Bethlehem and US Steel awakened the Venezuelan government's interest, resulting in nationalization of the mines in 1975.

BELOW: interior courtyard of the Casa del Congreso de Angostura, built in 1766–77.

In 1960, the **Corporación Venezolana de Guayana** (CVG) was created by presidential decree to develop the Guayana Region – initially just in Bolívar and Delta Amacuro, with later inclusion of Amazonas and even parts of Anzoátegui and Monagas. With the exclusion of petroleum, CVG controls the development of all the natural resources and basic industries in that region, as well as being responsible for the development of public utilities, and economic, sporting, social, and cultural affairs. It was 1997 when privatization of some of the CVG companies began, principally in the area of the aluminum and steel industries.

Boom town

Ciudad Guayana ❸ was born in 1961, when the CVG fused Puerto Ordaz and San Félix with the industrial zone of Matanzas – at a sufficient distance west of Puerto Ordaz so that the city would not be affected by industrial contamination. The cities are linked by three bridges over the Caroní River. The population of this thriving metropolis is now about 700,000, and is expected to reach 2 million by 2030. Matanzas is the site of gargantuan steel, aluminum, and iron ore plants.

Puerto Ordaz was built in 1952 by the Orinoco Mining Company as its administrative headquarters for shipping iron ore abroad. At the wharf, you can see ore, which has been whisked by train from Cerro Bolívar, being loaded onto barges, and bauxite arriving from upriver at Los Pijiguaos. Many industrial executives make their homes in this part of town, while workers tend to live in San Félix, but wherever inhabitants live, they rarely use the name "Ciudad Guyana"; likewise, there is no mention of it in airline or bus timetables as everyone continues to use the former names of Puerto Ordaz and San Félix.

From **Parque Cachamay** (closed Mon; token admission fee) which occupies 52 hectares (128 acres) next to the Hotel Inter-Continental Guayana, there is a great view of Cachamay and Llovizna Falls on the Caroní.

A visit to the very pretty **Parque Llovizna** (Tues–Sun 9am–5pm; free), via the San Félix–El Pao road, offers a closer view of the falls. Nearby are the ruins of the **Caroní Mission Church**. The Spanish Capuchin monks who founded their first mission in the area in 1724 became successful cattle and horse breeders, and established towns and schools; these are all on land belonging to Edelca (Electrificación del Caroní), which maintains them beautifully.

Downstream from Ciudad Guayana are the **Castillos de Guayana la Vieja** ❹ (closed Mon; token admission fee), two forts built to protect San Tomé, Guayana's first Spanish settlement, against English, French, and Dutch pirates. They are actually in Delta Amacuro state, but access is possible only by road from San Félix since their construction was designed to prevent access from the river.

The forts are poised on rocks high above the river. San Francisco was built in 1678–84, on the site of the former monastery of San Francisco de Asís. The second fort, San Diego del Alcalá (or *El Padrastro* – the obstacle), built in 1747, is perched on a nearby hill. But even this was not enough of an obstacle to prevent pirate assaults, and eventually the settlement was moved upriver for safety.

Giant dam

Another side trip from Ciudad Guayana follows the Ciudad Piar highway for about 90 minutes south along the Caroní River to **Guri Dam** ❺. Guayana's industrial development has relied on hydroelectric power provided by this giant, whose phased construction began in 1963. With the inauguration of Macagua II

Maps:
Area 274
City 276

BELOW: one of the many waterfalls near Puerto Ordaz.

Dam in 1997, another phase of the project, the complex's capacity is now 12,540 megawatts – among the world's largest. It supplies 70 percent of national electrical needs, including those of Ciudad Guayana's steel and aluminum plants, plus power for parts of northern Colombia. It will also soon supply Manaus, in Brazil. Excellent free tours are available daily at Macagua II (10am and 2.30pm; it also has a visitors' center, open daily 10am–2.30pm; free) and at Guri (9am, 10am, 2pm, 3pm). Many local tour operators offer excursions with transportation to the dam.

Guri's reservoir, the continent's fourth largest lake, is also a popular sportfishing venue, featuring two of Venezuela's best freshwater game fish: feisty *pavón* (peacock bass) and *payara*.

Northwestern attractions

A gold miner weighs his day's find.

An enjoyable expedition can be made along the **Caura River**, where several tourist camps now operate, offering packages with rustic lodging, meals, and excursions (the highlight of which is a trip to a waterfall called **Salto Para** by an indigenous Ye'Kwana community). This impressive cascade is reached via a three-hour trek through the jungle from a rustic base camp on a sandy riverfront beach. As a bonus, at the Indian settlement by the falls, visitors can buy exquisite, authentic crafts.

BELOW: an aerial view of the Guri Dam on the Caroní River.

Continuing westward from Maripa, where the road crosses the Caura River, to Caicara de Orinoco then south toward Puerto Ayacucho, you will see mammoth mountains of *laja*. In the area of the **Paraguaza River**, not far from the border of Amazonas state, there are various communities of Panare Indians, most of whom wear traditional dress – men in what looks like a red diaper with a huge woolen pom-pom on each hip, and barebreasted women with a short sarong-style skirt). This road is paved and can be traveled in any car.

En route to the Gran Sabana

From Ciudad Guayana to El Dorado is 296 km (184 miles). The latter is not only the last town of any size until you get to Santa Elena de Uairén near the Brazilian frontier, but marks the beginning of the count-down to the Gran Sabana.

Upata ❻ is basically a "dormitory" community of Ciudad Guayana, where many workers in the basic industries live. It is also considerably more economical, thus many travelers en route to the Gran Sabana choose to stay over in its large, comfortable, but economical Hotel Andrea rather than in Ciudad Guayana, where options are quite expensive or quite ghastly.

Guasipati, El Callao, Tumuremo, and El Dorado are all "gold towns," getting progressively rougher as you proceed southward. Hotels, the few that are available here, are all pretty basic and generally do not cater to tourists.

El Callao ❼ enjoys two claims to fame – seemingly unrelated, but intimately linked: gold and Carnival. When news spread about incredibly high-grade ore found near the Yuruarí River in 1849, the gold rush was on. Prospectors established a settlement there in 1853 called Caratal, subsequently moved it to the banks of the Yuararí River and renamed it El Callao. Among these fortune hunters were great numbers from the British and French Antilles who introduced their languages and customs. One of the latter was celebration of Carnaval, an expression of their culture through the music and dancing of the calypso.

Gold has had its ups and downs, with exploitation ceasing for many years before a recent revival. However, Carnaval in El Callao has been an on-going tradition with lively calypso music and people dancing in the streets. The dark-skinned *Madamas* wear elaborate dress typical of the islands, and there are dozens of *comparsas* (groups costumed according to particular themes), and an all-pervading party atmosphere.

El Dorado

Founded at the confluence of the Cuyuní and Yuruári Rivers, a basin containing Venezuela's most important gold deposits, **El Dorado** ❽ has always been linked with gold. Legends about gold here started long before the first actual discoveries by miners. Persistent stories about a lost Inca empire with a treasure-filled palace sent many of the conquistadores on the gold trail.

Today, a stroll through the town will show that gold reigns supreme. Nearly every establishment announces "Gold bought and sold," offering *bateas* (large shallow wooden bowls used for panning) or gold jewelry. El Dorado also has a reputation as a dangerous place because of confrontations between formal and informal miners. It is also the site of the infamous maximum-security prison known as "Las Colonias," made famous by its imprisonment of Papillon (nickname of Frenchman Henri Charrière, author of the famous autobiographical novel of the same name). Today, as then, it is considered a hell-hole. ❑

Map on page 274

At El Dorado, the kilometer markings on the road are "reset," starting at 0 km. From that point on, locations for all sites through Gran Sabana en route to Santa Elena de Uairén are indicated by their distance in kilometers from that point.

BELOW: a dip in the Orinoco.

LA GRAN SABANA

*The Great Savannah, long the stuff of legends and novels, contains
the dramatic Angel Falls and is full of magical landscapes.
The big growth area today is adventure tourism*

Map
on page
286

Caracas

How could a place that contains the Angel Falls – the highest and longest free drop of water in the world – the imposing Roraima *tepuy*, inspiration for Sir Arthur Conan Doyle's *The Lost World*, and rivers that flow over beds of semi-precious jasper not fail to act as a magnet for those seeking intimate contact with one of Mother Nature's greatest works? For this reason La Gran Sabana (the great savannah) and Canaima are two of Venezuela's most popular vacation destinations for adventure and ecotourism.

Unfortunately, despite fierce opposition from environmentalists and local indigenous peoples, large electricity pylons and transmission lines have been built through Canaima National Park and the mesas of La Gran Sabana, and in 2001 hydro-electric power began to be transported to Brazil. Not only have the power lines had an irreparable impact on the delicate ecosystems and beautiful scenery of the region, but they have also allowed the possibility of full-scale mining within the supposedly protected Imataca forest reserve. At the dawn of the 21st century, it remains to be seen whether the Venezuelan government can successfully address the major environmental challenges of preserving its natural resources and reducing pollution and deforestation in the face of considerable economic, social, and political difficulties.

Identity crisis

Depending on the reference, prime attractions such as Angel Falls and the Roraima *tepuy* are sometimes identified as being in La Gran Sabana, while at other times in Canaima – both are correct. The 3 million hectares (7.4 million acres) of **Parque Nacional Canaima Ⓐ** (decreed as such in 1962) overlap most of the vast area known as **La Gran Sabana**.

"**Jungle Rudy's**" **Campamento Ucaima**, opening in the mid-1950s, was the pioneer camp in the area near the lagoon and the tiny Indian village that shared the name of Canaima. The camp was established on the banks of the Carrao River with majestic *tepuyes* (the local Pemón name for flat-top mountains with vertical rock walls) in the background. **Campamento Hoturvensa**, more commonly referred to as Campamento Canaima, was established by Avensa airlines in 1979 at the edge of the lagoon, with an enviable view of the falls "thrown in." The camps by **Canaima Ⓑ** village are in the northwestern extreme of the national park.

The promotion by these two operators, especially that of Hoturvensa with the clout of an airline for widespread publicity, put Canaima on the map. So much so that, to most people, "Canaima" is not the entire national park, it is the Hoturvensa camp; while "La Gran Sabana" is everything else in southeastern Bolívar.

PRECEDING PAGES: the towering *tepuyes* on the savannah. **LEFT:** Kavac tourist camp at the foot of Auyántepui. **BELOW:** Pemón woman with her daughter.

The popularly understood separation of the two is further accentuated by the fact that the only practical access to Canaima is by air, while "visiting La Gran Sabana" by any means other than by road – enabling easy visits to the beautiful waterfalls and other attractions along its full length – is not even considered.

Hoturvensa and Ucaima are considered the "premium" camps at Canaima. To provide less expensive alternatives, various others have opened. In order of attractiveness, the best choices are: **Parakaupa**, run by one of Jungle Rudy's daughters and with its own restaurant; **Wey Tepuy** and **Churún Vena** (installing a restaurant); and, without eating facilities, **Kaikusé** and **Kusari**, though visitors here can arrange to eat at one of the above camps or to use the **Restaurante de Simón** – next to Churún-Vena in the village – which offers tasty, economical meals. All except Ucaima are close to each other and the airstrip. A further attractive option is the camp on Isla Anatoly, opposite Campamento Canaima. Facilities are simple but it has a delightful location near a pink-sand beach, close to the Saltos Hacha (email: bernaltours@terra.com.ve).

The star attraction of the park is **Angel Falls** ⓒ, named after its discoverer, Jimmie Angel *(see page 288)*, which makes its dramatic plunge off the edge of **Auyántepui** ⓓ, the largest *tepuy* in La Gran Sabana, covering 700 sq. km (270 sq. miles). This cataract is renowned for being the highest (978 meters/3,210 ft) falls with the longest free drop of water (807 meters/2,648 ft) in the world.

In the language of the Pemón, *Auyántepui* means Devil's Mountain. According to their mythology, a group of evil spirits called *marawitón* live on the summit together with a higher spirit, *Tramán-chitá*. Angel Falls is *Parecupá-merú* (*merú* means falls); however, it is often mistakenly referred to as *Churún-merú* – the name of another impressive cataract at the end of Devil's Canyon.

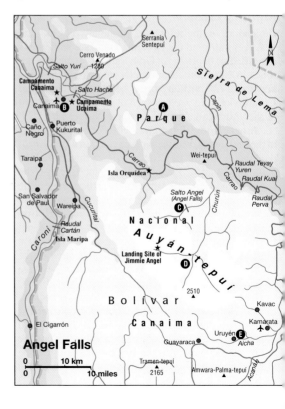

Map on page 286

Canaima's camps are the departure point for excursions to Angel Falls, but none has a view of them – or even Auyántepui, since they are about 50 km (30 miles) away. To see the famous cataract, you must sign up for a river excursion or view it by plane. The premium camps generally offer packages that include lodging, meals, and excursions. All major travel agencies offer these, while those that are more specialized create their own package deals, which offer a variety of combinations – from backpacker specials, sleeping in hammocks, to a far more luxurious option. Independent travelers can arrange tours in Canaima itself, with companies offering combinations from a half-day to several days.

Other northwest options

Uruyén ❺, near the southern base of Auyántepui (the opposite side from Angel Falls) has a simple, attractive camp (owned and operated by indigenous Pemón) and an airstrip. This side is the departure point for travelers wishing to climb the *tepuy*. Nearby, the camp of Kavac is an attractive Indian *pueblito* (village). Local Pemón take visitors on treks to the waterfalls, savannah and *tepuyes* of the area, as well as on exhilerating hikes through the Kavac Canyon to the beautiful cataract at the end. **Arekuna** is a pretty premium camp on the shores of the Caroní River, and from here there are opportunities to explore the river, go trekking, and visit local communities.

Route through La Gran Sabana

Before completion in 1991 of the excellent paved highway traversing the length of La Gran Sabana to Santa Elena de Uairén (now finished as far as Boa Vista in Brazil), a trip to La Gran Sabana was indeed an adventure. The first road was

Camping en route to Auyántepui, a tough trek of at least five days to reach the summit.

BELOW: Angel Falls.

Jimmie Angel

The accidental discovery of the world's highest waterfall by the Missouri-born pilot Jimmie Angel has become an essential part of the mythology of the Gran Sabana. In 1921, Angel met the Alaskan geologist and explorer J.R. McCraken in a bar in Panama. McCraken told Angel about a mountain in South America with a river of gold. Angel told him he'd take him there for $3,000; to Angel's surprise, McCraken accepted. Angel landed in a remote spot in Bolívar state indicated by the Alaskan, who filled his sack with gold until Angel insisted on leaving as darkness was approaching.

Obsessed with the desire to find this treasure spot again, Angel dedicated the rest of his life in this pursuit.

McCraken had given only verbal directions as they flew, but Angel was sure the spot was on top of Auyántepui. In 1930, he returned with mining engineer Dick Curry, but couldn't land. On October 10 of that year, he tried anew, but foul weather again impeded landing.

In 1935, he convinced geologist F.I. "Shorty" Martin to get financing from the Case Pomeroy Company. They landed in Kamarata Valley and, on March 25, 1935, discovered the canyon of Auyántepui, now known as Devil's Canyon. "I saw a waterfall that almost made me lose control of the plane. The cascade came from the sky! But I still didn't have any luck in landing," said Angel.

However hard he tried, he couldn't find a place to land, so in 1937, he made an ascent accompanied by the Spanish sea captain and expert topographer Felix Cardona Puig, and the engineer and explorer Gustavo Heny to survey possible landing sites. He then organized his fifth attempt, on this occasion accompanied by his wife Marie Sanders, Heny, and Joe Meacham (owner of an Arizona nightclub). He landed on the top on October 9, 1937 in a Flamingo monoplane, *Río Caroní*. But it sank in the swampy ground, and he and his group had to hike down. The trek took them 11 days, but fortunately Heny was familiar with the route, and he led the group safely down to Kamarata.

Despite his continual search for the "river of gold," Angel never found the spot again.

He died in Panama in 1956 as the result of injuries suffered in a plane crash. He had left instructions that upon his death, he wanted to be cremated, with his ashes scattered over the falls that bore his name. This final, consoling wish was carried out.

In 1970, the Venezuelan Air Force (FAV) rescued his Flamingo in order to restore it for their 50th anniversary. It remained in the Museo Aeronáutico de Maracay until 1980, when it was moved to Ciudad Bolívar.

The American explorer and journalist Ruth Robertson, who made the first accurate measurements of the height of the falls in 1949, is credited with the naming of this natural phenomenon as "Angel Falls." Though much has been written about others who knew of the falls long before Jimmie Angel, he continues to be popularly credited with their discovery – perhaps because of his colorful character, or simply because this name best conveys a romantic image of the sparkling cascade of water, as if it were falling from the heavens. ❏

BELOW: Jimmie Angel's monoplane. After being rescued from the top of Auyántepui, it now waits to be returned to the spot where it landed.

Map on page 274

not cut through until 1973. Just dirt then, travel was possible only in dry weather in convoys of several 4x4 vehicles, which could help each other in fording rivers or when stuck in deep sand or mud. Now, visitors in any normal vehicle can admire a marvelous variety of beautiful landscapes, unique flora, numerous waterfalls, and settlements of the indigenous Pemón on a comfortable, easy drive of just 227 km (141 miles) from Km 88 to Santa Elena de Uairén. Major travel agencies offer all-inclusive tour packages for land travel, usually three to four days, typically including a visit to El Dorado and to a camp of informal gold miners, then on to hit all the standard stops en route to Santa Elena de Uairén.

If you are planning to fly to Ciudad Bolívar or Ciudad Guayana, then rent a vehicle there (normal car or 4x4), confirmed reservations paid well in advance are imperative, especially in high season. If driving, the ideal place to stay the night before starting through the Gran Sabana is in Las Claritas (Km 85). Although the town itself is the epitome of an Old West-style mining town, full of makeshift buildings and brothels, there are a couple of good lodging options within walled or fenced compounds: Campamento Anaconda (tel: 286-22 3131; fax: 286 22 6572) and Campamento Gran Sabana (tel/fax: 288 92 2001/ 2002). Book in advance as accommodations are difficult to find in high season.

Into the Canaima National Park

The road enters the Canaima National Park and La Gran Sabana a short distance south of Las Claritas, with the first landmark, **Piedra de la Virgen** ❾. Continue through the dense forest of the **Sierra de Lema**, and at Km 119.7 you will come to the **Salto de Danto** waterfalls. As you emerge from the forest, the vast expanse of the high savannah stretches out in a breathtaking panorama: rolling

TIP

The rainy season is the best time to visit the Angel Falls to be sure of not finding the falls reduced to a trickle. Climbing Auyántepui, however, is best in the dry season, November through April.

BELOW: dining patio at Canaima jungle camp.

TIP

Roberto Marrero has spent years producing extremely detailed maps and guidebooks to this area, including his *Guide to the Gran Sabana*, which is available from good bookstores in Caracas and in Gran Sabana, and is published in Spanish and English. An excellent website is www.gransabana.com for maps, photos and recommended itineraries.

BELOW: a low river level reveals a rich plant life.

hills covered with grasses, rivers bordered by *moriche* palms – and the first distant *tepuyes* to be seen on this drive. All along the way are groupings, normally of extended families of native Pemón dwellings (they are the only people permitted to reside in the national park or erect buildings), along with various lodgings, always located by a river to provide a source of water. These include rustic camps with just empty *churuatas* to provide shelter from the elements for backpackers (Salto Kawi – Km 194.5; Quebrada de Pacheco – Km 238; Río Soroape – Km 243); ones with beds and some services (Salto Kama – Km 201.5); and even one place that not only has quite nice rooms with bath, but a large restaurant with good food and a gasoline station (**Rápidos de Kamoirán** – Km 174; the only one with phone contact, tel/fax: 286 51 2729).

Near the National Guard outpost of **Luepa** (Km 147) is the side road to **Kavanayén ⑩**, with a relatively large Capuchin mission that offers basic dormitory-style accommodations. The route there is paved as far as the military airstrip, but a 4x4 vehicle is recommended to cover the rest. En route, a side road leads to **Iboribo**, the departure point in large motor-powered dug-out canoes for **Chinák-merú**, a beautiful waterfall on the Aponguao River, with a broad rock face over which a wall of water plunges.

The fragile landscape of the savannah hosts fascinating flora, including numerous carnivorous plants such as colonies of the tiny ruby sundew with its bright red "jaws" and huge expanses of vivid fuchsia-colored ground orchids.

Back on the main road, the next big attraction southward is **Salto Kama ⑪** (Km 201.5). The waterfall faces west and is best photographed in the afternoon light, when rainbows form in the mist produced from its high drop. **San Francisco de Yuruaní** is the departure point for scaling **Roraima ⑫** or **Kukenán** *tepuyes* – the latter is considered the hardest, and it is compulsory to use the indigenous guides for both ascents. The normal round-trip excursion takes about six days, with different options and prices.

Quebrada de Jaspe (Km 273.5) is among the most unusual places on this drive, with its river bed and base of the stair-step falls of semi-precious jasper. The water is shallow – mostly only knee-deep – and you can easily walk in the river to the base of the falls.

Santa Elena de Uairén ⑬, first settled in 1922 and now with a population of some 15,000, besides having a military frontier outpost, is the source of supplies for local diamond miners and tourists. The town offers plenty of lodging and dining options.

Diamond territory

A popular trip from Santa Elena is to the diamond mining towns of **El Paují ⑭** and **Icabarú ⑮**, 75 km (47 miles) and 115 km (71 miles) west, respectively. The famous 154-carat Bolívar diamond was found nearby in 1942. The dirt road, despite repairs a couple of years ago, has not been maintained at all since then, and the journey takes 10 grueling hours, even in a 4x4. Quick, comfortable light commercial flights are the best option. Rutaca provides an air taxi service to both destinations daily, with flights from about 7am–5pm every time five passengers accumulate, for about US$35 per person each way.

Map on page 274

Locals warn against visiting Icabarú, pointing out it is a very rough and dangerous miners' camp where tourists are not made to feel welcome. El Paují, however, is quite a contrast – and a surprise. Rather than fortune-hunters, most of the residents are "refugees from stress" and artsy types: former high-pressure executives who came for a break – and decided to make the visit permanent; artists, musicians, and dancers who find endless inspiration in the tranquility and beauty of nature. These same people have opened some half dozen unique choices for comfortable lodging full of imaginative details. Most offer guided tours to visit local attractions.

Among the best choices in El Paují are Hospedaje Chimantá, Las Brisas, Campamento Manoa (for both lodges, call Luis Scott, tel/fax: 288 95 1431), and Casa de Cultura y Posada Amariba (tel/fax: 212 978 0084; email: amariba@cantv.net). Since there are no telephones here, you should make arrangements via Anaconda Tours (tel: 288 95 1016), located next to the principal bakery (Panadería Trigopán) on Calle Bolívar in Santa Elena, which has radio contact. Via Icabarú, another good choice is Campamento Kawaik (tel: 295 42 3841; email: kawaik@intercon.net.ve). All these camps are ecologically conscious.

Roadside welcome.

Side trip to Brazil

South from Santa Elena, you can cross over into Brazil to La Línea ("The Line"), just across the international border between Venezuela and its neighbor. In La Línea you can shop for Brazilian wines or leather-sheathed Bowie knives, or you can try a typical Brazilian *churrasco* – an all-you-can-eat meal, with skewers of beef, pork, chicken, and sausages served with a variety of side dishes, washed down with liter-sized bottles of Antarctica beer. ❑

BELOW: heading into mining country.

A CASTLE IN THE CLOUDS

Standing guard over the savannah like a medieval fortress, Mount Roraima harbors life-forms that inspired Conan Doyle to write The Lost World

Clammy mists swirl around labyrinths of blackened rocks sculpted into nightmarish shapes: bulbous heads, stretched and twisted limbs, spiny torsos, and gaping jaws. This could be a Salvador Dalí landscape brought to life, or a macabre graveyard of petrified Mesozoic reptiles.

In fact, this is the surface of Mount Roraima, the tallest and most famous of the dozens of *tepuyes* (plateaus) that dominate the horizon of the Gran Sabana in southern Venezuela, and the source of inspiration for Arthur Conan Doyle's classic adventure story, *The Lost World*.

Elsewhere on Roraima are huge sinkholes, lined with spiky plants. A canyon on its eastern rim is carpeted with sparkling quartz crystals, earning the name *El Valle de los Cristales* (Crystal Valley). Providing a chance for hikers to wash in fresh water, another area has several pools in the rock, predictably nicknamed *El Baño* (The Bathroom). As for camping facilities on top of Roraima, visitors have to squeeze onto sandy ledges under narrow over-hangs, optimistically known as *El Hotel*. With only one known path in its entire perimeter, local guides are absolutely essential in this rocky maze – not just to get you up but to lead you back down. Roraima's splendid isolation is likely to remain safe for a few more million years.

▷ **LOCAL RESIDENTS**
A straw-roofed house of the Pemón, who are the only authorized guides to take you up the *tepuyes*, which they regard as sacred.

△ **VIEW FROM THE EDGE**
After one of the frequent rainstorms over Roraima, new waterfalls spring out from its rim and cascade onto the forest below.

▽ **ANCIENT OUTLINE**
Flying over the lush forest fringing the *tepuyes*, even the tannin-stained rivers seem to hint at the presence of prehistoric inhabitants.

△ **CLINGING TO LIFE**
Clusters of plants take root together in whatever crevice or patch of soil has survived the torrential rainfall on the summit of Roraima.

PRIZE PLANTS

oggy sinkholes are filled
ith plants, over half of
hich are endemic species
nd some of them exclusive
the summit of one *tepuy*.

CARNIVOROUS PLANT LIFE

Roraima's rain-drenched surface supports few animals. Plant life up here, however, is plentiful and well adapted to the cold and wet climate. The black rock itself turns out to be pale underneath but coated with a species of algae that thrives in these sodden conditions. The heavy rainfall has washed away most of the soil and what little remains is low in nutrients. The plants that grow here are mostly insect-eaters, such as marsh pitchers, sundews, and bladder worts, which cling to the crevices in the rock where soil has found a niche. One species of bromeliad has also evolved carnivorous habits, absorbing nutrients through its leaves from the bodies of insects drowned in pools formed in its vase.

◁ **TOWERING GIANTS**
A typical *tepuy* towers some 1,500 meters (5,000 ft) over the savannah, fringed by tropical forest.

▷ **NATURAL SCULPTURE**
The blackened rocks take on monstruous shapes as a result of millions of years of continuous erosion.

AMAZONAS

This spectacular state includes areas where only scientists and missionaries are allowed to travel independently. But camps allow others to explore the interior as package tourists

Map on page 298

Amazonas state, located in the southernmost extreme of the country, covers nearly 184,500 sq. km (71,000 sq. miles) yet has a population of only 120,000, the majority belonging to 15 indigenous groups. Bordered on the north by Bolívar state, with Colombia on the west, Brazil to the south, and Brazil and Bolívar state on the east, Amazonas includes rainforests sheltering exotic plants and rare animals, hundreds of rivers, and broad savannahs. Delicate border disputes have occurred more than once, and threats to its surprisingly fragile environment are always a concern, but it is also a place where travelers can enjoy one of the world's great wilderness adventures.

Natural abundance

About 8,000 species of plants grow in Amazonas – 7,000 of them indigenous. Orchids, bromeliads, and mosses drape the rainforest, with a canopy so thick and immense it seems impenetrable. Jaguars prowl deep in the jungle, along with ocelots, deer, tapir, giant anteaters, peccaries, and half a dozen species of monkey – although it is unlikely that you will spot them. The fearsome bushmaster snake grows up to 4 meters (12 ft) in length; the deadly fer-de-lance and the better-known anaconda are not quite so lengthy.

There are some 680 species of birds, including magnificently colored toucans, parrots, and macaws. And there are insects galore: a hundred different families with their various relations, including brilliant, neon-colored butterflies and 6-inch (15 cm) cockroaches. Scorpions and tarantulas are found on the rainforest's floor, and its rivers harbor electric eels, piranha, alligators and crocodiles, *pavón* (peacock bass), freshwater dolphin, and the fast-disappearing Arrau tortoise, which is prized for its flesh.

Delicate ecosystem

Although Amazonas is teeming with life, the rainforest ecosystem is very delicate. If the land is cleared for large-scale farming, the shallow nutrients are leached out and washed away by the rains, leaving a desert-like landscape. Miners leave behind rivers contaminated with mercury and holes that fill with rainwater to become breeding areas for mosquitoes.

Nearly 6.3 million hectares (15.6 million acres) of the state are protected under special administration by the Environment Ministry: this includes 18 natural monuments (12 of which are *tepuyes*), four national parks, the Sipapo forest reserve, the upper Orinoco-Casiquiare biosphere reserve, and the Cataniapo River protected hydrographic basin. Unfortunately, actual protection is virtually non-existent due to the extreme difficulty of access to most areas.

PRECEDING PAGES: bridge across a jungle river. **LEFT:** Yanomami children. **BELOW:** a screeching macaw.

Amazonas

Among these is the **Cerro La Neblina** (Misty Mountain), the highest point within the **Parque Nacional Serranía de La Neblina** and, at 3,014 meters (9,888 ft), the tallest peak in South America that is not in the Andes. Because of its remoteness along the southern border, it was not discovered until 1953.

Map on page 298

Commercial resources

Amazonas contains a wealth of lumber, medicinal plants, dyes, resins, gums, and fibers, and the rivers hold great hydroelectric potential. But such riches have been only marginally exploited. Amazonas also has the largest gold deposits in South America and has recently drawn thousands of miners – many coming over the border illegally from Brazil. Venezuela has not suffered the same sort of environmental catastrophe as its southern neighbor, but the situation is volatile.

The same kind of pre-Cambrian plateaus known as tepuyes (from the Pemón word for mountain) are usually called cerros (Spanish for hill) in Amazonas.

Despite the difficulties, the area has attracted explorers for centuries. The Orinoco was probed as early as 1531 by conquistador Diego de Ordaz, who dreamed it would lead to El Dorado. Dozens of other explorers combed the 2,574 km (1,600 mile) river and its tributaries, but the source of the Orinoco remained a mystery until 1950. In that year, a team of Venezuelans, French, and North Americans traced the last 190 km (120 miles) of the Orinoco's course to the Sierra Parima at the Brazilian border. The origin of the seventh largest river in the world is a stream that trickles from a mountain that expedition members named Delgado Chalbaud (elevation 1,047 meters/3,435 ft).

Amazing river

The Orinoco River exhibits a rare phenomenon in Amazonas. During certain times of the year, instead of receiving waters from the smaller Río Casiquiare, it feeds part of its own volume into this inferior channel. The Casiquiare then runs in the opposite direction from the Orinoco's main course, empties into the Río Negro and on into the Amazon. German naturalist Alexander von Humboldt *(see page 173)* documented this curiosity when he came to the area in 1800, and it amazes engineers even today.

BELOW: hiking through the rainforest.

Most travelers to Amazonas will be satisfied with tours organized by legally registered camps and travel agencies that offer anything from quick tours around Puerto Ayacucho to lengthy expeditions deep into the interior. To be avoided are the tours offered by "pirates" – freelancers who often hang around in the airport attempting to lure incomers with their "bargain" prices; these people are neither legally authorized to offer their services nor equipped to handle any emergencies.

Anyone wishing to go into the interior independently must get authorization from the Office of Indian Affairs (ORAI), a lengthy and onerous process, which also involves approval from the Environment Ministry, National Guard, and Amazonas State Government. Permission is normally granted only to scientists and missionaries.

Transportation in this remote region is mainly by air taxi and dugout canoes called *bongos* or *curiaras*. The only paved roads are the highways that come from Caicara de Orinoco (Bolívar state) and San

Fernando de Apure (Apure state), which then continue southward to Puerto Nuevo, which is located a few kilometers beyond Samariapo and the Maipures Rapids.

Few towns

Arrows made by native Yanomami from the Casiquiare River region.

BELOW: baby croc.

The *criollo* towns are clustered along the Orinoco, Atabapo, Guanía, and Negro rivers, bordering Colombia. **Puerto Ayacucho ❷** is by far the biggest, with a population of about 80,000. The place where most travelers begin their journeys, Puerto Ayacucho was founded in 1924, and was originally the base camp for workmen building the road south to Samariapo. It links the two ports along a section of the Orinoco that cannot be navigated due to rocks and the treacherous Atures rapids. Being both a port on the Orinoco and a border post, Puerto Ayacucho has a heavy military and navy presence. The average temperature in Puerto Ayacucho is 27.6°C (82°F). In the dry season (December through April), the town gets very dusty, while during the rains it is extremely humid.

The airport offers daily flights to Caracas and other cities, while charter operators fly tourists, scientists, and missionaries to the interior. Tourist information is available at the airport and at the tourist office in the Palacio del Gobierno on Avenida Río Negro, next to Plaza Bolívar. Look out for the free booklet, *Guía de Servicios Turísticos*.

Many native peoples live in Puerto Ayacucho or come to the market to trade. **Plaza Rómulo Betancourt** on Avenida Río Negro has become the port's informal indigenous market, where Guahibo, Piaroa, and Curripaco Indians sell bead necklaces, carved wooden animals, and other crafts; most trading happens on Thursday, Friday, and Saturday. Avenida Orinoco is the site of a daily market, mainly focusing on food and clothing, which tends to be busiest on weekends.

Fresh produce and river fish, *tortas de casabe* (large, circular cakes of the traditional bread made from grated yucca root), and *katara* (a spicy sauce containing heads of *bachacos* – leaf-cutter ants with formidable mandibles, said to be an aphrodisiac), are on sale here.

The **Museo Etnológico del Territorio Federal Amazonas** (Tues–Sat, Sun am only; small admission fee), facing the plaza, is outstanding, showing all aspects of everyday life and customs of the five ethnic families of Amazonas' indigenous peoples.

Jungle pleasures

There's much to see in this wild corner of the country. About 35 km (22 miles) north of Puerto Ayacucho is **Pozo Azul ❸**, a deep, clear lagoon fed by a little stream. It's safe to swim here, but lately the area has not been well maintained. A much better choice is the popular **Tobogán de la Selva ❹**, a natural rock slide in a river surrounded by jungle, the same distance in the opposite direction from the capital, just off the road to Samariapo. This 20-meter (60-ft) granite rock forms a natural slide and is set in a recreational area with nature trails and refreshment stands.

Cerro Pintado ❺ has the largest known petroglyphs in Venezuela, including a 50-meter (164-ft) snake that is said to represent the Orinoco.

The paved road south from Puerto Ayacucho ends at Puerto Nuevo. Between this and another small port town, **Samariapo** , several kilometers before it, are the impressive Maipures Rapids. Lying at the southern extreme of these rapids, about 20 minutes by boat from Samariapo, is **Isla Ratón**, which is the largest land mass in the Orinoco River. It must also be one of the hottest places on earth: the sun beats down all day as its clusters of multi-colored houses stand unprotected against the burning rays.

Cerro Autana, the sacred mountain of the Piaroas, is 80 km (50 miles) southeast. This 1,200-meter (3,940-ft.) column of pre-Cambrian rock has a spectacular cave near its summit. Open at both sides, its galleries form a huge domed salon 40 meters (130 ft) high and 395 meters (1,300 ft) long.

Deep in Amazonas, along the Upper Orinoco, **La Esmeralda** ❼ rests in the shadow of the Cerro Duida (2,396 meters/7,860 ft). Some 128 km (80 miles) upstream lies the Yanomami mission of **Platanal** ❽.

Tourist camps

All the tourist camps in the interior of the country offer all-inclusive packages for lodging, meals, and excursions. They include: **El Yaví**, near Cerro Yaví, in the northeastern extreme of the state; **Yutaje**, some 40 km (25 miles) southwest of Yaví, near a pair of twin falls from which it takes its name; **Camani** and **Junglaven**, near the headwater of the Ventuari River; **Ventuari**, east of San Fernando de Atabaupo; and **Manaka Jungle Lodge**, near the junction of the Ventuari and Orinoco rivers.

Camp **Mawadianajodo** is in the Ye'Kwana village of the same name, near the *tepuyes* Duida and Marahuaca in the center of the state. Camps around Puerto Ayacucho include Camturama, Tucán, Orinoquía, and Nacamtur. ❏

Map
on page
298

TIP

Expediciones Aguas Bravas offers a unique adventure of rafting in the Atures rapids near Puerto Ayacucho – sitting in the front gives the wildest ride, and don't take a camera unless it is totally waterproof and shockproof (tel: 21 0541/21 4458).

BELOW: a red howler monkey.

Amazon Peoples

About 120,000 people live in Amazonas state, 40 percent of them members of 14 distinct indigenous groups in five linguistic families – Piaroa, Guahibo, Yanomami, Arawak, and Ye'Kwana (the first three independent; the last pertaining to the Caribe family) – each with its own language and culture. Only the most isolated, the Yanomami for example, living deep in the jungle near Brazil, have been able to resist encroachment from the outside world. In 1991, in a precedent-setting decree, President Carlos Andrés Pérez set aside a large stretch of Amazonas as a permanent homeland for them: the Casiquiare–Alto Orinoco Biosphere Reserve. Nevertheless, to date the reserve exists only on paper, with no official demarcation, regulation of visitors, or development plan – much less any consultation with the indigenous peoples it affects.

Many of the Venezuelan Indians have suffered invasion of their lands by miners and ranchers, been poked and prodded in the name of science, and urged by the government to assimilate into *criollo* society. Only a few groups are becoming politicized. Although the Venezuelan Constitution of 1999 gave all indigenous peoples the right to demarcate their lands by September 2002 to protect themselves from exploitation by oil and gold prospectors, the Yanomami are geographically remote and ill-equipped to engage in the elaborate negotiations that are taking place, and stand to lose much of the territory they traditionally believe to be their hunting grounds.

The Yanomami and other Indian groups have been endangered by the white man's gold fever ever since the days of the conquistadors. More recently, since the late 1980s, illegal gold miners, primarily slipping across the border from Colombia and Brazil, have invaded the dense rainforests, looking for a latter-day El Dorado. Occasional violent clashes have occurred. Moreover, incursion by outsiders has often exposed these primitive populations to new diseases against which they have no immunity – such as yellow fever, an outbreak of which claimed the lives of numerous Yanomami in 1998.

Amazonas is also a battleground for souls. The first Catholic missionaries (Jesuits) arrived in the mid-1700s, followed by Capuchins and Franciscans. However, from 1845 until the arrival of the Salesians in 1933, the Catholic church was practically non-existent. In 1940 the Hijas de María Auxiliadora nuns arrived. Between 1976 and 1988, the Sisters of San José de Tarbes, Sisters of Nazareth, and Sisters of Madre Laura began working in the interior of the territory. In the 1940s, the Protestant New Tribes missionaries sent families to live in the Indian villages. They learned the indigenous languages and have put five of them into written form. The government has taken advantage of this to communicate with the groups by printing booklets on health issues and other matters of social concern.

Visitors will have plenty of chances to see native peoples in their typical dwellings and engaged in their usual activities, but they may be surprised by what they see.

Publicity photos invariably show primitive **Yanomamis** – nearly naked, the females with sticks piercing their noses and the skin below their lower lip. But, because their remote

southern homeland is in an area declared off limits to tourists, seeing them is unlikely. They belong to the Yanomama family – the first group to populate the continent and currently the most numerous indigenous population in the state, though, interestingly, their presence in Venezuela only dates from the 20th century, having migrated from the bordering area of Brazil.

Farmers, hunters, fishermen, and gatherers, the Yanomami had, until recent times remained completely removed from the influence of modern culture. It has only been since 1950 that some of them have established relatively continual contact with missionaries and scientists. For this reason, people are fascinated with the group whose mode of living and customs have changed little since the Stone Age. Unique to the Yanomami is the custom of grinding the bones of the dead after cremation, and consuming the powder in a special brew, believed to keep the spirit of the deceased with them.

Guahibos (or *Hiwi*, in their own language) are primarily concentrated in Colombia, in the areas adjacent to the northwestern extreme of Amazonas state, but since the beginning of the 20th century have expanded their presence to the east side of the Orinoco around Puerto Ayacucho, to become the second-largest indigenous group in Amazonas. They are known for their archery prowess, ceramics, and *katara* (hot sauce made with the heads of *bachacos* – leaf-cutter ants).

Piaroa are mainly seen from the capital southward to the Sierra Guayapo and between Las Mercedes and San Juan de Manapiare along the Ventuari River, the extension of their population spreading progressively farther east since the early 1900s. In Piaroan, they call themselves *Uhuothoj'a*, meaning "people who live in the forest" – the traditional lands of the Piaroa are the vast mountain forests, though they always build their palm-thatched *churuatos* (huts) in communities near rivers and side-creeks, called *caños*.

Among the Piaroa crafts, the items most appreciated by collectors and tourists are the masks emulating animals (such as monkeys and peccaries), used in their *warime* ceremony. Though denominated "masks," they are worn on top of the head with the wearer's face covered by a long fringe of palm or bark.

The **Ye'Kwana** – aka Maquiritare or Makiratare – are known as expert boat-builders (using single hollowed-out tree trunks), and as navigators. They are also known for their physical strength. Their territory extends from the headwaters of the Ventuari River south to the Orinoco. The Ye'Kwana have never lived in large concentrations, but have dispersed strategically to allow efficient exploitation of forest resources. They use a highly democratic system and are tranquil individuals, who are more likely to leave a community than provoke a confrontation.

Arawak, living along the southwest border from the Orinoco to Brazil, are known as gatherers of jungle products, such as rubber. Common traits are subsistence based on cultivation on small farms *(conucos)* cleared in the jungle; hunting, gathering wild fruits, and fishing; a rich magic-religious culture with shamanism (hallucinogens such as *yopo* are inhaled to induce supernatural visions); and multi-family living structures. ❏

LEFT AND RIGHT: native Piaroa.

INSIGHT GUIDES
TRAVEL TIPS

Insight FlexiMaps

Maps in Insight Guides are tailored to complement the text. But when you're on the road you sometimes need the big picture that only a large-scale map can provide. This new range of durable Insight Fleximaps has been designed to meet just that need.

Detailed, clear cartography
makes the comprehensive route and city maps easy to follow, highlights all the major tourist sites and provides valuable motoring information plus a full index.

Informative and easy to use
with additional text and photographs covering a destination's top 10 essential sites, plus useful addresses, facts about the destination and handy tips on getting around.

Laminated finish
allows you to mark your route on the map using a non-permanent marker pen, and wipe it off. It makes the maps more durable and easier to fold than traditional maps.

The world's most popular destinations
are covered by the 125 titles in the series – and new destinations are being added all the time. They include Alaska, Amsterdam, Bangkok, Barbados, Beijing, Brussels, Dallas/Fort Worth, Florence, Hong Kong, Ireland, Madrid, New York, Orlando, Peru, Prague, Rio, Rome, San Francisco, Sydney, Thailand, Turkey, Venice, and Vienna.

✵ INSIGHT GUIDES
The world's largest collection of visual travel guides

CONTENTS

Getting Acquainted

The Place

Area: 916,442 sq. km (352,143 sq. miles), divided into 23 states, one Federal District, and 72 islands which are Federal Dependencies.
Capital: Caracas
Population: 23 million
Language: Spanish; 2 percent indigenous languages.
Religion: 96 percent Roman Catholic; complete religious freedom, with many different faiths represented; separation of church and state.
Time Zone: GMT -4 hours
Currency: Bolívar (Bs)
Weights and Measures: metric
Electricity: 110 volts, 60-cycle system, single-phase AC current.
International Dialing Code: 00 58

Climate

A tropical climate predominates, making Venezuela a perfect year-round travel destination. The average daytime temperature is 27°C (80°F), varying only a few degrees from the "winter" (the seemingly backward reference attributed to the rainy season – the *warmest* time of year, roughly May–Oct) to the coolest months (Dec–Feb) in the dry season.

In the northern part of the country, rains in the wet season usually consist of a short downpour in the afternoon, with the sky quickly clearing again. The geographical location, particularly altitude, affects the averages. The highest points in the Andes are perpetually covered with snow and anywhere in the Andes gets cold at night. The average temperatures in January and July are:

Caracas 18°C/65°F–21°C/70°F
Mérida 18°C/65°F–19°C/67°F
Puerto La Cruz
26°C/79°F–27°C/80°F

Coro, in the driest state of Falcón, rarely gets rain. Bolívar, Delta Amacuro, and Amazonas states, get the most. The dry season is the best for visits; any time is fine for the coast. The dry season is the best time for birding and access in the *llanos* or the Gran Sabana, while the rainy season is the best time to visit Angel Falls.

The Government

A democratic republic since 1958, until the Constitution of 1999 Venezuela's president was chosen by direct popular vote every five years and could only be re-elected after a lapse of 10 years. The president appoints all Cabinet members. In 1989, the first direct elections were held for state and local officials.

The legislative branch (Congress) consists of the Senate and Chamber of Deputies; members are elected at the same time as the president.

The judicial system is based on Napoleonic Law (no trials, rather hearings before a judge), with a Supreme Court and system of lower courts.

Highlights

- Highest mountain: Pico Bolívar in Mérida state (5,007 meters/ 16,427 ft).
- Longest (12.5 km/7.5 miles) and highest (4,765 meters/ 15,630 ft) cable car in the world (in Mérida.)
- Longest river: Orinoco (2,574 km/1,600 miles).
- Largest lake in South America: Maracaibo in Zulia state; crossed by the longest pre-stressed concrete bridge in the world (8 km/4.8 miles).
- Highest waterfall in the world: Angel Falls (978 meters/ 3,212 ft).

The election of former coup leader Hugo Chávez Frías in 1998 as president brought with it major changes in the country's political structure and raised concerns over the growing concentration of power in the central government and, more specifically, in the hands of the president himself.

Once in office, Chávez insisted that the only way his "Bolivarian revolution" could be carried out to save Venezuela from the crisis "brought on by the corruption of the past 40 years" (since the institution of democracy) was by being immediately granted "special powers" to decree economic, social, and political laws. He also demanded a new Constitution. Heavily weighed with *chavistas*, Congress passed an "Enabling Law" giving him these powers and a National Constitutional Assembly (NCA) was authorized, with Chávez determining how it would be formed. It became the de facto government led by the *comandante*. Under his guidance the NCA stripped Congress and the state legislators of almost all their functions, replacing the former two-house legislative system (of Senate and Chamber of Deputies) with a provisional single body, the National Legislative Commission, popularly referred to as the *congresillo* – or "little Congress." Its leaders were personally chosen by Chávez. The Supreme Court was replaced by a tribunal with its make-up decided by the *congresillo*. Decentralization was set in reverse, with formerly autonomous regional functions and agencies placed under the control of distinct Cabinet ministries, whose leadership is likewise decided by the president. Under the new Consitution, the term of the president was also lengthened from five to six years, with immediate re-election possible.

The Economy

With the great increase in petroleum prices, oil currently accounts for over 70 percent of central government's revenues and

Public Holidays

January 1 New Year's Day
Carnaval the Monday and
Tuesday prior to Lent
Easter *Semana Santa* – Holy
Week. Thursday and Friday of
that week are holidays
April 19 Declaration of
Independence
May 1 International Workers' Day
June 24 Anniversary of the Battle
of Carabobo, turning point in the
War of Independence
July 5 Independence Day
July 24 Birth date of the
Liberator, Simón Bolívar
October 12 *Día de la Raza*,
Columbus Day
December 25 Christmas Day

80 percent of GNP. Abundant raw
materials and cheap electricity
through the hydroelectric
development of the Caroní River
(with current generating capacity
amongst the highest in the world:
12,910 MW – and more dams being
built), aluminum, iron ore, and steel
are other important contributors.

Despite ideal conditions, not even
a fraction of the great potential of
agriculture and tourism has been
developed, and since the early
1990s Venezuela has been
suffering a deepening economic
crisis, often exacerbated by so-
called "cures".

Political uncertainty prior to the
1998 presidential elections led to
capital flight and paralyzation of the
economy. If anything, these
problems increased during the first
18 months of the administration of
President Chávez, plunging the
country into the worst recession in
recent history despite soaring oil
prices. By mid-2000 capital flight
was estimated at around $66
million per day.

Chávez insisted that
unemployment had decreased and
production and investments were
increasing, but the figures painted a
different picture.

The National Federation of
Industry announced that from May
1998 to May 2000 some 6,000

small and medium businesses
closed, making over 300,000
workers redundant. Adding its own
grim statistics, the National
Federation of Construction workers
reported 500,000 unemployed in
their sector. Consumption of basic
foodstuffs dropped by 12 percent.

Meanwhile, banks nervously
reported that overdue loan
payments increased by more than
50 percent and overdue credit card
payments in the five largest banks
increased 173 percent in 1999.
The bankruptcy of the Cavendes
financial group and the
disappearance of more than a
dozen smaller financial institutions
were causing nervousness with
memories of the 1994 banking
crisis still fresh in many minds.

The domino effect has produced
a steady increase in unemployment
at every echelon, contributing to a
growing "informal" sector (largely
making ends meet by selling
anything and everything in the
streets) which in 2000 accounted
for 52 percent of the "occupied"
(earning) sector of the population.

Despite the lowest level of
inflation for 23 years and a huge
windfall from an increase in oil price
from US$9 to US$25 a barrel,
falling to US$20 in 2001, poverty
has continued to rise with over 80
percent of the population living on
or below the poverty line.

Although the minimum monthly
wage was increased to Bs190,080
in April 2002, in a surprise hike to
appease public discontent, inflation
levels and the cost of imported
goods have begun to rise sharply.
And for the first time in 30 years
even the rich (approximately 7.5
percent of the population) are
feeling the pinch and protesting
about the mismanagement of the
economy of the world's fourth-
largest oil producer.

Since the devaluation of the
bolívar in February 2002 and
Chávez's failed bid to take control
of the state oil company, the
Venezuelan government finds itself
close to bankruptcy, compounded
by continuous capital flight and
global recession.

Planning the Trip

Visas & Passports

Regulations sometimes change
overnight, so double check with
your nearest Venezuelan consulate
(see page 311). At the moment, no
visa is needed (the form for a
tourist card, good for 90 days, is
distributed by air or sea carriers, or
can be obtained at the immigration
checkpoint) for tourists visiting from
the UK, the USA, Canada and
Australia.

If a longer stay is anticipated,
tourist visas, valid for up to one
year, are issued at Venezuelan
embassies or consulates abroad.
Most nationalities are restricted to
a maximum of three tourist cards or
visas in one year. Transit visas,
valid for up to 72 hours, have
similar costs and criteria as the
tourist visa, and a copy of an
onward air ticket is required. No
inoculations are needed, but a
yellow fever certificate and
protection against malaria and
typhoid are recommended if you
intend traveling in the jungle.

Transient visas are required for
anyone planning to work in
Venezuela, even for a short period.
They can usually only be obtained
outside the country and visitors
wishing to change from a tourist
visa to a transient visa technically
have to travel outside of the country
to obtain their papers from a
Venezuelan consulate. Because of
the delays involved, visitors wishing
to remain in Venezuela for some
time often arrive in the country with
tourist cards, converting to
transient visas by leaving and re-
entering the country (usually by
going to nearby Curaçao or Aruba)
once their papers are ready. There

are two types of transient visa: the **business visa** *(transeúnte de negocio)* which allows short-term business interests to be pursued, and the **regular transient visa**. The first is issued exclusively at Venezuelan consulates and are valid for 120 days or one year, at the discretion of the issuing consul and are not renewable in Venezuela. Regular transient visas must be applied for in Venezuela by a third party. These can be obtained by a company for a member of its staff, or by an individual seeking to bring a child or spouse to Venezuela.

Customs

PROHIBITED ITEMS

It is illegal to carry narcotics into Venezuela and penalties for foreigners are severe, ranging from immediate deportation to lengthy jail sentences. An ounce of marijuana is considered just as serious as a kilo of cocaine by Venezuelan courts.

Also strictly prohibited from entry are firearms, ammunition, explosives (only Venezuelan citizens may apply for licenses to carry firearms), fresh flowers, sugar cane plants, citrus and other fresh fruits, cotton plant seeds, animal products, medications, archeological items and pirated copies of copyrighted articles.

PETS

Any pet entering Venezuela must have a general health certificate issued, signed, and stamped by a licensed veterinarian not more than 15 days prior to entry into Venezuela. Additional vaccination certificates, obtained within the preceding year, are also required. Dogs need a valid vaccination certificate for rabies, parvovirosis, distemper, hepatitis, and leptospirosis. Cats need one for rabies, panleucopenia, calicivirus, feline rinitis and rhinotracheitis. This documentation must be presented for validation by the appropriate Venezuelan consulate in the country of departure.

Other requirements include an export permit, to be obtained 15 days before departure, with all documents in hand, from the Ministerio de Producción y Comericio (Production and Commerce Industry which absorbed the former Agriculture Ministry), in Caracas, tel: (212) 509 0497/0378; www.mpc.gov.ve

Health

DISEASES

Up to the 1930s, **malaria** claimed 10,000 lives a year from a population of some 3 million. By 1960, it had been eradicated from most of the country except for certain residual areas, mainly in Amazonas. Complacent that the disease had been licked, spraying for mosquitoes ceased and malaria stations were abandoned. The error of this move has now become evident with a resurgence not only of malaria, but of dengue fever, also mosquito-borne.

Current statistics are less than precise, as under government administration statistics rely only on entities which report to them, and the Health Ministry does not check with each state to fill in the gaps left by those who haven't filed reports.

Though reports are incomplete, as of June 2002 (in descending order), the states with the most number of reported cases of malaria were Bolívar, Sucre, and Amazonas. It is essential to obtain proper advice and suitable medication from a physician in your home country and also to take protective clothing with you.

Since 1998 the incidence of cases of dengue fever (both classic and hemorrhagic) has been increasing yearly, primarily in poor urban areas. As of June 2000, the states with the greatest number of reported cases of dengue fever were: Apure, Guárico, Mérida, and Yaracuy; with Anzoátegui and Zulia "on alert" due to growing numbers of cases; Distrito Federal and Vargas also have problem areas following the catastrophic flood of December 1999.

Your physician may recommend anti-malaria prophylactics (which have to be started prior to arrival) if you are planning extended visits to either Bolívar or Sucre. Otherwise, to combat both malaria and dengue fever (there is no vaccine or other similar prophylactic for the latter), the simplest protection is strong insect repellent applied both to the skin and clothing.

While few visitors will be entering the area of the upper Orinoco near La Esmeralda and Parima in Amazonas, if you do, be aware that in late 1998, there was a serious outbreak of **yellow fever**, **leptopirosis**, and **hepatitis B** among the Yanomami Indians there. Provisional statistics for 2000 indicated that the yellow fever crisis had improved but as of 2002 the World Health Organisation highlighted Venezuela as an endemic area.

For further details call the department of Epidomología, Ministerio de Sanidad in Caracas, tel: (212) 481 7915.

Duty Free

Personal possessions that are more than six months old, including items such as cameras, computers, binoculars, and sports equipment, along with new goods up to a value of US$1,000, 200 cigarettes, 25 cigars, 2 liters of liquor and 4 small bottles of perfume may be imported without incurring import duties.

All receipts should be kept for verification purposes. The value of new goods must be detailed on a customs declaration form *(declaración de aduanas)* provided by airlines or travel agents. Personal medications are permitted.

Venezuelan Embassies and Consulates Abroad

Australia (with jurisdiction for New Zealand and Fiji): M.L.C. Tower, 1st Floor, Suite 1, ACT-2606, Canberra, tel: 824827/ 4828/4895; fax: 2811969; email: venezuela@linkpro.com.au; www.linkpro.com.au/venezuela/
Canada: 32 Range Road, Ottawa ON–K1N 8J4, Ontario, tel: (613) 235-5151/2; fax: (613) 235-3205; embavene@travel-net.com; www.travel-net.com/~embavene/ Suite 400, 205 rue Peel, Montreal, tel: (514) 842 3417/3418/0732.
India: N-114 Panchshila Park, New Delhi, tel: 651915/4122
Jamaica: 30–36 Kuntsford Boulevard, Mutual Security Bank Building, 5th Floor, Kingston, tel: 96-25510/19 & 96-65570; fax: 92-67442
Kenya: House 3rd Floor, Mama Ngina Street, Nairobi, tel: 332300; fax: 337487

Trinidad & Tobago: Venezuelan Centre, 16 Victoria Avenue, Port of Spain, Trinidad. Tel: (62) 79 821/823, fax: (62) 42 508.
United Kingdom: 1 Cromwell Road, London SW7 2HW, tel 207 581-2776/8063 & 584-4206; fax 207 589-8887; email: embvenuk-despacho@dial.pipex.com; www.venezlon.demon.co.uk
United States: 1099 30th Street, NW, Washington DC 20007, tel: (202) 342-2214/342-6822; fax: (202) 342-6820; email: embajada@embavenez-us.org; www.embavenez-us.org 545 Boylston Street, 6th Floor, Office 603, Boston, Massachusetts 02116, tel: (617) 266-9355/266-9368; fax: (617) 266-2350; email: pp002353@interramp.com; www.venezuela.mit.edu/consulado. boston/

2700 Post Oak Boulevard, Suite 1500, Houston, Texas 77056, tel: (713) 961-5141/2; fax: (713) 961-1485; email: consulvenhou@pdq.net 1101 Brickell Avenue, North Tower, Suite 901, Miami, FL 33131, tel: (305) 577-0302/577-4214; fax: (305) 372-5167; email: conmiami@icanect.net; www.consuve.com/ 1006 World Trade Center, 2 Canal Street, New Orleans LA 70130, tel: (504) 522-3284/524 6700; fax: (504) 522-7092; email: cvenezu@aol.com 7 East 51st Street, New York NY 10022, tel: (212) 826-1660–67/826-1669 73; fax: (212) 644-7471 455 Market Street, Suite 220, San Francisco, CA 94105, tel: (415) 512-8340/8342; fax: (415) 512-7693; email: vensfo@ix.netcom.com

WATER

Urban water supplies are treated and chlorinated; however, it is still generally not advisable to drink water from a faucet since most of the supply lines are in poor condition. Bottled water is available throughout the country.

HIV/AIDS

The latest available statistics (from 1999) show that Venezuela has over 62,000 carriers of Aids (a figure that many sources consider to be very conservative).

If toying with the idea of a little Latin loving, do so only with adequate protection. Condoms are widely available (called preservativos and available in pharmacies and stores like Condomania in CCCT in Caracas), thanks to private initiatives by concerned community and gay groups. For the department of the Health Ministry that deals with Aids, tel: (212) 481 2275/36.

MEDICATION

No prescriptions are necessary to purchase any medications except those containing narcotics. Moreover, medications – whether name brands or generics – are generally considerably cheaper than exactly the same ones abroad.

Money Matters

Because of the constantly fluctuating rate of exchange, it is advisable not to change more currency in bolívars than you anticipate using.

Cash is best to carry around, preferably in small denominations.

Lost Credit Cards

In Caracas (direct dial 212): American Express (24 hours), tel: 206 2795 Diners, tel: 202 2323 MasterCard, tel: 607 7111/202 1111 Visa, tel: 501 9592

Outside of main hotels, restaurants, and expensive stores in the largest cities, few places accept travelers' checks, foreign currency, or credit cards. Even many of the major travel agencies in Caracas do not accept cards or, if they do, may add a surcharge of 3–15 percent. Cards accepted in Venezuela, in descending order of frequency, are: Visa, MasterCard, American Express, Diners.

ATMs are widely available and give good rates of exchange, but are sometimes targeted by gangs of thieves.

CURRENCY EXCHANGE

Currency can be exchanged at **casas de cambio** (most banks only exchange currency for their clients). A set percentage of commission (regardless of amount) is reflected in the difference between the buy/sell offer, rather than a flat fee. Thus, you do not get hit with a fat "minimum commission," as is the case in many other countries.

It is not recommended to exchange currency in hotels since they give unfavorable rates. There are several *casas de cambio* in the international airport in Maiquetía.

In Caracas, **Italcambio** is the main chain of exchange house. Their most convenient location is on Avenida Luis Roche, one block south of the Altamira Metro stop; however, the office with the fastest service and longest hours (Mon–Sat 10am–9pm, Sun 1–7pm) is in the mammoth Centro Sambil shopping center (two long blocks south of the Chacao Metro stop on Nivel Autopista, a few meters west of the elevators of Plaza del Arte).

EMERGENCY MONEY

Western Union, formerly working with DHL, are now represented by Grupo Zoom which has more than 40 offices in Caracas alone. For information, check the website on www.westernunion.com. Intercambio offer an alternative service called Moneygram and also have a national network. Details are available on www.italcambio.com.

The sales tax has been reduced to 14.5 percent. However, a 1 percent tax is now added to all tourism-related services (plane tickets, lodging, and tours), which goes to a fund for tourism promotion and training. Sometimes this is included in quoted prices, at other times not. Be sure to ask. (This is normally only charged at the more expensive places since its application depends on the annual sales of the business in question, with those below a certain level exempt.)

What to Bring

CLOTHES

Lightweight, casual clothing is best. At formal restaurants and Caracas discotheques, jacket and tie are sometimes required for men. Bring light clothing in natural fabrics if possible for evenings, and heavier clothing if you are planning any mountain treks.

SUN PROTECTION

You can easily obtain high strength sun block at any pharmacy, and insect repellent (Off, Avispa, and Osiris work best) on grocery store shelves. A hat or cap and sunglasses are equally essential.

WET WEATHER GEAR

Bring a lightweight rain poncho for wet season or jungle trips, a sturdy plastic garbage bag for personal belongings in the rain and in wet-bottomed boats, and a compact fold-up umbrella. Slip-on plastic sandals are also invaluable.

MEDICINES

You are strongly advised to bring any personal medications you may need with you as, although drugs are cheap in Venezuela, your particular medication may be hard to obtain.

FILM

Print film is widely available and reasonably priced, but slide, black and white, or high-speed film is scarce outside the largest cities.

Getting There

BY AIR

The Simón Bolívar International Airport is in Maiquetía, 28 km (17 miles) from Caracas across a mountain range. The international and domestic termini are very close to each other and there are shuttle buses every 10 minutes. Several airlines fly to Venezuela – check with your travel agent.

Other cities that have international airports include Maracaibo, Valencia, Barcelona/ Puerto La Cruz, San Antonio de Táchira, Las Piedras (Paraguaná Peninsula, Falcón), Maturín and Margarita Island.

Immigration & Customs

On arrival tourists will have to present their passport, visa (if required), or tourist card, and entry card or customs declaration. The last two are normally distributed in the plane before landing; otherwise, after disembarking you will have to seek them out at a designated desk near the immigration check-in counters.

In Maiquetía, they have a unique system for checking out passengers at customs. You press a button, and if it comes on green, you pass through; if the light is red, customs agents go through everything you have. As this system is operated manually, one assumes that the idea is that if someone appears nervous the agents flash a red light.

Airport Transfer

There are airport **shuttle buses** which run between both the national and international airports in Maiquetía and Caracas with stops by the Gato Negro Metro station (use this stop only during daylight hours) and at their terminal two blocks west of the Bellas Artes Metro station and Caracas Hilton (Calle Sur 17, in the underpass below Avenida Bolívar). The fare

Note on Prices

Because of the constant changes in the value of the **bolívar** and history of government-imposed devaluations, prices in this guide are given in **US dollar** equivalents to try to provide as accurate pricing as possible. Even many hotels, travel agencies, and tour promoters now quote all of their prices in dollars "or the equivalent in bolívars at the exchange of the day" to avoid problems with price fluctuations when dramatic changes occur.

Flying to Venezuela

Here are some off the principal international airlines serving Venezuela, with Caracas contact numbers:

Air Canada – (212) 285 0484
Air France – (212) 283 5855
Alitalia – (212) 285 6108
American – (212) 209 8111
Avianca – (212) 953 5732
British Airways – (212) 266 0122
Continental – (800) 359 2600
Iberia – (212) 267 8666
KLM – (212) 285 3333
TAP Air Portugal – (212) 951 0511
United – (212) 278 4545

costs less than US$2 and generally takes just under an hour. On weekends and during holidays, traffic jams can double that time.

There is a shuttle bus service between the airport and downtown Porlamar (Centro Comercial AB on Avenida Bolívar), Margarita International Express (operating 5.30am–last flight; the fare is equivalent to about $6 per person).

A welcome new service at Maiquetía airport is that provided by the taxi co-operative Anfitriónes de Venezuela. Prices are fixed and tickets can be bought in either the domestic or international terminal. The **taxis** that park at the curb of the departure area in Maiquetía airport have a monopoly and charge nearly double the going rate. To avoid paying over the odds, another option is to call Tele-taxi on (212) 753 4155/9122 (pre-paid phone cards are sold in dispensers next to the banks of phones in the terminal). This company has a stand at the airport's gasoline station and they make pick-ups at curbside on the upper arrivals level (tell them what you are wearing and by which exit you will be standing). It costs about US$18 either way between the airport and Caracas Hilton. Pick-up at your lodgings can also be arranged by phone with them or another company *(see Getting Around on page 323)*.

A word of caution: never use the *piratas* who flood the terminal at incoming flight times, offering "Taxi, taxi." They are operating illegally, most are not licensed taxi drivers, and there have been many instances of hold-ups by them.

BY SEA

The waters of Venezuela are a favorite among visitors in yachts and sailboats for the wonderful snorkeling and diving, beautiful islands, and lack of tropical storms or hurricanes – *but* almost all have tales of problems with permits, port officials, and disasters that have occurred due to non-functioning lighthouses.

Cruise Lines

While a few cruise lines have resumed stops in **La Guaira** since the disastrous December 1999 flood, the area continues to be a zone totally unsuitable to visit on foot (both for safety reasons and lack of nearby attractions), or even in vehicles, making inland excursions essential if you choose to leave the ship.

An ambitious new waterfront market-cruise port is still under construction in Porlamar (**Isla Margarita**). In the meantime, cruise ships are arriving in **Guamache** (near Margarita's ferry dock), but there are long delays for transfers by ship–shore shuttle and the tourist areas are at least 30 minutes away by taxi or bus.

BY ROAD

An entry permit is required for motorists driving into the country. This is obtainable from your local Venezuelan consulate *(see page 311)*. Take a photograph and money to cover the administration fee (about US$10).

Travel Agencies

The top seven travel agencies in the country, all based in Caracas, with direct dial of (212) are:

Italcambio
Tel: 562 9555/9591
Fax: 562 4591
E-mail: info@italviajes.com
www. italviajes.com
Molina
Tel: 278 1400/1202
Fax: 285 0224
E-mail: general@molina-viajes.com, molintours@cantv.net
www.molina-viajes.com
Omega
Tel: 285 9685/283 9711, (800) 66 342
Fax: 284 5753
E-mail: info@omega.com.ve
www.omega.com.ve
Quo Vadis
Tel: 263 1733/261 7782
Fax: 263 1716
www.quovadis.com.ve
Saeca
Tel: 993 8121/6604/0841/2888
Fax: 993 2208
E-mail: info@saeca.com
www.saeca.com
Turismo Maso Internacional
Tel: 266 9566, 267 3577, 267 3600
Fax: 262 2204
E-mail: masovac@telcel.net.ve
www.travelya.com; www.turismo-maso.com
Turisol
Tel: (800) 88 747, 263 9333
Fax: 206 3978
E-mail (CCCT office): turiccct@telcel.net.ve
www.turisol.com

Traveling On

Flights: The airport in Maiquetía is the national hub for almost all domestic and international flights. Departure tax for international flights is US$52 and liable to change; for national flights, it is roughly US$2.

Reservations must be reconfirmed 72 hours ahead for international flights. For national flights, you must be at the airport 1 hour ahead of departure, for international flights, 2 hours. During peak seasons (Christmas, Carnaval, Holy Week), it is wise to plan on arriving an extra hour early to take account of the chaos that prevails

Specialist Tours

Alpi Tour, Caracas – tel: (212) 283-1433/1733, fax: (212) 285-6067; e-mail: alpitour@viptel.com; www.alpi-group.com. Peacock bass fishing (catch and release), VenNature tours with expert anthropologists, botanists, entymologists, etc. Excursions with a professional photographer to learn how to take the best nature photos, visits to typical artisans plus charter flights, yachts.
Arassari Trek, Mérida – tel/fax: (274) 252-5879; www.arassari.com. Formerly known as Bum-Bum Tours, this company has an excellent reputation for trekking, white-water rafting, horseback riding, mountain-biking, caving, birding, "herping" (for frog and reptile fanciers), and ecotourism tours.
Eco-Voyager, tel/fax: (212) 762-1496/763-3612; www.ecovoyager.com. Highly recommended, with a variety of individual and group programs as well as birding, fishing and diving options.
Natoura Turismo Adventura, Mérida – tel: (274) 252-4216; fax: (274) 252-4075; email: natoura@telcel.net.ve; www.natoura.com. Adventure and eco tours in the Andes, excursions by jeep and on horseback, mountain bikes, climbing, birding and trout fishing, natural history tours, hang-gliding and paragliding, student discounts.
RAS Flying Safaris, through Alpiturismo, Caracas – tel: (212) 285-5273; email; safari@telcel.net.ve. Custom-designed air safaris in a six-seater Aztec

geared to those who want to see the most possible in the shortest time with very personalized service; *llanos*; meals, beverages, lodging, land tours included.
Sesto Continente, tel: (414) 924-1853; email: divelosroques@scdr.com; www.scdr.com. Specializes in organized diving trips to various spots.
Sociedad Conservacionista Audubon de Venezuela, Caracas – tel: (212) 992-3268/2812; fax: (212) 991 0716; email: ecoturismo@ audubondevenezuela.org http://audubondevenezuela.org/ Handles bookings for ecotourism destinations, with emphasis on places for birding. 9am–12.30pm.
Tobogán Tours, Puerto Ayacucho – tel: (248) 21-4865; fax: 21-4553; e-mail: tobogan@cantv.net. Excursions to all parts of Amazonas.

In the UK

A travel agency specializing in Venezuela is **Geodyssey**, based at 29 Harberton Road, London N19 5JS, tel: (020) 7281-7788; fax: (020) 7281-7878; email: enquiries@geodyssey.co.uk Also, **Last Frontiers** have excellent first-hand knowledge of Venezuela and, like Geodyssey, can tailor-make itineraries throughout the country. Tel: (01296) 633000; www.lastfrontiers.com.
For a comprehensive list of operators promoting Venezuela, contact the **Latin American Travel Association,** tel: (020) 8715-2913; www.lata.org

at the airports at that time. If you are not there in good time, you risk losing your reservation.

ISLA MARGARITA

This is a hopping-off point for nearby islands. Boats run to Coche and Cubagua (which are the other

islands of Nueva Esparta state) and Los Testigos, Los Frailes, and La Tortuga.
    Aereotuy offers flights from Isla Margarita to La Blanquilla, direct routes for day tours (or overnight) to Kavac and Canaima with fly-over of Angel Falls, and to Los Roques. International flights also originate and arrive here.

Practical Tips

Documents

Do not go *anywhere* without documentation (i.e., passport with tourist card or visa). There are checkpoints *(alcabalas)* all along the highways, where you may well be asked to show your documents, and checks are even made in the city. Such checks are aimed at picking up illegal aliens. If you do not have your documents, you will be taken to jail or at least held by the authorities until you can prove your legal status – not a pleasant experience.
    Make a photocopy of your passport (with visa) and any other important documents you are carrying with you, including your airline ticket and your driver's license. Make sure you also have a list of phone numbers to call in case you lose your credit cards or travelers' checks.

Business Hours

Most offices and stores, and even many supermarkets, close for lunch (anything from 1–3 hours, from around 11.30am to about 3–3.30pm). Most business offices begin work 8–8.30am and end 4.30–6pm. The exception is commercial establishments in small towns in the interior, which are usually open every day and from very early morning until dark, since most are owner-operated and thus not bound to labor laws limiting hours of work shifts for employees.

Banks

Many banks now have continuous hours: 8.30am–3.30pm. During the Christmas shopping season, banks offer special extended hours, which

Important Numbers

The nationwide emergency number: 171
Information: 113
National long-distance operator: 100
National collect calls: 101
International long-distance operator: 122
INDECU (Institute for the defense and protection of consumers – where you can make complaints about abuses): (800) 43 328; www.indecu.gov.ve

are published in the local press. Some banks have external tellers offering service after closing hours.

Banks are often closed on Monday for "mandatory bank holidays" which don't necessarily bear any relation to national holidays.

Shopping Malls

With the exception of Centro Sambil in Caracas, and hypermarkets such as Makro, Rattan, and Construcentro, stores in malls normally don't open until 9.30 or 10am, close for lunch, end the day at 7pm, and are closed Sunday.

Media

TELEVISION

The following are the commercial channels: 2 (Radio Caracas Televisión), 4 (Venevisión), 10 (Televen); Commercial pay-TV: 12 (Omnivisión); Government-owned: 8 (Venezolana de Televisión).

The parabolic antennas on nearly every rooftop tell at a glance the popularity of satellite TV. The service is now provided in nearly every larger hotel countrywide. DirecTV is available in even the remotest places.

RADIO

AM stations tend to be more oriented toward popular Latin music, while the repertoire of many FM stations is almost exclusively

North American or European recordings. Some stations with a difference include:

Exitos FM 99.9: popular English-language songs of the 60s, 70s, and 80s
FM 95.5: jazz
Emisora Cultural FM 97.7: classical, jazz, and discussion programs (occasionally in English), with limited number of commercials
KYS FM 101.5: the "station of contemporary adults" plays mostly English-language songs and every Saturday at 10am and Sunday at 8pm, features Casey Kasem's Countdown of the American Top 40.

PRINT

Newspapers

The only English-language daily newspaper published in Venezuela is *The Daily Journal* (founded in 1945), available nationwide in the principal cities. Its "Week in Review" supplement printed on Monday provides a useful summary. *Margarita Post* is a very informative weekly, with both local and international news, published in English on Thursday and available free in major hotels, the airport, and other tourist-oriented locations on Isla Margarita, also on-line: www.margaritaonline.com.

The *Miami Herald*, *USA Today*, *New York Times*, *Wall Street Journal*, *Financial Times*, and various other English-language newspapers, are often available (at higher price than face value) from newsstands and in the bookstores of Caracas' luxury hotels. *El Nacional* and *El Universal* are the two most important national papers.

MAGAZINES AND BOOKS

Newsstands of premium hotels plus large bookstores in major cities sell a wide selection of imported English-language magazines and some paperbacks, all at roughly double the normal price. Nationally published magazines in English or bilingual text include:

Business Venezuela, published monthly in English by the Venezuelan American Chamber of Commerce, focuses on business themes, but also has an annual issue dedicated to tourism, usually available in either June or December.

Escape, an informative monthly tourism magazine with presentation in English and Spanish.

Entonces, a quarterly tourism and entertainment magazine, in a combination of English and Spanish.

VenEconomy (by subscription, tel: (212) 761 8121, fax: 762 8160), a monthly magazine printed in two versions – one English and one Spanish, plus weekly bulletins, with focus on the hot current economic topics.

Three Caracas bookstores specialize in English-language books and magazines: **The American Book Shop**, Edificio Belveder, Local B. Avenida San Juan Bosco, between cross streets 1 & 2, Altamira, Mon–Fri 9am–6.30pm, Sat 9am–5.30pm; **The English Book Shop**, Concresa, 1st floor – same level and a few doors from Electricidad de Caracas, Prados del Este, Mon–Fri 1–6.30pm, Sat 11am–6.30pm, the most expensive; and **Read Books**, Plaza Urape, next to the Urológico San Román and the Anglican Church of Caracas, Urb. San Román, Mon–Sat 10am–7pm, the most economical – all books sold at regular US/UK prices; houses its own café.

Entertainment Guides

Every Thursday, included free in *El Universal* newspaper is a useful guide to Caracas (in Spanish), *Guía de la Ciudad*, with information on the week's highlights on art galleries, on stage, on TV, at conferences, activities for kids, movies, restaurants, cafés, and the hottest night spots.

In the weekend edition of the *Daily Journal* there is a useful guide to forthcoming entertainment and outdoor events.

Telecommunications

Since the privatization of CANTV, and the removal of its monopoly, telephone services in the country have greatly improved.

Payphones

Most payphones accept only the pre-paid phone cards or *tarjetas telefónicas*. These are sold at newsstands, by the blind – mostly at the entrances to Metro stations, at CANTV offices, hotels, and stores. In various denominations up to about US$7, they can be used for direct-dial national and international long-distance calls; you can also put in a new card without interrupting your connection.

Emergency calls: The nationwide emergency number, 171, can be dialed toll-free from payphones but unless you have good working Spanish, get a local to help you make a call.

Communications Centers

Known as CANTV *Centros de Telecomunicaciones,* these offer services that can be paid for with credit cards as well as cash: national and international calls, sending or receiving faxes, making photocopies, sale of pre-paid telephone cards, and information on car rental, hotels, airlines, and restaurants. They are generally open 8am–8pm, and can

be found in the following places: the Simón Bolívar International Airport in Maiquetía; Centro Plaza shopping center, Avenida Francisco Miranda, two blocks east of the Altamira Metro station, 5th level; and at international airports.

Cell Phones

Cell (mobile) phones are used by everyone from executives and housewives to motorcycle delivery boys. There are now also pre-paid phone cards available for certain models of cellular phones. In Caracas, cellular rentals are available through: Organización Rent-a-Phone, Hotel Caracas Hilton, tel: (212) 503 4329, fax: 503 4328, (414) 921 8844; e-mail: rapcb@telcel.net.ve; www.rentaphone.com.ve (For other cities, check Yellow Pages under *teléfonos celulares, alquiler).*

The Internet

Premium hotels geared primarily toward business travelers have in-room plug-in for computers to be able to transmit/receive e-mail, etc. Cyber cafés and computer or telecommunications-oriented stores in malls of major cities offer Internet services for the general public. Even a number of small *posadas* now also provide this service for a modest charge.

Collect Call Numbers

You can make collect calls from public or private phones, dialing directly to an operator in the country that you are calling:
Australia (800) 1-1610
Canada (800) 1-1100
Germany (800) 1-1490
Holland (800) 1-1330
Hong Kong (800) 1- 1852
Israel (800) 1-1390/1391
Japan (800) 1-1810
Puerto Rico (800) 1-1120/1122
Singapore (800) 1-1650/1651
Switzerland (800) 1-1410
UK (800) 1-1440/ 1441
United States (800) 1-1120/1121

Postal Services

The mail service through IPOSTEL within Venezuela is less than reliable or speedy – particularly within Caracas, where letters can take months to move even between post offices just blocks apart.

Outgoing post, however, is more reliable. For Europe or the US, mail averages about 10 days but can take up to three weeks. A few major hotels have mail drop boxes and sell stamps, but otherwise, all mail must be taken to a post office for weighing, stamping, and posting. No tape or staples may be used for closings on envelopes.

Changes to Telephone Numbers

A restructuring of national telephone numbers was initiated in June 2000 by which every phone number in the country will be changed over the course of the next several years. The first phase involved the change of all area codes to three-digit numbers.

Greater Caracas, previously 02 (or just 2 for incoming long distance calls), is now **212**. All other direct-dial area codes (which had a zero plus two digits) now have a 2 replacing the zero.

For all cell phones, the 0 of the code indicating the company identification (eg., Movilnet – 016,

Telcel – 014) was replaced with a 4 (eg., the access code to dial Movilnet numbers is now 416).

For national long-distance calls to normal CANTV numbers, calls to cell phones, or calls to non-geographical numbers (eg, 800, 900, 500, etc.), a **zero** will have to be dialed before the area code (eg., before: Maracay – (043) 259 2034, after: 0 (243) 259 2034; Movilnet numbers – before: (016) 211 3999, after: 0 (416) 211 3999; toll free – before: (800) 234 5678, after: 0 (800) 234 5678).

Dialing for international long-distance numbers will remain the

same: with the need to dial **00** prior to country code, area code, and the personal number.

The next phase is more complicated, since all personal numbers will be converted to 7 digits (Caracas is the only place in Venezuela which has them now).

If you have problems reaching a number, you can verify if a change has occurred by dialing the nationwide *transferencias* number: **531 0333**. An electronic voice asks you to dial in the current number with area code, and tells you whether or not it has been changed and, if so, to what.

For extra insurance (since you get a numbered and signed receipt), for a small extra charge, you can have your letter certified *(certificado)* or ask for a return receipt *(con aviso de recibo)*.

Express Mail

IPOSTEL also offers express services: EEE *(Envío Especial Expreso)* for mail within Venezuela and EMS (Express Mail Service) for international mail with dispatches of letters and documents sent sealed in a special waterproof, registered envelope; packages of up to 20 kg (44 lb), with tariffs cheaper than commercial couriers. National delivery takes a day or two. For international mail: to America and Europe – 72 hours for capital cities, 96 hours for principal cities, 120 hours for rural zones; to Asia, Africa and Oceania – 96 hours capitals, 120 hours principal cities, 144 hours rural zones. All principal IPOSTEL offices in Caracas offer the services; for other locations, call toll-free to the Unidad de Atención al Cliente: (800) 26 378 or (800) 64 367.

Packages

All packages must be sewn into opaque, colored material, the idea being to discourage pilfering. No string or tape can be used.

Private Couriers

For important documents or packages, especially if speed and security are vital, national and international courier services are the method of choice, though costly. Some of the main agents in Caracas, all offering national and international door-to-door service unless otherwise noted, are:
Aerocav: Tel: (212) 205 0623/7; www.tnt.com, www.aerocav.com (cargo and COD service too).
DHL Worldwide Express: Tel: (212) 205 6000, 235 9060, 235 2049; toll-free (800) 34 574, (800) 34 592; www.la-reg.dhl.com (offices also in Hotels Tamanaco Inter-Continental and Caracas Hilton; in CCCT).

Domesa International: Tel: (212) 484 5133, 481 5911 (an office in the Chacaíto Metro station); www.domesa.com.ve.
FedEx: Tel: (212) 205 3333; toll-free (800) 0800 463 3339.
MRW: Tel: toll-free (800) 30 400; www.mrw.com.ve. International service plus guaranteed next-day service in all of Venezuela. NB: part of their income is donated to support a free service for Venezuelans studying abroad.
P.O. Box International: Tel: (212) 993 3549, 993 7525, 992 5305; fax: 992 3469; toll-free (800) 76269 (international service, air and sea cargo only).
United Parcel Service (UPS): Tel: (212) 241 6454, 204 1441; www.ups.com
World Courier: Tel: (212) 263 5447, 263 7667; e-mail: opsccs@cantv.net; website: www.worldcourier.com.
Grupo Zoom: Tel: (212) 242 7111.

Local Tourist Offices

The former Tourism Ministry is now part of the new Ministry of Commerce and Production, with the president of Corpoturismo (the National Tourism Corporation) holding the position of vice minister.

Their offices are located on the 35th–37th floors of the west tower of Parque Central in Caracas.

Post Offices

The most convenient post offices *(correos)* in Caracas are in:
C.C. Arta, next to the Chacaíto Metro station (2nd floor)
Centro Ciudad Comercial Tamanaco (CCCT), Level C–1 (by the CANTV office), in Chuao, close to the Hotel Euro-building, Hotel CCT Best Western (in the same building), Hotel Tamanaco Inter-Continental, and Hotel Paseo Las Mercedes
Parque Central (Edificio Mohedano, Level Bolívar – by Residencias Anauco Hilton, the Hotel Caracas Hilton, and the Bellas Artes Metro stop).

The office for tourist attention is on the 35th floor (tel: 571 3089/309 0247; www.venezuela.com/corpoturismo and www.venetur.com.ve). However, you may be hard-pressed to make yourself understood by any of the "English-speaking" personnel and the verbal information is less than reliable.

To obtain any printed matter (maps, brochures, posters), a written request must be submitted and appointment made.

Amazingly, there is not a single tourist information kiosk anywhere in Caracas (despite an indication on their website of one in Parque Central). They do have a booth in the international airport at Maiquetía, but this does not have regular hours.

Each state now has its own tourism office. Several are quite efficient (such as Mérida and Yaracuy) and others practically worthless. The contact details for the state tourism offices are as follows:
Amazonas:
● Dirección de Turismo, Avenida Río Negro, Palacio de Gobierno (next to the Plaza Bolívar), Puerto Ayacucho, tel/fax: (248) 21 0033.
Anzoátegui:
● Corporación del Turismo del Estado Anzoátegui (Coranztur), Palacio de Gobierno (P.B.), Avenida 5 de Julio at Calle Flores, Barcelona, tel: (281) 742 974
● Tourist kiosk, Paseo Colón, Puerto La Cruz, tel: (281) 688 170
Apure:
● Corporación Apureña de Turismo, Edif Julio Chávez, Mezanina B, Paseo Libertador (behind the statue of San Fernando), San Fernando de Apure; tel: (247) 41 2362/3320, fax: 28 309, 41 3035.
Aragua:
● Instituto Autónomo de Turismo del Estado Aragua, Museo de Antropología, Plaza Girardot, Avenida Bolívar between Calles Soublette and Mariño, Maracay; tel/fax: (243) 46 6155.
Barinas:
● Corporación Barinesa de Turismo (Corbatur), Avenida Marqués del

Foreign Consulates in Caracas

(All in Caracas, direct dial code 212)
Australia: Qta Yolanda, Avenida Luis Roche, between 6th and 7th Transversals, Altamira.
Tel: 261 4632; fax: 261 3448; e-mail: caracas@defat.gov.au
Canada: Edif Omni, Avenida 6 between 3rd and 5th Transversals, Altamira. Tel: 264 0833.

UK: Torre Las Mercedes, 3rd floor, Avenida La Estancia, Chuao.
Tel: 993 4111/5280;
fax: 993 9989;
e-mail: embcaracas@ven.net;
www.britain.org.ve
United States: Calle F at Calle Suapure, Colinas de Valle Arriba.
Tel: 975 6411; fax: 975 8971;
www.usembassy.state.gov/ven

Pumar, Nº 5–42; tel: (273) 27 091; tel/fax: 28 162; e-mail: corbatur@telcel.net.ve.
Bolívar:
● Dirección de Turismo, Gobernación del Estado Bolívar, Avenida Bolívar, Quinta Yeita Nº 59; tel: (285) 21 613, 22 362; fax: 24 535.
Carabobo:
● Calle Ricaurte with Calle Anzoátegui, Sede Desarrollo de la Costa, Gobierno de Carabobo, Puerto Cabello; tel/fax: (242) 61 4222/4622.
Cojedes:
● Unidad de Turismo-Dirección de Planificación y Desarrollo – Gobernación del Estado Cojedes, Avenida Ricaurte, Edif. Carry, upper level of Banco Lara, San Carlos; tel/fax: (258) 33 0917, tel: 33 5450/5370.
Delta Amacuro:
● Dirección de Turismo del Estado Delta Amacuro, Edif San Juan (3rd floor), Ofic 18, Calle Bolívar, Tucupita; tel/fax: (287) 21 0179/216 852.
Falcón:
● Secretaria de Turismo del Estado Falcón, Paseo Alameda, between Calles Falcón and Palmasola, Coro; tel: (268) 511 132.
● Dirección de Turismo-Estado Guárico, Avenida Principal de la Morera (beside Radio Guárico); tel/fax: (246) 32 1153.
Lara:
(all in Barquisimeto)
● Dirección de Turismo del Estado Lara, Avenida Libertador Este, Edif Fundalara (3rd floor); tel: (251) 53 9321; fax: 53 7544.

● Aeropuerto Internacional Jacinto Lara (no phone).
● Passengers' Terminal (no phone).
● Paseo Botánico El Cardenalito (highway at the eastern entrance of Barquisimeto).
Mérida:
● City of Merida: Corporación Merideña de Turismo (Cormetur), Avenida Urdaneta at Calle 45 (next to the airport); tel: (274) 263 0814/ 5918/4710; fax: 263 2782; (800) 63 743.
● Airport: tel: (274) 63 9330.
● Terminal de Pasajeros Sur, tel: (274) 63 3952.
● Jardín Acuario: Avenida Andrés Bello (across from Centro Comercial Las Tapias); tel: (274) 66 0143.
● Mercado Principal: Avenida Las Américas (2nd floor); tel: (274) 44 9366.
● By the cable car station: Calles 24 and 25, facing Plaza Las Heroinas.
Miranda:
● Corporación Mirandina de Turismo (Corpomitur), Centro Comrecial Parque Humboldt, Nivel Oficina, Oficina 2, Prados del Este, Caracas; tel: (212) 979 4075, (234) 23 2237 (Higuerote); fax: (212) 976 0806.
Monagas:
● Dirección de Turismo Estado Monagas, Avenida Alirio Uguarte Pelayo, elevado de Boquerón (next to IPAN), Hacienda El Sarrapial, Maturín; tel/fax: (291) 643 0798.
Nueva Esparta:
● Corporación de Turismo Nueva Esparta, Centro Artesanal Gilberto Menchini, Local 18, Calle Jóvito Villalba, as you enter Los Robles; tel/fax: (295) 62 2514/3098/ 4194; e-mail: corpotur@enlared.net

Portuguesa:
● Pro Turismo – Dirección de Turismo, Avenida I.N.D., in front of Fundadeporte, Guanare; tel: (257) 251 0324.
Sucre:
● Calle Sucre Nº 49 (between the Plaza Bolívar and Iglesia Santa Inés), Cumaná; tel: (293) 431 6183.
Táchira:
● Avenida España at Avenida Carabobo, Edif Cotatur, San Crístobal; tel: (276) 357 9655; fax: (276) 357 1004; e-mail: cotatur@funtha.gov.ve; www.cotatur.gov.ve
Trujillo:
● Corporación Trujillana de Turismo: Avenida Principal La Plazuela Nº 1–23, Trujillo; tel: (272) 236 1277; tel/fax: 36 1281.
Valera
● Avenida Bolívar between Calles 10 and 11; tel: (271) 54 286.
● Vargas: Dirección de Turismo del Estado Vargas, Piso 2, Ofc 6, beside Iglesia San Sebastián, Maiquetia; tel: (212) 331 2666.
Yaracuy
● San Felipe: Fundación Yaracuyana de Turismo (Funyatur), Avenida Alberto Ravell, Centro de Convenciones Henrique Tirado Reyes; tel: (254) 231 8993; fax: 231 9666; e-mail: funyatur@telcel.net.ve; www.gobernacion.yrc.gov.ve
● Yaritagua: Centro Turístico Los Carrascosa, Carrera 8 at Calle 19; tel: (251) 82 3033/3633; tel/fax: 82 3781.

Women Travelers

In terms of security, there is normally no problem for women travelers if they take normal common sense precautions.

Since old macho traditions die hard, it is still generally considered improper for a woman to go into a bar alone. By night, even in the large hotels, a woman going into the bar alone at night is normally viewed as available – thus fair game for all wolves – or a prostitute. Many discotheques refuse entry to women on their own.

Most single women travelers prefer to choose restaurants or the theater for evening entertainment and to stay on business floors in hotels where the same stigma does not apply for using the bar of the executive lounge.

Traveling With Kids

Most lodging facilities offer discounts for children. In general, camps, *hatos* (ranches), and other adventure and ecotourism destinations are not appropiate for younger children. In fact, some places refuse to admit children under a certain age, either for safety reasons or out of consideration for other guests. At Hato Piñero, for example, children are only allowed stay in the low season, and not at all if they have birders booked.

One of the best destinations for children is the Andes, since there are many places to let them run around, along with many attractions that are geared specifically to them (such as Valle Hermosa – tel: 274-63 7561), or that are as enjoyable to kids as adults, such as the reconstructed old Andean village, Los Aleros, or the science museum and aquarium in Mérida.

Non-smokers

Venezuelans smoke a lot and everywhere. Only a few of the luxury hotels have certain designated non-smoking rooms. It is very rare to encounter a restaurant that has a non-smoking section (and if it does, it is normally only a token gesture, without any physical separation from the smoking section). A few offices (mostly of foreign companies) are smoke-free.

Business Travelers

Nearly all the luxury hotels have **Executive Floors** set aside for business travelers whose rooms are often outfitted with connections for computers, e-mail, etc., and which have their own lounge and bar where continental breakfast is often served. These all offer secretarial services, the use of faxes and copiers, rooms for small meetings, etc. The Caracas Hilton and the Tamanaco Inter-Continental also have Japanese-speaking personnel and even have special Japanese menus. These hotels may have a weekly or monthly cocktail party specifically with business travelers in mind.

Various facilities have come to be offered principally, or in some cases even exclusively, for corporate clients who make extended stays. These include:

In Caracas:
Altamira Suites, tel: (212) 284 0748/220 9311, fax: 283 5574; email: info@alsuites.com
4ta Avenida Suites, tel: (212) 285 5252, fax: 285 5280; email: admveba@hotmail.com
Hotel CCT Best Western (all suites), tel: (212) 700 8000, (800) 45 835, fax: (212) 700 8090; email: ventas@bwhotelcct.com
Embassy Suites, tel: (212) 276 4200, (800) 13 313; fax: 266 65566, email: reserva@embassysuites.com.ve
Hesperia Garden Suites, tel: (212) 266 9844, 267 3333; fax: 266 6776; email: alemaral@hotmail.com; www.hoteles-hesperia.es/

In Valencia
Guaparo Suites, tel: (241) 25 0522, fax: 25 0412; www.guaparohoteles.com
Ucaima Suites, tel: (241) 22 7011, fax: 22 0461; email: ucaima@ucaima.com
Corporate rates are normally available only to companies that have made a formal request in writing and that have a certain minimum number of room nights per year. It is best to phone and find out the policy.

Chains such as **Inter-Continental** and **Hilton** afford priority treatment for frequent travelers. Maiquetía's international airport has several executive lounges, which are at the disposition of frequent-flier card-holders of various airlines.

Aserca Airlines specifically targets business travelers, offering all first-class services.

Travelers With Disabilities

Unfortunately, there is very little consideration for the disabled in Venezuela, even in the capital; in the interior, it is virtually non-existent. Few sidewalks, much less building entrances, are equipped with ramps, and sidewalks are often full of holes or obstacles, making wheelchair access difficult if not impossible. Elevators rarely have Braile indications on buttons; few bathrooms have facilities for wheelchair access.

One notable exception to the rule is in the **Sala Braile of the Museo de Arte Contemporáneo de Caracas Sofía Imber – MACCSI** (Parque Central, Nivel Lecuna, tel: (212) 572 8289/0075; www.maccsi.org.ve). In this special unit, created in 1981, they offer guided visits (where participants can appreciate sculptural pieces by touch, with accompanying explanations by the guides, and they even have paintings with overlay of Braile), directed reading (in their own Braile library focusing on topics related to art), workshops in Braile, and special vacation plans that are geared to the needs of non-sighted art lovers.

Tipping

A tip *(propina)* of 10 percent is normally added to all restaurants checks. It is customary to leave 5–10 percent extra, depending on the quality of service.

Taxi drivers are not usually tipped unless they carry bags or perform some special service.

Airport porters expect US$1 per bag and, in Maiquetía, this is generally considered to be a fee rather than a gratuity.

In top hotels, the standard for bellhops is US$1–5, depending on the amount of luggage; for chamber staff, the tip is the equivalent of US$1 per night; for special services performed by the *concierge*, tip US$3–5, though what you pay is likely to vary depending on the price of the place you are staying.

Medical Treatment

Good-quality hotels have physicians on call. Check with the concierge. There are no specifically English-speaking medical facilities in Venezuela, but many doctors and dentists, particularly specialists, speak fluent English. English-speakers are more likely to be found in private clinics than public facilities.

Public hospitals are more accustomed to handling emergencies, but some of the facilities can be sorely lacking in space, equipment, and even the most basic medical supplies.

In smaller towns in the interior of the country, there is normally only one hospital or *"ambulatorio"* – walk-in clinic. Specific addresses are not needed: anyone will be able to point you in the right direction.

Pharmacies

Venezuela has an excellent system to ensure that at least one pharmacy *(farmacia)* is open 24 hours in every sector of every town right across the country. These are identified by a lighted *Turno* sign and with the names of those *de turno* (on duty) in the vicinity posted on the doors of all the other pharmacies. Full lists are printed daily in Spanish-language papers.

Except for barbiturates, prescriptions are not required to buy any medications in the

Emergencies

The nationwide emergency phone number is **171** (when you dial, operators will direct your call to the appropriate service). This number can be dialed from public pay phones without the need to introduce coins or prepaid cards.

country. At the US Embassy, Health Unit personnel can offer advice about medications (eg. locally available remedies for common ailments, Spanish terms for medicines, illnesses, etc) and suggest English-speaking doctors.

Security & Crime

With the increase in the nation's economic problems, crime has likewise risen. However, there is no need to be overly alarmed: the grim statistics of Monday morning body counts in Caracas newspapers are not representative of the general situation visitors are likely to encounter in areas frequented by most tourists, since (sadly) 99 percent of these violent crimes are committed in the slum areas, where local people have hit rock-bottom.

Robbery

The targets of robbery are more likely to be people who appear to be "good catches." Common sense is the best guideline for avoiding problems: do not flash money around. If your hotel has secure safety deposit boxes with individual keys (not just a "place where it will be guarded" in an office), leave any valuables you will not be needing there. Always carry your documentation, but leave photocopies in a secure place.

Men should always try to carry their wallets in front rather than in a hip pocket (many people prefer around-the-waist pouches). Women should hold purses firmly under an arm and take special caution with cloth bags – in Centro, the old downtown area, there are people particularly adept at slitting them with razor blades to remove wallets or other valuables without your noticing. Don't wear expensive jewelry or any other obviously valuable objects while out in the street. When not using them, tuck cameras in a bag or purse.

Be constantly aware of what is going on around you and who is nearby – not just for suspicious looking characters on foot, but

motorcyclists who specialize in snatching purses, gold chains, etc. as they go by.

Keep away from questionable areas in Caracas, even by day: any of the *barrios* (slum) areas, anything west of Avenida Baralt, south of El Silencio, or north of Avenida Urdaneta; by night: Sabana Grande, anywhere in Centro, or Plaza Venezuela.

Car Crime

When you are traveling by car, always keep the doors locked. When you park, never leave anything inside. If you have to place objects in the trunk, do so before parking – so no one will see you "hiding" something. And never leave your vehicle unlocked in the street, even if it is "only for a minute." Should you be the unfortunate victim of a hold-up, *do not* try to resist. The criminal will almost certainly be armed and would probably not hesitate to injure you.

Three popular ploys currently being used for robberies of cars and/or occupants are: hurling rocks to break the windshield, another car purposely bumping into you, or people flagging you down with a supposedly broken down car. Especially if you are in an isolated area or it is after dark, do not even consider stopping. In the case of a "bump," take down the license plate number if possible, but the priority should be to get to the nearest populated area.

Hitchhiking

It is *not* recommended ever to hitchhike or pick up anyone (not even police) asking for or thumbing a ride. Too many people have been victims of attacks and robberies.

Checkpoints (Alcabalas)

These are encountered along the highways throughout the country. If you are stopped, you will probably be asked for personal identification, driver's license, *carnet de circulación* (registration) for the vehicle, and

National Guardsmen

Visitors are often taken aback by the sight of police and National Guardsmen toting machine guns and automatic weapons. Do not worry – it's not the sign of an imminent insurrection, just the weapon of choice for national and local security forces.

requested to open the trunk for an inspection. Don't panic – this is a nuisance, but is normal and legal. If they ask you to give them or someone else a ride (a very common request), you are neither obliged nor wise to do so.

Safety Deposit Boxes
Most high-quality accommodations either have safety deposit boxes in rooms or you can hand valuables in at the reception area for safe-keeping.

Etiquette

Dress
Though shorts are seen even on the streets of Caracas (formerly a real taboo except at beach towns), they are still not considered in good taste. Topless sunbathing is illegal, but fairly common at some beaches on Margarita (such as El Agua and Caribe).

Forms of Address
Spanish-speakers from other countries are often surprised at the immediate use by many Venezuelans of *"tú"* (the familiar use of you) and being addressed with terms normally reserved for intimate relationships. While this is a common practice, it is recommended that visitors stick to the more formal *"Usted"* form of you to avoid causing offence.

Photography
If you are planning to take a direct photo of a person, you should ask permission first. This is especially true in the case of indigenous people, who are often quite opposed to being photographed.

Getting Around

By Air

For domestic travel, every state has at least one airport for commercial flights, except for Delta Amacuro, where Tucupita airport has been out of service for some years. Travelers wishing to reach this state by air will have to fly in to Monagas' Maturín airport, then use public transportation or rent a car to reach the delta.

Avensa/Servivensa, Aserca, and Aeropostal dominate the domestic market. However, a number of regional or specialized airlines offer alternatives for specific routes and types of services on a regular basis (in addition to scores of charter services). Compare prices as there is often a surprising difference.

Public Transportation

Because the majority of the population cannot afford cars, you will find cheap public transportation available virtually everywhere. In the larger cities it is a breeze to get around effortlessly. There are large buses *(transportes* or *colectivos)*, *por puestos* (mini-buses or cars that run on set routes), *libres* (taxis) that circulate constantly and, in Caracas, the Metro (underground train).

By Bus

Urban Buses
Buses and *por puestos* (these are super cheap: the maximum ticket price anywhere within a city is about 20 US cents) post main stops and the end point of the route in the front window of their vehicles.

Rates are controlled and indicated for buses and *por puestos*. They do not operate by schedules, but rather circulate constantly; just flag them down in the *paradas* (designated bus stops along the streets).

Intercity Buses
Arrangements for intercity bus travel must be made at the *Terminal de Pasajeros* (passenger terminal), found in all towns and cities, except for the luxury lines, which have their own terminals – see below.

There are two teminals serving Caracas: **La Bandera**, at the Avenida Nueva Granada and the El Valle *autopista* intersection, near Los Próceres, with the La Bandera Metro stop nearby; and the **Terminal del Oriente "General Antonio José de Sucre"** for eastbound routes, located a short distance east of Caracas. The most convenient bus stop for transfers coming or going – buses are clearly marked "Terminal del Oriente" – is next to the Petare Metro station; for information, tel: (212) 243 2606/3253, daily 6am–11pm.

Some long-distance runs have only one or two scheduled departures per day, so call or check posted hours. In fact, most buses and *por puestos* have no set departure time, leaving only when the last seat is filled. For some buses, you can buy tickets in advance (a must, if you can get them, for peak seasons of Christmas, Carnival, Holy Week when huge lines and lack of seats are the norm).

The most common practice for popular destinations with frequent services is to just go to the terminal and take the next departing bus that looks in decent condition. Dozens of hawkers for both buses and *por puesto* cars shout out destinations, creating a circus atmosphere. Prices are fixed.

Luxury Buses
A welcome addition to bus services are the interurban bus routes of "luxury" lines. They have fixed departure times, tickets can be

Distances

If you are driving straight through with only normal brief stops for gasoline, restroom visits, a quick bite to eat, taking the most direct/quickest route, any major city in the country is one day's drive from Caracas. Flying time is under 2 hours for the most distant commercial flight from Maiquetía.

purchased in advance, buses are new and air-conditioned, with TV or video, bathroom, and they even have trip attendants. The only drawback is that they also have permanently closed curtains, making it impossible to view the landscape and you are forced either to watch the TV or sleep in the dark interior. The principal lines include the following (for others, see *Transporte de Pasajeros* in the Yellow Pages):

Aeroexpresos Ejecutivos
Avenida Principal de Bello Campo, Caracas
Tel: Caracas (212) 266 2321 266 3601/2214; Puerto La Cruz (281) 67 8855
Email: info@ aeroexpresos.com.ve; www.aeroexpresos.com.ve
With services running between Caracas, Maracay, Valencia, Barquisimeto, Maracaibo, Puerto La Cruz, and Maturín.

Expresos Camargüi
Avenida Principal de San Martín, behind Edif Bloque Dearmas, Caracas
Tel: (212) 471 4614.
Has routes between Caracas and Puerto La Cruz, Cumaná, Cariaco, Carúpano, Punta de Mata, Maturín, Anaco, Cantaura, El Tigre, Ciudad Bolívar, Temblador, Tucupita, and Ciudad Guayana. Expresos Camargüi also offer a taxi service to the terminal.

Expresos Los Llanos
Terminal La Bandera, near the La Bandera Metro stop, Caracas.
Tel: (212) 243 6140.
This company has perhaps the most extensive service in the country, with routes connecting Caracas with all major coastal cities from Maracaibo to Carúpano and just about every point in the interior from San Antonio de Táchira and Mérida to Barinas, San Fernando de Apure, Barquisimeto, Ciudad Guayana, Santa Elena de Uairén, Tucupita, and Güiria – and several points in between.

Peli Express
Behind Pro Venezuela, near Plaza Venezuela Metro stop, Caracas
Tel: (212) 794 1442/0077, Puerto La Cruz (281) 86 0623, 81 8767/ 6286, 80 3772, (414) 980 3705.
Offers a service between Caracas, Puerto La Cruz, and Valencia.

Rodovias
Avenida Libertador, 100 meters from Colegio de Ingenieros Metro stop, Paseo Amador Bendayán, Caracas
Tel: (212) 577 6622/7011/7765; e-mail: info@rodovias.com.ve; www.rodovias.com.ve.
Rodovias has daily services for Puerto La Cruz, Cumaná, Carúpano, Maturín, Ciudad Bolívar, Ciudad Guayana, and Valencia.

By Ferry

Conferry, in Caracas, (tel: 212-782 8544) offers a service for cars or passengers between Puerto La Cruz (tel: 281-267 7847/8253) and Cumaná (tel: 293-66 1903), and Margarita Island (tel: 295-61 9235; www.conferry.com).

Buy tickets well ahead in peak vacation periods. If you are driving, you must line up 2 hours' ahead of scheduled departure time (ferries are notoriously non-compliant with schedules). Two types of ferries are offered: *Convencional* has two sections – the extremely basic *segunda* (or *turista*) class, with open "windows" permitting fresh air to waft around, plastic seating and long tables, a TV, and a snack bar, and *primera* (with air conditioning, theater-type seats, and a fancier snack bar); and the Margarita Express, supposedly more rapid (not always the case), more elegant, and considerably more expensive. The Margarita Express has no choice of seating except inside an enclosed salon with deep-freeze-level air conditioning, making a sweater or blanket necessary.

In 2002, a new catamaran service operated by Conferry began operating between the port of La Guaira, near Caracas, and Margarita. This has been warmly welcomed by Caracas residents. Check with Conferry as delays to new routes are regrettably common *(see details above)*.

Gran Cacique Express (Puerto La Cruz, tel: 281-63 0935; Margarita, tel: 295-98 339, fax: 800-22 726, e-mail: naviarca@telcel.net.ve) has a passenger service only, with transfer between Puerto La Cruz–Margarita in under 2 hours; VIP service.

Naviarca (tel: 293-31 5577/433 0909) also has a car/passenger service, Cumaná–Araya and Cumaná–Margarita. If you are taking your car, try to go in the morning, as an open barge-like ferry and afternoon winds and waves leave your car bathed with salt water. Neither of these routes has set schedules: the services simply depart when the ferry is full.

There is a very inexpensive passenger-only service between Chacopata (on the Araya Peninsula, Sucre state) and Coche Island, continuing to Margarita, where it lands in Porlamar.

Driving

Driving in Caracas is an exercise in self-preservation and frustration, and a test of your nerve. The city is chaotic, congested, and filled with manic, aggressive drivers who consider traffic regulations mere suggestions. However, once you escape this madhouse, driving in the interior is pleasant and the highways are considered to be the best in Latin America.

In many areas, driving is the *only* way to get a chance to appreciate landscapes, explore quaint villages, mingle with the locals, and check out crafts and foods sold along the roadside, all of which is usually missed when taking other forms of transport.

Night Driving

Driving at night is not advisable since lighting, lane markings, and warnings of obstacles are poor to non-existent, and there are frequently animals in the road.

Traffic Laws

Enforcement of driving laws is virtually non-existent in Venezuela. It was hoped that the new Ley de Tránsito (Traffic Law) would finally bring about changes, especially since the fines it outlines for non-compliance were initially viewed as an attractive source of income for local governments, but not even that incentive has motivated traffic police to resolve the anarchy that reigns in the streets.

Driving is on the right. Legally, use of seat belts is required, motorcyclists must wear helmets, and use of cellular phones by drivers in motion is prohibited. However these regulations (along with speed limits – few of which are even posted) are ignored with impunity owing to non-enforcement.

Street Parking

Street parking in big cities, especially Caracas, is often next to impossible. Vehicles are parked everywhere – on sidewalks, by fire hydrants, blocking driveways, etc. Occasional operativos are carried out, usually on Friday or before holidays, more for the rapid accumulation of funds than to promote compliance with the law, when illegally parked cars (and often legally parked ones) are towed away. They are supposed to write in chalk on the pavement the location of the official lots of the transit police where your car has been taken, but this is not always done. This, coupled with the high incidence of car theft (90 per day stolen in Caracas), means it's best to use an enclosed parking lot or garage (estacionamiento) and use public transportation from then on.

Valet Parking

Many establishments offer valet parking. While convenient, it is not necessarily safe: there have been many cases of items stolen from the cars, keys duplicated and later used to steal the cars, car thefts of prized models by the attendents, and vehicles damaged by the parqueros. Claims to insurance companies are normally rejected, since you voluntarily handed over your keys to an unknown person.

Car Rental

Car rental agencies have counters at all major airports and hotels. Those near "adventure areas" also rent 4WD vehicles. During peak vacation periods, reservations should be made well in advance. Rental fees are very high, with the lowest basic rate available for an economy compact at about US$85

Car Rental Agencies

These numbers are available nationwide, toll-free for reservations:

Auto 727 – Tel: (800) 25 084, email: reservaciones@auto727.com
Avis – Tel: (800) 22 776, email: avisven@cantv.net
Budget – Tel: (800) 28 343, (212) 263 4359; www.budget.com.ve
Hertz – Tel: (800) 43 781, email: rafbell@cantv.com
Other large agencies without toll-free numbers are:
Aco – Tel: (212) 991 2744
Dollar – Tel: (212) 979 0630/4132

per day. However, as a slight compensation, gasoline is the cheapest in the world.

Get full insurance coverage since Venezuelans are notoriously aggressive drivers and are usually uninsured. Make sure the carnet de circulación (registration) is in the car when delivered or you could run into problems at the frequent alca-balas (police or National Guard checkpoints) scattered all along the nation's highways.

To rent a car you must have a credit card and valid driver's license. The following companies have a minimum age restriction: 25 years for Hertz; 23 with Avis.

Taxis

Registered taxis have yellow license plates with black letters and can be hailed in the street. Meters are not used, so agree on a price (bargaining is OK) before you get in. There is usually a minimum base price agreed upon by all the taxi lines in an area, even if you are only going a block, and the price goes up from there – ask several cabs if you suspect one is trying to take advantage of your being a foreigner. Even in heavy traffic, no trip within the city with one of the circulating taxis should cost more than the equivalent of about US$15.

For your own safety, avoid the **piratas**, who are illegally operating freelancers (check for yellow plates, since many mount the boxy "Taxi" signs on top of their car).

Taxis with sitios – lines that have a specific place where they park (usually with a phone box for clients to call them for pick-up) – charge more than the taxis that simply circulate looking for fares.

Taxi lines operating out of the luxury hotels charge considerably more than other lines with sitios.

Longer Taxi Hire

You can also hire taxis by the hour or day, for city sightseeing or going to nearby destinations (such as the beaches), for much less than renting a car and you don't have to worry about getting lost, parking, or defensive driving.

If you don't speak Spanish, check the Language section on page 360 of this guide for some basic phrases.

Tours

All major travel agencies (the larger hotels in the country all count travel agencies among their services) offer numerous options for both local tours and trips farther afield. These include many all-inclusive charter flights, principally with the destination of Isla Margarita *(see Specialist Tours on page 314.)*

There are also many lodgings, tour operators, and travel agents who have their own websites and can be contacted via e-mail.

The Latin American Travel Association, based in London (tel: 020 8715 2913; www.lata.org) is dedicated to the promotion of Latin America as a travel destination. It produces a useful free factual guide to the region, including Venezuela, with a list of tour operators, ground handlers, airlines, and hotels that operate there.

Maps

Metro Guía, in La California Metro station, just outside the turnstiles, sells maps, guidebooks, Metro tickets, and phone cards. **Librería Tecni-Ciencias**, one of the capital's most complete bookstores (CCCT, Centro Lido – near Chacaíto Metro, Torre Phelps – facing Plaza Venezuela, Centro Sambil) has many maps of Venezuela, including Roberto Marrero's series on the Gran Sabana.

Speed Limits

Speed limits are all posted in kilometers per hour, although it is rare to ever see limits posted or anyone paying any attention to speed limits. Unless otherwise indicated by signs, limits are:
•Urban streets and roads: 40 kph (25 mph) except near schools, hospitals, and military installations, where the limit is 15 kph (9 mph)
•*Autopistas* (highways): 80 kph (50 mph) in the left lane, 60 kph (37 mph) in right lane
•Rural roads: 60 kph (37 mph) during the daytime, 50 kph (30 mph) at night.

Caracas A–Z

This section covers everything you need to know about visiting Caracas. It is followed by an A–Z of Isla Margarita *(see page 330)*. For information about the rest of Venezuela, turn to page 337. Unless otherwise noted, all phone numbers in this section have area code 212.

Choosing a Hotel

With the emphasis on business travelers, decent mid-priced lodging is difficult to find. Though dozens of these hotels are found in the Plaza Venezuela to El Rosal area, surrounding the popular Sabana Grande Boulevard, they are almost exclusively by-the-hour places (with *por ratos* – just for a while – rates clearly posted) frequented by prostitutes and their clients. Hotels in *Centro* are likewise not recommended because of the high degree of insecurity at night.

Hotel Listings

Hotels are listed alphabeticaly.

Atlantida
Avenida La Salle, beside La Nunciatura Apostólica, Los Caobos.
Tel: 793 3211
Fax: 781 3696
E-mail: atlantida@telcel.net.ve
Near Plaza Venezuela and Sabana Grande shopping and restaurant areas; fax, internet, and e-mail services. **$$$$**

Avila
Avenida George Washington, San Bernardino
Tel: 555 3000
Fax: 552 8367
E-mail: havila@cantv.net

Very traditional, in a tranquil residential area, with extensive grounds and swimming pool. **$$**

Hotel Hilton Caracas
Avenida Sur 25 con Avenida Mexico, Apartado 6380, Caracas 1010-A
Tel: 503 5000
Fax: 503 5003
www.hiltoncaracas.com.ve
In the financial and cultural heart of the city, 35 minutes from the airport and with views of Caobos Park. 738 renovated rooms and suites and three restaurants. **$$$$**

CCCT-Best Western
Centro Ciudad Comercial Tamanaco (CCCT), Avenida La Estancia, Chacao
Tel: (800) 46 835, 902 8000
Fax: 959 6697/9972
E-mail: hotelcct@cantv.net
Within the huge, CCCT shopping center; suites with kitchen; swimming pool, gymnasium, sauna, tennis; rental of in-room faxes, computers, cell phones. Price includes breakfast. Weekend discount of 40 percent. **$$$**

Centro Lido
Avenida Francisco de Miranda, El Rosal
Tel: 952 5040
Fax: 952 2944
E-mail: hotelcentrolido@yahoo.com
In the sophisticated Centro Lido shopping center. Very pretty, but pricey boutique hotel. All rooms have two phone lines with voice mail, fax and laptops, Jacuzzi. A special weekend "honeymoon" (but you don't have to be newlyweds) package for two people has a 50 percent discount. **$$$$**

Continental Altamira
Avenida San Juan Bosco, Altamira
Tel: 261 0644
Fax: 262 0243
E-mail: reservaciones@hotel-continental.org
In the heart of one of the capital's best restaurant zones, two blocks above Plaza Francia and Altamira Metro. Swimming pool. 20 percent discount plus free breakfast buffet at weekends. **$$$**

El Cid
Avenida San Felipe, entre 1ra y 2da Transversal, La Castellana.
Tel: 263 2611
Fax: 263 5578

E-mail: cumarucidhotel@cantv.net
Modest fully equipped suites with
kitchen. Quiet side street in heart
of La Castellana–Altamira
restaurant and banking district,
opposite new Letonia Center.
Peruvian restaurant. 25 percent
discount on weekends. **$$**

El Condor
3ra Avenida Las Delicias
Sabana Grande
Tel: 762 9911–15/762 7621
Fax: 762 8621
Easy access to shopping, though
not the best area by night. Good
Italian restaurant. **$**

**Eurobuilding Caracas
Hotel & Suites**
Avenida La Guarita, Chuao
Tel: 902 2187–88
Fax: 907 2189/993 9285
E-mail: euro@ven.net
Great expanses of marble and glass
give this hotel a rather sterile look.
Short walk from Las Mercedes
restaurant, gallery zone, and CCCT
shopping mall. Three styles of
Sunday brunch. Spanish nouvelle
cuisine in luxury restaurant. 50
percent discount on weekends. **$$$$**

Gran Meliá Caracas
Avenida Casanova at the end of

Calle El Recreo, Sabana Grande
Tel: (800) 63 542/762 8111
Fax: 762 3737
E-mail: caracas@gran-melia.com.ve
www.solmelia.es
Gigantic super luxury hotel with 432
rooms, a separate tower of apart-
suites, convention area for 3,000;
two pools. There is a 45 percent
discount on weekends. **$$$$**

Hotel Shelter Suites
End of Avenida Libertador with Calle
José Félix Sosa, Chacao
Tel/fax: 265 3866–9
Directly opposite C.C. Centro
Sambil (a huge shopping center);
good Italian restaurant. Ten percent
discount on weekends. **$$**

JW Marriott
Calle Mohedano with Avenida
Venezuela, El Rosal
Tel: 957 2222
Fax: 957 1111
www.marriott.com
Large hotel with cocktail lounge,
hair salon, gift shop, business
center, restaurant. In-house leisure
options include outdoor pool,
solarium, health club, whirlpool,
and sauna. **$$$$**

Lincoln Suites
Avenida Francisco Solano López,
between Avenida Los Jabilos and
Jerónimo, Sabana Grande
Tel: 761 2727
Fax: 762 5503
In the heart of Sabana Grande
boulevard shopping and restaurant
area. Internet connection, small
living area, classiest lodging in this
zone. Weekend rate. Not the best
area at night. **$$$**

Paseo Las Mercedes
End of Avenida Principal de Las
Mercedes, in C.C. Paseo Las
Merecedes
Tel: 991 0033
Fax: 993 0341
Great location: shopping in mall in
front of the Tamanaco Inter-
Continental, in the heart of one of
the city's principal cultural zones.
Lobby has chic bar and café; pool.
30 percent weekend discount. **$$$**

Tamanaco Inter-Continental
End of Avenida Principal de Las
Mercedes
Tel: 909 7000
Fax: 909 7116

E-mail: caracas@interconti.com
"Grand dame" of the capital's
luxury hotels. Built in the 1950s
when its now privileged location
overlooking the Las Mercedes zone
of prime restaurants and galleries
was "out in the country," it still
enjoys a reputation as a status
hotel for social and business
affairs, though lately service has
slipped. There is a weekend
discount of nearly 60 percent. **$$$$**

Hoteles del Amor

Throughout the county, you will
come across a great number of love
hotels (usually referred to as
"*moteles*"), some enormous and
very showy, but all easily identified
by their separate very discreet
entrance and exit with the
"reception" just a booth to pay at
the entrance. These are not
brothels (you bring your own
partner), but places where lovers
can go for a private encounter in
surroundings that are often very
luxurious.
    These have come about as much
from the fact that many young
adults cannot afford to live
independently, and are forced to
live with their parents (often even
once they are married) with no
private space for intimate
encounters, as by the high level of
extramarital activity that seems to
be a national sport. Since they are
geared toward short-time use, you
cannot come and go. Keys are left

in a bin as you leave, with re-entry possible only if you pay again.

Eating Out

Caracas is reputed to have more restaurants per capita than any other city in Latin America. Your problem will not be finding a place to eat, but deciding where.

The two principal zones for a large concentration and variety of restaurants are **Las Mercedes** and the **Altamira–Los Palos Grandes–La Castellana** (divisions between these last three exist only on maps; they all run together in a tightly packed area). **La Candelaria**, the Spanish sector in Centro, is known for its ethnic restaurants and tascas, but is best visited just for lunch since the zone is not safe by night. The same goes for **Avenida Francisco Solano**, which parallels the "Gran Avenida" pedestrian boulevard of Sabana Grande, with its many Italian and Spanish specialty eateries.

If you are into very serious sampling among the capital's hundreds of choices, you might pick up Miro Popic's annual Guía Gastronómica de Caracas (Spanish–English; available at bookstores, around US$15). It reviews virtually every place serving food in Caracas, and includes nightspots and places in surrounding areas.

For the latest "in" places, see the weekly reviews of restaurants, cafés, and nightspots in Feriada in Sunday's El Nacional, and Guía de la Ciudad in Thursday's El Universal.

The monthly magazine Exceso includes reviews of all the principal restaurants, cafés, and nightspots in Caracas.

Restaurant Listings

Below is a sampler of the variety available among all styles and prices ranges.

Ara
Centro Lido (8th floor), Avenida Francisco de Miranda, El Rosal
Tel: 953 3270
Bistro-style menu. Roof-top setting

with open-air Oriental garden. Chic clientele. Regular live music and comedy. Closed 3–7pm and Sunday. **$$$**

Arabica Café
Multicentro Los Palos Grandes, Avenida Andrés Bello, between Avenida Francisco de Miranda and 1ra Transversal
Tel: 285 6748
Estate-grown coffees, mouth-watering pastries, light fare. Nifty loft inside with newspapers and magazines for leisurely reading, plus outdoor seating. Open daily 7am–11pm, candlelit by night. **$$**

Bar Basque
Alcabala a Peligro, La Candelaria.
Tel: 576 5955
Considered for years one of, if not the best restaurant in Caracas. Tiny place with Basque home cooking; an institution for well over three decades. Closed Sun and Aug. Reservations recommended. Zone best visited only by day. **$$**

Centro de Arte La Estancia
Avenida Francisco de Miranda, La Florida (1 block east of Altamira Metro).
Tel: 208 6622, 285 6793
Oasis of tranquility in the center of one of Caracas's busiest zones. Set within the walls of a former coffee plantation, with beautiful gardens (guided visits offered) and a restored hacienda housing a gallery with constantly changing exhibits focusing on design. There is also an outdoor café with refined atmosphere featuring occasional live music. Closed Sun. **$–$$**

Cleopatra
Avenida Principal del Bosque, at Calle Santa Clara
Tel: 731 1769
For well over 30 years, Cleopatra has been serving up delicious Lebanese fare at reasonable prices and with fast service. **$$**

Chez Wong & Grill
Avenida Principal de La Castellana (facing the plaza), Edif Iasa, first floor
Tel: 266 5015/264 6332
After years in its original location on Avenida Francisco Solano in Sabana Grande, with the changing atmosphere of that zone, this

precedent-setting establishment owned and operated by Yuman Ley Wong and his son moved to a more inviting location and changed its name. Creative Chinese cooking head and shoulders above others of its genre, with regional specialties such as smoked duck with tea leaves and jasmine. Forget about fried rice and chow mein here! **$$$**

Da Guido
Avenida Francisco Solano near Las Acacias, Sabana Grande.
Tel: 763 0937
Unpretentious but consistently good traditional Italian cooking; run for well over 20 years, with a faithful following. Best visited only by day due to the undesirable flavor of the zone after dark. **$$**

Das Pastelhaus
Calle La Paz and Calle Santa Rosalía (at the corner of the plaza), El Hatillo
Tel: 963 5486
Delicious German pastries downstairs; the upper terrace serves both Italian and French-style (with white sauce rather than tomato sauce) pizzas. Closed Mon. **$$**

Delicatesses Indú
Calle Villaflor, between Boulevard and Avenida Casanova, Sabana Grande
Tel: 762 0669
For years this places has maintained a standard of high-quality vegetarian Indian cooking. No alcohol or smoking allowed. There is an economical fixed-price lunch menu. Closed Sun. **$$**

El Buffet Vegetariano
Avenida Los Jardines Nº 4, La Florida
Tel: 730 7490/7512
Healthy, generously served cafeteria-style vegetarian fare; family atmosphere. Daily fixed-price menu. No smoking or alcohol. Open weekdays 11.30am–2.30pm. **$**

El Portón
Avenida Pinchincha and Calle Guaicaipuro, El Rosal
Tel: 952 0027/0302
Traditional Venezuelan-style specialties, particularly beef; usually with live música criolla weekends and evenings. **$$**

Price Categories

Prices for restaurants in Caracas are quoted in US$, but payable in bolívars at the exchange rate of the day. Prices based on a three-course meal for one, without alcoholic beverages.
$ = under $10
$$ = $10–$20
$$$ = $20–$30
$$$$ = over $30

Fritz & Franz
Avenida San Juan Bolsco with third cross street, Edif La Placette, Altamira
Tel: 265 5724
Traditional German cuisine. The restaurant is surrounded by many popular nightspots. Open noon–10.30pm, closed Mon. **$$**

Fuente de Soda Papagallo
C.C. Chacaíto, Chacaíto
Tel: 962 1008
An institution, with an enormous menu, consistently tasty meals, and speedy service. The fixed-price lunch menu is a real bargain, and the pizzas are great. Excellent value. Great place for people-watching. Open 8am–midnight. **$$**

L'Attico
Avenida Luis Roche and 2da Transversal, Altamira
Tel: 265 8555
American-style casual restaurant (open-sided balcony is the best spot) and lively bar with occasional live music. Great burgers, varied menu, from clam chowder and cornbread to Tex-Mex and Italian fare. Open Sun 9am–1 or 2am, other days noon–the last client leaves. (Check out their Boston Bakery downstairs, tel: 263 2457, for special homemade breads, pastries, and light fare.) **$$**

Le Petit Bistrot de Jacques
Avenida San Felipe, La Castellana (facing McDonald's)
Tel: 263 8595
Traditional French bistro with a faithful following for its authenticity and consistency. Closed Sunday. The adjacent Bistrot Express has take-out and deliver service, tel: (800) 84 282. **$$$**

Marco Polo Ristorante
Avenida Francisco de Miranda, Torre La Primera, Campo Alegre (two blocks east of Chacaíto Metro)
Tel: 953 5131
Long-time favorite for traditional Italian cuisine in an elegant setting. Live music for Saturday lunch (accordion and singer), and opera-style show that uses the entire restaurant for its "stage" Fri and Sat after 9.30pm. Open daily noon–3.30pm, 7.30–11pm. **$$$**

Maute Grill
Avenida Río de Janeiro, Las Mercedes.
Tel: 991 0892
Skip the American West motif A/C bar and head to the rear for the restaurant part surrounding a traditional Venezuelan-style tree-filled patio. Excellent beef. **$$**

News Caffé
1ra Transversal at 1ra Avenida (behind Centro Plaza), Los Palos Grandes
Tel: 286 5096
Interesting combination of well-stocked bookstore and multiple sections with distinct atmospheres, popular with a chic clientele. Restaurant with creative menu, café, bar, live music Thur–Sat at 9pm; open daily 10am–1am. **$$**

Samui
Multicentro Los Palos Grandes, Avenida Andrés Bello, between Avenida Fancisco de Miranda and first cross street, Los Palos Grandes (no sign, next to Arabica Café
Tel: 285 4600
Rated by *The New York Times* as "the best Thai restaurant in South America" – with good reason. Beautiful interior, outstanding food and presentation. Closed Sun. **$$$$**

Urrutia
Avenida Francisco Solano, corner of Manguitos, Sabana Grande
Tel: 763 0448
Calle Madrid, corner of Monterrey, Las Mercedes
Tel: 993 9526
More than 30 years of consistent excellence in its original location in Sabana Grande, and now with a second site in the posher Las Mercedes zone called Casa Urrutia, serving traditional Spanish dishes, with emphasis on seafood. Las Mercedes location closed Sun. **$$$**

Nightlife

Like most places, the main time for enjoying nightlife is on weekends, but in Caracas, bars, discos, and other hang-outs also do a healthy business any night of the week.

Bars and Music

For more traditional nightlife of dancing, drinking, music, and cafés, Las Mercedes is the best area, with a great variety of dynamic places, and with the best security. *Caraqueños* are an extremely fickle audience, always seeking something new, different, and with infallible service. If a place begins to slacken, you can be sure it will be gone soon. In Las Mercedes, there is every type of place – from **Taz Sports Bar** (open 24 hours a day, live music) to a score of *terrazas* (open-air cafés that don't come alive until late at night) or a growing number of places with gourmet ice cream such as **4-D**, **Bravíssimo**, and **Gelatería Parmalat**.

While an older audience hits places like **Tapas de Madrid** for the evening, the younger crowd is out cruising to see where the action is, very likely changing places several times in an evening.

Check out listings at www.planetaurbe.com to find out where the hottest places are to be found.

Best Nightspots

Al Trote
Avenida Andrés Bello, between first and second cross streets, Edif Everí
Tel: 286 3426
"In" place popular with a diverse clientele ranging from the arty crowd to yuppies. Two levels with modern New York styling, alternative music from electronic to jazz; light snacks.

El Maní es Así
Calle El Cristo
Sabana Grande district
Tel: 763 6671
Famous for live salsa and an

Tascas

Tascas are popular Spanish-style bars serving drinks

intimate atmosphere. Open daily from 5pm till very late.

El Sarao
C.C. Bello Campo, basement
Tel: 267 2503
Overflowing on weekends with people who love to dance to salsa, merengue, and other infectious Latin rhythms. Open daily 5pm–dawn.

Juan Sebastián Bar
Avenida Venezuela, El Rosal
Tel: 951 5575
The best jazz bands; a clientele that comes for the music, not to see and be seen.

Pal's Club
CCCT, Nivel C-1 (entrance from parking lot), Chuao
Tel: 959 1690
Elegant place for upscale crowd, with cyberbar, dining area, bar, and dance floor.

Patatu's Drive Pub & Grill
C.C. Los Chaguaramos
Tel: 662 5085
Tex-Mex cooking; 1960s-style live music (and interior decoration to match) Tues–Thur, Sat; Ladies Night: 7.30– 9.30pm Wed–Thur. Other nights music for three generations. Closed Sun.

Cultural Activities

Caracas has a dynamic cultural agenda. To find out what's going on, check the free weekly calendar in *El Universal* newspaper (in Spanish). *The Daily Journal* (in English) carries a calendar of events every day, with its Friday listings the most exhaustive. There are also culture/events pages published daily in the Spanish-language newspapers.

Theater
The majority of live presentations take place in the complex of the Bellas Artes zone in Los Caobos:
Ateneo de Caracas
Tel: 573 4622
Theater, movies, gallery, music.

Casa del Artista
Boulevard Amador Bendayán,
Quebrada Honda (by the mosque),
near Colegio de Ingenieros subway.
Tel: 576 5518/8865
Cultural complex that is headquarters of the Union of Artists of Venezuela.
Rajatabla
Tel: 572 6109
Alternative theater.
Teatro Teresa Carreño
Tel: (800) 67372/574 9122
The country's principal theater, which features everything from opera to rock concerts.
　　The venue for larger events (especially pop concerts) is usually the **Poliedro** (tel: 681 3333). Take La Rinconda exit from westbound El Valle *autopista* (indicated as the route for Maracay). The principal luxury hotels also hold concerts in their main salons.

Art
The greatest concentration of private galleries is found in **Las Mercedes**, with Sunday (roughly 11am–2pm) the principal day for openings and the favorite time for art lovers to make the rounds (mainly because this is the only day you can easily find parking). The **Bellas Artes** zone offers the following important galleries (for further details, *see page 140–1*):
Museo de Arte Contempóraneo de Caracas Sofía Imber
Tel: 573 8289
One of the best on the continent.
Museo de Bellas Artes
Tel: 578 1819
Mainly temporary exhibitions. Excellent view from the sculpture terrace.

Festivals

There are many annual festivals, ranging from dance, theater, and jazz to Latin music and chamber music. Since dates and locations of presentations vary, it is best to keep an eye out for announcements in the local media and banners strung across principal avenues.

Galería de Arte Nacional
Tel: 578 1818
Four centuries of Venezuelan art. Other important sites for art and cultural events scattered through the city include:
Casa Rómulo Gallegos (CELARG)
Tel: 285 2990
Avenida Luis Roche at third cross street, Altamira
Museo Alejandro Otero
Tel: 682 0941
La Rinconada
Fundación Corp Group Centro Cultural
Tel: 206 3246/1149
Torre Corp Banca, La Castellana
Museo de Arte Colonial Quinta de Anauco
Tel: 551 8650
Avenida Panteón, San Bernardino
Sala Mendoza
Tel: 571 7120
Avenida Andrés Belllo, Edif Las Fundaciones, PB, Local 10
Gallery with over 40 years in the spotlight, bookstore focusing on international art publications, beautiful artistic and indigenous crafts, café, gallery.
Centro de Arte La Estancia
Tel: 208 0412
Avenida Francisco de Miranda, La Floresta

Science
Museo de Ciencias Naturales
Tel: 571 1265/577 5094/577 5103/577 5786
Fax: 573 2368
E-mail: informacion@museo-de-ciencias.org
www.museo-de-ciencias.org
Plaza Los Museos, Parque Los Caobos, Bellas Artes
Along with permanent and changing exhibits relating to natural sciences, the museum has free weekly lectures on various scientific themes (upon request, they will send by email schedules of upcoming talks). Closed Mon, free.

For Kids

Caracas provides a fair number of activities specifically geared toward children. Various restaurants (such as **Cristal Ranch**, Avenida Principal,

Las Mercedes) have clowns and other entertainment for kids on Sunday afternoon.

Museo de los Niños (Wed–Sun; closed noon–2pm) is the most outstanding offer in the capital for kids (and fascinating for adults too); the enormous hands-on children's museum in Parque Central should not be missed (see page 140).

Parks such as **Caricuao Zoo**, including a kids' petting zoo (near the Zoológico Metro stop) and **Parque del Este** (Metro stop of same name); and the **Museo de Transporte** next door are ideal destinations. **Parque los Caobos** nearly always has informal clown performances on Sunday.

Teatro Tilingo (tel: 793 7249; Avenida Andrés Bello, Parque Aristides Rojas, Maripérez) offers theater for kids every weekend (Sat 3pm; Sun 4.30pm); as does **Sala Cadafe** (tel: 208 8355; Edif Cadafe, Avenida Sanz, El Marqués; Sat 4pm; Sun times vary – call in advance).

The **Cinemataca Nacional** (tel: 576 1491, Galería de Arte Nacional, Los Caobos) has movies especially for children on Sunday at 11.30am.

The **Centro Ciudad Comercial Tamanaco** (CCCT) in Chacao has enough attractions to keep kids amused for hours (see Shopping, below, for details).

Emergency Services

MEDICAL

Ambulances of the fire department of the Federal District. Tel: 545 4545/577 9209.

Aeromed Aeroambulancias: Transfer of patients in critical condition on national and international highways, and in airplanes specially equipped for intensive care; transfer on land by ambulances to assistance center at the destination. 24-hour emergency service. Tel: 993 2541, 992 8980, (416) 625 1391.

Centro Móvil de Medicina Permanente Emergency service with doctors who can make 24-hour house calls, tel: 483 7021/6092.

Hospitals

Clínica El Avila: Avenida San Juan Bosco 6th Transversal, Altamira. Tel: 276 1111/1013 (private).

Clínica Cardiológica San Pablo: Calle La Peña at Calle La Guairita, Lomas de Las Mercedes. Emergency – tel: 991 2121/5454 and 999 2211/2301.

Clínica de Emergencia Infantil: (children's emergencies) Edif Topacio, Avenida Avila, between avenidas Caracas and Gamboa. Tel: 577 6136/7381/8211/9854 (private).

Hospital Universitario: Universidad Central de Venezuela. Tel: 606 7111 (public).

DENTAL

The following clinics have some English-speaking staff:

Centro de Especialidades Odontológicas: Avenida Principal, Chuao, children's services: tel: 991 6122/6801; adult services: tel: 991 6422/6877.

Clínica Odontológica Oreadi: CCCT, Oficina 218 Chuao. Tel: 959 1948/1971.

Centro Odontológico El Prisma: El Pirámide (same exit as for C.C. Concresa, right next door), Prados del Este, first floor by the gasoline station, tel (416) 625 1795, 979 4280/2245. 24-hour emergency service.

Transportation

THE METRO

The **Metro** (subway/underground train) is the pride of Caracas, with three lines providing stops all along the main corridors for business, shopping, and cultural attractions. A complementary system of Metrobuses combines Metro travel with buses that cover extensive routes from each stop.

Tickets can be purchased for the Metro alone or combinado, good for a Metro ride and continuing service on Metrobus (or vice versa). Much more economical (and saving you from waiting in long lines) are the multi-abono and multi-abono combinado tickets, valid for 10 rides at a flat fee. Tickets are also available at many newsstands, identified with a large M.

The Metro runs from 5am–11pm (with the exception of a few stations in run-down areas, which close earlier, and are better avoided anyway) and is very clean, with excellent security.

TAXIS

For reliable late night/early morning taxi service in Caracas (such as early-morning pick-ups to get you to the airport, or pre-arranged pick-ups from isolated areas at specific times) there are several 24-hour service radio-link taxi lines.

Coventaxis Tel: 576 6865/6533/577 0368

Taxi Movil-Enlace Tel: 577 0922/3344. American Express accepted.

Taxitour Tel: 794 1264/1365 & 793 9744, (800) 82 948. Visa, MasterCard accepted.

TaxiVen Tel: 985 0296/5715.

TeleTaxi Tel: 753 9122/4155. Visa, MasterCard, and American Express are accepted.

If speed is of the essence, traffic is at a standstill, and you are feeling brave, another option is **Pronto Taxi**, which pioneered a motorcycle taxi service in Caracas. Passengers are provided with helmets and even raincoats and the use of an enclosed compartment for personal items if the weather is nasty. Tel: 793 4981, 263 7959. One of the main places where the riders gather is the east end of the Chacaíto pedestrian boulevard (see also page 323).

Shopping

SHOPPING MALLS

There are numerous shopping malls (centros comerciales) in Caracas. The biggest and best are: **Centro Sambil** (Avenida Libertador) and **Centro Ciudad Comercial Tamanaco** (CCCT), both in Chacao. The first, reputed to be the largest mall in Latin America, has, along with 540 stores, a marine aquarium, an annex of the Museo Jacobo Borges art museum, a recreation center with bowling alley, a Play Adventure amusement park, Tierra Increible (with galactic adventures, robot dinosaurs, and interactive displays), discotheque, theaters, and many other attractions.

CRAFTS

For gorgeous museum-quality Venezuelan crafts, no place compares with **Casa Caruba** (tel: 283 9368; Avenida Andrés Bello, between the first and second cross streets, Edif Everi, Los Palos Grandes; Mon–Fri 10am–1pm, 3–7pm; Sat 10am–7pm, closed Sun), though prices are very high. These are works of art created by fine Venezuelan craftsmen, from wood carvings and hammocks to jewelry and furniture.

The colonial village of **El Hatillo** (Metrobus from the Altamira Metro stop) is the best place to spend a full day's leisurely browsing on foot. For several blocks in each direction from the traditional Plaza Bolívar, the vintage buildings are jammed with small shops that house everything from mini-galleries and workshops creating one-of-a-kind gold jewelry, to ceramics, books, unique clothing, spices, and antiques. A prime attraction is **Hannsi**, indisputably the place with the best selection of Venezuelan handicrafts in the country (its representation of indigenous art is particularly outstanding). Almost every place is closed Monday – if you are offered tours on a Monday to the town, just say no.

There are restaurants for every taste – **Sake** (Japanese), **Casaccia** and **La Terraza** (Italian), **L'Arbalette** (Swiss), **Houlihan's** (American), **Don Juseff** (Arabic), **Mi Fogón** (Venezuelan), **La Romana Hatillana** and **Hatillo Grill** (meats), **Papasitos** and **Padrisimo** (Mexican), **Sukothai** (Thai), **Vara Grill** (shish kebabs), **Oker's** (Basque), as well as some half dozen pizza places.

Isla Margarita A–Z

Unless otherwise stated, the telephone numbers in this section are preceded by the area code 295.

Choosing a Hotel

Most of the large hotels and resorts are offering bargains to boost occupancy severely affected by the economic crisis and lack of airline services to Margarita. These special deals are usually all-inclusive packages with meals, drinks, and often tours and airline tickets thrown in. Venezuelan travel agencies all have such plans, but the biggest bargains are frequently available in charter packages sold abroad by huge tour wholesalers.

Among the travel agencies most frequently offering special plans for the big hotels and resorts are: **Airone Tour Operator**, tel/fax: (212) 267 7590/2755/4940, fax: (212) 263 0387, e-mail: airone@cantv.net **Aseyreca – A-1 Tours**, tel: (212) 693 3581/8061, fax: (212) 693 3581,e-mail: aseyreca@aseyreca.com.ve **Candes Turismo**, tel: (212) 953 4710, fax: (212) 953 6755, email: info@candesturismo.com.ve. One of the oldest and best-known travel companies in Venezuela. **Deep Marine**, tel: (212) 762 8847, 763 3784, (414) 274 8236; e-mail: ventas@deepmarine.com, www.deepmarine.com, **Online**, tel: (212) 794 1859/1025, fax: (212) 782 6889; e-mail: on-line@cantv.net; www.viajesonline.com.ve **Trotamundos Internacional**, tel: (212) 285 2410/5237, 576 0078, fax: (212) 285 2498/576 6083; e-mail: trotamundos@ cantv.net; www. trotamundos.com.

Unión Tours tel: (212) 501 7019/7081, fax: 501 8245, e-mail: uniontours@bancunion.com

The listings below are alternatives to the multitude of large resorts heavily promoted by most agencies. As in other areas of the country, choices of decent mid-priced traditional hotels are sadly wanting. A number of entrepreneurs are now offering small *posadas* (inns) with personalized service aimed at independent travelers generally looking for something different from all-inclusive packages with homogenized meals and group tours. For value for money, these options are a far better choice than cheap hotels.

Places in Porlamar are listed first, then establishments in other areas in alphabetical order.

Hotel Listings

PORLAMAR

Hotel Bella Vista Cumberland
End of Avenida Santiago Mariño
Tel: 61 7222/4157
Fax: 61 2557
E-mail: hbellavista@yahoo.com
Pioneer of the luxury tourist hotels, built in the late 1950s. The only downtown facility directly on the beach; swimming pool, and other services commensurate with its status. Adjacent to the prime duty-free shopping area, near main restaurants and night entertainment. **$$$**
Hotel Hilton Margarita
Avenida Los Uveros, Costa Azul
Tel: 62 3333/4111
Fax: 62 0810
E-mail: pmvhitw.res@hilton.com
www.hilton.com
Luxury beach-front facility (though the beach is not particularly appealing owing to lots of seaweed) with lovely swimming pool, the usual quality services in keeping with its category, shopping arcade, tennis courts, casino next door. **$$$$**
Howard Johnson Tinajero Suites & Beach Club
Calle Campos, between Marcano and Cedeño, Sector Bella Vista

Tel: 63 8380/9949/8499/9619
Fax: 63 9163
Reservations Caracas:
Tel: (212) 242 1255
Fax: (212) 243 6414
E-mail: hjtinajeroccs@cantv.net
Three blocks from 4 de Mayo (one
of the main streets for stores and
restaurants) yet on a quiet side
street, and it has a pool. Suites
with one or two bedrooms, fully
equipped kitchen, Jacuzzi, satellite
TV. **$$$**

La Samanna
Avenida Bolívar at Francisco
Esteban Gómez, Urb Costa Azul
Tel: 62 2662
Fax: 62 0989
Reservations Caracas:
Tel: (212) 284 9006
Fax: (212) 285 7352
E-mail: info@samanna.com
www.samanna.com
Luxury lodging aimed toward clients
using their adjoining
Thalassotherapy Center to
counteract stress, physical
ailments, and for beauty
treatments. Four restaurants
including Japanese and dietetic;
piano bar, 40 stores. **$$$$**

Margarita Princess Suites
Avenida 4 de Mayo
Tel: 263 6777, 261 8732/3476
Fax: 263 0222
Caracas office:
Tel: (212) 572 9232/9019
Fax: (212) 574 3821
E-mail: hotelprincess@telcel.net.ve
www.enlared.net/princess
Downtown location. Suites with 1–2
bedrooms, 1–2 bathrooms, cable
TV, balcony, restaurants, bar, in-
room refrigerator, travel agency,
pool, executive services. Breakfast
included. **$$$**

SAN JUAN BAUTISTA

Hotel Restaurant La Casona
Calle Miranda, San Juan Bautista
Tel: 59 333
Fax: 59 133
E-mail: casona@enlared.net
www.think-venezuela.net/ casona
Quiet village near airport and ferry.
Large yet cozy complex offering 24
extremely appealing fully equipped

apartments with private balcony,
complete kitchen, quality details
throughout; large swimming pool
surrounded by tropical garden,
ample restaurant, and bar. Price
includes breakfast. **$$$**

COCHE ISLAND

Isla de Coche Hotel
San Pedro del Coche
Tel: 99 1431/1435
Fax: 99 1132
Aimed princpally at windsurfers.
Located on the beach, but with pool
as well. Restaurant, TV. **$$$**

Coche Speed Paradise
Playa La Punta, Isla de Coche
Tel: (295) 63 9810; (414) 995
2182/2183
www.coche-paradise.com
Geared toward windsurfers, but
facilities appealing to all types. On
the beach, but also with swimming
pool. 64 cabins surrounded by palm
trees. Sold as an all-inclusive
package covering transfers between
El Coche and Playa Yaque, where it
has a sister hotel, Hotel Windsurf
Paradise. Meals, open bar. **$$$**

JUAN GRIEGO AND VICINITY

Apartments of Marie-Noelle
Casa Nº 11, Calle La Marina, Playa
Zaragoza, Pedro González
Tel: (416) 681 8119
Two very attractive, impeccable
beachfront apartments with lots of
decorative touches, fully equipped
kitchen and dining area; every
imaginable detail to make you feel

Price Categories

Prices are quoted in US$, but
payable in bolívars at the
exchange rate of the day. Prices
based on double occupancy,
standard room, without breakfast
(unless otherwise noted).
$ = under $20
$$ = $20–$50
$$$ = $50–$100
$$$$ = over $100

at home (huge stacks of towels,
books, coffee, tea, etc.). **$$**

**Barceló Dunes Hotel & Beach
Resort**
Playa Puerto Cruz, Pedro González
Tel/fax: 63 1333
E-mail: redunes@telcel.net.ve
www.barcelo.com
Huge beachfront resort with tennis,
gymnasium, diving lessons in the
pool, boat excursions to nearby
beaches, and kids' club. Price
includes all meals, snacks, and
open bar. **$$$$**

Laguna Honda Inn B&B
Urb Laguna Honda on the main road
between Juan Griego and
La Asunción
Tel: 53 1150
E-mail: lloydok@hotmail.com
Very warm, homey setting.
Delightful owners (firebrand
venezolana and her British spouse)
personally attend guests.
Comfortable, spotless rooms. Cozy
central atrium with bar (for guests
only), living area with cable TV.
Tours. Breakfast included. **$$**

Las Casitas de Freddy
End of Calle Bolívar (steet beside
the church), Pedrogonzález
Tel: 58 0154, (212) 372 1993
Eight modern apartments (with full
kitchen, AC, TV, 2 bedrooms, 1–2
bathrooms) within walled compound.
Pool, Jacuzzi, barbeque, restaurant
(only open in high season). **$$**

PAMPATAR

Allegro Resort Lagunamar
Apostadero, via Guacuco north
of Pampatar
Tel: 62 0711/1763
E-mail: lagunmar@telcel.net.ve
www.allegroresorts.com
Large rooms and suites, enormous
grounds, beach, water sports, huge
swimming pools, tennis,
gymnasium. Isolated location;
without private transportation,
you're stuck there or must take
taxis (no shuttle provided to get
there either). All-inclusive (three
meals, national beverages). **$$$$**

Posada La Bufonera
Calle Almirante Brión, Pampatar
Tel/fax: 62 8418/9977

Very pretty beachfront rooms decorated in a rustic style, equipped kitchen, in-room safe, beach chairs and umbrellas; enclosed compound. Restaurant next door. **$$**

PARAGUACHI

Conjunto Turístico Vacional
Las Aves
Avenida 31 de Julio (the main highway Via Playa El Agua), just past El Salado
Tel: 42 3415/0773, (212) 323 1433, (212) 242 8738
E-mail: yoline@telcel.net.ve
Outstanding walled compound with four extremely handsome fully equipped apartments decorated in a rustic style; lush gardens with central Jacuzzi and barbecue. Clients are covered free with full health insurance plan while on the island. There is a free airport/ferry transfer in high season for clients contracting lodging with optional breakfast and dinner package. **$$$**

PLAYA EL AGUA & VICINITY

Hotel Cocoparaiso
North end of the waterfront street, Playa El Agua
Tel: 49 0117/0274
Fax: 49 1054
www.cocoparaiso.cjb.net
Large attractive rooms and bungalows with bar, small

Price Catagories

Prices are quoted in US$, but payable in bolívars at the exchange rate of the day. Prices based on double occupancy, standard room, without breakfast (unless otherwise noted). When verifying current prices, ask if taxes are included – if not, you pay 15 percent more.
$ = under $20
$$ = $20–50
$$$ = $50–100
$$$$ = over $100

refrigerator, terrace with hammock, safety deposit box, sound equipment, hairdryer. No TV. Swimming pool, *caney*-bar, gymnasium, breakfast included in rate. Low season – **$$**, high season – **$$$**

Hostería El Agua
Avenida 31 de Julio, by the south entrance to waterfront boulevard of Playa El Agua
Tel/fax: 249 7297
E-mail: hosteriaelagua@hotmail.com
An appealing place with a distinct European flair. There are 15 spotless rooms with private bathroom, breakfast included. Services include laundry, tours, taxi, transfers; dinner available. English spoken. **$$**

PLAYA EL YAQUE

Las Brisas del Yaque
End of the waterfront street then half a block to left
Tel: (414) 995 6504
Fax: 63 9730/995 0908
E-mail: hectorwindsurfin@hotmail.com
Walled complex with 10 four-person villas – decorated in a modern tropical style, with fully equipped kitchen, two bedrooms, two bathrooms. Price 50 percent more in high season than low season. **$$$–$$$$**

Windsurfer's Oasis
The waterfront street
Tel: 63 9375/9216
Fax: 63 9098
Reservations in Caracas, tel: (212) 242 8764; fax: (212) 242 9068
E-mail: oasiselyaque@cantv.net
Modern three-story hotel, located right on the beach, swimming pool for adults with Jacuzzi, pool for kids, snack bar, rental of windsurf equipment and classes available. **$$$**

Yaque Motion – Windsurfer's Guest House
The waterfront street
Tel/fax: 63 9502/9742
E-mail: gugu@elyaquemotion.com
www.elyaquemotion.com
In an enclosed compound. Attractive rooms; upper terrace with

restaurant, bar. Guests can use the equipped kitchen. Mountain bike rental. Camping allowed. Surfboard storage. Breakfast included in high season. English spoken. **$$**

PLAYA FERMÍN/ EL TIRANO

Hostería Marymonte
In front of Playa Fermín on Via El Cardón
Tel: 48 066
Fax: 48 557
E-mail: marymonteca@cantv.net
www.marymonte.compucen.com
Nine pretty, connected (but cantilevered for privacy) cabins, each with its own terrace and hammock. Swimming pool, restaurant. English spoken. Sun umbrellas and loungers are available to take to the beach. **$$**

PLAYA PARGUITO

Villa Cabo Blanco
One block from the beach, huge sign marks turn from via El Tirano–Playa El Agua road
Tel: 267 1487/416 7145
Fax: 262 7419
E-mail: info@villa-caboblanco.com
www.villa-caboblanco.com
Eight extremely attractive villas, each catering for 2–8 people, with fully equipped kitchen, terrace, satellite TV, sound system and AC. Pool, bar; lush gardens. French, English, German spoken. **$$$**

ROBLEDAL

L'Auberge L'Oasis
Calle El Tanque (south edge of Robledal, on the Macanao Peninsula)
Tel/fax: 91 5339
E-mail: charles@enlared.net
Ideal for sailors, with calm bay in front. Inviting inn, and comfortable, spotless rooms. Restaurant open to public (excellent French cooking). Breakfast included. French and English spoken. **$$**

Restaurants & Nightlife

The greatest concentration of restaurants, clubs, bars, bingo halls, discos, and other spots for nightlife is on Avenida 4 de Mayo and Avenida Santiago Mariño. This is particularly convenient for visitors without private transportation, who can either check out the options on foot or easily hail a passing taxi or *por puesto* bus. A good number of the restaurants are known as much for nightlife as for dining: the emphasis is on food during the day and early evening, but from 11pm until dawn, the focus shifts to the bar for music (live or recorded) and dancing.

All of the luxury hotels have their own discotheques and usually feature theme nights with appropriate music and show or activities (Pirate Night, Caribbean Night, etc.), for an older clientele.

At Playa El Agua, casual open-sided restaurants line the beach, many have live music, most feature seafood on their menus. In Juan Griego, the beachfront likewise has the best restaurants. Playa Caribe has become a very popular place with the young crowd for night entertainment in its casual, open-sided waterfront bars (most with music and dancing after dark), but it is very isolated, and you need private transportation to get back to your place of lodging.

Places where you have to dress up are practically unheard of – even the Hilton is without a fancy restaurant, acknowledging that people come to Margarita specifically to relax and to get away from the formalities of working life.

The free promotional literature passed out to arriving passengers at the airport and in various free magazine-style guides available in hotels often contain special coupons for restaurants and night spots good for discounts, free drinks or snacks, entry without cover charge, etc. Most places have happy hour around 7–8pm.

Price indications apply only to restaurant service.

PORLAMAR

Andy's
C.C. Galería Fente (in front of Jumbo) Avenida 4 de Mayo
Tel: 64 4162
With micro-brewed beer produced by *gringo* from Colorado (winner of "The Great American Beer Festival" awards for his "Red Lady Ale"). Food, live music, and with great prices anytime, but even better Mon and Thur with half-price promo. **$$**

Cheers
Avenida Santiago Mariño.
Tel: 61 0957
Ample (but still packed), divided into several different sections. Good food by day; casual, sociable atmosphere at night, with live music; in the midst of an area with various popular spots where people do a lot of bar-hopping. **$$**

Cocody
Avenida Raúl Leoni, sector Bella Vista
Tel: 61 8431
A taste of France in the Caribbean, romantic terrace with tropical atmosphere. **$$$**

Dady's Latino
Avenida 4 de Mayo, in the new Jumbo Ciudad Comercial (shopping center)
Tel: (414) 785 9161
Split personality – focus on dining by day (complete with tuxedoed waiters and table-side preparation – somewhat out of sync with clients in shorts!) and pulsating discotheque after dark, popular with the younger crowd for music that ranges from techno to salsa. Open noon till 2 or 3am. **$$**

Dino's Grill
Calles Igualdad and Martinez
Tel: 642366
Inexpensive and popular grill open 7am–2pm. **$$**

La Atarraya de las 15 Letras
Calle San Rafael at Charaima
Tel: 61 5124
Typical *margariteña* and *criolla* cuisine. **$**

Latino's
Behind Señor Frog's (Avenida Bolívar, C.C. Costa Azul, Urb Costa Azul)
Tel: 62 7793

Very popular discotheque emphasizing salsa music and other Latin beats that attracts clients of all ages.

Margaritaville
Enter beside Señor Frog (Avenida Bolívar, C.C. Costa Azul), continuing several blocks to the coast
Large, extremely appealing complex of indigenous-style *churuatas* with very attactive outdoor/indoor restaurant, handicrafts shops, and more – definitely worth a visit.

Mosquito Coast Bar & Grill
Avenida Santiago Mariño, Paseo Guanaguao
Tel/fax: 61 3525
For years, the most popular spot on the island. Older crowd comes early for Tex-Mex food, 7–8pm happy hour. Younger crowd drifts in around midnight for energetic dancing in a more wacky atmosphere than usual dark discos. Open 7pm–dawn.

Piano Blanco
Calle J.M. Patiño (half a block from Avenida Santiago Mariño).
Tel: 64 0936.
Long-standing piano bar, drawing a slightly older crowd, featuring *boleros,* salsa, music of the 1960s. Restaurant with French and Italian specialties. Open noon–3am, Sunday from 6pm. **$$$**

Señor Frog's
Avenida Bolívar at Calle Amapolas, C.C. Costa Azul, Local 1, Urb Costa Azul
Tel: 295 620 0270

Extremely popular lively bar/restaurant with crazy atmosphere, loud music, dancing, margaritas by the pitcher, barbecue ribs, etc. Cover charge. **$$**

Sevillana's
Avenida Bolívar, sector Bella Vista
Tel: 63 8258
Spanish cuisine with live music and flamenco dancing. **$$$**

The English Bulldog
Avenida 4 (Bolívar), C.C. Costa Azul (next to Señor Frog's)
English-style pub and grub open from 7pm. **$$**

Woody's
Avenida 4 de Mayo
Good music, reasonably priced food and drinks, relaxed atmosphere. **$**

PLAYA CARDON/ PLAYA FERMIN

La Langouste del Cardón
Boulevard Playa Cardón
Tel: 48 550
Tanks with live lobsters to eat all year long, haute cuisine, French wines. **$$$$**

La Trattoria al Porto
Calle La Marina, El Tirano.
Tel: 48 208
Almost a cult following for its authentic Italian food. Homey atmosphere, wines, terrace overlooking the sea. Open only weekends and holidays outside of high season. **$$$**

Price Categories

Prices are quoted in US$, but payable in bolívars at the exchange rate of the day. Prices based on a three-course meal for one, without alcoholic beverages. Places emphasizing nightlife are without price rating since emphasis is on liquor consumption. Nevertheless, with Margarita being a free-port, drinks here are normally considerably cheaper than on the mainland.
$ = under $10
$$ = $10–$20
$$$ = $20–$30
$$$$ = over $30

PLAYA EL AGUA

Mambo Tango Beach Club
Playa El Agua (by Flamenco Hotel)
Tel: 49 1207
Fax: 49 0107
By day the Mambo Tango is a beach club (open from 8am), offering sun umbrellas, a restaurant, lockers, and showers. From 8pm until dawn, the place becomes a dinner and dancing Caribbean Show package. **$$–$$$**

PEDRO GONZALEZ

Tock & Tock
Calle Bolívar, beside the church
Tel: 53 0382
This cozy place serves delicious, inspired Venezuelan gastronomy at very reasonable prices. **$$**

PLAYA CARIBE

Mosquito Beach Club
Playa Caribe (2 km/1 mile east of Juan Griego)
This is where the young and beautiful go to play. Seafood, burgers, and salads, among other low-key options, are on the menu. For beach-goers there are bathrooms, changing rooms, showers, loungers, and sun shades. Things get more lively at night-time, with music and dancing. Bilingual staff. **$$**

Currency Exchange

Caribe Express
Avenida Santiago Mariño, C.C. Fermín, Local 4, Porlamar
Tel: 263 9051/9153
Cussco
Calle Velásquez at Santiago Mariño, Porlamar
Tel: 261 3379
Febres Parra
Hotel Bella Vista, lobby, Local 21, Porlamar
Tel: 263 3811
For You
Avenida Santiago Mariño, Porlamar
Tel: 261 4442

Honorary Consuls

Canada – tel: 61 3475, 64 0086
Denmark – tel: 63 7143/3002
France – tel: 87 0660/0111
Germany – no local rep, call Embassy in Caracas: (212) 265 2827
Italy – tel: 61 6666
Spain – tel: 61 5435/5446, 64 0487
Switzerland – tel: 62 8682/5672
United Kingdom – tel: 62 4665, (414) 995 1267

Tourist Information

Corporación de Turismo de Nueva Esparta, the state tourism office, Centro Artesanal Gilberto Menchini, Los Robles.
Tel/fax: 62 2514/3098/4194; E-mail: corpotur@enlared.net
Fondene (Fund for the Development of Nueva Esparta State). Headquarters in the old customs house in Pampatar, by the fort.
Tel: 62 2494/2342
Fax: 62 2814.
Fondene also have a tourist information stand at the airport, tel: 62 2342/2494.
There are also several websites promoting Margarita including www.margaritaonline.com, www.la-isla.com, www.margaritaislandguide.com and www.veweb.com.

Emergency Services

MEDICAL

Centro Diagnóstico Porlamar, Calle Díaz at Calle Marcano, Porlamar. Tel: 63 2778 (pediatric emergencies).
Hospital Luis Ortega, Avenida 4 de Mayo at Calle San Rafael, Porlamar.
Tel: 261 1101/0356 (public).
Centro Clínico Margarita, Calle Marcano at Calle Díaz.
Tel: 61 5635/4611/4443 (private).
Centro Médico Nueva Esparta, Via La Sierra, La Asunción.
Tel: 42 0011/0822/242 1711 (private).

DENTAL

Dr Salomon Klugermann DDS
(Graduate of University of Michigan
School of Dentistry),
Calle Petronila Mata, Quinta Nº
D–12, Urb Playa El Angel, Pampatar,
tel/fax: 62 5146/1301.
Emergencies and regular care,
English spoken.
Dr Lorena Godoy
Avenida Francisco Esteban Gómez
at Avenida Bolívar, C.C. La Samana,
Local 27, Porlamar, tel: 62 7563;
emergencies, tel: (416) 681 6008.
English and French spoken.

Cultural Activities

For information about special
activities, consult the **Dirección de
Cultura de la Gobernación de
Nueva Esparta**, tel: 42 2105/2600,
e-mail:
culturamargarita@hotmail.com
Museo Casa de la Aduana, in the
Fodene building, facing the colonial
fort on the main street passing
through Pampatar, tel: 62
2494/2342. Changing exhibits of
contemporary art. Free.
**Museo de Arte Contemporáneo
Francisco Narváez**, Calle Igualdad
at Calle Díaz, Porlamar, tel: 61
8668/4142. Permanent exhibition
of the works of its namesake along
with temporary exhibitions.
Tues–Sat 8.30am–5pm,
Sun 10am–3pm. Free.
Museo Marino, Boca de Río,
Macanao Peninsula, tel: 93 231.
Exhibits concerning Margarita's
sea-faring traditions, along with
marine life, a small aquarium,
videos about oceanography, and
more. Daily 9am–4.30pm.
Admission charge.
Museo Nueva Cádiz, next to the
Plaza Bolívar, La Asunción. Displays
of items related to Margarita's early
history, intricate ship models,
extensive shell collection. Free.
Museo Virgen del Valle, beside the
Basilica Menor de la Virgen del
Valle, El Valle. Religious museum
with incredible collection of
offerings left for the patron saint of
Margarita and eastern Venezuela.
Admission charge.

Outdoor Activities

You can take a ride in an **ultra-light
plane** in Porlamar (Tues–Thur) or at
Playa El Agua (Fri–Sun). Tel: 62
5030, 61 7632.
Diverland, via Porlamar–Pampatar
is a large amusement park, which
also includes **Waterland** (with an
excellent dolphin show), open
Wed–Sun 6pm–midnight. Admission
price is for unlimited use of all the
rides. Happy Hour for kids under 9;
free entrance 6–7pm.
Parasail – the Flyer offers
parasailing from the beach in front
of the Margarita Hilton, Playa
Moreno. Tues–Sun 10am–4pm. Tel:
62 1904.
Operators offering **diving** include:
Margarita Divers, contact Aldonza
Manrique, tel/fax: 62 1280 or 995
3341, www.margaritadivers.com
Scuba Doo Diving Center, tel: 64
6272/4755, fax: 61 8258, e-mail:
octopus@enlared.net
Windsurfing. Playa El Yaque (its
waters are rated among the best in
the world) has numerous places
offering equipment rental and
lessons.
Horseback Riding Cabatucán
offers riding in the rugged Macanao
Peninsula in a package with French
dinner while watching the sunset.
Tel: (016) 681 9348, e-mail:
cabatucan@telcel.net.ve
Isla Bonita Golf Club, Pedro
González, tel: 65 7370, e-mail:
ibonitagc@cantv.net. Part of the
Hotel Hesperia Isla Margarita, this
18-hole golf course is open daily.

Tours

Jeep safari and horseback riding
tours of Macanao Peninsula with
bilingual guide, insurance, visit to
La Restinga, Museo Marino, lunch,
open bar. C.C. Tours, Calle Tubores,
Porlamar. Tel: 64 0297.
Moon Dancer party boat (with
music, all food and booze included)
has a full-day cruise departing from
the Concorde Marina daily at 10am.
Tel: 67 1972/1625/1724, e-mail:
maloka@telcel.net.ve,
www.moondancer.com.ve
Many local tour operators offer boat
tours to Coche, one of them on a
large yacht (*Cata Fiesta* – with food,
open bar, lively show) and another
on a sailboat (*Catatumbo* – food,
open bar, entertainment, but a
slightly more refined atmosphere).
Aereotuy offers many exclusive
tours with departure from
Margarita: Los Roques, La
Blanquilla Island, Grenada and
Tobago, Canaima and Angel Falls,
Uruyén and Arekuna in Canaima
National Park, two different lodges
in Delta Amacuro. Tel: 63 2211/
2094/0307; fax: 61 7746;
www.tuy.com
Rutaca offers day tours from
Margarita to Canaima–Angel Falls,
Uruyén, Los Roques, Trinidad,
Tobago; plus flights to Barcelona,
Güiria, Ciudad Bolívar, Carúpano.
Tel: 69 1346/1245/1747/1301–5.

Transportation

Along with a multitude of taxis that
can be contracted for single rides or
by the day, an ample service is
provided by the cheaper *por puesto*
cars and buses.

BUSES

The following are the principal bus
routes with departures from
Porlamar (destination listed first,

Fun for Kids

Play Aventura, entertainment
center in C.C. Rattan Plaza,
Pampatar, has special areas for
kids (huge module with slides,
labyrinths, tubes, pool filled with
plastic balls; video games) and
teens (with video games,
simulators, pool tables, air
hockey, music, etc.).
Mundo Animal (Animal World),
via Playa El Agua, sector
Salamanca, near La Asunción,
tel: 42 2552. At a veterinarian
clinic, this is a petting zoo where
kids may pet, brush, feed, and/or
play with the friendly species of
the animal kingdom and observe
the more scary, exotic ones.

Airlines

Aereotuy – tel: airport 269 1129/1480; Porlamar 263 2211/0307.

Aeroejecutivos – tel: Pampatar 263 2642.

Aeropostal – tel: airport 269 1172/1374, (800) 28466 (7.30am–8pm), Porlamar 63 1341.

Aserca – tel: airport 269 1480/1149, (800) 88 356, www.asercaairlines.com

Avensa – tel: airport 269 1301–5; Porlamar 261 7111.

Avior – tel: airport 269 1314/1014

Laser – tel: airport 269 1329, 69 1116, (800) 23 732.

Oriental de Aviación – tel: Porlamar 269 1054, 61 2019, fax: 269 1254, (800) 67 436.

Rutaca – tel: airport 269 1346/1245/1747.

Zuliana de Aviación – tel: Porlamar 63 2852/2936.

then departure points – all next to or near the Plaza Bolívar; routes are usually posted in the front window; fares to anywhere are under US$1):

La Asunción and Playa Guacuco: Línea Matasiete on Calle Fajardo, between Avenida 4 de Mayo and Calle Igualdad.

Playa Parguito, Playa El Agua, Manzanillo: Línea Antonín del Campo, Calle Guevara, between Marcano and Cedeño.

Tacarigua, Santa Ana, Juan Griego: Unión Juan Griego, Avenida Miranda, between Igualdad and Marcano.

El Valle, Las Piedras: Línea Mariño, Calle Marcano between Calle Guevara and Avenida Miranda.

La Guardia: Línea La Guardia, Calle La Marina, between Libertad and Arismendi.

San Juan, Fuentideuño: Unión de Conductores San Juan, Calle San Nicolás, between Arismendi and Mariño.

Terminal de Ferry in Punta de Piedras: Unión Tubores, Calle Maneiro, between Mariño and Arismendi.

Laguna de La Restinga, Península de Macanao: Línea La Restinga, Calle La Marina, between Calle Mariño and Boulevard Guevara.

TAXIS

Taxi Ejectivo (nights) tel: 63 9568.
Taxi Impacto, tel: 63 7798/7113.
Taxi.net, tel: 64 2114/4103.
Union Latina (Mosquito Coast), tel: 63 6002.

CAR RENTAL

Avis
Tel: Airport 269 1236/1223
Beach Car Rental
Tel: 297 1953/1837/1736, 269 1369/1469
Budget
Tel: 261 6413/61 2490
Hertz
Tel: 261 4490/69 1274/269 1237
Miami Car
Tel: Airport, 269 1483/1253; Hotel Bella Vista, 261 2490
Oriental Car Rentals
Tel: Airport, 269 1199; Playa El Agua, 49 0029; Main office, 74 3192/61 2667; fax: 74 1448.
Ramcar
Tel: Airport 269 1482; Hotel Bella Vista 263 5425; www.buscaribe.com/ramcarii

FERRIES

Conferry
Tel: (295) 261 9235/ 6780/6397, fax: 261 4364; (800) 33 779; www.conferry.com. You can reserve tickets though their toll-free 800 number.
Gran Cacique II
Tel: (295) 298 339/430/439. Service between both Cumaná (passengers & cars) and Puerto La Cruz–Margarita (passengers only).
Naviarca
Tel: 298 139/232. Service between Cumaná–Margarita, Margarita–Isla de Coche, Cumaná– Araya (passengers and cars).

MOTORCYCLES

A number of companies in Porlamar rent motorcycles:

Hotel Bella Vista Cumberland (in the parking lot)
Tel: 261 7222, ext. 260.

Hotel La Perla
Tel: 63 5902, ext. 3009.

Hotel Crystal Garden
Tel: 62 0211.

Port L'Mar Suites
Tel: 61 7444, ext. 734.

Nicol's Rent Motors
Avenida 4 de Mayo at Calle Amador Hernández.

Harley-Davidson Rental & Boutique, Avenida 4 de Mayo (in front of C.C. Jumbo). Tel: 261 8178.

Shopping

The principal shopping area for **duty-free shopping** in Porlamar is along Avenida 4 de Mayo and the bordering downtown area to the north, the waterfront to the south, on the east by Avenida Santiago Mariño and Calle Arismendi to the west. The Rattan hypermarket and Mundo Graffiti (Avenida 4 de Mayo near Santiago Mariño) are the focal points. There are duty-free stores in Juan Griego too, but the quality and variety of the merchandise is inferior to that in Porlamar.

Opening Hours

Most shops are open Mon–Sat 9am–1pm and 3–7pm; but in high season Mon–Sat 9am–7pm, Sun 9am–1pm. During Christmas time, many of the stores remain open much later.

Sunday

Sunday is *not* a good day for public transportation. Many drivers traditionally take that day off to be with their families, so buses and taxis are few and far between.

On Sunday, holidays, and at night, taxis charge 25 percent over the day rate.

Where to Stay

Choosing a Hotel

Corpoturism (the National Tourism Corporation) has a star rating system (1–5) which has been applied to most hotels. Suites and alternative options are normally not officially graded.

There is generally a significant gap between quality of four- to five-star hotels and three-star or below. Most one- to two-star choices offer very basic accommodations.

There has been a strong entrepreneurial movement to fill the gap with "alternatives" to traditional hotels, where smaller size and personalized service are emphasized, and where value for money is excellent. These are primarily in the form of *posadas* (inns), cabins, and camps. They come in all styles and price ranges, from extremely basic to truly exceptional facilites that put five-star hotels to shame.

Alternative Lodging

The definitive guide (English and Spanish, side-by-side, with over 1,000 options, in every state, plus Los Roques, Las Aves, and La Tortuga) to alternative lodging, completely updated annually since 1995, is *Elizabeth Kline's Guide to Camps, Posadas & Cabins in Venezuela*, available in bookstores throughout Venezuela and, in the US, via notkalvin@yahoo.com.

Reservations

All camps, *hatos* (ranches), and places with meals included require advance reservations. In any case, it is always best to call ahead to see whether deposits are required,

Price Categories

Prices are quoted in US$, but payable in bolívars at the exchange rate of the day. Prices based on double occupancy, standard room, without breakfast (unless otherwise noted).
$ = under $20
$$ = $20–$50
$$$ = $50–$100
$$$$ = over $100

check availability, and get specific directions for arrival, etc. This is particularly true during high season, which can vary depending on the location. All places are busy over Christmas, Carnaval, Easter week, and the August to October school vacation, for example. The high season for *llanos* camps is in the dry season (mid-Nov–mid-April).

El Litoral

This is the area of the Caribbean coast nearest to Caracas and the Simón Bolívar National and International Airport in Maiquetía, which serves Caracas.

Due to the natural disaster which devastated this area in December 1999, there are still few lodging options functioning in and around Macuto and Caraballeda because of continuing problems with the infrastructure.

Virtually all beaches were destroyed by mudslides, and vast areas are still in a state of ruin. The only higher-class option functioning at full capacity west of the airport is Puerto Viejo. However, the zone around Puerto Viejo is pretty unsavory, and it thus stands as an "island" from which exploration is not advised.

Hotel Puerto Viejo Best Western
Avenida Principal Puerto Viejo, third and fourth cross streets, Sector Playa Grande (west of Catia La Mar).
Tel: (212) 352 4044
Fax: 352 1311
E-mail: gracie@telcel.net.ve
www.hotel-puertoviejo.com

Nice hotel in the Best Western chain, and the only lodging close to the airport, but in a rather seedy area. All the amenities of a luxury hotel plus beachfront, three swimming pools (including a salt-water pool), tennis courts, satellite TV, marina. Significant discount for business travelers midweek and for tourists on weekends. Breakfast included. **$$$$**

Aloe Spa
Between La Sabana and Caruao, Miranda state.
Tel: Spa (212) 313 1014;
Tel: Caracas (212) 952 3741
E-mail: reservations@aloespa.com
www.aloespa.com

A great place for total relaxation; there is a cozy atmosphere with guests attended to by the spa's owners. Massage, steam baths with aromatic herbs, hydrotherapy, clay treatments, and hatha yoga are all offered. The beach is on-hand and there are nearby hot springs. Plan includes meals and treatments. There are handsome, artistic details throughout. Gourmet vegetarian fare is offered, and the restaurant is open to the public (by reservation) with epicurean cuisine emphasizing seafood, but also including meat on request; bar. Progressive discounts for two or more guests. **$$$**

Los Roques

Because new construction is prohibited due to the archipelago's national park status, all lodging is in the form of *posadas* (some 60), converted from the houses of local fishermen. Except for a few very basic options with shared bathroom, lodging is very expensive compared to other locations in Venezuela – even with breakfast and dinner included. Most also provide a cooler with lunch. Some will even take clients to nearby cays or beaches. The average cost is around US$60–200 per person/per night double occupancy – not including cost of the flight (about another US$150). Many offer a discount in low season. Pricing for the following is **per person.**

Aereotuy Posadas
Tel: (800) 23 736
E-mail: tuysales@etheron.net
www.tuy.com
This airline has six *posadas* with pretty, airy rooms with two different pricing categories and offers packages with flight and excursion to nearby cays included. **$$$$**

Bequeve Los Roques
Tel: (212) 731 0636
www.losroques-bequeve.com
Stylish well-run *posada* with eight attractive rooms, superb food, and day-trips to the other islands. **$$$$**

La Cigala Posada
Tel/fax: (414) 200 4357
www.lacigala.net/cigala
Large social area with covered areas as well as open gardens, inviting modern design, several rooms with ample loft; known for its good food. **$$$$**

Posada Caracol
Tel: (414) 313 0101
E-mail: info@posadacaracol.com
www.posadacaracol.com
A stylish option run by Italian family and located right on the beach. **$$$$**

Posada La Corsaria
Tel: Carolina Pacannis, (414) 930 0796; William Pacannis, (212) 267 6321/993 5879
E-mail: command@telcel.net.ve
Handsome decoration incorporating vivid tropical colors and lots of artistic details. Excursions available to nearby cays. **$$$$**

Posada Mediterráneo
Tel: (414) 929 3305;
Agencia Elero in Caracas, (212) 975 0906/0082/0237
www.posadamediterraneo.com
Has a very streamlined Mediterranean look. Rooftop terrace has a bar and telescope. Transfer to cays included. Bone fishing packages available. **$$$$**

Posada Gremary
Tel: (414) 927 8614/(212) 337 2765
Rooms are simple but with nice touches, some with private bathroom. Shared living room with DirecTV. In high season, package includes transfer to nearby cay. **$$–$$$**

Posada Acuarela
Tel/fax: (414) 932 3502
Reservations Caracas, tel: (212) 793 7117
Fax: (212) 781 5756
Imaginative details like models of fish suspended on transparent lines. Internal gardens (including one with a palm tree in the roofless shower!). Transfer to cays. Italian, French, and English spoken. **$$$$**

El Oriente

ANZOATEGUI

Via Boca de Uchire-El Hatillo
Posada Sol, Luna y Estrellas
Calle 8, Urb Marylago (8 km/5 miles east of the Boca de Uchire church)
Tel: (416) 610 9257, (414) 208 5595
Located right on a tranquil, pretty beach. Very appealing cross between rustic and Mexican *hacienda* style; with swimming pool, bar, barbecue, beach volleyball, and *bolas criollas*, mini soccer, TV, some rooms with AC. All meals included. Half price for kids. **$$$**

El Dorado Suites
Avenida Principal Mesones with Calle 2, Zona Industrial Mesones, Vía Distribuidor Los Mesones-Barcelona.
Tel: (281) 76 9166/9245
Fax: (281) 76 9366
Rooms and suites (with Jacuzzi), pool, restaurant, bar. Gymnasium, sauna. Good prices, despite its appearance (because of its entrance/reception) as a by-the-hour place. **$$**

Lecherías–El Morro
Golden Rainbow Maremares Resort & Spa
Avenida Américo Vespucio with Avenida R–17, El Morro.
Tel: (800) 73 767, (281) 81 1011/3022
Fax: (281) 81 3028
Huge resort with several lagoon-size pools, golf (though the course is in poor shape), restaurants, bars, nightclub, complete health spa, stores, marina. Discount for guests over 55. **$$$$**

Types of Lodging

Not all lodging is in towns or in hotels in Venezuela. Especially in the interior, the alternatives are more common than traditional hotels. These include:
cabaña cabin, cottage
campamento camp
hato cattle ranch
posada inn, small and usually family-run lodging characterized by personalized attention
churuata indigenous-style dwelling, usually with earthen walls, palm thatch roof (often used for restaurants, bars, and social areas)
caney like a *churuata*, but without side walls

Puerto La Cruz
Gaeta Hotels
Beach hotel
Tel: (281) 65 1822/65 0411
Fax: (281) 65 0065
City hotel
Tel: (281) 65 0536
One facing the beach, on Paseo Colón, another two blocks south of the beach (the "city" hotel and cheaper). Plain but comfortable rooms, good location, Continental breakfast included. **$$–$$$**

Hotel Cristina Suites
Avenida Municipal
Tel: (281) 67 4712
Fax: (281) 67 5058
Caracas
Tel: (212) 953 7122
Eight blocks from beach. 250 junior and luxury suites, mini-bars in all rooms, satellite TV. Piano bar/disco, two pools, gymnasium, sauna, games room, laundry, stores, baby-sitting, emergency medical center, organization of excursions. **$$$$**

Hotel Caribe Mar
Calle Ricaurte Nº 12, half a block south of Paseo Colón (at its western extreme)
Tel: (281) 67 3291/4973/ 5722/5846
Fax: 67 2096
Good option for tight budgets in this generally expensive city. 73 rooms and suites, room service, satellite

TV, basement parking garage, restaurant, bar, safety deposit boxes for rent. Near ferry terminal, Paseo Colón. **$$**

Hotel Turístico Puerto La Cruz
Paseo Colón
Tel: (281) 65 3611/3402
Fax: (281) 65 3117
Reservations Caracas:
Tel: (212) 266 9729
E-mail: hotel@hesperia-puertolacruz.com
www.hesperia-hoteles.es
Now part of the Hesperia group, this luxury facility is the only hotel in Puerto La Cruz on the beach, next to the marina, and the first of the upscale hotels built in Puerto La Cruz. Large pool, various restaurants, very popular bar, disco, shopping arcade. **$$$$**

Route of the Sun: PLC-Cumaná
Colorada Bungalo's Hotel Club
Urb Playa Colorada
Tel: (414) 981 3966/67 0093
Eight spacious and very attractive three-level bungalows for four with fully equipped kitchen, two bathrooms, covered parking for each unit. Pool, barbecue. **$$**

Quinta Jali B & B
Calle Marchant, Urb Playa Colorada
Tel: (416) 681 8113
Comfortable rooms great for low-budget travelers (some with private bath, AC or fan – specify if you have a preference, no price difference). Honor system for drinks from fridge. Breakfast available by prior arrangement. French spoken. **$**

Villa Majagual
Tel: (293) 221 120/(414) 773 0023
Set on a hillside on the private Majagual peninsula in Mochima National Park, 6 km (4 miles) from Santa Fe, this delightful *posada* has 12 *cabañas*, private beach, excellent food, and outstanding views. **$$$**

Hotel Las Palmeras
Tel: (414) 773 6152
Small hotel in walled compound in quiet setting, one block back from the beach. Simple but ample and comfortable rooms with private bath. Rooftop terrace. A little English spoken. Personalized service. **$**

Playa Santa Fe Resort & Dive Center
Santa Fe, beachfront, Santa Fe
Tel/fax: (414) 773 3777
E-mail: santafe@telcel.net.ve
USA
Tel: (530) 546 3756
Fax: (530) 546 2064
E-mail: cpclean@sierra.net
www.santaferesort.com/lodging/lodging.html
Handsome complex, right on the beach, with large airy rooms, numerous social and garden areas, small gymnasium, barbecue, tours, and diving offered. Friendly owner; English spoken. **$$–$$$**

Posada Gaby
Final Avenida Principal of Mochima
Tel: (414) 993 2725/773 1104
Cumaná
Fax: (293) 33 0462
The best option in Mochima. On the shoreline with its own dock; optional boat trips, rental of diving and snorkeling equipment, pedal boats, and "banana." Breakfast available. **$$**

Cumaná
Hotel Cumanagoto Hisperia
Tel: (293) 30 1400, 51 5198
Fax: (293) 52 1877
E-mail: hotel@hesperia-cumanagoto.com
www.hesperia-cumanagoto.com
Luxury hotel recently reopened after complete remodeling. Private beach, swimming pool, tennis courts, golf course, health spa, gymnasium, bar, and restaurants. Breakfast is included in the price. There is a discount of about 30 percent in the low season. **$$$–$$$$**

Price Categories

Prices are quoted in US$, but payable in bolívars at the exchange rate of the day. Prices based on double occupancy, standard room, without breakfast (unless otherwise noted).
$ = under $20
$$ = $20–$50
$$$ = $50–$100
$$$$ = over $100

Hotel Los Bordones
Avenida Universidad
Tel: (293) 51 3111
Fax: (293) 51 5377
Beachfront setting with tropical decor, rooms and suites with satellite TV, mini-bar. Daily aerobics by pool, stores, tennis, disco, dining, bar, tennis. Low season discounts up to 50 percent. **$$$**

Hotel Minerva
Avenida Cristóbal Colón
Tel: (293) 31 4471/66 2712
Fax: (293) 66 2701
Faces shoreline, but it's not a swimming beach. Restaurant, bar, small pool, satellite TV. **$$**

Bubulina's Hostal y Restaurant
Half a block west of Iglesia Santa Inés
Tel/fax: (293) 31 4025/33 4137
Tel: (293) 33 2287/2345, (414) 393 2393, (414) 764 4031
Excellent choice for colonial zone, inviting restaurant/bar (open to the public from 6pm, closed Sun). Breakfast included in price. **$$**

Araya Peninsula
Medregal Village
Via Los Cachicatos-Guacarapo
Tel: (414) 993 5643/993 0700
Fax: (414) 993 4890
E-mail: medregal@telcel.net.ve
www.guayanaweb.com/medregal
Attractive beachfront compound with large restaurant, enormous pool with adjacent bar in palm-roofed *churuatas*, emphasis on water sports. Price includes full American breakfast buffet. **$$**

Posada Araya Wind
Village of Araya
Tel: (414) 774 5485/993 71442
Next to photogenic ruins of colonial fort and beautiful beach, aimed mainly toward windsurfers. Comfortable rooms, some with AC, Breakfast available in garden. **$**

Carúpano
El Colibrí
Avenida Sur, about four blocks north of Avenida Circunvalación (the southern by-pass from the *redoma* (traffic circle) by Hotel El Yunque)
Tel: (294) 32 3583
Quiet residential zone. Three very handsome two-story villas with fully

equipped kitchen surrounded by lush gardens, central swimming pool, and a separate restaurant, all within a walled compound. German, Dutch, English spoken. Excellent value. **$$**

Posada Nena
Playa Copey
Tel: (294) 31 7624
Fax: (294) 31 7297
E-mail: posadanena@bigfoot.de
www.venezuela-urlaub.de
Extremely attractive, cozy place facing the beach. The grounds are paved with seashells and shaded by palm trees. Outstanding food, intimate bar, and pool table are offered. The upper rooms to the rear with screened walls are of note. Unique tours offered. English spoken. Excellent value for money. **$$**

Posada La Colina
Calle Boyacá Nº 52 (behind Hotel Victoria)
Tel: (294) 32 0527
Fax: (294) 32 2915
E-mail: merle@telcel.net.ve
Pretty rustic style, hilltop setting, sea view. Rooms with handsome bentwood furniture, tropical-style decor. Both casual poolside dining and formal restaurant and bar. Breakfast included. **$$**

Rancho Grande Posada-Restaurant
Opposite Carúpano's industrial zone, just west of the city
Tel: (414) 994 0962
Large impeccably maintained family-run complex with extensive grounds that has grown steadily to now include standard rooms, cabins (equipped with a small refrigerator, but no kitchen), restaurant serving excellent food, bar. Activities available include *caneys* with pool and ping pong tables, playground, go-cart track, rental of bicycles and horses. A great place for families. **$$**

Río Caribe

Hotel Mar Caribe
Avenida Rómulo Gallegos
Tel/fax: (294) 61 494
Walled compound next to the beach in the heart of town, rooms surround large pool. Restaurant, bar, frequent live music. **$$**

Posada Caribana
Avenida Bermúdez Nº 25
Río Caribe
Tel: (294) 61 162/242
Fax: (294) 61 124
Caracas, tel: (212) 265 9150, 263 3649; fax: (212) 263 9455
E-mail: caribanainn@cantv.net
Restored colonial house with very stylish rooms, central open courtyard, inviting shared living area. Restaurant/bar to rear with dining on terrace or inside with AC. American breakfast included **$$**, Plans with meals and transfer to Playa Medina, **$$$**

Villa Antillana
Calle Rivero Nº 32
Tel/fax: (294) 61 413
Owner-operated *posada* in pretty traditional house adorned with many paintings by well-known artists, handsomely decorated rooms, comfortable social area with sound equipment plus TV and videos. Optional services include therapeutic massages, floral treatment, excursions to hot springs. Breakfast included, other meals are available on request (the food is delicious here). **$$–$$$**

Price Categories

Prices are quoted in US$, but payable in bolívars at the exchange rate of the day. Prices based on double occupancy, standard room, without breakfast (unless otherwise noted).
$ = under $20
$$ = $20–$50
$$$ = $50–$100
$$$$ = over $100

Via Playa Medina

Posada La Ruta de Cacao
2 km east of Río Caribe,
Tel: (414) 994 0115
E-mail: rutacacao@oem.es
Complex with extensive garden areas, ample rustic-style duplex cabins, *churuata*-style restaurant/bar, horseback riding. Optional tours and transfers can be included in the package. Price per person with breakfast **$**, with breakfast and dinner **$$**

Hacienda Bukare
14 km (8¾ miles) east of Río Caribe, Via Playa Medina, Bukare
Tel: (294) 65 2003, (414) 226 8201
Fax: (294) 65 2004
E-mail: bukare@cantv.net
In Europe
Reservations through Geodyssey (London)
Tel: (44) 20 7281 7788
Fax: (44) 20 7281 7878
E-mail: enquiries@geodyssey.co.uk
www.geodyssey.co.uk
Beautifully restored *hacienda* on a working cacao plantation with social area, restaurant (with outstanding meals at very reasonable prices), and bar. Separate building houses pretty rooms, each with private balcony facing tropical forest. Swimming pool. Transfers and tours available. Friendly owners are hosts. English spoken. **$$**

Playa Medina

Cabañas Playa Medina
On the beach
Info & reservations: Corpomedina in Carúpano
Tel: (294) 31 5241
Fax: (294) 31 3021
Right on one of the most beautiful beaches in Venezuela. Rustic-style cottages amid palm trees, most with two levels, living room, bedrooms, refrigerator. Plan includes meals, beverages, and transfers to and from Carúpano airport. Optional tours available. **$$$$**

Via El Pilar–Bohordal

Campamento Agro Ecológico Río de Agua
Near Bohordal.
Info & reservations: Corpomedina in Carúpano 312283
Tel: (294) 31 5241
Fax: (294) 31 3021
E-mail: tmarep@telcel.net.ve
Unique camp on 1,000-hectare (2,470-acre) water buffalo ranch, with emphasis on ecotourism. No TV, phones, or electric generators. Energy from solar panels, bio-gas plant. Abundant avifauna observed during tours by dugout canoe. Lodging in *churuatas*. Meals, juices, tours included. **$$$$**

MONAGAS

Caripe & Vicinity
Cabañas Bellerman
Via San Agustín–Teresén
Tel: (416) 692 3360
Tel/Fax: (292) 51 326
E-mail: cababellermann@cantv.net
Some 7 km (4 miles) from
Guácharo Cave. Very pleasant
cabins (with one or two bedrooms)
nestled on a wooded hillside;
equipped kitchen, playground, store
selling homemade liqueurs and
preserves. Pets allowed. Friendly
owners. **$$**

Hacienda Campo Claro
Teresén
Tel: (292) 55 1013
A 70-hectare (173-acre) functioning
farm, with options to hike and ride
horses. The pleasant stone cabins
have equipped kitchens and
individual rooms. There is a
barbecue area and meals are
available. **$$**

Hacienda Turistica La Cuchilla
3 km past La Cuchilla,
near El Guácharo
Tel: Hacienda, (416) 891 7503,
Luis Leopardi, (292) 51 331,
Mariflor Leopardi, (292) 51 469)
www.haciendalacuchilla.freeservers.
com
La Cuchilla has a tranquil wooded
setting on a working coffee
hacienda where visitors can watch
the process of preparing coffee
beans during the harvest months of
Nov–Jan. Nicely decorated cabins
(with equipped kitchen) and rooms.
Meals available. **$$**

Maturín
Hotel Morichal Largo
Via La Cruz, Km 3
Tel: (291) 51 4222/6122,
(800) 52 746
Fax: (291) 51 5544
E-mail (reservations):
hmlrooms@telcel.net.ve
www.morichallargo.com
Located on the outskirts of the city,
a luxury hotel with all the
accompanying amenities but a
rather cold aspect. Two huge
swimming pools, tennis courts,
gymnasium, racquetball, and sauna
offered. **$$$$**

Hotel Stauffer Maturín
Tel: (291) 43 1111/0622/
1211/1422
Fax: (291) 43 1455/0804
E-mail: stauffer@telcel.net.ve
www.stauffer-hotel.com
Prime location, next to mega-mall.
Very attractive low-rise design.
Central pool with ample gardens,
large handsome rooms. European-
style service. **$$$$**

Posada Rancho San Andrés
Via San Félix, Via Aribí (20 minutes
south of Maturín)
Posada, tel/fax: (416) 691 1067
Office, tel/fax: (291) 41 6278
Other contacts: tel: (291) 43 0298,
(414) 760 0094, (414) 760 0095,
(416) 691 1067
E-mail: janssenfred@cantv.net
Very pretty camp on 1,000 hectares
(2,470 acres), with cozy rooms plus
individual cabins, large restaurant
next to pool, wildlife excursions,
horseback rides, bikes. English
spoken. Breakfast included. **$$**

Midwest

ARAGUA

Colonia Tovar
Cabañas Breidenbach
Sector El Calvario
Tel/fax: (244) 55 1211
Modern cozy apartment-style units
for 2–6 people, some with
fireplaces and fully equipped
kitchen, and TV. **$$**

Hotel Selva Negra
One block below the church
Tel: (244) 55 1415/1072
Fax: (244) 55 1338
Pioneer hotel in the colony, founded
in 1936. Regular rooms and cabins
spread over extensive wooded
grounds, traditional *fachwerk*
design, highly regarded restaurant
with typical German cuisine. **$$$**

Posada Don Elicio
Sector La Ballesta.
Posada:
Tel: (244) 55 1254,
Tel/fax: (244) 55 1073
www.posadadonelicio.com
Reservations Caracas:
Tel: (212) 284 5310,
(414) 929 1346
Fax: (212) 284 2429

Among the most beautiful lodges in
Venezuela, extremely cozy,
decorated in the best of taste.
Excellent food, terrace seating or
inside dining, extensive grounds,
intimate bar. Breakfast and dinner
included in price. **$$$$**

Spa Renacer Center
Sector La Cava, Qta Mi Refugio
Colonia Tovar:
Tel: (244) 55 1504
Reservations Caracas tel: (212)
987 3342/985 6716/(416) 821
2860/(414) 230 6591
E-mail: renacerspacenter@cantv.net
Spa treatments guaranteed to
relieve stress and stimulate the
senses with wonderful aromas
(each room has a theme with
corresponding fragrances), flower-
filled gardens, and soft sound of
flowing water everywhere; the
personnel wear genuine smiles.
Basic plan includes lodging, use of
sauna and Jacuzzi, and three meals
daily. **$$$$**

Maracay
Caribbean Eco Tours
Calle El Piñal Nº 64, El Limón
Tel/Fax: (243) 83 4925,
(414) 444 1915)
E-mail: caribean@telcel.net.ve
Excellent choice in the tranquil
mountain setting of an exclusive
residential zone, 10 minutes from
the entrance to Henry Pittier
National Park. Walled complex with
ample gardens, very pleasant guest
rooms, cable TV. Inviting
terrace/dining area, bar, swimming
pool. All meals available, prepared
by a Dutch chef, good selection of
wines (at cost!), fruit juices and soft
drinks included in the price of
meals. Other optional services
include cellular phone rental,
laundry, Internet and e-mail
connections, airport transfers, ecotourism excursions in the park and
tours to all parts of Venezuela.
Friendly owners attend guests. **$$**

Hotel Pipo Internacional
Avenida Principal El Castaño
Tel: (243) 41 3111/2022/3343
Fax: (243) 41 6298
E-mail: hpipoin@telcel.net.ve
www.hotelpipo.com
The best in the city. Cool mountain

location, just minutes from entrance to Henri Pittier National Park. Twelve-story tower, many thoughtful details (bedside control switches, phone in bathroom), large pool, gymnasium, sauna, disco. **$$$**

Hotel Byblos Continental
Avenida Las Delicias (opposite Redoma del Toro).
Tel: (243) 42 1224/0311/4010/5401
Fax: (243) 42 2679
E-mail: byblos@truevision.net
In the heart of the main street for restaurants, nightlife, shopping; near the zoo. 87 attractive rooms in tower, plus suites, small pool, disco, restaurant, bar. **$$–$$$**

Hotel Princesa Plaza
Avenida Miranda, between Fuerzas Armadas and Bermúdez
Tel: (243) 33 1008, 32 1454/2052/0177, 33 2357
Fax: (243) 33 7972
E-mail: hotelprincesaplaza@cantv.net
www.hotelprincesaplaza.com
Excellent central location, just one block from the Plaza Bolívar and Teatro de la Opera, on a quiet side street. Disco, restaurant with international and French cuisine, satellite TV, beauty shop. **$$$**

Via El Limón–Cata–Cuyagua
Posada Cuyagua Mar
One block from the main plaza in Cuyagua
Tel: (212) 861 1465,
(243) 92 0001, (416) 620 4491,
(414) 937 4507
Surprisingly large with 26 simple, pleasant rooms surrounding tree-filled grounds, terrace, restaurant. Price includes breakfast and dinner. Short drive to beach – one of the best in Venezuela for surfing. **$$**

Via Las Delicias–Choroní–Puerto Colombia:
Hotel Hacienda El Portete
Calle El Cementerio, between Choroní and Puerto Colombia Posada
Tel: (243) 91 1255,
(414) 345 7768
Reservations Maracay
Tel: (243) 45 9271/0734
E-mail: elportete@cantv.net
www.elportete.com

Complex on 60 hectares (150 acres) including Playa El Diario, with swimming pools for adults and chidren, children's play area, video room, DirecTV, conference area, restaurant, bar, stage for live performances. Price includes breakfast, with other meals optional. **$$$**

Posada La Casa de Los García
Calle El Cementerio, between Choroní and Puerto Colombia
Posada tel: (243) 991 1056/1257
Caracas tel: (416) 635 6894
Tel/fax: (212) 662 2858
E-mail: posada-garcia@etheron.net
www.posada-garcia.rec.ve
300-year-old house converted into a *posada*, maintaining its traditional styling; flower-filled center courtyard. Nicely furnished rooms. Price includes breakfast. Dinner and all-inclusive plans available upon request. **$$$**

Posada La Meson Xuchytlan
Calle Principal, Puerto Colombia
Tel: (243) 91 1234
Reservations Caracas tel/fax: (212) 977 1794,/(414) 928 0952
E-mail: xuchytlan@bahiachoroni.com
Gorgeous Mexican *hacienda*-style architecture, furnishings, antiques and original art. Suites have private garden patio with jacuzzi; family-style rooms have two levels. Price includes ample breakfast buffet. Regular room – **$$**, suite – **$$$**

Posada Lemontree II
Calle José Maitín, Nº 3
Tel/Fax: (243) 91 1123 (specify Lemontree II since there is a Lemontree I of much lower quality).
E-mail: lemontree@bahiachoroni.com
Walled compound with quiet setting,

attractively remodeled house offering six rooms with private bath, hot water, and garden area. Services include telephone, fax, vans, boat and hiking excursions with bilingual guides, diving, restaurant, crafts shop. Pretty and economical. English spoken. **$–$$**

CARABOBO

Valencia
Apart-Hotel Ucaima
Avenida Boyacá, beside C.C. La Viña Siglo XXI, La Viña
Tel: (241) 22 7011/4853/7381
Fax: (241) 22 0461
E-mail: ucaima@ucaima.com
Next to shopping center. Rooms and large suites with kitchen, lighted tennis courts, swimming pool, satellite TV, restaurant, bar, parking, and room service. Breakfast is included in price. Great value. **$$$$**

Guaparo Suites
Avenida Hispanidad, between Guaparo Redoma and freeway
Tel: (241) 24 3182/7978, 25 0522
Fax: (241) 25 0412
E-mail: gsuite@telcel.net.ve
www.guaparohotels.com
Appealing new suites with fully equipped kitchenette, AC, TV, handsome furniture, in-room safe. Rooftop terrace with Jacuzzi, bar, game room with pool tables. Located close to main restaurant/shopping zone. **$$$$**

Hotel Coronado Suites
Calle 149 con Avenida 101, Urb Carabobo (one block from Avenida Bolívar Norte)
Tel: (241) 21 8255/1970
Fax: (241) 22 5155
E-mail: frerub@cantv.net
72 suites and 16 rooms, satellite TV, in-room teleports for computers, restaurant, bar, room service, solarium with Jacuzzi, and office service for business travelers.
$$$–$$$$

Hotel Don Pelayo
Avenida Díaz Moreno, between Calle Rondón and Vargas
Tel: (241) 57 9372/9378
Fax: (241) 57 9384
143 pleasant rooms and suites,

satellite TV, AC, restaurant, coffee shop, bar, parking garage; but not an area to be moving around on foot at night. **$$**

Hotel Inter-Continental Valencia
Avenida Juan Uslar, La Viña
Tel: (241) 24 7070, 20 3000
Fax: (241) 824 9265
E-mail: valencia@interconti.com
The most prestigious hotel in the city, mainly for business travelers, but also popular for its entertainment program. Quiet residential zone, but walking distance to a nice shopping center. Swimming pool, gymnasium, restaurants, stores, popular bar with large dance floor (house band plus DJ). **$$$$**

Hotel Stauffer Valencia
Avenida Bolívar Norte, El Recreo Valencia
Tel: (241) 23 4022/7919/9374
Fax: (241) 23 5044/4908/8487
Reservations Caracas
Tel: (212) 793 3101/3410/3627
Fax: (212) 782 0944
E-mail: stauffer@telcel.net.ve
www.stauffer-hotel.com
Ideal for visitors without private vehicle: on principal avenue of Valencia for restaurants, entertainment. Shopping center in the base of the tower, plus restaurants and movie theater. Pool. Full breakfast and tax is included in the price. **$$$–$$$$**

Puerto Cabello
Hotel Suite Caribe
Avenida Salóm Nº 21 (the continuation of the freeway entering the city), Urb La Sorpresa
Tel: (242) 64 2286/3970/3456
Fax: (242) 64 3910
E-mail: hotelscaribe@telcel.net.ve
Tower hotel with regular rooms and two-room suites, satellite TV, disco, pool, sauna, gymnasium, restaurants, and bar. **$$$**

Bejuma–Aguirre
Posada La Calceta
Bejuma
Tel/fax: (249) 92 522
Tel: (249) 94 1041, (416) 840 9867, (414) 497 9988
Caracas
Tel/fax: (212) 962 0738, (414) 940 3254

E-mail: info@posadalacalceta.com
www.posadalacalceta.com
In a large working *hacienda* in the mountains. Ample, well-appointed rooms. Great attention to detail, tasty meals included plus tours. Huge pool, horseback riding. Store with excellent selection of Venezuelan crafts plus demonstrations by local artisans. German and English spoken. **$$$** per person per night

Hacienda La Concepción
First entrance to Aguirre
Spa: tel: (414) 941 9999
Reservations Caracas: tel: (212) 943 4570, (414) 279 4500
Fax: (212) 993 5275
E-mail: efrain@hoffman-spa.com
www.hoffmann-spa.com/haciendamco.htm
Spa under the direction of specialist in alternative medicine. Various anti-stress programs. **$$$$**

YARACUY

San Felipe
Posada Turística Granja Momentos
Via Club La Montaña
Tel: (254) 31 0153
Very inviting option, enhanced by very friendly owners/hosts. Two separate cabins plus two rooms (shared bathroom) in their home. Large *churuata* where delicious meals are available. Pool, barbecue. **$$**

Yarigagua
Centro Turístico Los Carrascosa
Tel/fax: (251) 482 3781/3033
Carrera 8 at Calle 19, (two blocks south of the Plaza Bolívar)
Marvelous multi-functional establishment within a huge beautifully restored 19th-century house, with enormous rooms, museum, coffee shop, office of state tourist foundation, restaurant, bar, swimming pool. For visitors to Barquisimeto, this is not only a very distinct and convenient alternative (just 15 minutes away by freeway), but outstanding value compared with options in Lara's capital. **$$**

FALCON

Tucacas
Aparto Posada del Mar
Calle Páez at Avenida Silva
Tel: (259) 812 0524, (414) 940 1071, (416) 642 1819
Tel/fax: (259) 812 3587
E-mail: posadadelmar@cantv.net
www.apartoposadadelmar.com
Very handsome, spacious apartments for 4–6 with fully equipped kitchen (including penthouse unit with private terrace, and barbecue) plus standard rooms. Beachfront, *caney* with barbecue, pool with Jacuzzi, sauna with ocean view, boat service to cays. **$$$**

Casa de Descanso 2 más 3
By the Km 62 marker, near the entrance to town
Tel: (242) 83 0896
Well-kept, spotless rooms in a quiet, inviting family home (guests are attended by the very pleasant owners). Private bath, AC, cable TV. living area, enclosed porch. **$$**

Posada Jonathan
Calle Sucre at Calle Principal
Tel: (242) 83 0239/3315, (414) 943 1529
Simple but comfortable and economical rooms, plus a suite with equipped kitchen. **$–$$**

Between Tucacas & Chichiriviche
El Solar de la Luna
Bella Vista
Posada: tel: (242) 88 1010, (416) 647 2741, (416) 644 0915
Caracas: tel: (212) 986 2861
One of the best *posadas* in Venezuela. Beautiful rustic-style house with nine guest rooms, each different and a work of art. Vivid colors, crafts, and paintings. Terrace with dining area and garden centered round Jacuzzi with panoramic view of the coast. Exquisite food. Breakfast and dinner with wine included. Excursions to cays available. **$$$**

La Pradera
Sanare
Tel: (416) 642 2014, (414) 943 2339
Extremely cozy rooms, all with

either four-poster bed or bunks with curtains to enclose them. Terrace with pool table. Imaginative menu (restaurant open to public). Breakfast and dinner included. **$$** per person

Villa Mangrovia
Lizardo Spit
Morrocoy National Park
Tel: (414) 941 5176
Fax: (049) 914 70
or book through Last Frontiers in the UK, tel: (01296) 653 000, www.lastfrontiers.com
Charmingly run place, these are the only accommodations within Morrocoy Park and pre-booking is essential as there are only four rooms. Excellent cuisine and drinks included in the price. **$$$**

Chichiriviche
Posada Morokkue
Avenida Principal, Playa Norte
Tel: (416) 642 4985/(259) 818 6492
Fax: (242) 86 492/(259) 815 1197
E-mail: info@morokkue.com
www.morokkue.com
Beachfront option with five very pretty rooms, central AC. DirecTV in the communal social area. Glassed-in restaurant/bar on the first floor and inviting furnished terrace upstairs, both with sea view. French and Italian spoken. Basic package includes breakfast and dinner, optional extra: island transfer and picnic lunch. **$$$** per person.

Villa Marina Apart-Hotel
Vía Fábrica de Cemento, Sector Playa Sur
Tel: (259) 818 6759/411
Fax: (259) 818 6503
Large, attractive complex with huge pool as focal point. 40 apartments with fully equipped kitchen. Pool tables, covered children's playground, ample gardens, and plants everywhere. **$$$**

Via Chichiriviche–Coro
Posada Granja El Ojito
Tocópero
Tel: (268) 774 1050
Fax: (268) 774 1130
E-mail: info@granjaelojito.com
www.granjaojito.com

Very appealing compound with first-class details throughout. 10 rooms with central AC, DirecTV, phone, hammocks in deep porch. pool, extensive green areas, tennis court, short walk via palm grove to beach, German, French, and English spoken. Restaurant and bar only for guests. Room alone **$$**, plan with meals **$$$**

Coro
Hotel Intercaribe
Avenida Manaure at Calle Zamora
Tel: (268) 51 1811/1944/1955
Fax: (268) 51 1434
Located near the historic zone, simple but comfortable rooms, satellite TV, small swimming pool, ice-cream parlor, restaurant, bar, beauty shop, room service, video games, playground, secretarial service. **$$**

Hotel Miranda Cumberland
Avenida Josefa Camejo at Avenida Carnevalli
Tel: (268) 252 3322/3311/3022
Fax: (268) 52 3096
E-mail: cumberland@cantv.net
www.hotelescumberland.com/falcon
Excellent location in front of the airport and within walking distance of the colonial zone. Handsomely remodeled recently, satellite TV, central AC, in-room safety deposit box. Restaurant, piano bar, sauna, conference rooms, pools for adults and kids. **$$$**

Posada Corocororico
Intercomunal, Sector La Sabana
Tel: (268) 78 517/537
Near Xerophytic Garden. Plain but clean and economical. Restaurant, bar, room service. Low season **$**, high season with breakfast only **$$**

Price Categories

Prices are quoted in US$, but payable in bolívars at the exchange rate of the day. Prices based on double occupancy, standard room, without breakfast (unless otherwise noted).
$ = under $20
$$ = $20–$50
$$$ = $50–$100
$$$$ = over $100

Paraguaná Peninsula
Hotel Península
Calle Calatayud, beside the Club Centro Hispano, Punto Fijo
Tel/fax: (269) 46 6708/5983, 45 9776/9734/9847
E-mail: hotelpeninsula@eldish.com
Enclosed compound, rooms with satellite TV, mini-bar. Laundry and fax service, bar, restaurants, room service, gymnasium, sauna, pool, jogging track, playground, stores, multi-purpose sports areas. **$$**

Hacienda La Pancha
Via Adícora–El Hato, Falcón
Tel: (414) 969 2649
Reservations Caracas tel: (212) 987 0081
Email: haciendapancha@hotmail.com
Service weekends only unless special arrangements made. No children under 16 due to fragile antiques and intimate ambience of a shared family home. Very pretty traditional colonial-style house atop hill, surrounded by xerophytic gardens. Guest rooms filled with creative touches, surrounding a central garden. Restaurant (open to the public on weekends, meals for lodgers by prior request) with outstanding French and Catalan cuisine. Price includes lodging, breakfast, and dinner **$$**

La Troja
Calle Santa Ana, Nº 2, Adícora
Tel/fax: (269) 88 048,
(212) 952 8352
Large, very pretty enclosed complex. Cabins for up to eight and large dormitories for summer camps, meetings. Restaurant. Volleyball, basketball, barbecues, mini-zoo, ample pool with terrace. Low season (room alone) **$$**; breakfast, dinner, excursion included in high season **$$$**

Posada de la Familia Kitzberger II – La Carantoña"
Calle Comercio, one block from the beach
Tel: (269) 88 004
Tel/fax: (269) 88 173
Recently refurbished rooms (with private bath, TV, some with AC) in a traditional house in the colonial zone. Cozy beer garden in enclosed rear patio. Good choice for tight budgets. With fan **$**, with AC **$$**

Lara

Barquisimeto

(See also entry under Yaracuy for Centro Turístico Los Carrascosa, page 343)

Hotel Barquisimeto Hilton
Carrera 5, between Calles 5 and 6, Urb Nueva Segovia
Tel: (251) 54 3201/2945 & 53 6022, (800) 44 586 (8.30am–6pm)
Fax: (251) 51 8404, 54 4365
E-mail: brmhitwsal@hilton.com
Great view over Turbio River valley from back rooms and its popular poolside restaurant. Lighted tennis courts, disco, beauty spa, sauna, steam room, stores, private golf course (15 minutes from hotel), quiet neighborhood. **$$$$**

Hotel Principe
Calle 23, between Carreras 18 & 19
Tel: (251) 31 2111/1131
Fax: (251) 31 1731
In the heart of the banking district, just blocks from the historic zone and government offices. 150 rooms, satellite TV, pool, stores and services. Restaurant, bar. **$$**

Hotel Yacambú
Avenida Vargas, between Carreras 19 and 20
Tel: (251) 52 1077/4272, 51 3022/3729
Fax: 52 2474
48 rooms and suites. Impressive bathrooms considering its three-star status, cable TV, restaurant, bar. **$$**

Cubiro

Hotel Centro Turístico Cubiro
Avenida Principal ("La Vuelta")
Tel/fax: (253) 48 155
Regular rooms plus cabins for six with two bedrooms, TV, private terrace with great view of the valley, Barbecue. Restaurant service until 8pm, bar much later. Rooms **$**, cabins **$$**

Sanare

Posada Los Cerritos
Los Cerritos colonial zone
Tel: (253) 49 0016
In the midst of the restored colonial zone and near entrance to Yacambú National Park. Attractive complex with simple but comfortable rooms. Large pleasant restaurant, bar. **$$**

Carora

Posada Madrevieja
Avenida Francisco de Miranda (main street entering town)
Tel/fax: (252) 21 3787
E-mail: madrevieja@cantv.net
Inviting open-sided restaurant with good food. Separate building houses comfortable rooms. **$$**

Northern Zulia

Maracaibo

Apart Hotel Suite Golden Monkey
Calle 78 (Dr Portillo) between Avenida 10 and 11.
Tel: (261) 797 3285/6462/7423, (414) 961 7440
Fax: (261) 797 1040
Regular rooms plus apartments with kitchen (microwave, refrigerator, but no utensils). Restaurant, bar.
Rooms **$$**, apartments **$$$**

Gran Hotel Delicias
Avenida 15 at Calle 70, Las Delicias
Tel: (261) 97 6111
Fax: (261) 973 3037
www.granhoteldelicias.com
Recommended moderate-priced hotel with restaurant, disco, soda bar and pool, slightly away from the center of town. **$$**

Hotel Del Lago Inter-Continental
Avenida 2 El Milagro
Tel: (261) 792 4222, (800) 12 132
Fax: (261) 793 0392
E-mail: maracaibo@interconti.com
www.interconti.com
On shoreline of Lake Maracaibo, next to new shopping center. Popular poolside barbecue with live entertainment a weekend gathering spot, piano bar, gymnasium, racquetball, shopping arcade. **$$$$**

Hotel El Paseo Best Western
Avenida 1B at Calle 74, Sector Cotorrera
Tel: (261) 792 4422/4114/1929
Fax: (261) 791 9453
E-mail: elpaseo@iamnet.com; hotelelpaseo@cantv.net
www.hotelelpaseo.com
Tower topped by the country's only revolving restaurant (with bar and small dance floor, too) offering fabulous view over city and Lake Maracaibo. 53 large suites, satellite TV, pool. **$$$$**

Hotel Kristoff
Avenida 8 (Santa Rita), between Calles 68 and 69
Tel: (261) 797 2911–13, 97 2917–19, (800) 57 478
Fax: (261) 798 1614
E-mail: reservaciones@hotelkristoff.com
www.hotelkristoff.com
Handsome, economical alternative to other upscale hotels; rooms, suites, and *cabañas* (just larger suites) with mini-bar; satellite TV, nightclub, pool, playground. **$$$**

Maruma International
Maracaibo
Avenida Circunvalación 2
Tel: (261) 736 3622/0022, (800) 62 786
Fax: (261) 736 2886
Reservations Caracas
Tel: (212) 752 0009, 751 2353
Fax: (212) 751 2579
www.maruma.com
Near airport/industrial zone; new convention center next door. Elegant public areas, shopping arcade, pool, jogging track, gymnasium, sauna, tennis, horseback riding, racquetball courts. Good reductions on weekends. **$$$$**

Los Andes

This region has more lodging than anywhere else in Venezuela, the majority in the form of cabins or small *posadas*, and this list barely scratches the surface of a multitude of excellent options available. Reservations are almost always necessary, especially in high season, and required for places which include meals. The website www.andes.net is an excellent guide to the region.

TRUJILLO

Bocono and Vicinity
Posada Turística Estancia de Mosquey
Guanare–Boconó highway, a short distance before Boconó
Tel: (271) 652 1555/1886
Pleasant rooms, tranquil setting with extensive lush gardens,

covered terrace with barbecue for guests to use, kiddie pool, game room, Jacuzzi, steam bath. Restaurant service 8am–6pm. Attended by friendly owner. Excellent value. **$–$$** (depending on season)

Hotel Campestre La Colina
By river at northern exit of Boconó.
Tel/fax: (272) 52 2695/1960.
E-mail: guarache@cantv.net
Quiet setting, extensive lawn areas (plenty of romping space for kids). Rooms plus handsome cabins with separate bedrooms, private verandah. Restaurant/bar. Rooms **$$**, cabins **$$$**

Trujillo

Hotel Country Trujillo
Avenida Carmona, at exit of downtown via Monumento Virgen de la Paz.
Tel: (272) 236 3942/3646/3576
The fanciest among the few options in town, in tranquil setting. Recently refurbished rooms have cable TV, small refrigerator. Pool, restaurant, bar, room service. **$$**

Posada La Troja: El Portal del Encanto
Via Monumento Virgen de la Paz.
Tel: (414) 971 2990/723 1959
Unique alternative in rustic artisan style with lots of imaginative decorative details, separate units with sleeping lofts (trojas) are the stars. Popular restaurant in front terrace. **$–$$**

Valera–La Puerta and Vicinity

Camino Real
Sector La Plata, Valera
Tel: (271) 52 260/815, 53 795
Fax: (271) 51 704
E-mail: caminoreal@trujillonet.com
The best offer in the state's largest and most important city. Tower hotel in the center of town. Refined restaurant/bar. **$$$**

El Nidal de Nubes I
Via Valera–La Quebrada–Jajó
Tel: (414) 723 2844
E-mail: nidalnubes@hotmail.com
www.andes.net/nidaldenubes
Spectacular mountain-top setting with panoramic view true to its name (nest in the clouds). Cozy, imaginative rooms, restaurant, bar.

Grounds overflowing with flowers. Weekdays, room alone can be contracted; weekends-only package with substantial breakfast and dinner included. Tours available. Without meals **$$** per double room, package with meals **$$** per person.

Hotel Guadalupe Resort
Avenida Principal, La Puerta
Tel: (271) 83 294
Tel/fax: (271) 83 825
E-mail: guadalup@telcel.net.ve
www.hotelguadalupe.com
Large resort with rooms plus apartments with kitchen. Tennis court. Tours available. Impressive facilities but cold service. Rooms **$$$**, apartments **$$$$**

Casa Agripina
La Flecha (just south of La Puerta)
Tel: (271) 83 957
A delight. Extremely handsome units, all different and with fully equipped kitchens (some with fireplace); each with private kiosk with barbecue in central terraced garden brimming with flowers. Very personable owners. **$$–$$$**

Mérida

Santo Domingo & Vicinity

La Trucha Azul International Resort
Avenida Principal, Santo Domingo
Tel: (273) 88 066/150/079/080/087
Fax: (273) 88 067
Reservations Valencia tel: (241) 21 9296
E-mail: la trucha@latruchaazul.com
www.latruchaazul.com
Very pretty large resort with rustic style, creek and lush plantings. Excellent service. Regular rooms plus suites with fireplace. Discount of 30 percent in low season. Ask if they have any special packages. **$$$**

La Sierra
Avenida Principal, Santo Domingo.
Tel: (273) 88 110/113
Fax: (273) 88 050
Reservations Caracas tel: (212) 575 4835, fax: (212) 575 4853.
Luxury compound, the largest (for six) with fireplace. Restaurant with great view of valley, tasca, sauna. Low-season discount. **$$**

Hotel Los Frailes
Via Santo Domingo-Apartaderos

Reservations Hoturvensa tel: (212) 907 8130/8031/8134, fax: (212) 907 8140
E-mail: hoturvensa@cantv.net
Extremely pretty complex incorporates buildings of vintage farm on site of 1642 monastery in center of the páramo. Excellent restaurant and cozy bar. **$$$**

Posada La Casa de Mis Viejos
Calle Independencia (half a block above the plaza and church), Santo Domingo
Tel: (274) 88 268
Pleasant, economical option with typical rustic style, comfortable rooms with private bath, some with TV, enclosed parking. **$**

Price Categories

Prices are quoted in US$, but payable in bolívars at the exchange rate of the day. Prices based on double occupancy, standard room, without breakfast (unless otherwise noted).
$ = under $20
$$ = $20–$50
$$$ = $50–$100
$$$$ = over $100

Timotes–Mérida

This area of the páramo is one of the most picturesque in the country with beautiful mountains and ancient farmhouses.

Hotel Las Truchas
At northern entrance to Timotes
Tel/fax: (271) 89 158
Beautifully maintained and family-run since 1958. Cabins with fireplaces, and rooms. Restaurant serving typical Andean dishes; lovely cozy bar. **$$–$$$**

Posada San Rafael del Páramo
Just north of entrance to San Rafael de Mucuchíes
Tel: (274) 82 4198/82 0938
Very pretty hand-built house, with original part erected in 1868. Filled with imaginative decorative details, and very comfortable. Restaurant with terrace open in high season, excursions available on foot and horseback, rental of tents to use posada as base for exploring the páramo. **$**

Hotel Castillo San Ignacio
At north entrance to Mucuchíes
Tel: (274) 82 0751/0021
Mammoth stone castle that people love or hate since it is not at all typical of the region, but it does contain incredible workmanship, reminiscent of the medieval period with huge, heavy beams, etc. Each room is different, and all have first-class bathrooms and an elegant aspect. Excellent restaurant and inviting bar. **$$**

Hacienda Escagüey
Main highway, Escagüey (4 km south of Mucurubá)
Hacienda
Tel: (414) 974 9712
Reservations Caracas tel: (212) 963 5608/7951
E-mail: escaguey@telcel.net.ve
Two distinct options: rooms in a 1878 *hacienda* or beautiful cabins built nearby in a high valley surrounded by a profusion of flowers. Breakfast and dinner included. Rooms or cabins **$$$**

Cabañas Micatá
Near Escagüey
Tel: (274) 89 1000/808 1502, (414) 974 1277, (414) 974 0700
Fax: (274) 89 1001
E-mail: cabanasmicata@hotmail.com
www.andes.net/micata
Handsome log cabins with first-class features, including refrigerator; most have fireplace and are surrounded by lawns and flowers. Swimming pool, restaurant, bar, communal room with pool table, table soccer, fireplace, satellite TV. No pets allowed. English is spoken by the owners/hosts. Breakfast and dinner included. **$$$**

Cabañas Mucuratay
Tabay
Tel: (274) 283 1002/0107, (414) 974 0769
Fax: (274) 83 1000
Large, inviting cabins (for 7–10 people, with two or three bedrooms), outstanding workmanship, fully equipped kitchen, TV, and hilltop setting with great view. Restaurant, bar, game room, gymnasium, and a children's playground. Low-season discount. **$$$**

Cabañas Turísticas Xinia & Peter
Via La Mucuy Baja
Tel: (414) 742 1833
Tel/fax: (274) 83 0214
E-mail: xiniaypeter@hotmail.com
Three spectacular cabins, each different and extremely cozy, with fully equipped kitchen, TV, built-in safe, beautiful decor, surrounded by verdant gardens. Excellent restaurant. Optional tours, transfers, and various special packages. German and English spoken by delightful owners/hosts. **$$–$$$**

Via El Valle–La Culata

Residencias Fabbro
Tel: (274) 44 6758
Wooded setting, walled compound with seven attractive cabins of different sizes (capacity 2–9), all with equipped kitchen, TV, the smallest with fireplace. Game room with pool table, ping pong, fireplace. Playground, barbecue grills, washer and drier for use by guests. Italian spoken by friendly owners/hosts. **$$–$$$**

Riverside
El Valle, Sector El Playón
Tel: (274) 44 6639
Pretty, well-kept, and very homey cabins set in impeccably maintained garden, fenced compound. Sauna. Friendly European owner sells great homemade sausage, preserves, and dried fruit. Mini-spa with beauty treatments, massages, etc. Excellent value. Low season discount. **$$**

City of Mérida

For less expensive lodging here, you are better off in *posadas* than the city's cheaper hotels. Check out www.andes.net for excellent information on accommodations.

Hotel Park Best Western
Calle 37, in front of Parque Glorias Patrias
Tel: (274) 263 7014/4866/0803
Fax: (274) 263 4582
E-mail: parkhotel@cantv.net
www.bestwestern.com
One of the best downtown hotels, 125 rooms and suites in tower hotel, with restaurant, bar, disco,

travel agency, stores. Significant extra cost for rooms with AC (unnecessary in this mountain climate). Breakfast included. **$$**; with AC **$$$**

Hostería & Spa La Sevillana
End of Avenida Principal La Pedregosa
Tel: (414) 741 5969, (274) 266 3227
Fax: 266 2810
E-mail: sevillana@telcel.net.ve
www.andes.net/lasevillana
Marvelous tranquil wooded setting, yet minutes from downtown Mérida, gorgeous rooms, excellent food, health spa. Social area with fireplace, bar. Beautiful gardens, hiking paths. Breakfast included (also plans with all meals available), discount in low season. English spoken. Price includes full American breakfast. **$$$**; with all meals **$$$$**

Posada de Luz Caraballo
Avenida 2, Nº 13–80, opposite Plaza Sucre (Milla)
Tel: (274) 252 5441
Fax: (274) 252 0177
www.andes.net/luzcaraballo
Luz Caraballo has 36 simple but immaculate rooms with TV, hot water; consistently dependable, friendly service; restaurant with bar service, snack bar. Limited parking. Low-season discount. **$–$$**

Posada Los Bucares de Mérida
Avenida 4, Nº 15–5, at Calle 15
Tel/fax: (274) 252 2841/0566
E-mail: losbucarespos@hotmail.com
Typical vintage house with central courtyard, spotless comfortable rooms with hot water, some with TV; use of refrigerator; *artesanía* shop and snack bar; rare ample private parking. Very friendly owners. **$**

Posada Papá Miguel
Calle Piñango, Nº 1, La Mesa de Los Indios (5 km north of Ejido)
Tel/fax: (274) 252 2529
E-mail: posada_papamiguel@hotmail.com
Delightful old house with additions in the same style, restaurant with delicious home cooking, bar, barbecue, shop with handmade crafts, special programs, traditional Christmas dinner, tours available (to

nearby hot springs, picturesque mountain villages, workshops of artisans, etc.). Very friendly owner speaks some English. Price includes welcome cocktail, breakfast, and dinner. **$$**

Estancia Victoria Margarita
Calle Principal Nº 122, San Juan de Lagunillas
Tel: (274) 221 3813/996 1653/ (414) 745 8689
E-mail: estanciavm@latinmail.com
Large fenced complex with the focal point a sprawling 300-year-old house that holds the living quarters of the owners/hosts. Restaurant, bar, games room, and large covered terrace used for conferences and special events. Appealing cabins in independent buildings to the rear. Separate bar built around a tree in the garden, playground, children's pool, *bolas criollas*. Excellent value. Rooms **$**, cabins **$$**

Cabañas "El Coronel"
Via El Morro (and "Los Pueblos del Sur")
Tel: (414) 974 1265/741 7150
Tel/fax: (274) 271 5225
E-mail: cabanascoronel@hotmail.com
Marvelous hillside setting with view of city of Mérida below and mountains. Nine cabins for up to eight people with equipped kitchen and TV, surrounded by gardens; quality, good taste, and attention to details are evident throughout. Swimming pool with changing rooms, barbecue, *bolas criollas* court, mini-soccer field. Salon for events with capacity of 100. Meal service available by prior arrangement for groups. The personable owner grows peaches, figs, orchids, and bromeliads. **$$**

El Tao
Near La Azulita.
Tel: (414) 960 5888
Fax: (274) 297 040
Unique ecological farm on 14 hectares (35 acres) with an emphasis on natural health programs, an appreciation of nature, and relaxation. Excellent birding opportunities. Without meals **$$**, with programs and meals **$$$**

TACHIRA

Northern Táchira

Finca La Huerfana
Páramo El Zumbador, Via El Cobre–La Grita
Tel: (416) 777 9393/ (414) 979 5350
This is a real gem, located on 80 hectares (200 acres) with river, forest, *páramo* with many trails. Extremely pretty rustic style, widely spaced cabins with fireplace, a large new multi-purpose building with bar and several levels for social area or meetings. Inviting restaurant (emphasis on natural foods). Shop with local crafts. Charming owners. English spoken. **$$**

Western Táchira

Hotel Aguas Calientes
Via Principal Ureña–Aguas Calientes
Tel: (276) 87 2450
Tel/fax: (276) 87 2665/87 1391
This hotel's main attraction is that 34 of the 36 rooms have natural "hot tubs" fed by thermal springs. Large swimming pool, extensive grounds. 15 minutes from San Antonio airport. **$$**

San Cristóbal

For inexpensive lodging, you are better off in *posadas* than cheap hotels.

Castillo de la Fantasía
Redoma España
Tel: (276) 56 4492/4959
Fax: (276) 56 4847
Definitely different. Built in the style of a European chateau. Each room distinct – from streamlined modern to rococo with ornately carved furniture, crystal chandeliers; huge bathrooms – most with Jacuzzi, elegant restaurant, inviting bar.
$$$–$$$$

Posada Los Pirineos
Avenida Francisco Cárdenas, Quinta El Cerrito, Nº 16–38, Urb Los Pirineos
Tel: (276) 55 6528
Fax: (276) 55 8366
Nicely decorated rooms, small refrigerator, AC, phone, guests can use kitchen, inviting third-story terrace, breakfast and laundry

service. During Christmas season, decorations cause traffic jams. **$$**

Posada Turística El Gran Chalet
Via Palo Gordo (from Avenida Principal of Zona Industrial Paramillo of San Cristóbal)
Tel: (414) 701 8050
Tel/fax: (276) 57 2162
A world of surprises awaits inside this large compound where the delightful owners are your hosts. Four appealing rooms and suites, one within the enormous chalet where they also live, the others in separate structures in back, all with TV, small refrigerator. Huge salon with bar for meetings or social events and a private fleet of every type of vehicle: an air-conditioned luxury bus with capacity for 47, a Colombian-style *chiva* (brightly painted open-sided wooden bus), limousine, 4x4, and a wide variety of restored classic cars including a 1944 Citron, BMW, Mercedes Benz, 1957 Oldsmobile, and 1939 Buick – part of their personal collection and utilized to provide optional transfers and tours for clients. Meals available by prior arrangement. **$$**

Los Llanos

Packages at the *hatos* (cattle ranches) all include lodging, meals, beverages, and excursions (by boat, horseback, or photo safari trucks) and are by no means cheap. By advance reservation only.

Hato El Piñero
Vía El Baúl, Cojedes state
Tel: office in Caracas (212) 991 8935/0079
Fax: (212) 991 6668
E-mail: hatopinerovzla@telcel.net.ve
www.branger.com
Pioneer among *hatos* in the *llanos* accepting tourists. Very pretty lodging in colonial-style building amid 80,000 hectares (197,684 acres), top-notch service, wildlife reserve, biological station, fauna check-list. No children under 12. You can drive there in a city car (about 5 hours from Caracas). Slight discount in low season.
$$$$ per person

Apure
Hato El Cedral
Between La Ye and Elorza
Tel: (212) 781 8995
Tel/fax: (212) 793 6082
E-mail: hatocedral@cantv.com
www.hatocedral.com
Former King Ranch with 50,000 hectares (123,553 acres). Incredible quantity and variety of wildlife, especially birds. New rooms with more luxury than their original simple cabins (now used only when demand exceeds capacity in the new part) with AC. Swimming pool, social room with videos about wildlife, fauna checklist. Best to visit in dry season. Access by car or charter to their own airstrip. Bilingual guides only by prior arrangement. Price includes meals and standard excursions. **$$$$** per person

Barinas
Posada Rosa Elena
Calle 13 at Carrera 7, Barinitas
Tel: (414) 564 3723
www.members.
xoom.com/reposada
Centennial home of the family of current owners/hosts, adapted for use as a *posada*. All rooms have private bath and handsome furnishings (some have AC). Seating areas with cable TV, *caney* with the bar and restaurant (only for *posada* guests). Emphasis is on guests interested in rafting and kayaking on rivers of Barinas (the USA Olympic team and fanatics from Spain are regular guests). Ask about prices/details for many optional plans including: peacock bass fishing, bicycle tours, excursions to a private ranch for observation of fauna. Optional transfers between the Barinas airport/bus terminal–*posada*. Lodging alone **$$**, plans with meals and rafting **$$$**

Portuguesa
Posada del Cabestrero
Guanare, Portuguesa state
Tel: (257) 253 0101
Within grounds of the Museo de los Llanos complex. *Posada* built in typical rustic ranch style, ample

room with private patio/garden with hammock, cable TV, small fridge. Price includes breakfast. **$$**

Guarico
Centro Recreacional La Fe
52 km (32 miles) south of the bridge at the exit of Calabozo, at Km 227 next to a National Guard *alcabala*
Tel: (414) 946 1372, (246) 871 2279, (247) 41 3929, ext. 499
Fax: (246) 71 3464
E-mail: soreliafranco@hotmail.com
Country-style building, with good taste and quality in evidence, plus excellent service: this place is a jewel. Six rooms with private, two with shared bathroom. Inviting restaurant (emphasis on spit-roasted meats) open to the public for lunch and dinner (breakfast by prior arrangement), live music on weekends. Packages with meals and excursions available. Room alone or with meals **$$**, plus excursions **$$$**

Near Nutrias
Centro Turistico El Gaban
About 18 km (11¼ miles) southeast of Dolores, Via Barinas–Nutrias (a total of 106 km (66 miles) from Barinas), El Gaban
Tel: (273) 5826 183 (evenings only)
Office in Barinas tel/fax: (273) 32 3921
Good choice for independent visitors. Attractive, well-maintained complex with pool surrounded by 24 simple but comfortable rooms with AC, TV, private bath. Restaurant with good food at reasonable prices, bar. *Manga* (narrow run) for *toros coleados* (aficionados of bull-

running), used during periodic contests, plus live *llanero* music, small zoo of endemic animals. Vistors can observe cow milking every morning at 7am. Optional excursions for wildlife observation (minimum 10 people) and horseback riding (for any number). Friendly personnel. **$$**

Guayana Region

DELTA AMACURO

Prices are for one person, per night
Delta Orinoco Lodge
Caño Guamal, northern delta
Camp
Tel: (414) 989 0452
Reservations Tucupita Expeditions in Tucupita
Tel: (287) 721 1953
Tel/fax: (287) 721 0801
E-mail: orinocodelta@cantv.net
www.orinocodelta.com
The most attractive and well-equipped camp in the delta, located next to a *caño* with abundant wildlife. Some 30 individual cabins with private bathroom, built like the native-style *churuatas* with palm roofs, all connected by an elevated boardwalk. Meals, wildlife excursions and visits to the communities of the Warao Indians included. **$$$$**
Campamento Boca de Tigre
Boca de Tigre, northern part of delta
Tel/fax: (291) 41 7084/6566
E-mail: bocatigre@telcel.net.ve
www.bocadetigre.com
Handsome camp built with Guyanese styling. Large buildings with 25 rooms. Option of arrival by seaplane from Maturín. Meals, tours to observe wildlife and indigenous settlements included in the rate. **$$$$**

BOLIVAR

Western Bolívar
Prices are per person, per night.
Campamento Río Caura
Las Trincheras, on banks of Caura River (4½ hours west of Ciudad Bolívar)

Reservations Cacao Lodge
tel: (212) 977 1234/2798
Fax: (212) 977 0110
E-mail: cacaotravel@cantv.net
www.cacaotravel.com
Sleep in hammocks in indigenous-style *churuata* (with shared bathroom), or alternatively in cabins with beds and private bathroom at higher cost. Optional five-night/six-day tour to Salto Para is a highlight: by the river, camping on a beach, hiking through the jungle to reach the beautiful falls next to Ye'Kwana Indian community. Choose lodging only, with some or all meals, or with meals and tours. English spoken. Lodging only **$$**, with meals/excursion **$$$**

Ciudad Bolívar
Laja Real: Avenida Jesús Soto, facing the airport
Tel: (285) 20 813, 27 955/944
Fax: (285) 28 778
Large pool, gymnasium, restaurant, piano bar, disco, stores, pre-check-in service for flights. Though this is four-star rated and more impressive looking, local operators recommend the Laja City over it. **$$$**
Laja City: A few blocks from Laja Real (Avenida Bolívar between Táchira and Germania)
Tel: (285) 29 920/919
Simpler, quieter, and better-maintained rooms than its sister hotel, and guests may use the facilities at the Laja Real at no extra charge. **$$**
Posada Angostura
Calle Boyaca
Located in the heart of the colonial city center, with just seven stylish bedrooms, A/C, and TV. Dining room and terrace with sea view. Bookable through www.cacaotravel.com

Ciudad Guayana
Hotel Inter-Continental Guayana
Avenida Guayana, Parque Punta Vista
Tel: (286) 920 1111
Fax: (286) 923 1914
E-mail: guayana@interconti.com
Great location overlooking river and Cachamay Falls, connected by jogging path to Cachamay Park. Private dock and boats for river tours, pool, business center, plus other services and amenities typical of its luxury classification. Weekend discounts. **$$$$**

Upata
Hotel Andrea
Avenida Raúl Leoni (south exit of town)
Tel: (288) 21 3656/3618/3735/2811/3032
Just 30 minutes south from Ciudad Guayana, this is a good alternative to lodging at Ciudad Guayana (which is either very expensive or of poor quality), and especially convenient for people heading for the Gran Sabana. Rooms are simple but comfortable. Chinese restaurant/bar, stores, guarded parking. **$$**

Route of La Gran Sabana
La Montañita
Km 70
(no phone)
Simply furnished but comfortable and well-maintained lodgings built and run by indigenous Pemón couple. Rooms have private bath and *churuatas*; meals and tours available. Pool table, bar, video for the use of guests only. Camping also allowed. **$**
Campamento Anaconda
Las Claritas (Km 85)
Reservations Anaconda Tours
Tel: (286) 23 1449, 22 3130
(416) 686 4373
Tel/fax: (286) 22 6572
Ideal for independent travelers before exploring Gran Sabana (starting at Km 88). Enclosed compound lodging alone available, or full packages with excursions and meals. Lodging only **$$**, all-inclusive (minimum 2 nights/ 3 days) **$$$$**
Rápidos de Kamoirán
Km 174
Tel/fax: (286) 51 2729,
(416) 686 5297
25 simple, pleasant rooms with private bath, electricity 6pm–midnight. Restaurant serves the best food in the zone. Store, gas pump. **$$**

La Gran Sabana
There is only one main road through La Gran Sabana. "Addresses" for lodging and attractions here are all indicated according to the distance in kilometers (there are roadside markers all along the way) from El Dorado (at Km 0), and running southward to Santa Elena (Km 316) by the Brazilian border. The same method is used for the westbound route from Santa Elena (Km 0) to El Paují and Icabarú. A useful website for planning travel in this region is www.gransabana.com

Santa Elena de Uairén
Cabañas Freidenau
Avenida Principal Urb Cielo Azul
Tel/fax: (288) 95 1353/1295
Large fenced compound with various sized cabins and mini-suites (for three, with covered parking) for up to nine (these with kitchen, but no utensils). Suites **$$**, cabins **$$$**
Cabañas Kiamanti
North edge of town
Tel/fax: (288) 95 1952/1041
15 comfortable modern A-frame style cabins surrounded by gardens of native plants in a tranquil hilltop setting. Restaurant, bar, game room, and central garden with resident macaws. Swimming pool, mini-soccer field. Sold in package with breakfast and dinner. Excellent value. **$$**
Campamento Ya-koo
Via Sampay
Tel: (288) 995 1742
Tel/fax: (288) 995 1332
E-mail: yakoo@cantv.net
www.ya-koo.com
On outskirts of town. Handsome *churuata*-inspired cabins with nice view from hillside hold 14 comfortable rooms with private bath, restaurant/bar for guests, many reference books about the area, tours available. Natural swimming pool formed by damming of river running through the property. German spoken. **$$**

Hotel Lucrecia
Calle Perimetral
Tel: (288) 95 1130/1385
Fax: (288) 95 1839
In a convenient location, with comfortable rooms with private bathroom, hot water, TV, and AC. Restaurant. **$$**

Villa Fairmont
Urb Akurima
Tel: (288) 95 1022
Spacious triple rooms with DirecTV, small refrigerator. Large restaurant in *churuata* (open to public 7am–midnight daily) with bar, pool tables, wood-fired pizza oven. Tours available. **$$**

Hotel Gran Sabana
Via Santa Elena de Uairén–Brazil
Tel: (289) 995 1810/1811/1812
Fax: (289) 995 1813
E-mail: servicios@hotelgransabana.com
www.hotelgransabana.com
New option offering by far the most elegant lodging in the zone: 60 rooms with AC, DirecTV, direct-dial phones, small refrigerator, bathrooms with hot water. Swimming pool, soda fountain. Breakfast included in the price. **$$$**

El Paují

Access recommended only by Rutaca air taxi from Santa Elena because of poor condition of access road.

Hospedaje Las Brisas
Eastern outskirts of El Paují
Tel: (288) 95 1030
Taking advantage of the beautiful surrounding landscapes, windows have been installed in the main room of cabins, and showers only have a partial wall so you can admire the view as you bathe. Restaurant. **$**

Hospedaje Chimantá
Near the only intersection in the village, near the airstrip
Tel: (288) 95 1994 (nights), (414) 886 1481
Tel/fax: (288) 95 1431
Rooms with many attractive and imaginative details such as use of *bateas* (wooden bowls used for panning gold) for washbasins. Restaurant/bar run by owner (good food, outstanding bread). **$$**

Price Categories

Prices are quoted in US$, but payable in bolívars at the exchange rate of the day. Prices based on double occupancy, standard room, without breakfast (unless otherwise noted).
$ = under $20
$$ = $20–$50
$$$ = $50–$100
$$$$ = over $100

Via El Paují–Icabarú

Campamento Kawaik
Km 90, via Icabarú, 15 minutes from El Paují
Tel: (295) 42 3841, (414) 995 6135
E-mail: kawaik@intercon.net.ve
Located on a river bank with views of the Akopán and Chimantá *tepuyes*. Consists of main building with communal and dining area and cabins, each with private bathroom and terrace. Very ecologically oriented: electricity is via solar energy, running water via gravity from a nearby spring, building materials were foraged from abandoned mining camps or transported in from Upata and Puerto Ordaz (thereby not cutting any trees in the zone). Price includes transfers El Paují–camp, lodging, all meals, and guided excursions in the zone. Access is recommended only by inexpensive air taxi to El Paují (due to the poor condition of the access road) followed by transfer from there in a 4x4 vehicle. Discounts for resident tourists and groups of five or more. **$$$$**

Canaima

Prices at camps are quoted per person per night, flight *not* included.

Campamento Ucaima (Jungle Rudy's)
600 meters/yards from Hacha Falls
Ciudad Guayana
Tel: (286) 962 2359
Reservations Caracas tel/fax: (212) 693 0618/0825
E-mail: ucaima@etheron.com
www.junglerudy.com
Pioneer in Canaima, with this very

inviting camp established in the mid-1950s. Located on the banks of the Carrao River with *tepuyes* in the background. There is an extensive lawn, mature trees, tropical plantings; spacious rooms, a very intimate feel and personalized treatment. Meals and tour included in the price. **$$$$**

Hoturvensa (Campamento Canaima)
Hoturvensa Caracas
Tel: (212) 907 8130/8054/8153/8049
Fax: (212) 907 8053/8140
At edge of the Canaima Lagoon, with the Hacha Falls and *tepuyes* in the background. Huge camp with 115 rooms in cabins. Cafeteria-style meals. Plan includes meals, boat ride in lagoon; all tours extra. **$$$$**

Campamento Parakaupa
Tel: (414) 864 5541
Tel/fax: (286) 961 4963
E-mail: parakaupa@etheron.net
www.etheron.net/usuarios/parakaupa
A short walk from Canaima airstrip, with views of Canaima Lagoon, Hacha Falls, and *tepuyes*. Run by Jungle Rudy's daughter. There are 12 comfortable rooms, a porch with hammock in front. Very tasty meals are included. No children under six allowed on excursions. Tours optional. **$$$$**

Posada Kusari
Tel: (286) 962 0443
Near the airstrip, a little beyond Parakaupa *(see above)*, on the left. 12 simple double rooms with private bath, cold water only, fan, porch with hammocks. **$**

Other Options

Campamento Arekuna
Reservations through Aereotuy
Caracas
Tel: (212) 761 6231/6247/8483
Fax: (212) 762 5254
E-mail: tuysales@etheron.net
Porlamar
Tel: (295) 63 0307
Fax: (295) 61 7746
E-mail: tuysales@etheron.net
www.tuy.com
Northwestern corner of Canaima

National Park, by the banks of the Caroní River. Attractive native-style cabins. Private landing strip. Some attractions can be visited on foot. Optional boat tours of falls, petroglyphs, Pemón communities, Canaima. Low-season discount. Includes flight (from Porlamar or Ciudad Bolívar), meals, tours. **$$$$**

Campamento Akare-Merú
Tel: (414) 304 7880,
(416) 607 3942,
(212) 576 6038/6855
E-mail: akarem@cantv.net
www.akaremeru.com
Spectacular camp in the middle of the Caroní River. During the rainy season, it is on an island; in the dry season it becomes a peninsula with freshwater beaches of pure white sand. Structures combine elements of Pemón architecture along with modern comforts (enjoy the wonderful view of the river and jungle as you take a shower), with creative details throughout using only natural materials. Library, living-dining area, restaurant with panoramic views. Solar energy. Price includes lodging, meals, national beverages, excursions. Optional charter flights to the *posada*. **$$$$**

Amazonas

Puerto Ayacucho & vicinity

Camps are definitely the best option in Puerto Ayacucho. Hotels are quite poor, and the residences (aimed principally at backpackers and use-by-the-hour) are cheap, but you definitely get what you pay for.

Residencia Internacional
Avenida Aguerrevere Nº 18
Tel: (248) 21 0242
Considered slightly better than the other *residencias*, but still very basic; 30 rooms, most with private bathroom. Some with AC. Small TV area and bar. **$**

Vía Puerto Ayacucho–Samariapo

Nacamtur
From the *redoma* (traffic circle) near the airport, via Samariapo, take the exit for Gavilán 4 km beyond; this

Price Categories

Prices are quoted in US$, but payable in bolívars at the exchange rate of the day. Prices based on double occupancy, standard room, without breakfast (unless otherwise noted).
$ = under $20
$$ = $20–$50
$$$ = $50–$100
$$$$ = over $100

place is 1 km from that turn.
Camp tel: (416) 547 5009
Messages tel: (248) 21 2763/4255 (answering machine), (248) 21 4066 (Anunción Cobos)
Fax: (248) 21 0325
This is the best alternative to Puerto Ayacucho hotels if you have a vehicle. There is paved access to the attractive compound with large suites in AC brick cabins. Huge restaurant, bar, disco. Short walk to caves and petroglyphs. Tours available. English spoken. **$–$$**

Yagrumo–Cataniapo
Km 21, via Galiván
Tel: (248) 21 0541/4458
Fax: (248) 21 1529
E-mail: yagrumocat@hotmail.com
In the middle of the jungle, but with access by city car. A great option for close contact with nature and tours totally distinct from the standard offer of every other camp. Lodging ranges from a *churuata* with hammocks and shared bathroom, to a cabin with beds, private bathroom, and living room. English and some German spoken. Economy "hammock & breakfast" plan for backpackers; or full package with lodging, all meals, and excursions. H&B **$**, cabin alone **$**, package **$$$**

Camps with Packages

Prices for the following are per person/per night, inclusive of transfer between airport, lodging, meals, standard tours – usually Ethnological Museum, petroglyphs, short hike in jungle, visit to Piaroa settlement, river excursion, Tobogán de la Selva.

Campamento Tucán
Behind Terminal de Pasajeros, Puerto Ayacucho
Camp
Tel: (416) 448 5273
Office
Tel: (248) 521 1378
Large fenced compound within the city, with access by paved road. Lodging in rooms or cabins set back in tranquil wooded property (some with AC, all with cold water only). If space is available or in the low season, rooms alone can be rented. Definitely the best option for in-town lodging. **$$$**

Camturama Amazonas Resort
Km 20 via Samariapo, Sector Garcitas
Reservations Caracas
Tel: (212) 941 8813, (248) 521 0266, (416) 821 1995
E-mail: magico@ven.net
www.angelfire.com/ve/camturama
Geared to those who prefer not to rough it: 46 nicely decorated rooms in modern cabins with AC and hot water. Restaurant. Large entertainment center with bar, disco, pool tables, etc. If there is space available in low season, they will rent rooms alone. There is an optional restaurant service with very reasonably priced meals (advisable to reserve). Rooms alone **$$**; plans (price per person): with meals but without any excursions **$$$**, with tours **$$$$**

Campamento Orinoquía
Km 20 via Samariapo, Sector Garcitas (next to Camturama)
Cacao Lodge
Tel: (212) 977 1234
Fax: (212) 997 0110
E-mail: cacaotravel@cantv.net
www.cacaotravel.com
On the banks of the Orinoco, individual cabins or Piaroa structures with private bath, or triple rooms next to huge *churuata* social building (dining room, bar, living area). German, English, Italian, and Portuguese spoken. Plans with just lodging and two or three meals. All tours sold separately, ranging from boat transfer to nearby beach (**$**) to two-hour fly-over of Autana (**$$$$**). Lodging plus meals **$$**

Note: To reach the following camps, there is an air taxi service Monday to Saturday from the airport in Puerto Ayacucho by Aguaysa (tel: 248-21 0020/0026/0443) and Wayumi (tel: 248-21 0635).

Campamento Yutaje
Northern Amazonas, north of San Juan de Manapiare
Tel: (248) 21 2550, 42 5002
Cabins and *churuatas* in a large cleared area surrounded by woodland and a river. River excursions. Price includes lodging, meals, beverages, and two excursions per day, but not soft drinks, ice, or flight to/from camp. **$$$**

Campamento Camani
On banks of Ventuari River, near San José de Camani
Tel: (248) 24 4865, 21 4553, 21 4865
E-mail: camani@enlared.net; info@camani.com
www.enlared.net/camani; www.camani.com
Located near to the airstrip, and by the river. Native-style cabins, swimming pool. Restaurant and bar. Horseback riding. Included in price: welcome cocktail, lodging, all meals, non-alcoholic beverages, tax, and nearby excursions. Optional: sport fishing plans and bar service. **$$$$**

Where to Eat & Nightlife

In the smaller towns and cities, there is not usually sufficient potential clientele to maintain a place dedicated only to nightlife. Thus, many places lead a "double life," with part of their facilities popular as a restaurant during the day and early evening; but, by night, putting on a different face – often with the addition of some form of entertainment or space cleared for a dance floor. For this reason, restaurants and nightlife have been placed under the same headings to avoid duplications or omissions, with the explanations clearly defining their multi-faceted or singular emphasis.

Because of the fact that most discotheques charge cover and/or require *"consumo mínimo"* (purchase of at least a half bottle of liquor and set-ups, with no sale of individual drinks, beer, or wine), many people prefer to go to a pleasant bar for nightlife.

Eating Out

With the exception of coffee shops in premium hotels, it is rare to find any restaurant open for breakfast. Venezuelans either eat breakfast at home or will stop at a *panadería* (bakery) for juice, coffee, and *cachitos* (ham rolls) or similar fast food, or at an *arepera* for a *tostada* (an *arepa* filled with anything from grated cheese to quail eggs or octopus) or at street stands for *empanadas* (deep-fried turnovers with fillings).

Most formal restaurants close after lunch, around 3pm, and do not re-open until 7–8pm, with dinner served until nearly midnight. Venezuelans usually have their evening meal late, whether at home or in restaurants, rarely sitting down to eat before 8.30–9pm.

Many places offer a *menu ejecutivo* (along with their regular menu) as a lunch option. This is a fixed-price menu, including soup or appetizer, main dish, dessert, and beverage – usually a great bargain and you get much faster service than when ordering à la carte.

In many villages in the interior, the best places to eat are not necessarily formal restaurants, but private homes where *la señora* prepares tasty home cooking that she also serves to the public to bring in extra cash or fill a need in places where no restaurants exist. You will often find hidden gems by asking where to go at the place where you are staying (particularly at *posadas*) since they are most familiar with the local offers.

El Litoral

Since the devastating mudslides, flooding, and high seas which struck the central coast with in December of 1999, few restaurants have remained in operation owing to physical damage, the destruction that surrounds them, the lack of potable water, and of course the shortage of clients. Though having suffered little damage, the area west of the airport has never been popular with tourists who must pass through the unpleasant Catia La Mar area before reaching any of the tourist hotels, restaurants, or beach clubs. Thus, virtually the only option in this sector is:

Dining Prices

Prices are quoted in US$, but payable in bolívars at the exchange rate of the day. Prices based on a three-course meal for one, without alcoholic beverages.
$ = under $10
$$ = $10–$20
$$$ = $20–$30
$$$$ = over $30

El Meson del Faro
Avenida Principal de Puerto Viejo,
Catia La Mar
Tel: (212) 351 1435/3553
Though the neighborhood is less
than appealing, this is the best
option on the central coast, with
excellent Spanish cuisine and
attentive service. **$$$**

Dining Prices

Prices are quoted in US$, but
payable in bolívars at the
exchange rate of the day. Prices
based on a three-course meal for
one, without alcoholic beverages.
$ = under $10
$$ = $10–$20
$$$ = $20–$30
$$$$ = over $30

El Oriente

ANZOATEGUI

Puerto La Cruz
The area in the center of Puerto La
Cruz on Paseo Colón and the block
to the south and west is solid with
bars, discotheques, show places,
gambling halls, restaurants... if you
can't find something to entertain
yourself here, you had best just go
back to your room and watch TV!

With the great number of offers
on this boulevard and the pleasant
area for strolling, most people
prefer simply to stop at whatever
place strikes their fancy as they
walk, rather than heading for a
specific destination.

Brasero Grill/La Boite del Brasero
East end of Paseo Colón
Tel: (281) 67 4850/266 0923
Restaurant features beef and
seafood. Bar. Upscale crowd. **$$$**

El Bacha
Paseo Colón
Tel: (281) 65 0206
Mouthwatering Arab pastries,
Middle-Eastern espresso. **$**

El Parador del Puerto
Paseo Colón
Tel: (281) 265 0391/3950.
Seafood specialty, elegant-looking
dark interior. **$$–$$$**

El Rancho del Tío
East end of Paseo Colón
Tel: (281) 65 3677
Huge place with sophisticated rustic
styling, open-sided terrace air-
conditioned closed part with live
music and separate bar. Prices a bit
higher than its neighbors. Beef and
seafood specialties. **$$–$$$**

Fornos
Paseo Colón
Tel: (281) 65 3860
Handsome, rather formal interior,
appealing antipasti cart, Italian
kitchen. **$$–$$$**

Fuentemar
Paseo Colón
Tel: (281) 68 7623
Long-established place on the
beach side, with both inside and
outside seating, but at the latter a
distinct soda-fountain-style menu.
Formal interior has seafood. **$$**

Lecherías–El Morro (Barcelona)
Caffé L'Ancora
Avenida Americo Vespucio (near
Maremares), Complejo Turístico
El Morro
Tel: (281) 81 0090
Popular casual setting with pizzas
(white and red sauces), Mexican
fajitas, interesting sandwiches, and
special desserts. Open
9am–midnight daily. **$$**

La Terraza Bar & Grill
C.C. Punta Marina, Avenida Americo
Vespucio, via Maremares
Tel: (281) 81 8212/0002
Very pretty outdoor setting on a
large terrace, protected by giant
umbrellas, overlooking the canals.
Salads, barbecue ribs, pizza,
fajitas, gourmet hamburgers. **$$**

SUCRE

Mochima
El Mochimero
On the waterfront, a few doors
down from the parking lot.
Pleasant, casual setting with open
sides. The previously very enjoyable
restaurant has had a complete
change of owner and style (now
both are Spanish). Fortunately, the
result has made the place even
better than before. **$–$$**

Santa Fe
**Bar-Restaurant Club Náutico
"Santa Fe"**
Tel: (293) 21 0026
Large *caney* right on the beach of
Santa Fe. Previously a raunchy beer
hall with dancing (locals still
refering to it as *La Pista* – dance
floor). With the take-over and
complete remodeling by new owner,
Aníbal, the offer is now delicious
seafood (to die for are the grilled
extra large prawns – *langostinos
especiales*) in a very appealing
setting with decidedly different
clientele than before. **$–$$**

Cumaná
El Colmao
Calle Sucre, opposite the
Plaza Bolívar
Tel: (293) 66 2351
International and seafood dishes in
a rather formal atmosphere.
Nothing out of this world, but
considered the best choice in the
city. **$–$$**

Carúpano
La Madriguera
Calle Independencia Nº 12–A
(diagonal from Plaza Santa Rosa)
Creative Italian cuisine in the
setting of a restored vintage house
in the heart of the city. Closed
Monday. **$–$$**

Posada Nena
Playa Copey
Tel: (294) 32 0527/31 7624
Fax: 31 7297
www.posadanena.com
Inviting setting with restaurant
(open breakfast, lunch, dinner) in
churuatas shaded by palms, sea
shells underfoot. Savory food,
varied menu with many creative
touches, occasional German
dishes. **$–$$**

Restaurant Rancho Grande
Via Cumaná–Carúpano, opposite
the industrial zone of Carúpano
Tel: (414) 994 0962
On the right with huge signs
announcing it. Large *churuatas*
house family-run restaurant
featuring well prepared beef,
chicken, fish choices, with music.
There is a good sized recreation
area, ideal for children. **$$**

Pariana Café
Avenida Bermúdez, two blocks from the beach
Tel: (294) 61 706/2
E-mail: pariana@cantv.net
Very hip locale managed by the dynamic duo of Tamara and Juan Sara, with emphasis on creative cuisine (including special gastronomic festivals with live music) in a vintage building finished with very eclectic decor mixing antiques with modern art and hand-crafted furniture. **$**

MONAGAS

Caripe and Vicinity
Las Delicias del Valle
Via Teresén–El Mirador, Caripe
Open sided restaurant with pretty view and tasty home-style cooking, freshly baked cakes. Open from about 8am–6pm.
El Posada del Gallego
Via El Guácharo–Maturín
Tel: (414) 761 1060, 760 2900
Large family-run restaurant and *tasca* featuring savory Spanish food prepared by Manolo and served in enormous portions with very reasonable prices; rabbit (they raise their own) is also a specialty. Live entertainment is provided on weekends by the chef's wife, singer Katy Duvall. **$**

Maturín
Maturín is not known for its great choice of dining spots, with the majority leaning to family-oriented pizza parlors or no-frills *pollo en brasa* (spit-roasted chicken – eat in or take out) places with plastic chairs and formica table tops. The best bet for anyplace with any degree of class is in the restaurants of the Morichal Largo and Stauffer.
Agora
Avenida Alirio Ugarte Pelayo
Mixed bag: popular disco, but also pool tables; open from 9pm.
Mister Pasta
Carrera 6 Juncal
Tel: (291) 42 9289
Popular, with good choice and excellent value for money. **$**

La Curagua
Hotel Morichal Largo, Km 3,
Vía La Cruz
Tel: (291) 51 4222/4322
The most formal restaurant (though still more resort style dress than jacket and tie) of those offered in this hotel. Frequent gastronomic festivals. **$$$**
Meeting Place
Avenida Ugarte Pelayo
Popular pool place with bar, videos, music, games
Río Macho Café
Frente al Banco Provincial, entre Avenida Bolívar y Avenida Luis del Valle García.
Very casual gathering place for hamburgers, barbecue meats, shish kebabs. Live music weekends.
Whisky's
Hotel Morichal Largo, Km 3, vía La Cruz
Tel: (291) 51 4222/4322
Bar with music and dance floor in the city's only luxury hotel, geared to a more upscale and older audience than other local offerings for nightlife.

Guayana Region

DELTA AMACURO

Tucupita
Hotel-Bar-Restaurant Pequeña Venezia
Sector San Salvador
11 km (7 miles) on road to El Volcán
Tel: (287) 21 0777/0578/2044
The specialty of the house is unique: *costillas de morocoto* – unusual because *morocoto* is a huge local fish and the ribs *(costillas)* are the size of pork ribs with very tasty meat with a chicken flavor. **$$**

BOLIVAR

Puerto Ordaz
The greatest concentration of long-standing restaurants and places for nightlife, as well as a number of newcomers, pepper "Centro" – in the area in the immediate vicinity of C.C. Trébol and the Civic Center, roughly in the area bordered by Vía

Caracas, Avenida Ciudad Bolívar, the prolongation of Avenida Las Americas (follow this avenue from the Alta Vista shopping area to take you right to the heart of this district), and Vía Venezuela. With the numerous new shopping centers that have developed in the Alta Vista, various modest offers are beginning to open there, primarily geared toward daytime shoppers looking for a quick lunch.
El Churrasco
Carrera Upata at Calle El Callao
Tel: (286) 22 5939
Good pizzas and typical barbecue meats grilled over a wood fire. **$**
Ercole
Torre Loreto, semi-sótano, vía Colombia
Tel: (286) 23 3356, 22 3319
One of the best-stocked wine cellars in Venezuela, gourmet dining in elegant Art Deco setting. Private club, but Guest Relations at the Hotel Inter-Continental Guayana can make reservations for visitors.
$$$–$$$$
La Cuisine Express
C.C. Anto, PB, Carrera Tumeremo con Avenida Las Américas
Tel: (286) 23 4076
Choice of deli fare, cheeses, mouth-watering pastries served at outside tables; open Mon–Sat 7am–8pm, Sun 7am–1pm. **$**
La Forchetta de Oro Ristorante (Da Sergio)
Edif Royal, PB, Calle Tumeremo
Tel: (286) 22 6384
Good choice for pinched budgets. Homemade pasta; live music. **$**
La Llovizna
Hotel Inter-Continental Guayana
Parque Punta Vista
Tel: (286) 22 2244, 23 0722/0011
Gourmet international menu, beautiful view of Llovizna Falls in this elegant dining room. **$$$–$$$$**

Don't Forget!

Most restaurants, bars, and other places with public restrooms do *not* provide toilet paper (or if they offer it, you have to pay for it), thus you should always carry this necessity with you.

El Tascazo
C.C. El Trébol III, PB
Tel: (286) 22 9851
Popular discotheque and *tasca*; also with restaurant specializing in seafood. **$$**

Piano Bar-Restaurant Miuty
Edif La Meseta, Local Sótano, Calle Guasipati
Tel: (286) 23 4690, 22 0485
International cuisine, but more popular for its night action in the bar and for its large dance floor. **$$**

Santa Elena de Uairén
El Churanay Akurima
Villa Fairmont, Urb Akurima
Tel: (288) 95 1022)
Various levels suggesting divisions between inviting restaurant (featuring *carne en vara*, seafood, and pizzas baked in wood-fired oven), popular bar, and wing with pool tables. **$$**

El Paují
Restaurant-Bar La Comarca
At the only intersection, in the center of the village.
Limited menu, but well prepared. However, the reason to head for this place is the fantastic bread – full of whole grains and honey, moist and heavy – baked fresh for each meal by owner Luís Scott. **$**

Amazonas

Puerto Ayacucho
Discoteca Hot City
Avenida 23 de Enero, Centro
Located in the front of Hotel City with deafening decibel level that appeals primarily to a young crowd.

Tasca-Restaurant "Cherazad"
Avenida Aguerrevere at Río Negro
Tel: (248) 21 0874
Restaurant with Arab and *criollo* dishes, and the pleasing combination of good food, huge portions, and reasonable prices. The mixed platter of Middle Eastern specialties are particularly good. **$**

Vía Pto. Ayacucho–Samariapo
Nacamtur
Via Gavilán (1 km from the highway)
Tel: (248) 21 2763)
Though outside Puerto Ayacucho (5

km/3 miles from the traffic circle by the airport), very popular, classier ambiance and more entertainment than in-town offers: *tasca*, restaurant, disco, pool table. **$–$$**

Midwest

ARAGUA

Puerto Colombia
El Restaurant de Billy (El Alemán)
(also known as El Kiki)
Facing the river and access to Playa Grande
Without any sign to identify it, simply known by the name and nationality of its owner, Billy, a German chef. The best place to eat in town with every type of food from seafood to international fare. **$**

Maracay
Bodegón de Sevilla
Avenida Las Delicias
Tel: (243) 41 8410
Handsome and very popular Spanish *tasca* and restaurant in Maracay's restaurant zone. **$$**

Label's
Avenida Las Delicias, sector La Rinconada
Tel: (243) 41 8401/3189
French and Spanish menu in restaurant, with adjoining *tasca* and disco with faithful night crowd. **$$**

La Terraza del Vroster
Avenida Las Delicias
Tel: (243) 32 1528
An institution for its consistency and good value. Huge informal restaurant. Generous portions and rapid service. **$$**

Los Caneyes
Hotel Pipo Internacional
Avenida Principal El Castaño
Tel: (243) 41 3111
Very pleasant casual restaurant in the rear of the hotel, surrounded by tropical gardens. Meat is the specialty here. **$$**

CARABOBO

Valencia
The greatest concentration of better restaurants, bars, *tascas*, dance places are on or adjacent to

Avenida Bolívar Norte. As more casual alternatives, dozens of *terrazas* (casual open-air eateries) and cafés have opened on the three main streets of Urb El Viñedo – usually jammed at night.

Al-Ferdaus
Avenida Carlos Sanda, El Viñedo
Tel: (241) 825 3946
Arab meals and sweets, all made in-house. **$$**

Asociación de Ganaderos
Avenida Claudio Muskus, Guaparo
Tel: (241) 823 9770
This casual, open-sided restaurant of the cattlemen's club has outstanding beef: their *lomito piece* – section of whole tenderloin done to perfection – and thin crispy onion rings are legendary. **$$**

Bar Camoruco
Hotel Inter-Continental Valencia, Avenida Juan Uslar, La Viña
For years one of the favorite spots for dancing, with good house band alternating with disco music of all styles, ample dance floor, with no cover or minimum, guarded parking and safe area.

Casa Valencia
Final Avenida Bolívar Norte, near the Guaparo *redoma* (traffic circle)
Tel: (241) 823 9517, 824 2814
Attractive large building in the style of a vintage house with each room used as a different dining area. Traditional *criolla* fare, meats. **$$$**

Central Social Chino Valencia
Urb La Trigaleña Sur (entrance from the freeway between Lomas del Este and El Trigal)
Tel: (241) 842 1677
Impossible to find more authentic Chinese fare than within the private club of the city's large Chinese community. Restaurant/bar open to the public. **$$**

Il Cantone
Avenida Bolívar Norte at Calle 145 Nº 145–17
Tel: (241) 823 6234, 824 2874
Italian eatery with modern decor and enduring popularity. **$$**

Las Cuevas de Luis Candela
Avenida Bolívar, C.C. Los Sauces (basement, entry from south side)
Tel: (241) 821 5028
Liveliest Spanish-style bar in town, with clients across all age and

social groups thanks to years of consistently fast, friendly service, reasonable prices, generous drinks, good food, as well as live music at night. **$$**

La Grillade
Callejón Peña Pérez (half a block east of Avenida Bolívar)
Tel: (241) 823 5773
La Grillade is the place to go for a special meal. Elegant, French specialties and also excellent grilled meats; ample salad buffet. The bar is a very popular evening gathering spot **$$$**

La Villa de Madrid
Avenida Bolívar Nº 152–75
Tel: (241) 823 9534/6654
One side is a popular Spanish restaurant; the other side is an equally favored bar with dancing at night (combo of live music and disco). **$$**

Marchica
Avenida Bolívar Norte Nº 152–210 (next to Centro Comercial y Profesional Avenida Bolívar Norte)
Tel: (241) 822 4183
The traditional lair of business leaders and political movers and shakers. With an emphasis on seafood. **$$$**

Puerto Cabello

Mar y Sol
Calle El Mercado
Tel: (242) 361 2572/4497
Long-standing favorite. View from terrace or enclosed air-conditioned part of the port's beach and waterfront. Lobster a specialty. **$$$**

Restaurant Lanceros
Malecón
Tel: (242) 361 8920
In the heart of the restored colonial zone with view of the water (upstairs is best). Nice atmosphere, seafood specialties. **$$**

YARACUY

Yaritagua

El Buen Sabor
Northern service drive bordering the freeway, between Calles 4 and 5, Urb Daniel Carias
Tel: (251) 82 1507
Cozy family-run restaurant with main

dining room inside, and several tables on the covered porch in front especially nice in the evening. Simple, but well-prepared dishes served in large portions – the *parrilla*, with beef cut in bite-sized pieces and sausage piled high over french fries or yucca is enough for two. Very low prices and attentive service. **$**

San Felipe

Misión Nuestra Señora del Carmen
Sector La Marroquina
Tel: (254) 41 565
Fabulous setting in an impeccable reconstruction of a former 1720 mission that stood on this site. Gourmet restaurant Los Bourbones featuring "Euro-Yaracuyana" cooking; El Monje Piano Bar with live music (jazz and romantic ballads); and casual El Trapiche restaurant in the patio (serving barbecued beef). Beautiful setting, but service can be painfully slow. **$$–$$$**

FALCON

Tucacas

Tuca Café
Calle Páez
Tel: (242) 83 3739, (416) 842 3718
Very pleasant surprise in an area with few decent options. Gallery in the front. Restaurant in back opens to garden. Creative touches to menu (which earned owner/chef Carlos Arena the grand prize for one of his dishes in a recent regional gastronomic festival); good salads. This is a noted gathering place for artists, musicians, and intellectuals from the area. **$**

Sanare

La Pradera
On the left, just south of the split for Coro-Chichiriviche
Tel: (242) 84 2001/2002, (416) 642 0581, (416) 642 2014
Recently expanded to improve service to a clientele appreciative of interesting cooking that departs from the usual grilled meat, fish and chicken of the area. **$**

Sierra de San Luis

Falconés
Vía Soledad–Curimagua (just east of Curimagua)
Tel/fax: (268) 51 8271
People come from all around the area to this hotel for its delicious meals served family-style. **$$**

Puerto Cumarebo

La Fuente
West side of Puerto Cumarebo, on the north side of the highway
Tel: (268) 72 141
Best option in the zone, with international menu, but particular emphasis on seafood. Be sure to order their *arepas de maíz pelado* (coarsely pounded maize). **$–$$**

PARAGUANÁ PENINSULA

Cabo San Ramón

Marisquería Cervecería San Ramón
From Pueblo Nuevo, north to Cabo San Ramón via Voz de Venezuela. Take the road passing behind the huge radio tower another 3 km. Right on the water. No class at all, but the most wonderful lobster you've ever tasted, taken straight from the sea and prepared to order for you. Their fish is likewise as fresh as it comes. Open on weekends only. **$–$$**

Via Adícora–El Hato

La Pancha
On the left side of the highway just a short distance outside of Adícora in this direction (signs announce it).
Tel: (414) 969 2649, (212) 987 0081
E-mail: haciendapancha@ hotmail.com

In a handsome colonial-style house perched atop a small hill, with a duck pond in front, central garden courtyard, and filled with antiques (no children under 16 allowed – this is special!) Catalan and French cooking with *criollo* touches (where "you will *never* find the standard grilled chicken or fish of every other place!" assures the owner). By reservation, open weekends only. **$$**

Lara

Barquisimeto
Barquisimeto Hilton
Carrera 5, between Calles 5 and 6, Nueva Segovia
Tel: (251) 53 6022/6232/6332
Three offerings from this hotel are very popular with locals: **Le Provençal** gourmet French restaurant (**$$$**); **Valle del Turbio** restaurant on a terrace overlooking the Río Turbio valley featuring weekend barbecue from noon; Wed from 7pm, typical Larense night with live music (**$$**); and **Disko Laser**, considered the best discotheque in town.

Café 90
C.C. Paseo, Avenida Lara con Los Leones
Located in the principal shopping zone, a popular coffee bar, with pizza and pasta on the menu. **$**

Círculo
Centro Financorp, Carrera 2, Nueva Segovia
Tel: (251) 54 0975
Excellent creative continental cuisine at very reasonable prices, sophisticated contemporary setting where all the movers and shakers gather. Closed Sun evening and Mon. **$$–$$$**

La Trattoría
Hotel Principe, Calle 23, between Carreras 18 and 19
Tel: (251) 31 2111
Handy downtown location, near museums, financial, and shopping zones. Italian. **$$**

Pastelería/Café Majestic
Carrera 19, between Calle 30 and 31
Tel: (251) 31 7687
Very pretty and ample seating area

with elegant furniture, lace curtains, thoroughly tempting pastries; open Mon–Sat 8am–8pm. **$**

Tequila Club
Carrera 18, between Calles 31 and 32
Tel: (251) 32 2434/1314
Special nights: University crowd Tuesday; Vikings Wednesday; Tequila on Thursday with *mariachis*, drawings and many other surprises.

Tiuna
Final Avenida Lara Este
Tel: (251) 54 6471/2832
Long-established casual place with restaurant specializing in grilled meats (**$$**); while its bar side is a popular spot for its *tasca* and dancing.

Villa del Mar
Avenida 20 at Calle 9
Tel: (251) 51 1079
Huge seafood restaurant; its bar offers live music and dancing Wed–Sat.

Northern Zulia

Maracaibo
The largest concentration of restaurants is in the area by the junction of Calle 77 (Avenida 5 de Julio) and Avenida 4 (Bella Vista).

Babelonia
Avenida 9, between Calle 78 (Doctor Portillo) and 79
Tel: (261) 98 1318
Good Arabic food, open lunch and dinner. Closed Mon. **$$**

Bibas "El Café del Teatro"
Calle 70 at Avenida 3F (beside Centro de Bellas Artes)
Tel: (261) 92 8791, (414) 961 4485
Popular spot after events in the adjacent Bellas Artes center. Cocktails, grill, salad bar; live jazz

on Wed; directed gastronomy on Sat. Open from 5pm Mon–Sat, but people don't start showing up until around 7–8pm.

Celia
Calle 75, between Avenida 3F and 3G, Edif Marsans
"Fit for life" low-fat selections, good vegetarian dishes. Lunch only. **$**

Da Maurizio
Avenida 4 (Bella Vista), Nº 68–30, between Calles 67 and 68
Handsome setting, authentic Italian cuisine. Owner Maurizio Lombardo speaks fluent English and is always on the premises. **$$**

El Gaucho
Avenida 3Y, between Calle 77 and 78.
Tel: (261) 98 2110.
Featuring Argentine-style mixed grill. Indoor/outdoor dining. Open daily 5pm–2am. **$$**

El Mesón de Sancho Tasca Restaurant
Avenida 16 and 66, opposite the new Rectorate of the University of Zulia
Tel: (261) 51 2746
Economical fixed-price menu daily, karaoke on Friday and Saturday, very reasonably priced liquor. Open Mon–Sat noon–10pm. Closed Sun. **$**

El Zaguán
Calle Carabobo (Calle 94) at Avenida 6, Nº 6–15
Tel: (261) 23 1183
Traditional Venezuelan fare, lively bar, garden seating where occasional live music is presented. Closed Sun. **$$**

Fein Kaffe
Calle 78 at 3F
Tel: (261) 91 4296
As pleasant for the art everywhere – from tabletops to walls – as for the wide assortment of light American-style deli fare and pastries; adjoining gourmet shop. **$**

Koto Sushi
Avenida 11, between Calles 75 and 76, Nº 75–40
Tel: (261) 98 8954
Japanese specialties featuring sushi, sashimi, tempura, yakitori. Closed Mon. **$–$$**

Mi Vaquita
Calle 76 at 3H
Tel: (261) 91 1990

A fixture in Maracaibo since 1963, popular for its beef specialty restaurant and for its large, lively bar with music and dance floor. **$$**

Mandarin
Calle 68A, Nº 3H–08
Tel: (261) 91 7209/2120/0060
Elegant Cantonese and Mandarin cuisine. Karaoke happy hour in bar Mon–Fri 3–7pm; Thur–Sat 11.30am–3am. **$$**

Los Molinos Tasca Restaurant
Avenida 9B at Calle 75
Tel: (261) 97 8930,
(418) 615 2226
Tasca-restaurant with wide variety of food (paella is a specialty), live music with *mariachis*, flamenco show, dance music. **$$**

Paparazzi Café
Calle 72, between Avenida 17 and 18
Tel: (261) 83 2430/4249
Advertised as "Italian gastronomy at delicious prices," this popular place is open daily from 7am. **$**

Restaurant Peruano Marisquería
Avenida 15 (Las Delicias) at Calle 69
Tel: (261) 98 1513
Cozy family-run place with Peruvian dishes and seafood. **$**

Los Andes

TRUJILLO

Boconó
La Vieja Casa
Calle Miranda (half a block west of the Plaza Bolívar)
Tel: (272) 52 3077
Delightful restaurant-cum-museum with Andean home cooking. Each room of the Old House is a dining room packed with memorabilia. Open daily except Tues 3–7pm. **$**

MERIDA

Fresh trout is a specialty throughout Mérida, prepared in many different forms. And smoked trout is available at many roadside stores; it makes a fabulous snack while you are driving. On the route through the *páramo*, nearly every restaurant has "typical Andean

cooking" – a good opportunity to try it since once in the larger towns, the emphasis is on international fare.

Timotes
Hotel Las Truchas
North entrance of town
Tel: (271) 89 158, 88 066
Pretty restaurant serving typical Andean fare; super cozy bar that makes a good choice for a quiet romantic encounter. **$$**

Santo Domingo
El Punto Criollo
Avenida Principal (the highway), beside the hospital, on the third floor
Good food, pleasant atmosphere, and reasonable prices. **$**

Posada/Restaurant Los Andes
Calle Independencia Nº 9
Tel: (274) 82 0151
People come from all around to relish the tasty, economical home-style Andean cooking. Hearty soups are a meal in themselves. **$**

Castillo de San Ignacio
Northern entrance to town
Tel: (274) 82 0751/0021
The unique atmosphere of a medieval castle, waitresses in period dress, and a menu with varied international dishes offer diners a unique experience. **$$**

City of Mérida
A great many restaurants are concentrated along Avenida Los Próceres and its northern extension, Via Chorros de Milla. More modestly priced ones, catering to the large student community, are found throughout the heart of Centro in the vicinity of the Plaza Bolívar.

El Bodegón de Pancho
Avenida Los Américas, C.C. Mamayeya, PB, Local C–1
Tel: (274) 244 9819
Generous bar, huge place, friendly crowds, mostly in the 21–35 age range, good music for dancing (mostly merengue and salsa).

La Cucaracha
C.C. Las Tapias, Avenida Andrés Bello
Tel: (274) 266 1312

There are four options under one roof of The Cockroach: *tasca*, pub, pool, and discotheque (playing primarily American rock music).

La Fonda de Tía Mila
Calle Chorros de Milla
Tel: (274) 44 3308
Popular place with *carne en vara* (beef roasted on long poles over a wood fire) and trout popular items from the menu. **$–$$**

La Fonda Vegetariana and Restaurant El Tinajero
Calle 29, between Avenidas 3 & 4
Tel: (274) 52 2465
Fixed-price menu of the day or à la carte. Falafels, vegetable *hallacas* (tamales), etc. Open 7am–9pm. **$**

La Gitana
C.C. San Antonio, Avenida Andrés Bello (opposite Plaza del Ejército)
Tasca with formal atmosphere, popular with an older crowd; good *tapas*. Live background music on weekends.

La Patana
C.C. San Antonio, Avenida Andrés Bello (opposite Plaza del Ejército)
Tel: (274) 66 2746
Nightspot popular with people of all ages due to its varied program of live nightly music, ranging from *boleros* to jazz.

Los Tejados de Chachopo
Via Chorros de Milla
Tel: (274) 44 0430
With an interior filled with antiques and memorabilia, waiters dressed in vintage fashions, and a maze of rooms, Los Tejados specializes in typical Andean fare. A fun place. **$$**

Los Llanos

With population centers few and far between, restaurants tend to be scarce, and those one finds are all about the same, without any particular distinction to single them out; all with beef as the usual principal offer. *Carne en vara* (large pieces of beef skewered on a long pole and roasted over a wood fire) is a particular specialty. Many of these places have live *música criolla* (Venezuelan-style Country & Western music) on weekends.

Táchira
San Cristóbal
For restaurants and nightlife, Avenida Libertador in the Las Lomas Sector, and Barrio Obrero around Plaza Los Mangos (between calles 10–14 and carreras 22–23) have the greatest choices. Many unique stores add to the interest.
Discoteca Tempest
Edif Primo Centro, *sótano*
Avenida Libertador
Popular discotheque playing current hits, with a mostly young crowd.
Hato Viejo
Calle Principal Barrio El Lobo (right at first stop light on Avenida Los Agustinos), diagonal from the *manga de coleo*
Tel: (276) 56 4251
Large casual place with faithful clientele, divided into bar/restaurant; meat a specialty, reasonable prices. **$–$$**
La Vaquera
Avenida Libertador, Sector Las Lomas (access only from Avenida Libertador southbound)
Tel: (276) 43 6769
Perennial favorite popular for its seafood and beef. **$$**
Nuevo Nan King
Avenida 19 de Abril, Sector La Concordia.
Tel: (276)46 5357/4433.
Huge Chinese place with the look of a temple. A fixture in the capital since 1967. **$–$$**

Casinos and Bingo

With the restrictions imposed by the recent law applying to casinos and bingo halls, most former casinos have been forced to change to bingo. Some favorites include:
Gran Casino Margarita, next to the Margarita Hilton Avenida Los Uveros, Playa Moreno, Costa Azul. Tel: 62 3333/4111. The most elegant of the lot.
Bingo Charaima, Avenida 4 de Mayo, Porlamar. Huge bingo parlor also features salsa show, live music, and dancing.
Bingo Reina Margarita, Avenida 4 de Mayo, Porlamar.

Language

General

It is very rare to find anyone among the general public in Venezuela who can speak or understand any language other than Spanish – even in Caracas. Thus, if you are a non-Spanish speaker, it is best to be armed with a basic dictionary and willingness to do a bit of acting out to make yourself understood. Happily, most Venezuelans bend over backward to facilitate communication if you make any attempt at all to speak their language.

Pronunciation and Grammar Tips

Unless an accent mark indicates otherwise, stress on all words ending in vowels, "n" or "s" is on the penultimate syllable; while all words ending in other consonants are stressed on the last syllable.

"You" has both familiar *(tú)* and formal *(usted, Ud.)* forms in the singular, while *ustedes* is used for "you" plural for both.

VOWEL PRONUNCIATION

a – as in rather, bar.
e – at the end of a word is pronounced like the "e" in they, but in words that end with a consonant like the "e" in set or wet.
i – as a cross between the "i" in tip and the "i" in machine.
o – as in *hole.*
u – as in *rude*, but silent after "q" and in the groups "gue", "gui", unless marked by a diaresis *(antigüedad, argüir)* when the sound is like "gway" or "gwe").

CONSONANTS

These are pronounced more or less like those in English, the main exceptions being:
b and **v** – are usually pronounced the same (just as with **ll** and **y**, which are both pronounced as "y" in yes (unless the y comes at the beginning of a word, when it is usually pronounced as the "j" in Jordan).
c – before a, o, or u is like the "k" in keep; before i or e, like the "s" in same (as opposed to the Castilian pronunciation; most Venezuelans don't say they speak Spanish – *español*; rather, they say they speak *castellano* – Castilian). Thus, *censo* (census) sounds like senso.
g – before e or i sounds like a guttural h (as the "ch" in the Scottish *loch*); at the start of a breath group and after n *(gloria, rango)*, the sound is that of the g in get; in other positions it is like the "g" in go.
h – is always silent.
j – has a strong guttural sound like the "ch" of the Scottish word *loch*, except at the end of a word *(reloj)* when it is silent.
ll – sounds approximately like the "lli" in million (though it is often pronounced like a j).
ñ – sounds like ny, as in the familiar Spanish word *señor.*
q – is followed by u as in English, but the combination sounds like "k" in kick instead of like "kw" since the u is silent. *¿Qué quiere Usted?* is pronounced: Keh kee-ehr-eh oostehd?
r – has a single trill or vibration, though it is often rolled for effect at the start of a word.
rr – is always strongly trilled or rolled.
x – between vowels sounds like the "x" in box, or like the "g s" in big stick.
y – alone, as the word meaning "and", is pronounced "ee"; but when indicated as the letter, or the indication of a split in a road, or at the beginning of a word it is pronounced like the "j" of Jordan; while in the middle of a word it sounds like the "y" in yes.

Note that **ch** and **ll** are separate letters of the Spanish alphabet; phone books have ch and ll in English alphabetical order. However, in dictionaries, ch follows all other c entries. The same applies to ll.

NOUNS

Nouns are either masculine or feminine. Masculine nouns usually end in "o"; with article *el* for singular, *los* for plural and adjectives usually with corresponding "o" singular or "os" plural ending. Feminine nouns usually end with "a"; with article adjective *la* for singular, *las* plural and adjectives usually with corresponding "a" singular or "as" plural ending).

Yes *Sí*
No *No*
Thank you *Gracias*
Many thanks *Muchas Gracias*
You're welcome *No hay de que/Por nada*
Alright/Okay/That's fine *Está bien*
Please *Por favor*
Excuse me (to get attention) *¡Perdón!/¡Por favor!*
Excuse me (to get through a crowd) *¡Permiso!*
Excuse me (sorry) *Perdóneme, Dicsúlpeme*
Wait a minute! *¡Un momento!*
Could you help me? (formal) *¿Puede ayudarme?*
Certainly *¡Claro!/¡Claro que sí!*
Can I help you? (formal) *¿Puedo ayudarle?*
Can you show me...? *¿Puede mostrarme...?*
I need... *Necesito....*
I'm lost *Estoy estraviado*
I'm sorry *Lo siento*
I don't know *No sé*
I don't understand *No entiendo*
Do you speak English/French/German? (formal) *¿Habla inglés/francés/alemán?*
Could you speak more slowly, please? *¿Puede hablar más lentamente, por favor?/Hable más despacio, por favor*

Could you repeat that, please? *¿Puede repetirlo, por favor?*
Slowly *despacio/lentamente/poco a poco*
here/there *aquí* (place where), *acá* (motion to)/*allí, allá, ahí* (near you)
What? *¿Qué?/¿Cómo?*
When/why/where/who/how/which? *¿Cuándo?/¿Por qué?/¿Dónde?/¿Quién(es)?/¿Cómo?/¿Cuál?*
How much/how many? *¿Cuánto?/¿Cuántos?*
Do you have...? *¿Tiene...?/¿Hay...?*
I want.../I would like.../I need... *Quiero.../Quisiera.../Necesito...*
Where is the lavatory (men's/women's)? *¿Dónde se encuentra el baño (de caballeros/de damas)?*

Venezuelans tend to be very title conscious. Take a clue from the way a person presents him/herself or how the person is presented by another and address him/her in kind. Then, if they wish to be more informal, they will usually so indicate. But, some people can get very touchy if you ignore their title when addressing them, particularly upon first meeting.

Doctor (male) or *Doctora* (female) is used for lawyers as well as physicians. People who have doctorate degrees usually use the title *Doctor* as well. People who have earned an undergraduate university degree use the title *Licenciado/a* (*Lic*). When in doubt about their degree, you're better off to err on the side of flattery by using *Doctor*.

Other common titles are *Economista* – economist, *Arquitecto/a* – archiitect, *Ingeniero/a* – engineer, *Poeta* – poet, *Maestro/a* – for educators, well-known artists, and musicians.

Thus, a person is addressed as Ingeniero José López, or Licenciada María Ramírez. If they use these titles, always use them in formal correspondence as well.

Subject pronouns are often eliminated (except for emphasis) since the verb ending indicates whether you are indicating I (*yo*); you singular, familiar (*tú*); you formal (*usted*, often written as *Ud.* – always with U capitalized if abbreviated); he (*él*), she (*ella*), it (*ello*); we (*nosotros*); you plural (*ustedes*); they (*ellas* – f., *ellos* – m.). For example: *Soy americano.* (instead of *Yo soy americano*) – I am American.

Men or women who have passed beyond 50 are often addressed affectionately with a title of respect: *Don* (masc), *Doña* (fem). In this case, in conversation, it is usually with first name only (though in writing of upon presentation, with the whole name): *Don Pedro*, or *Doña Blanquita*. *Doña* is also often used alone by strangers addressing an older woman when they do not know her name.

Unless you are sure a young woman is married, address her as *Señorita* (Miss) rather than *Señora* (Mrs).

Hello! *¡Hola!*
Hello (Good day) *Buenos dias*
Good afternoon/night *Buenas tardes/noches*
Goodbye *Ciao/¡Adios!*
I am called... *Me llamo...*
What are you called? (formal) *¿Cómo se llama usted?*
Mr/Miss/Mrs *Señor/Señorita/Señora*
Pleased to meet you *¡Encantado!/¡Un placer!*
I am English/American/Irish/Scottish/Australian *Soy inglés/norteamericano(a)/canadiense/irlandés/escocés/australiano(a)*
Do you speak English? (formal) *¿Habla inglés?*
I'm here on holiday *Estoy aquí para vacaciones*
Is it your first trip to Venezuela/Caracas? *¿Es su primera viaje a Venezuela/Caracas?*

Do you like Venezuela/Caracas/ my city? (formal) ¿Le gusta a Venezuela/Caracas/mi ciudad?
I like it a lot ¡Me gusta muchísimo!/¡Me encanta!
It's wonderful ¡Es maravilloso(a)/fabuloso(a)!
How are you? (formal/informal) ¿Cómo está? ¿Qué tal?
Fine, thanks Muy bien, gracias
See you later Hasta luego
Take care (informal) ¡Cuídate!

Telephone Calls

the area code el código de área
I'd like to make a collect call Quisiera hacer una llamada que paga el destinario
Where can I find a telephone that takes pre-paid cards? ¿Dónde puedo encontrar un teléfono que toma tarjetas?
Where can I buy/Do you sell telephone cards? ¿Dónde puedo comprar tarjetas telefónicas? /¿Se vende aquí tarjetas telefónicas?
May I use your telephone to make a local call? ¿Puedo usar su teléfono para hacer una llamada local?
Of course you may ¡Por supuesto que sí!/¡Como no!/¡Claro!
Hello (on the phone) ¡Aló!
May I speak to...? ¿Puedo hablar con...?
Sorry, he/she isn't in Lo siente, no se encuentra
Can he call you back? ¿Puede devolver la llamada?
Yes, he can reach me at... Sí, él puede llamarme en (number)
I'll try again later Voy a intentar más tarde
Can I leave a message? ¿Puedo dejar un mensaje?
Please tell him I called Favor avisarle que llamé
Hold on Un momento, por favor
Can you speak up, please? ¿Puede hablar más fuerte, por favor?

In the Hotel

Do you have a vacant room? ¿Tiene una habitación disponible?
I have a reservation Tengo una reservación

I'd like... Quisiera...
a single/double (with double bed)/ a room with twin beds una habitación individual (sencilla)/ una habitación matrimonial/una habitación doble
king-size, queen-size/bunk beds/sofa bed cama king, queen/litera/sofá-cama
hammock hamaca (close weave), chinchorro (open weave)
mosquito netting mosquitero
for one night/two nights por una noche/dos noches
a room on the first floor/second floor/top floor/upper floor (of two)/that faces the street/in the rear/with sea view una habitación en la planta baja/en el primer piso/en el último piso/en la planta alta/que da a la calle/en la parte de atrás/con vista al mar
Does the room have a private bathroom or shared bathroom? ¿Tiene la habitación baño privado o baño compartido?
Does it have hot water? ¿Tiene agua caliente?
No, it has cold water only No, sólo tiene agua normal
Does it have a kitchen (with utensils)? ¿Tiene cocina (equipada)?
Do you provide towels? ¿Ustedes proveen toallas?
Could you show me another room, please? ¿Puede mostrarme otra habitación, por favor?
Is it a quiet room? ¿Es una habitación tranquila?

Swearing

Startling to many visitors, even natives of other Spanish-speaking countries is to hear swear words (groserías) and vulgarities seemingly in every other sentence (with no consideration that they are anything offensive or inappropriate) by the majority of the population – even among children – for whom ¡coño! and ¡no joda! (c——, and no f——) are more common than "darn it" or "really?!" in English.

What time do you close (lock) the doors? ¿A qué hora se cierren las puertas?
I would like to change rooms Quisiera cambiar la habitación
This room is too noisy/hot/cold/ small Esta habitación es demasiado ruidosa/caliente/ fría/pequeña
How much is it? ¿Cuánto cuesta?
Okay, I'll take it Está bien
Where... is the emergency exit/are the stairs? ¿Dónde... se encuentra la salida de emergencia/se encuentran las escaleras?
Is everything included? ¿Es un paquete todo incluido?
Does the price include tax/breakfast/meals/national beverages (beer, non-imported liquor)? ¿El precio incluye el impuesto/desayuno/comidas/ bebidas nacionales?
Do you accept credit cards/ travelers' checks/dollars? ¿Se aceptan tarjetas de crédito/ cheques de viajeros/dólares?
Is there a surcharge to pay by credit card? ¿Hay un recargo si cancelo con tarjeta de crédito?
I need a bell hop Necesito un botón
Please take the bags to my room Favor llevar el equipaje a mi habitación
What time is breakfast? ¿A qué hora está servido el desayuno?
Please wake me at... Favor despertarme a...
Come in! ¡Pase!, ¡Adelante!
I'd like to pay the check now, please Quisiera cancelar la cuenta ahora, por favor
Can you call me a taxi, please? ¿Puede llamarme un taxi, por favor?

USEFUL WORDS

bath el baño
dining room el comedor
key la llave
safety deposit box caja de seguridad
elevator/lift el asensor
toilet paper papel higiénico
soap el jabón

shampoo el champú
push/pull empuje/hale
towel la toalla

Bars, Beverages, and Snacks

What would you like to drink?
  ¿Qué quiere tomar?
I'd like... Quisiera...
coffee... un café...
American-style guayoyo
with a lot of milk con leche
with a little milk marrón
strong fuerte
cappuccino capuchino
small/large pequeño/grande
without sugar sin azúcar
tea... té...
with lemon/milk con limón/leche
herbal tea té manzanilla
hot chocolate chocolate caliente
fresh orange juice jugo de naranja
  natural
orangeade naranjada
soft drink refresco
mineral water still/carbonated
  agua mineral sin gas/con gas
with/without ice con/sin hielo
cover charge entrada
Spanish-style bar that usually
  features appetizers tasca
appetizers served in a tasca tapas
minimum consumption consumo
  mínimo
beer hall/pub cervecería
discotheque disco/discoteca
nightclub club nocturno
a bottle/a half bottle una
  botella/media botella
tall drink, highball un trago
cocktail un cóctel
a glass of red/white/rosé wine
  una copa de vino tinto/rosado/
  blanco
beer una cerveza
a gin and tonic ginebra con
  aguaquina
Scotch and soda/water un whisky
  con soda/agua
rum and cola (with lime) un ron
  con Coca Cola (Cuba libre)
Would you like something else?
  ¿Quiere algo más?
No thank you, bring me the check
  please No gracias, triágame la
  cuenta por favor
Is service included? ¿Incluye el
  servicio?

I need a receipt, please Necesito
  un recibo, por favor
Keep the change Es completo
Cheers! ¡Salud!
This is my treat (I'll pay) Yo le
  brindo
That is very kind of you Gracias,
  es muy gentil

SNACKS

ice cream helado
sandwich sandwich
turnover (filled with meat, cheese,
  etc.) una empanada

IN A RESTAURANT

I'd like to reserve a table Quisiera
  reservar una mesa, por favor
Do you have a table for...? ¿Tiene
  una mesa para...?
I have a reservation Tengo una
  reservación
breakfast/lunch/dinner
  desayuno/almuerzo/cena
Could we have another table,
  please? Podemos tener una
  mesa diferent, por favor?
I'm a vegetarian Soy
  vegetariano(a)
Is there a vegetarian dish? ¿Hay
  un plato vegetariano?
May we have the menu? ¿Puede
  traernos la carta (or el menú)?
wine list la carta de vinos
What would you like as a
  starter/main dish/dessert?
  ¿Qué quiere usted para el primer
  plato (or para empezar)/el plato
  principal or el segundo/el postre?
What would you recommend?
  ¿Qué recomiende?
home-made casero(a)
Could you please bring me a
  fork/knife/small spoon/large
  spoon/napkin/ashtray? ¿Por
  favor, puede traerme un
  tenador/un cuchillo/una
  cucharita/una cuchara/una
  servieta/un cenicero?
fixed price menu menú
  ejecutivo/menú de degustación
special of the day plato del
  día/sugerencia del chef
The meal was very good La
  comida fue muy buena

Menu Decoder

EXTREMESES, PRIMER PLATO (FIRST COURSE)

sopa/crema soup/cream soup
hervido de res/pescado/pollo
  broth with large chunks of meat/
  fish/chicken and vegetables
mondongo tripe soup
sopa de ajo garlic soup
sopa de cebolla onion soup
ensalada... salad...
  mixta mixed
  de palmito with palm hearts
  de aguacate con tomate
    avocado and tomato
  de berros watercress
  con aceite y vinagre/aceite de
    olivo with oil and vinegar/
    olive oil
pan con ajo garlic bread

SEGUNDO/PLATO PRINCIPAL (MAIN COURSE)

La Carne (Meat)

a la brasa/a la parrilla charcoal
  grilled
a la broaster/en vara spit roasted
a la plancha grilled
ahumada smoked
albondigas meatballs
asado(a)/horneado(a) roasted
bistec thin cut of beef
brocheta/pincho shish kebab
carne (carne de res) beef
cerdo/cochino/puerco pork
chivo/cabra goat
chorizos spicy paprika sausage
chuleta chop
churrasco a large boneless steak,
  usually rump, round, or chuck
conejo rabbit
cordero lamb
costillas ribs
empanizado(a) breaded
frito(a) fried
guisado(a) stewed
hamburguesa hamburger
higado de res beef liver
jamón ham
lengua tongue
lomito tenderloin
milanesa breaded and fried thin
  cut of meat
pernil leg of pork

punta trasera **rump roast or steak**
rebosado(a) **batter fried**
riñones **kidneys**
salchicha **sausage**
perros calientes **hot dogs**
solomo **chuck steak**
ternera **veal**

Ordering Beef

Beef tends to be cooked one notch rarer than American style. (If it comes too rare, ask: *¿Puede cocinarla un poco más, por favor?*):

crudo **raw**
vuelta y vuelta **rare**
término medio **medium rare**
tres cuarto **medium**
bien cocida **well done**

Aves (Fowl)

alas **wings**
chicharrón de pollo **chicken cut up in small pieces and deep fried**
codorniz **quail**
mollejas de pollo **chicken gizzards**
muslo **thigh**
pato **duck**
pavo **turkey**
pechuga **breast**
piernas **legs**
pollo **chicken**

Mariscos/Pescado (Seafood/Fish)

almejas, guacuco **clams**
anchoa **anchovy**
atún **tuna**
bacalao **cod**
bagre **catfish**
botuto **conch**
calamares **squid**
cangrejo **crab**
caracoles **snails**
carite **mackerel**
cazón **baby shark**
corvina **blue fish**
huevas **fish eggs (in the egg sac, not caviar)**
langosta **lobster**
langostinos **shrimps**
lebranche **black mullet**
lenguado **sole or flounder**
lisa **silver mullet**
mariscos **shellfish**
mejillones **mussels**
mero **grouper, sea bass**

ostras **oysters**
pargo **red snapper**
pulpo **octopus**
róbalo **haddock, snook**
salmón **salmon**
sardinas **sardines**
sierra **king mackerel**
trucha **trout**
vieras **scallops**

Vegetales (Vegetables)

ajo **garlic**
ajoporro **leeks**
alcachofa **artichoke**
auyama **pumpkin or squash**
batata **yam**
berenjena **eggplant/aubergine**
brócoli **broccoli**
calabacín **zucchini/courgette**
caraotas **black beans**
cebolla **onion**
coliflor **cauliflower**
espárrago **asparagus**
espinaca **spinach**
guisantes **peas**
habas **broad beans**
hongos, champiñones **mushrooms**
lechuga **lettuce**
maiz, jojoto **corn, corn on the cob**
pepino **cucumber**
pimentón verde **green (bell) pepper**
remolacha **beets**
repollo/col **cabbage**
repollos/coles de bruselas **brussels sprouts**
vainitas **green beans**
zanahorias **carrots**

Frutas (Fruit)

aguacate **avocado**
cambur **banana**
cereza **cherry**
ciruela **plum**
dátil **date**
fresa **strawberry**
guayaba **guava**
higo **fig**
lechoza **papaya**
limón **lime**
mandarina **tangerine**
manzana **apple**
melecotón **peach**
melón **canteloup**
mora **blackberry**
naranja **orange**
parchita **passion fruit**
patilla **watermelon**
pera **pear**

piña **pineapple**
platano **plantain**
toronja/pomelo **grapefruit**
uvas **grapes**

Miscellaneous

arróz **rice**
azúcar **sugar**
espaguetis **spaghetti**
guasacaca **sauce made with avocado, onion, parsley, cilantro (coriander leaf).**
huevos (revueltos/fritos/hervidos) **eggs (scrambled/fried/boiled)**
mantequilla **butter**
mermelada **jelly**
mostaza **mustard**
pan **bread**
pan integral **wholemeal bread**
pan tostado **toast**
pasticho **lasagna**
pimienta negra **black pepper**
queso **cheese**
sal **salt**
salsa de tomate **ketchup**
salsa picante **hot sauce**
tocineta **bacon**
tortilla **omelette**

Tourist Attractions/Terms

aguas termales **hot springs**
artesanía **handicrafts**
balneario **swimming spot**
campamento **camp**
capilla **chapel**
castillo/fortín **fort**
catedral **cathedral**
cayo **cay/key**
Centro **old center of town**
cerro **hill**
comunidad indígena **indigenous community**
convento **convent**
galería **gallery**
iglesia **church**
isla **island**
jardín botánico **botanical garden**
laguna **lagoon**
lago **lake**
mar/Mar Caribe **sea/Caribbean Sea**
mercado **market**
mirador **view point**
montaña **mountain**
monumento **monument**
museo (histórico/arqueológico/ etnológico/de ciencias/del niño/de arte/de bellas artes)

museum (historical/
archeological/ethnological/
science/children's/art/fine arts)
oficina/module de turismo tourist
office/module
parque de atracciones amusement
park
parque infantil playground
parque nacional national park
parque park
pico peak
piscina swimming pool
playa beach
plaza town square
postal postcard
puente bridge
quebrada stream or gulch
río river
ruinas ruins
sanctuario sanctuary
teleférico cable car
tepuy mesa of ancient rock found
in Bolívar and Amazonas
torre tower
zona colonial colonial zone
zoológico zoo

Road Signs

alcabala, punto de control
police/military checkpoint
autopista freeway
bajada/subida peligrosa
dangerous downgrade/incline
calle ciega dead-end street
calle flechada one-way street
canal derecho right lane
canal izquierdo left lane
carretera highway, road
carretera negra paved highway
caseta guard house at the
entrance to a residential area
cauchero/se reparan cauchos tire
repair shop
cede paso yield/give way
circunvalación by-pass road/
peripheral road
conserve su derecha keep to the
right
conserve su canal do not change
lanes
cruce de ferrocarril (sin señal)
railroad crossing (without
signal)
despacio slow
desvío detour
disnivel uneven pavement
distribuidor freeway interchange
doble vía two-way traffic

Enciende luces en el túnel Turn on
lights in the tunnel
encrucejada intersection
entrada prohibida no entry
estacionamiento parking lot
estacionarse sólo en los hombrillos
parking only on the shoulders
falla de borde the edge of the road
is missing
final de doble vía/autopista end of
two-way traffic/freeway
fuera de servicio not in service
hundamiento sunken road
garaje no pare garage no parking
intercomunal interconnecting
freeway between two towns
*no estacione/prohibido
estacionarse aquí* no parking
no gire en U no U-turn
no hay paso, vía cerrado road
blocked, no way through
no hay salida no exit
no pare no stopping here
no toque la coroneta no horn
honking
*obreros, hombres/máquinas en la
vía* men at work/machinery in
the road
¡ojo! watch out!
pare stop
paso de ganado cattle crossing
paso de peatones pedestrian
crossing
peaje toll booth
peligro danger
pendiente fuerte, curva fuerte
steep hill, sharp curve
prepare su pago get your money
ready to pay at an upcoming toll
booth
rampa de frenos emergency
ramp on steep declines for
vehicles that have lost their
brakes
redoma traffic circle
*reductor de velocidad, obstáculos
en la vía, muros en la vía, policia
acostada* speed bump(s)
resbaladizo al humedecerce
slippery when wet
salida/próxima salida exit/next
exit
semáforo traffic light
sólo tránsito local local traffic
only
tome precauciones caution
un solo canal single lane
velocidad controlada speed
controlled or restricted

vía en reparación/en recuperación
road under repair
zona de construcción construction
zone
zona de derrumbes zone subject
to landslides
zona de niebla (neblina) fog zone
zona de remolque tow away zone
zona escolar school zone
zona militar military zone

Traveling

4x4, double-traction vehicle,
Four-wheel-drive vehicle
rústico
airline *línea áerea*
airport *aeropuerto*
arrivals/departures *llegadas/
salidas*
bus stop *parada (de autobus)*
boat dock for small boats/large
boats *embarcadero/muelle*
bus terminal *terminal de pasajeros*
bus *transporte, autobus*
car *carro, automóvil*
car rental *alquiler de carros sin
chofer*
charter flight *vuelo charter*
connection *conexión*
dug-out canoe without motor/
with motor *curiara/bongo*
ferry *ferry*
first class/second class *primera
clase/segunda clase, clase de
turista*
flight *vuelo*
luggage, bag(s) *equipaje, maleta(s)*
mini-bus or car with passenger
service on a fixed route, with
passage sold by the seat *por
puesto*
one-way ticket *boleto de ida*
open barge-like ferry *chalana*
platform *el anden*
round-trip, return ticket *boleto de
ida y vuelta*
runway *pista de aterrazaje*
sailboat *velero*
ship *barco*
subway *Metro*
taxi *taxi, libre*
traditional fishing boat *peñero*
yacht *yate*
Next stop please (for buses) *En la
próxima parada, por favor*
Which is the stop closest to
XXX? *¿Cuál es la parada más
cerca a XXX?*

Could you please advise me when we reach my stop/the stop for XXX ? *¿Por favor, puede avisarme cuando llegamos a mi parada/a la parada para XXX?*
Is this the stop for XXX? *¿Es ésta la parada para XXX?*

Terms for Addresses/Directions

a la derecha on the right
a la izquierda on the left
al lado de beside
alrededor de around
arriba/abajo above/below
avenida (Av) avenue
calle/carrera street
cerca de near
cruce con/con at the intersection of (two streets)
cruce hacia la izquierda/ la derecha turn to the left/ right
debajo de under
delante de in front of
derecho straight ahead
detrás de behind
edificio (Edif) high rise office building
en frente de/frente de/frente a in front of (many Venezuelans incorrectly use this to mean beside – it is best to double check to verify this)
en in, on, at
en la parte de atrás in the rear area (as behind a building)
encima de on top of
entre between
esquina (Esq) corner
PH – penthouse/PB – planta baja/ PA – planta alta/mezanina/ sótano penthouse/first floor/upper floor (of 2)/ mezzanine/basement
residencia (Res) residential tower, small pension
torre tower
transversal(es) cross street(s)
una cuadra a block

At the Airport or Travel Agency

customs and immigration *aduana e inmigración*
travel/tour agency *agencia de viajes/de turismo*

ticket sales *venta de boletos (pasajes)*
I would like to purchase a ticket for... *Quisiera comprar un boleto (pasaje) para...*
What departure times are available? *¿Cuáles son las horas de salida disponibles?*
When is the next/last flight/departure for XXX? *¿Cuándo es el próximo/último vuelo/la próxima/última salada para ....?*
What time does the plane/bus/ boat/ferry leave/return? *¿A qué hora sale/regresa el avión/ el autobus/la lancha/ el ferry?*
What time to I have to be at the airport/terminal/dock/ bus station/entrance? *¿A qué hora tengo que estar en el aeropuerto/el terminal/ el muelle/el terminal de pasajeros/ la entrada?*
How much does the ticket cost? *¿Cuánto cuesta/vale el boleto (el pasaje)?*
Is that price for one-way or round trip? *¿Es el precio de solo ida o de ida y vuelta?*
Is the tax included? *¿Se incluye el impuesto?*
Can I pay with a credit card? *¿Puedo pagar con tarjeta de crédito?*
Do they have any special plans/ packages/discounts? *¿Ellos tienen algunos planes/paquetes/ descuentos especiales?*
They offer an all-inclusive package *Ellos ofrecen un paquete todo incluido*
What is included in the price? *¿Qué está incluido en el precio?*
The package includes lodging, all three meals, snacks, national beverages, a welcome cocktail, excursions, transfers, a free gift, a bilingual guide *El paquete incluye alojamiento, las tres comidas, meriendas (or pasapalos), bebidas nacionales, un cóctel de bienvenido, excursiones, traslados, un regalo, un guía bilingüe*
Where do I pay the departure tax? *¿Dónde se paga el impuesto de salida?*

How much is the departure tax? *¿Cuánto cuesta el impuesto de salida?*
Where do I check in my luggage? *¿Dónde puedo chequear mi equipaje?*
Do you have luggage to check in? *¿Tiene equipaje para chequear?*
I only have hand luggage *Sólo tengo equipaje de mano*
Where is the office/counter for XXX airlines? *¿Dónde se encuenta la oficina/el mostrador de la línea áerea XXX?*
I would like a seat in first class/ business class/tourist class *Quisiera un asiento en primera clase/business, ejecutivo/ clase de turista*
From which gate does it depart? *¿Cuál es la puerta de salida?*
Where is the baggage arrival area? *¿Dónde llega el equipaje?*
Where do I report lost luggage/ make a complaint with XXX airline? *¿Dónde se encuentra la oficina de reclamos para XXX línea áerea?*
I need to change my ticket *Necesito cambiar mi boleto*
How long is the flight/will it take to get there? *¿Cuánto tiempo es el vuelo/dura el viaje?*
Is the flight arriving/leaving on time/late? *¿Es el vuelo saliendo/ llegando a tiempo/atrasado?*
Is this seat taken? *¿Está ocupado este asiento?*
Excuse me, but this my seat *Perdón, pero este es mi asiento*
Do I need to change planes? *¿Tengo que cambiar aviones?*

Driving

Where can I rent a car? *¿Dónde puede alquiler un carro?*
I would like to rent the most economical model/ a luxury car/ a 4x4 *Quisiera alquiler el modelo más económico/un carro de lujo/un rústico*
Is mileage/comprehensive insurance included? *¿Está incluido el kilometraje/seguros comprensivos?*

Where is the registration/ spare tire/jack/emergency triangle? ¿Dónde se encuentra el carnet de circulación/caucho de repuesto/gato/triángulo de emergencia?
Does the car have an alarm? ¿El carro tiene alarma?
How do you turn it on/off? ¿Cómo activarla/desactivarla?
Do you have a road map/a city map for XXX? ¿Tiene un mapa vial/plano de la ciudad para XXX?
How do I get to XXX? ¿Cómo se llega a...?
Turn right/left Cruzar (or girar, doblar) hacia la derecha/ izquierda
at the next corner/street en la próxima esquina/calle
Go straight ahead Siga derecho
You can't miss it No hay perdida
You are on the wrong road No está en la vía correcta
You have to return to the last town/split in the road Hay que regresar al último pueblo (a la última ciudad)/bifurcación, "Y" (pronounced Jay)
Please show me where am I on the map Por favor, indícame dónde estoy en el mapa
Where is ...? ¿Dónde se encuentra...?
Where is the nearest...? ¿Dónde se encuentra el/la XXX más cerca?
How long does it take to get there? ¿Cuánto tiempo requiere para llegar?
When and where do I have to return the vehicle? ¿Cuándo y dónde tengo que devolverlo el vehículo?
driver's license licencia de conducir
service station, gasoline station estación de servicio, bomba de gasolina
Fill it up please with 87/91/95 octane gasoline llenelo con 87/ 91/95 por favor
diesel diesel, gas-oil
My car won't start Mi carro no prende
My car is overheating Mi carro está recalentando

My car has broken down Mi carro está accidentado
I need a tow truck Necesito una grúa
Where can I find a car repair shop (for XXX type of car)? ¿Dónde se encuentra un taller mecánico (para XXX marca)?
Can you check the...? ¿Puede revisar/chequear...?
There's somethng wrong with the... Hay un problema con....
oil/water/air/brake fluid/light bulb aceite/agua/aire/liga para frenos/bombillo
trunk/hood/door/(side) window maletín/capó/puerta/ventana
fender (front/back)/bumper guardafango (delantero/trasero)/ parachoques

Emergencies

Help! ¡Socorro! ¡Auxilio!
Stop! ¡Párate!
Watch out! ¡Cuidado! ¡Ojo! ¡Epa!
I've had an accident He tenido un accidente
Call a doctor Llama a un médico
Call an ambulance Llama una ambulancia
Call the... Llama a...
...police la policía (for minor incidents)
...transit police la policía de tránsito (for traffic accidents)
...judicial police la PTJ or CPTJ (for serious crimes: robbery, rape, car theft, etc.)
Call the fire brigade Llama a los bomberos
This is an emergency, where is a telephone? Es una emergencia. ¿Dónde se encuentra un teléfono?
Where is the nearest hospital? ¿Dónde se encuentra el hospital más cerca?
I want to report a theft (something stolen when you were not present)/a robbery (armed, hold-up) Quisiera reportar un hurto/un robo (armado)
Thank you very much for your help Muchísima gracias por su ayuda

NOTE: If you call the **171** nationwide emergency number, they will dispatch the appropriate

The Car

...accelerator el acelerador
...alternator el alternador
...battery el acumulador, la batería
...brakes los frenos
...carburator el carburador
....clutch el embrague
...engine el motor
...fanbelt el correo del ventilador
...front end el tren delantero
...gear box la caja
...headlights los faros
...radiator el radiador
...shock absorber el amortiguador
...spark plugs las bujías
...starter el aranque
...steering wheel el volante
...tire(s) los cauchos
...transmission la caja
...windshield la parabrisa
...wires los cables

emergency personnel. Before you call, however, verify exactly where you are located so that you can tell them. If you are in a traffic accident, **never** move your vehicle, no matter how much you are blocking traffic, until the traffic police (tránsito) have arrived and indicated you can do so. If you have a rental vehicle, call the company immediately in case of breakdown, accident, or theft for instructions on what to do.

Health

Is there an open pharmacy nearby? ¿Hay una farmacía de turno cerca?
Where can I find a hospital/clinic? ¿Dónde puedo encontrar un hospital/una clínica?
I need a doctor/dentist Necesito un médico/dentista (odontólogo)
I don't feel well Me siento mal
I am sick Estoy infermo
Where does it hurt? ¿Dónde duele?
It hurts here Duele aquí
I suffer from... Padesco de...
I have a headache/stomach ache/ cramps Tengo un dolor de la cabeza/del estomago/de vientre

My throat hurts *Duele mi gargantua*
I feel dizzy *Me siento mareado*
Do you have (something for)...? *¿Tiene (algo para)...?*
a cold or flu *gripe o virus*
cough *tos*
diarrhea *diarrea*
constipation *estrenamiento*
fever *fiebre*
aspirin *asparina*
heartburn *ácidez*
insect/mosquito bites *picaduras de insectos/mosquitos*

Shopping

antiques shop *antigüedades*
apartment/apartment building *apartamento/residencia*
bakery *panadería*
bank *banco*
barber shop *barbería*
beauty salon *peluquería, salón de belleza*
bookstore *librería*
butcher shop *carnicería*
currency exchange bureau *casa de cambio*
department store *tienda por departamentos*
dry cleaners *tintorería*
florist *florestería*
gift shop *(tienda de) regalos*
greengrocer's *frutería*
hardware store *ferretería*
house *casa, quinta*
shopping center *centro comercial, mall*
jewelry store *joyería*
laundry *lavandería*
library *biblioteca*
liquor store *licorería, distribuidor (de licores)*
market *mercado*
newsstand *kiosco*
office building *edificio, centro empresarial, centro profesional*
pastry shop *pastelería*
post office *correos*
shoe repair shop/shoe store *zapatería*
small grocery store *bodega, abasto*
small shop *tienda*
supermarket *supermercado, automercado*
toy store *juguetería*

Clothing/Shoe Sizes

North American	European or South American
Shirts (Men)	
15	38
15 ½	39
16	40
16 ½	42
17	43
Blouses (Women)	
10	38
12	40
14	42
16	44
18	46
Shoes (Men)	
8	41
9	42
10	42
11	44.5
12	46
Shoes (Women)	
6 ½	36.5
7	37
8	38
8 ½	38.5
9	39

Useful Phrases

What time do you open/close? *¿A qué hora abre/cierre?*
Open/closed *Abierto/cerrado*
Can I help you? *¿Puedo ayudarle?*
What are you looking for? *¿Qué busca?*
I'd like... *Quisiera...*
What size do you need? *¿Qué talla busca?*
I'm just looking *Estoy sólo mirando, gracias*
How much does it cost? *¿Cuánto cuesta?*
Please write it down for me *Por favor escribirme el monto*
Where can I try it on? *¿Dónde está el probador de ropa?*
It doesn't fit *No queda bien*
Do you have it in another color/size? *¿Tiene en otro color/talla (clothing), tamaño (objects)?*
smaller/larger *más pequeño/más grande*

It's too expensive *Es demasiado caro*
Do you have something less expensive? *¿Tiene algo más económico?*
Are you going to buy it? *¿Quiere llevarlo?*
Where do I pay for it? *¿Dónde está la caja?*
I want to return this *Quiero devolver esto*
No refunds given *No se aceptan devoluciones*
Anything else? *¿Quiere algo más?*
a little more/less *un poco más/menos*
That's enough/no more *Está bien/no más*

Colors

light/dark *claro/oscuro*
red *rojo*
yellow *amarillo*
blue *azul*
brown *marrón*
black *negro*
white *blanco*
beige *color crema*
green *verde*
wine *vino tinto*
gray *gris*
orange *color naranjo*
pink *rosada*
purple *purpura*
silver *plateado*
gold *dorado*

Numbers

1 uno
2 dos
3 tres
4 cuatro
5 cinco
6 seis
7 siete
8 ocho
9 nueve
10 diez
11 once
12 doce
13 trece
14 catorce
15 quince
16 dieciséis
17 diecisiete
18 dieciocho
19 diecinueve

20 veinte
21 veintiuno
25 veinticinco
30 treinta
40 cuarenta
50 cincuenta
60 sesenta
70 setenta
80 ochenta
90 noventa
100 cien
101 ciento uno
200 doscientos
300 trescientos
400 cuatrocientos
500 quinientos
600 seiscientos
700 setecientos
800 ochocientos
900 novecientos
1,000 mil
2,000 dos mil
10,000 diez mil
100,000 cien mil
1,000,000 un millón
1,000,000,000 mil millones
1,000,000,000,000 un millardo

NOTE: In Spanish commas are used instead of decimal points and vice versa. For example $19.30 = $19,50; 1,000 meters = 1.000 metros; and 9.5% = 9,5%.

Temporal

morning *la mañana*
afternoon *la tarde (noon–7pm)*
late afternoon, dusk *atardecer*
evening *la noche (7pm–midnight)*
midnight *la medianoche*
dawn *la madrugada*
sunrise *amanecer*
sunset *puesta del sol*
last night *anoche*
yesterday *ayer*
the day before yesterday *anteayer*
today *hoy*
tomorrow *mañana*
the day after tomorrow *pasado mañana*
now *ahora*
early *temprano*
late *tarde*
a little while *un rato*
a second *un segundo*
a minute *un minuto*
an hour *una hora*
a half hour *media hora*
a day *un día*

a week *una semana*
a year *un año*
weekday *día laboral*
weekend *fin de semana*
holiday *día feriado*
long weekend *un puente*

Months

January *enero*
February *febrero*
March *marzo*
April *abril*
May *mayo*
June *junio*
July *julio*
August *agosto*
September *septiembre* (or setiembre)
October *octubre*
November *noviembre*
December *diciembre*

Conversion Charts

Metric–Imperial

1 centimeter = 0.4 inch
1 meter = approx. 39 inches
1 kilometer = 0.62 miles
1 gram = 0.04 ounces
1 kilogram = 2.2 pounds
1 liter = 1.76 UK pints
1 hectare = 2.47 acres

Imperial–Metric

1 inch = 2.54 centimeters
1 yard = 0.9 meters
1 mile = 1.6 kilometers
1 ounce = 28.35 grams
1 pound = 0.45 kilograms
1 pint = 0.47 liters
1 acre = 0.4 hectare

Days of the Week

Monday *lunes*
Tuesday *martes*
Wednesday *miércoles*
Thursday *jueves*
Friday *viernes*
Saturday *sábado*
Sunday *domingo*

Further Reading

There is a notable lack of current comprehensive information in print in English about Venezuela. However, there are numerous photographic "coffee table" books (nearly all produced by foreigners), many with both English and Spanish captions. These are available in all major bookstores.

General

Guide to Venezuela, by Janice Bauman and Leni Young, Ernesto Armitano Editor (1996). One of the book's most interesting aspects is the multitude of historical notes that are well researched, and also written in a readable style.
Living in Venezuela, published in English biannually by the Venezuelan American Chamber of Commerce (tel: 212-263 0833; www.venamcham.org). This is the most complete and up-to-date orientation book available about Venezuela, covering every possible aspect: vital statistics, history, government, economic overview, geographic regions, getting around, community organizations, education, clubs, health services and issues, legal matters, communications, leisure and travel, and more.
Guide to Camps, Posadas and Cabins, by Elizabeth Kline (2001). Widely available in Venezuela, this is the definitive guide to accommodations in the country.

There are some excellent websites for researching and planning a trip to Venezuela including:
www.auyantepui.com
www.think-venezuela.net
www.venezuelaturistica.com
www.venezuelatuya.com

Nature

Birding in Venezuela, by Mary Lou Goodwin (1998), is published by, and available through, Venezuela's Audubon Society, tel: (212) 92 3268/ 2812; www.audubondevenezuela.org. Written with a very personal approach by a founding member of South America's oldest Audubon Society, this is not only the definitive guide to exactly where to go to see certain species (down to exactly which path to take and what tree they are usually seen in), but is full of useful suggestions for lodging, places to eat, names and phone numbers of local birders, and comments about ecological issues. Technical, helpful, entertaining, all in one package.

A Guide to the Birds of Venezuela, by Rodolphe Meer de Schauensee and William H. Phelps, Jr; Princeton University Press (1978). The bible for birders, with detailed descriptions and illustrations for all entries.

In the Rainforest, Catherine Caufield (1991). Commentaries about life and nature in the rainforest.

Churún Merú, Ruth Robertson (1975). Recollections of the American journalist and adventurer who was the first person to measure the height and drop of Angel Falls accurately.

Quest for the Lost World, Brian Blessed (1999). The actor describes his travels in Venezuela in a humorous, evocative, and beautifully illustrated book.

Politics and Economy

Indictment of a Dictator: The Extradition and Trial of Marcos Pérez Jiménez, by Judith Ewell (1981).

Venezuela, the Democratic Experience, edited by John D. Martz and David J. Meyers (1986).

Venezuela's Voice for Democracy: Conversations and Correspondence with Romulo Betancourt, by Robert J. Alexander (1990).

Venezuela's Movemiento al Socialismo: from Guerrilla Defeat to Innovative Politics, by Steve Ellner (1988).

Fiction

The Lost World, by Sir Arthur Conan Doyle. A classic portraying an imaginary world on the summit of Roraima *tepuy* where, because of its isolation, dinosaurs continued living after their disappearance from the rest of the world.

The General in His Labyrinth, by Gabriel García Márquez (1990). Novel about the final days of Simón Bolívar by the famous Nobel Prize-winning Colombian writer.

The Man from Maracay, by Barry Oldham (Industrias Capsvar S.A. 1998). Action thriller written by a long-time British resident and journalist about the intrigue of kidnappings and confrontations with guerrillas along the Venezuelan–Colombian border.

Other Insight Guides

There are nearly 200 titles in the *Insight Guide* series, with the same high standard of text and photo-journalism.

Insight Guide titles on South American destinations include Argentina, Buenos Aires, Brazil, Rio de Janeiro, Chile, Ecuador, Peru, and South America.

There are also titles on Central America, including Guatemala, Belize & the Yucatán, Mexico, and Mexico City, and a number of Caribbean titles including Costa Rica, Dominican Republic & Haiti, Trinidad & Tobago, Jamaica, Puerto Rico, Bermuda, Barbados, Caribbean (the Lesser Antilles), Caribbean Cruises, and Cuba.

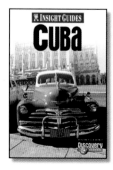

Insight Pocket Guides are a companion series in which local host authors show you specific itineraries that will make the most of your stay. The books come with a full-size fold-out map. Among the 100-plus titles are Jamaica, Barbados, Bermuda, Bahamas, Cancún & the Yucatán, the Cayman Islands, Costa Rica, Peru, Puerto Rico, Mexico City, and the Baja and Yucatán peninsulas.

ART & PHOTO CREDITS

Photography by EDUARDO GIL except for
Thomas Altinger back cover center bottom, 4BL, 51, 83, 195T, 255T, 277, 286, 287T, 291, 291T
Ask Images/Art Directors & Trip 4/5, 4BR, 17, 272/273, 278T
M Barlow/Art Directors & Trip 132, 132T
André and Cornelia Bärtschi back flap top, 101, 253, 256, 257, 297, 300, 301
R Belbin/Art Directors & Trip 243
Charles Brewer-Carias 296
Marvi Cilli 111, 114
R Daniell/Art Directors & Trip 251
Alain Dhone/Sipa Press/Rex Features 53
Ray Escobar 50, 68/69, 140,
Veronica Garbutt 49, 142T, 151
John Gottberg 90, 107
Andreas M Gross 173
Dave G Houser 20, 289
Volkmar Janicke back cover center, top & center left, spine top and bottom, 1, 2B, 5BR, 126/127, 128, 135L, 137T, 144, 204T, 206T, 231T, 237T
Elizabeth Kline front flap bottom, 24, 32, 80, 81R, 81R, 95, 104, 105, 108, 131, 138T, 146, 147T, 151, 163T, 168T, 171T, 172, 176, 179T, 181, 184T, 196, 197, 198T, 199, 200, 201, 208, 209, 210,

211, 212, 212T, 213, 218T, 222T, 229, 242, 243T, 244
Courtesy of *Lost World Adventures* 287, 299
Francisco Márquez/Naturpress 191
Buddy Mays/Travel Stock 269
Keith Mays 10/11, 16, 34, 54, 94, 96/97, 99, 100, 102, 103, 106, 109, 120/121, 129, 133, 190, 193, 202, 224/225, 248
B Masters/Art Directors & Trip 300T
S Mead/Art Directors & Trip 2/3, 271
P Musson/Art Directors & Trip 21, 181T, 227, 232, 235
Fernando Ortega/Naturpress 155, 156T, 157, 162T, 230, 245
Mike Osborne 110, 113, 115
Tony Perrottet 18/19, 39, 88, 116/117, 141, 143, 145, 154, 216, 275, 278, 280T, 288, 304
RCTV 70, 71, 73
Brian Rogers/Biofotos 250
Matthew Stockman/Allsport 98
Topham Picturepoint 8/9
Eduardo Vigliano 74, 75
Graham Wicks/Cephas 264, 266/267

Picture Spreads

Pages 84–85 *All pictures by* Elizabeth Kline *except bottom right-hand corner:* Volkmar Janicke

Pages 186–187 *Top Row, left to right:* P Musson/Art Directors & Trip, Volkmar Janicke, Volkmar Janicke, M Cerny/Art Directors & Trip
Centre Row, left to right: Volkmar Janicke, P Musson/Art Directors & Trip
Bottom Row, left to right: Elizabeth Kline, P Musson/Art Directors & Trip, Thomas Altinger
Pages 258–259 *Top Row, left to right:* Fernando Ortega/Naturpress, Fernando Ortega/Naturpress, Elizabeth Kline, Mireille Vautier
Centre Row, left to right: Brian Rogers/Biofotos, Fernando Ortega/Naturpress
Bottom Row, left to right: Thomas Altinger, Thomas Altinger, Thomas Altinger
Pages 292–293 *Top Row, left to right:* Thomas Altinger, Huw Hennessy, Thomas Altinger
Centre Row, left to right: Huw Hennessy, Huw Hennessy
Bottom Row, left to right: Thomas Altinger, Huw Hennessy, Elizabeth Kline, Huw Hennessy

Maps Colourmap Scanning Ltd
© 2002 Apa Publications GmbH & Co.
Verlag KG (Singapore branch)

INSIGHT GUIDE
Venezuela

Cartographic Editor **Zoë Goodwin**
Production **Sylvia Suddes**
Design Consultants
Carlotta Junger, Graham Mitchener
Picture Research **Hilary Genin, Monica Allende**

Index

Numbers in italics refer to photographs

66 I was first drawn to the Insight Guides by the excellent "Nepal" volume. I can think of no book which so effectively captures the essence of a country. Out of these pages leaped the Nepal I know – the captivating charm of a people and their culture. I've since discovered and enjoyed the entire Insight Guide series. Each volume deals with a country in the same sensitive depth, which is nowhere more evident than in the superb photography. 99

Sir Edmund Hillary

INSIGHT GUIDES

The classic series that puts you in the picture

The world's largest collection of visual travel guides & maps